HISTORY

OF THE

UNITED STATES

FROM

THE COMPROMISE OF 1850

BY

JAMES FORD RHODES

VOL. I

1850-1854

NEW YORK

HARPER & BROTHERS PUBLISHERS

1899

CONTENTS

OF

THE FIRST VOLUME

CHAPTER I

CHAPTER III

CHAPTER IV

CHAPTER V

HISTORY OF
THE UNITED STATES

CHAPTER I

My design is to write the history of the United States from the introduction of the compromise measures of 1850 down to the inauguration of Grover Cleveland, thirty-five years later. This period, the brief space of a generation, was an era big with fate for our country, and for the American must remain fraught with the same interest that the war of the Peloponnesus had for the ancient Greek, or the struggle between the Cavalier and the Puritan has for their descendants. It ranks next in importance to the formative period—to the declaration and conquest of independence and the adoption of the Constitution; and Lincoln and his age are as closely identified with the preservation of the government as Washington and the events which he more than any other man controlled are associated with the establishment of the nation. The civil war, described by the great German historian whose genius has illuminated the history of Rome as " the mightiest struggle and most glorious victory as yet recorded in human annals,"[1] is one of

[1] History of Rome, Mommsen, vol. iv. p. 558.

I.—1

those gigantic events whose causes, action, and sequences will be of perennial concern to him who seeks the wisdom underlying the march of history. While we now clearly see that the conflict between two opposing principles causing the struggle that led to the Missouri Compromise, and renewed from time to time after that settlement, was destined to result in the overthrow of one or the other, yet it was not until the eleven years preceding the appeal to arms that the question of negro slavery engrossed the whole attention of the country. It then became the absorbing controversy in Congress, and dominated all political contests; the issue came home to every thinking citizen, and grew to be the paramount political topic discussed in the city mart, the village store, and the artisan's workshop. It was less than three years before the secession of South Carolina that Seward described our condition as "an irrepressible conflict," and Lincoln likened it to a house divided against itself that could not stand. It is not difficult to trace the different manifestations of the opposing principles in these years. The signs of the times are so plain that he who runs may read them.

It will be my aim to recount the causes of the triumph of the Republican party in the presidential election of 1860, and to make clear how the revolution in public opinion was brought about that led to this result. Under a constitutional government, the history of political parties is the civil history of the country. I shall have to relate the downfall of the Whig party, the formation of the Republican, and the defeat of the Democratic party, that, with brief intermissions, had conducted the affairs of the government from the election of Jefferson, its founder and first President. The year that this party returned to power under the leadership of Grover Cleveland is a fitting close of this historical inquiry; for by that time the great questions which had their origin in the war had been settled as far as they could be by legislation or executive direction. Time only, that old common arbitrator, could do the rest. It is noteworthy that when the Democrats regained the national administration, it was under a leader in no way identified with the position of his party on the issues of slavery and the war. His nomination was an admission that the old questions were settled; his election showed the belief by the people that the Democratic party could be safely trusted to cope with the administrative and economical problems that were likely henceforward to engage the attention of the country.

The compromise measures of 1850 were a compromise with slavery and the last of those settlements that well-meaning and patriotic men from both sides of Mason and Dixon's line were wont to devise when the slavery question made unwelcome intrusion. To know the reason of these enactments and to understand their scope and purpose, a retrospect is necessary of so much of the history of our country as relates to the slavery question in politics.

Negro slaves, as is generally known, were brought to Virginia in the infancy of the colony. For fifty years after the landing of the first cargo at Jamestown only a few negroes were imported. But America had large new tracts of land and few agricultural settlers; and these economical conditions and the moral attitude of Christendom being given, slavery was in the natural course of things certain to be extended.[1] At first the rigor of the law was aimed at the restraint of intermarriage and of illicit intercourse between the races: public whipping, and admonition in the church, were visited upon the guilty white man.[2] But towards the last quarter of the seventeenth century, the laws

---

[1] See Society in America, Harriet Martineau, vol. i. p. 347.

[2] Short History of English Colonies, Lodge, p. 67 ; History of United States, Hildreth, vol. i. p. 521 ; vol. ii. pp. 178, 429 ; Hening, The Statutes at Large. Being a Collection of the Laws of Virginia from 1619–1792. Vol. i. pp. 146, 552 ; vol. ii, p. 170.

of the colonies began to be stringent, foreshadowing in
their severity the inhuman slave codes of the Southern
States under the Union ; yet while the Virginia slave legislation was ferocious, the custom was more lenient than the
law.[1] In South Carolina, however, the advantage of negro
labor might be seen at its best, for it had a climate better
suited to the African than the northern colonies, and it was,
moreover, essentially a planting state. The rice plant had
at an early period been introduced from Madagascar, and
the rice of Carolina was soon esteemed the best in the
world. The cultivation of rice and indigo was unhealthy
but highly remunerative labor, and it became the great object of the emigrant " to buy negro slaves, without which,"
the Secretary to the proprietors of Carolina wrote, " a
planter can never do any great matter." [2] In less than a
century after the settlement of South Carolina, capital invested in planting could easily be doubled in three or four
years. The mechanic left his trade and the merchant his
business to devote themselves to agriculture.[3] Slaves could
be bought for about forty pounds each, and as they produced in twelve months more than enough rice and indigo
to pay their entire cost, they were a profitable investment,
and the temptation was great to work them beyond their
physical endurance. The planters lived in fear of a rising
and massacre, and the legislation regarding the slaves was
harsh and cruel. The degradation of the negroes was great ;
dispensing for the most part with the ceremony of marriage,
their sexual relations were loose and irregular.[4]

In the neighboring colony of Georgia, the last of the thir-

---

[1] Lodge, p. 69.

[2] An Account of the Province of Carolina, London, 1682, cited from
the Historical Collections of South Carolina, by B. R. Carroll, vol. ii.
p. 33.

[3] Bancroft, vol. ii. p. 392. The edition used is that of Appleton & Co.,
1887, having the author's last revision. South Carolina was settled in
1670.

[4] Lodge, p. 182.

teen to be settled, the introduction of slaves was prohibited. Oglethorpe, the founder of the colony, said: "Slavery is against the Gospel as well as the fundamental law of England. We refused, as trustees, to make a law permitting such a horrid crime." [1] But the promised lucrative returns from negro labor were more powerful than respect for the law, and the Georgia planters began to hire slaves from Carolina. It was not long before slaves direct from Africa were landed at Savannah, while the laws against their introduction ceased to be observed. Whitefield, believing slavery an ordinance of God, designed for the eventual good of the African, and also having an eye to its present advantage to the colonist, argued earnestly for the introduction of slaves into Georgia; [2] and his practice conformed to his doctrine, for he bought a plantation on which, at the time of his death, there were seventy-five slaves; these he bequeathed to a lady whom he called one of the "elect." [3] The Methodist evangelist acted in consistency with the age, and so did his contemporary, Jonathan Edwards, the exponent of Calvinism in New England, who left, among other property, a negro boy. Nor did the pure life and liberal opinions of Bishop Berkeley lead him to a position on slavery in advance

---

[1] Bancroft, vol. ii. p. 287.   [2] Ibid., p. 299.

[3] Life and Times of John Wesley, Tyerman. In this work a curious letter from Whitefield in 1751 is printed, from which I make the following extracts: "As for the lawfulness of keeping slaves I have no doubt. It is plain hot countries cannot be cultivated without negroes. What a flourishing country Georgia might have been, had the use of them been permitted years ago. . . . Though it is true they are brought in a wrong way from their own country, and it is a trade not to be approved of, yet as it will be carried on whether we will or not, I should think myself highly favored if I could purchase a good number of them in order to make their lives comfortable, and lay a foundation for breeding up their posterity in the nurture and admonition of the Lord. I had no hand in bringing them into Georgia, though my judgment was for it. . . . It rejoiced my soul to hear that one of my poor negroes in Carolina was made a brother in Christ."

of his time. He conformed to the practice of the best people and held slaves.[1]

Farther northward, slavery appeared stripped of some of
its evils. The treatment of the negroes was more humane,
and legislation secured them a greater degree of personal
protection. In the colonies that afterwards became the
Middle States they were rarely worked as field hands, and
though sometimes employed in the iron furnaces and forges
of Pennsylvania,[2] their chief use was as domestic servants.
In New York it was deemed a mitigation of punishment
that refractory slaves, instead of being whipped, were sold
for the West Indian market. In New England slavery was
not a prominent feature except in Rhode Island, where Newport was largely engaged in the slave-trade; and at the outbreak of the Revolution, when one in fifty of the population of New England were slaves, the general tendency of
public opinion was against the institution. The laws in
regard to the slaves were mild, and limited their punishment; they were invariably employed as house-servants,
and were taught to read the Bible.[3]

In the colonies where moral feeling was not stifled by
golden returns from the culture of rice and tobacco by
slave labor, and where slaves were rather a domestic convenience than a planter's necessity, the notion that the practice
was an evil began to make itself manifest. The legislators
of the Providence Colony, in the middle of the seventeenth
century, enacted that no negro should be held to perpetual
service, but that all slaves should be set free at the end of
ten years; yet the law was not enforced, for it was far in
advance of public sentiment.[4] William Penn made earnest
though unavailing efforts to improve the mental and moral
condition of the negroes and to secure a decent respect for

[1] History of England in the Eighteenth Century, Lecky, vol. ii. p. 17.
[2] Iron in all Ages, Swank, p. 143.
[3] Lodge, p. 442; Hildreth, vol. ii. p. 419.
[4] Bancroft, vol. i. p. 293.

their family relations; in his last will he directed that his own slaves should be given their freedom. In 1688 a society of German Friends, who had left the country of the Rhine to enjoy the freedom of their religion under the Quaker law-giver, passed a solemn resolution declaring that it was not lawful for Christians to buy or hold negro slaves.[1]

Yet these did little to stem the current of opinion that, sustained by official and royal favor, rated the negro simply at his money-value as merchandise. William III., though establishing religious liberty and a constitutional government in England, was not in advance of his age in his views of the slave-trade. One of the early royal instructions issued in the name of William and Mary enjoined the colonial governors to keep open the market for salable negroes, and in the same reign an act of Parliament declared that "the trade is highly beneficial and advantageous to the kingdom and colonies."[2] Before and during the war of the Spanish Succession, with which the eighteenth century begins, the English government did its best for the protection of the negro traffic; it issued mandates to the Governor of New York and other governors to provide "a constant and sufficient supply of merchantable negroes."[3] Of the utmost significance was the treaty of Utrecht (1713), made at the close of this war. By compact with Spain, it provided that England should have the monopoly of supplying negro slaves to the Spanish-American provinces. The company formed to carry out the contract promised such enormous profits that Queen Anne reserved for herself one-quarter of the common stock; and it is noteworthy that almost the only feature of the treaty that gave general satisfaction in England was the article that encouraged the "kidnapping of tens of thousands of negroes, and their consignment to the most miserable slavery."[4] But all of the best minds of Eng-

---

[1] Bancroft, vol. i. p. 572.
[2] Ibid., vol. ii. pp. 77, 278.
[3] Ibid., p. 209.
[4] Lecky's England, vol. i. p. 138.

land were not of this way of thinking.   Baxter, the Christian patriot, had in the previous century reminded the slave-
holder that the slave " was of as good a kind as himself,
born to as much liberty, by nature his equal;" and it is a
grateful remembrance to lovers of English literature that
Addison and Steele protested against the inhumanity of
holding in bondage the African.[1]

Virginia for many years took a creditable attitude towards the question of slavery, although it is probable that
before the Revolution negro labor was for her an instrument of wealth.   By the middle of the eighteenth century
a large number in this colony favored the prohibition of the
slave-trade;[2] and this opinion, which with some undoubtedly had a moral prompting, was fostered by alarm at the
growing number of blacks, especially excited during the
French and Indian War.   " The negro slaves have been very
audacious on the news of the defeat on the Ohio," wrote
Governor Dinwiddie to the home administration after Brad-
dock's defeat in 1755.   " These poor creatures imagine the
French will give them their freedom.   We have too many
here."[3]   Six years later the Virginia Assembly imposed a
high duty on imported slaves, which it was hoped would be
prohibitory, but this act was vetoed by England;[4] and in
1770 King George III. instructed the Governor of Virginia,
" upon the pain of the highest displeasure, to assent to no
law by which the importation of slaves should be in any
respect prohibited or obstructed."[5]   At this time Virginia,
Maryland, and the Northern colonies favored strongly putting a stop to the foreign slave-trade ; and this feeling showed
itself in Virginia by a strong and respectful remonstrance
against the royal instructions, in which she had the sympa-

[1] Bancroft, vol. ii. p. 277.
[2] Ibid., vol. ii. p. 394.
[3] Montcalm and Wolfe, Parkman, vol. i. p. 229.
[4] Bancroft, vol. ii. p. 550; see Hildreth, vol. ii. p. 494.
[5] Bancroft, vol. iii. p. 410; Order in council of Dec. 9th, 1770.

thy of almost all of her sister colonies.[1]   But while the people of the Old Dominion were willing to prohibit the traffic
in human beings from Africa, to give their own negroes freedom was a different matter, and, while assenting without
dispute to the doctrine that slavery in the abstract was
wrong, they held that any question of its abolition should
be postponed to a more convenient season.   By no one is
this contradiction between speculation and practice more
frankly and clearly stated than by Patrick Henry in the
oft-quoted letter written two years before his memorable
oration.[2]

When the question of freedom and slavery was at issue,
the English judiciary had early been on the side of freedom.
Chief Justice Holt had, in 1697, affirmed that "as soon as a
negro comes into England he is free;" and, in 1702, that "in
England there is no such thing as a slave."[3]   But public
sentiment lagged behind the law, and later received the seal
of an extra-judicial opinion, which in practice permitted
American planters to bring their negroes to England and
hold them there as slaves.[4]   The Sommersett case, in which
the question of such a right was involved, came before the
Court of King's Bench in 1772, and Lord Mansfield delivered
the opinion.   He declared that slavery was of such a nature
that it could only be presumed to exist in a country where it
took its rise from positive law, and consequently it was a
state contrary to law in England.[5]   This decision, crystal-

---

[1] Bancroft, vol. iii. p. 410; Calendar of Home Office Papers, 1770–1772,
p. 600.

[2] See Bancroft, vol. iii. p. 412; Life of Henry Clay, Schurz, vol. i. p.
29; Hildreth, vol. iii. p. 393.

[3] Holt's Reports, 495; Campbell's Lives of the Chief Justices, vol. ii.
pp. 138, 139; see also Hildreth, vol. ii. pp. 125, 214.

[4] Hildreth, vol. ii. p. 426.

[5] Constitutional History of England, May, vol. ii. p. 273.   He remarks:
"It was a righteous judgment; but scarcely worthy of the extravagant
commendation bestowed upon it at that time and since.   This boasted
law, as declared by Lord Mansfield, was already recognized in France,

lizing a sentiment of humanity, was destined always to remain an honor to the great judge and his country's jurisprudence. It was a decision of prime importance to the English-speaking communities, who are more influenced by the dicta of high courts than by the assertion, however eloquent, of general ideas of abstract justice. There had been incomplete and unenforced legislation favoring the slave and judicial decisions unrespected, but no authority of such weight as Chief Justice Mansfield and his court had pronounced in terms which could not be misunderstood that henceforward, in one country governed by English law, freedom should be the invariable rule.

While Whitefield was conducting his Georgia plantation in the fashion of the time, John Wesley, having pondered deeply on the cruelty of slavery as he had seen it in America, characterized the slave-trade as " that execrable sum of all villainies ;" and in his " Thoughts on Slavery " denounced the practice in unmeasured terms. At the same time, Jefferson, holding opinions that would have made him an abolitionist had he lived in 1860, gave expression to them in his draft of instructions for Virginia's delegates to the first Congress of the Colonies, which was called to meet at Philadelphia in 1774. The abolition of slavery, he wrote, is the great object of desire in the colonies. "But previous to the enfranchisement of the slaves we have, it is necessary to exclude any further importations from Africa." To that end the repeated endeavors of Virginia had been directed ; but every such law had been vetoed by the king himself, who thus preferred the advantage of " a few British corsairs to the lasting interest of the American States and to the rights of human nature, deeply wounded by this infamous practice." [1] Washington shared the ideas of Jefferson. He presided at the Fairfax County Convention, and took part in framing the

Holland, and some other European countries; and as yet England had shown no symptoms of compassion for the negro beyond her own shores."

[1] Life of Jefferson, Parton, p. 138; Jefferson's Works, vol. i. p. 135.

resolves then adopted, one of which declared " that no slaves ought to be imported into any of the British colonies," and expressed " the most earnest wishes to see an entire stop forever put to such a wicked, cruel, and unnatural trade." [1] Franklin, as wise as he was humane, boldly argued in the Congress of 1776 that "slaves rather weaken than strengthen the state ;" [2] and that memorable body resolved " that no slaves be imported into any of the thirteen United Colonies." [3] The evil was appreciated, and the large majority of delegates felt that slavery ought to be restricted. It is estimated that already there had been brought into the colonies 300,000 slaves, and the blacks constituted one-fifth of the total population, [4] a larger proportion than has obtained at any subsequent period. [5] Yet these figures do not measure the extent of the slave-trade.   For the century previous to 1776 English and colonial ships had carried to the West Indies and the English continental colonies nearly three million negroes. A quarter of a million more had been bought in Africa, had died of cruel treatment during the passage, and had been thrown into the Atlantic. [6]

Burke boldly stated in the House of Commons that the refusal of America to deal any more in the inhuman traffic of negro slaves was one of the causes of her quarrel with Great Britain. [7] In the original draft of the Declaration of Independence, Jefferson gave expression to the same idea. One of his articles of indictment against George III. was: " He has waged cruel war against human nature itself, vio-

---

[1] Life and Writings of Washington, Sparks, vol. ii. p. 494.

[2] Life of Franklin, Parton, vol. ii. p. 130.   [3] Bancroft, vol. iv. p. 338.

[4] Ibid., vol. ii. pp. 274, 390. See also Burke's Speech on Conciliation with America.

[5] This is based on the figures of 1770; see Bancroft; also F. A. Walker's article in *The Forum* for July, 1891.

[6] Bancroft, vol. ii. p. 277.

[7] Cited in Hodgson's North America, vol. i. p. 57. Burke's Speech on Conciliation with America. Burke's Works, London edition of 1815, vol. iii. pp. 67, 68.

lating its most sacred rights of life and liberty in the persons of a distant people who never offended him, captivating and carrying them into slavery in another hemisphere, or to incur miserable death in the transportation thither. . . . Determined to keep open a market where men should be bought and sold, he has prostituted his negative for suppressing every legislative attempt to prohibit or restrain this execrable commerce." This passage, however, was struck out, Jefferson explained, " in compliance to South Carolina and Georgia, who had never attempted to restrain the importation of slaves, and who, on the contrary, still wished to continue it. Our Northern brethren also, I believe, felt a little tender under these censures; for though their people had very few slaves themselves, yet they had been pretty considerable carriers of them to others." [1]

" We hold," said the Congress of 1776, in the Declaration of Independence, " these truths to be self-evident : that all men are created equal ; that they are endowed by their Creator with certain inalienable rights ; that among these are life, liberty, and the pursuit of happiness." This clause created as much discussion during all the years of the slavery agitation as if it had been part of our organic law. The abolitionists, and afterwards the Republicans, asserted that it proved the solemn and deliberate belief of our Revolutionary fathers to be that all men were entitled to their freedom ; while, on the other hand, the apologists for slavery maintained that, in the minds of the illustrious author and his colleagues, the words " all men " certainly did not include the African race ; and a very clever argument to this effect was made by Chief Justice Taney in the Dred Scott decision. [2]

The affirmation by slaveholders of the equality of man is an inconsistency which cannot be denied. [3] But as Jef-

---

[1] Jefferson's Autobiography. Works, vol. i. p. 19.

[2] Infra, Chap. IX.

[3] " The grotesque absurdity of slave-owners signing a Declaration of Independence, which asserted the inalienable right of every man to liberty and equality."—Lecky's England, vol. vi. p. 282.

ferson and the Southerners who endorsed his words were in speculation far in advance of the social practice of their time, as they believed that their prohibition of the slave-trade would so curtail slavery that it would eventually die out, and as they little dreamed of the economical and political conditions that were destined to fasten it upon the South, the inconsistency was not so glaring as it appears to posterity.[1]

During the Revolutionary War, the slavery question is almost lost sight of in the struggle for independent nationality. Free negroes took part in the battle of Bunker Hill; and although a little later it was decided that colored men would not be accepted as enlisted soldiers, Washington reversed this decision, and they served in the American army at every subsequent period of the war.[2] The royal Governor of Virginia tried to excite the slaves to revolt against their masters by promising them their freedom, but had little success. Their Northern brethren desired liberty more ardently, as, during the victorious progress of Howe's army through Pennsylvania, the slaves prayed for his success, believing that he would set them free.[3] A scheme for the general enfranchisement of the slaves, with a view to diminish the aristocratic spirit of the Virginian and Southern colonists, was the subject of discussion in Parliament; but Burke reminded his Tory hearers that this was a game two could play at, and the American master might "arm servile hands in defence of freedom."[4] The great statesman spoke wisely. In Rhode Island the slaves were emancipated by law on the condition of their enlistment in the army for the war, and this project had the full approval of Washington.[5] At a later day, the question of arming the blacks

---

[1] See Justice Curtis on this, infra, Chap. IX., and Lincoln, Chap. IX.

[2] Bancroft, vol. iv. pp. 223, 322; Sparks, vol. iii. p. 218.

[3] Bancroft, vol. v. p. 180.

[4] Burke's Speech on Conciliation with America. Works, Bohn's edition, vol. i. p. 475.

[5] Bancroft, vol. v. p. 219.

in Carolina was seriously discussed, and the policy was warmly recommended to Congress by Hamilton; but as a matter of policy it was disapproved of by Washington. He argued: "Should we begin to form battalions of them, I have not the smallest doubt" the British would "follow us in it, and justify the measure upon our own ground. The contest then must be, who can arm fastest. And where are our arms?" [1]

The year following the Declaration of Independence, Vermont separated from New York and framed a State constitution, in which slavery was forbidden forever; but of the original thirteen colonies, Pennsylvania was the first to take steps to abolish the system, the Assembly voting in 1780 a scheme of gradual emancipation. [2] In the same year Massachusetts adopted a new constitution, and in the declaration of rights it was asserted: "All men are born free and equal, and have certain natural, essential, and inalienable rights." When the convention came to discuss how many of the old laws should remain in force, it was seen that any statutes that maintained or protected property in negroes were inconsistent with this clause; and it was therefore considered that its adoption abolished slavery. The common notion soon had the seal of judicial approval. The Supreme Court had occasion to pass upon the question, and decided that by virtue of this article slavery ceased to exist in Massachusetts. The colored inhabitants became citizens, and were allowed to vote if they had the requisite qualifications of age, property, and residence. At about the same time the Methodists of the United States, in solemn and regular conference, resolved that "slavekeeping was hurtful to society, and contrary to the laws of God, man, and nature." [3]

---

[1] Bancroft, vol. v. p. 370.

[2] Act of March 1st, 1780. Laws of the Commonwealth of Pennsylvania from Oct. 14th, 1700, to April 6th, 1802, vol. ii. p. 246.

[3] Bancroft, vol. v. pp. 416–422.

With the end of the war and the ratification of the peace with Great Britain, it became the duty of Congress to establish a government for a large extent of the ceded territory not comprised within the boundaries of any of the thirteen States. In 1784, Jefferson reported an ordinance that provided for the prohibition of slavery after the year 1800 in all the western country above the parallel of 31° north latitude. This proposed interdiction applied to what afterwards became the States of Alabama, Mississippi, Tennessee, and Kentucky, as well as to the Northwestern Territory.[1]

To his sorrow and lasting regret, this anti-slavery clause was lost by one vote. " The voice of a single individual," Jefferson wrote two years later, " would have prevented this abominable crime. Heaven will not always be silent ; the friends to the rights of human nature will in the end prevail."[2] In truth, the friends of human rights gained an important victory in the enactment of the Ordinance of 1787, which was a substitute for the Jefferson Act of 1784, differing from it, however, in that slavery was immediately prohibited, and in that it only applied to the Northwestern Territory, which later became the States of Ohio, Indiana, Illinois, Michigan, Wisconsin, and a part of Minnesota. Coupled with this stipulation was a clause providing for the rendition of fugitive slaves. The Ordinance partook of a compromise, and had the votes of all the members present but one ; four of the Southern States were represented. Every one of their delegates gave his voice for the anti-slavery article, and its adoption was not considered an anti-slavery triumph. In view of all the circumstances, it may be regarded as a wise adjustment of opposing interests, and its practically unanimous adoption was gained through the operation on individual minds of various and even conflicting motives.

---

[1] See the plan in Jefferson's handwriting in the State Department archives.

[2] Jefferson's Works, vol. ix. p. 276 ; Bancroft, vol. vi. p. 118.

In contriving the passage of this Ordinance, the friends
of freedom builded on a more magnificent scale than they
dreamed. A bulwark against the encroachments of slavery
was needed for the Northwest, as Indiana Territory (it then
included Illinois) afterwards petitioned many times for the
suspension of the anti-slavery article of the Ordinance, but
Congress refused the prayer. It is probable that had it
not been for the prohibitory clause, slavery would have
gained such a foothold in Indiana and Illinois that the two
would have been organized as slave-holding States. The
tribute paid by Webster contains the truth of history, and
is pregnant with philosophy. "We are accustomed," he
said, "to praise the law-givers of antiquity; we help to
perpetuate the fame of Solon and Lycurgus; but I doubt
whether one single law of any law-giver, ancient or modern,
has produced effects of more distinct, marked, and lasting
character than the Ordinance of 1787. . . . It fixed forever the character of the population in the vast regions
northwest of the Ohio, by excluding from them involuntary
servitude. It impressed on the soil itself, while yet a wilderness, an incapacity to sustain any other than freemen.
It laid the interdict against personal servitude, in original
compact, not only deeper than all local law, but deeper
also than all local constitutions." [1]

Washington, Hamilton, Madison, and Franklin did not
assist at the Congress that enacted the Ordinance of 1787;
they were at the federal convention in Philadelphia, engaged in framing the Constitution, that an eminent English
statesman has called "the most wonderful work ever struck
off at a given time by the brain and purpose of man." [2] To

---

[1] First speech on Foot's resolution, 1830, Webster's Works, vol. iii.
p. 263. On the Ordinance of 1787, see Bancroft, vol. vi. p. 287 *et seq.;*
Benton's Thirty Years' View, vol. i. p. 133; Hinsdale's Old Northwest,
chaps. xv. and xviii.; Dunn's Indiana, chaps. v. and vi.; Poole's article,
North American Review, April, 1876; Evolution of the Ordinance of 1787,
Barrett.

[2] Gladstone.

the effort to form a more perfect union of the States, slavery was a constant obstacle. It was the subject of two com-promises, although the words " slave," " slavery," and "slave-trade" do not occur in the Constitution ; for an adroit circumlocution was employed to avoid offending dele-gates who objected to the use of those terms.[1]

The first compromise referred to the apportionment for representatives in Congress. What rule should be applied to the half million or more of slaves in the five Southern States? Were the negroes persons or property ? The article of the Constitution, proceeding on the theory that they were neither absolutely the one nor the other, but that they par-took of both of these qualities, provided that in the appor-tionment for representatives, and for direct taxation as well, five slaves should count as three freemen ; as the expounder of this compromise said, the slave was regarded " as divested of two fifths of the man."[2]   In the mention of who shall or shall not be included in the enumeration, the provision closes with, "and three fifths of all other persons."[3]   The meaning is plain, but the word "slave" is avoided. This proportional adjustment was not new ; it had been adopted four years previously by the Confederation as a measure of the direct contributions of the States.

The second compromise related to the slave-trade. Under the Articles of Confederation the power to regulate this traffic and all species of commerce was left with the States. All the States but North Carolina, South Carolina, and Georgia had interdicted the slave-trade. These three positively would not accept the Constitution if this traffic was immediately and unconditionally prohibited.[4]   At the same time, the Northern States desired that Congress should

[1] History of the Constitution, Curtis, vol. ii. p. 305.

[2] The *Federalist*, No. 54.   Only New Jersey and Delaware voted against this scheme, but Massachusetts and South Carolina were divided.   Curtis, vol. ii. p. 164.

[3] Art. I., section 2.

[4] Curtis, vol. ii. p. 301 ; Bancroft, vol. vi. p. 320.

I.—2

have power to pass navigation laws by a simple majority, an action which the South contended ought to require two thirds of both branches of the Legislature. Finally mutual concessions were made. The North was given what it desired, and a provision was incorporated in the Constitution to the effect that the slave-trade should not be prohibited until the year 1808.[1] In due time, acts to enforce the understanding that was expressed in this article of organic law were passed, and the inhuman traffic was virtually brought to an end in the year named in the Constitution.

The existence of slavery dictated the provision for the rendition of persons who, "held to service or labor in one State," escape into another. It was by authority of this clause that the two Fugitive Slave laws were enacted. It is unquestionable that this stipulation was necessary for the adoption and acceptance of the Constitution;[2] and there were two precedents for it, one in the New England Confederacy of 1643,[3] and the other in the Ordinance of 1787. This clause was the subject of but little debate and passed unanimously.[4]

A defence of the work of our constitutional fathers, including the slavery compromises, is hardly necessary. Their choice lay between achieving a union of the States with those provisions, and failing to accomplish any union at all. It is a tendency of the Anglo-Saxon race to take the expedient in politics when the absolute right cannot be had, and in following it the delegates acted wisely.

Yet, could our fathers have known what was known to the abolitionists of 1833 and 1860, how different the course of history would have been! In 1787 it was supposed, and with apparent reason, that slavery would die out in all of

---

[1] Curtis, vol. ii. p. 303.

[2] Curtis, vol. ii. p. 451; Benton's Thirty Years' View, vol. ii. p. 773; The War between the States, Alex. Stephens, vol. i. p. 202; Alex. Johnston went over the ground thoroughly, and came to the same conclusion, *New Princeton Review*, vol. iv. p. 183.

[3] Bancroft, vol. i. p. 293; Curtis, vol. ii. p. 453.

[4] Elliot's Debates, vol. v. pp. 487, 492; Curtis, vol. ii. p. 456.

the States.   Seven had already abolished it, or were preparing to do so ; and he would not have been called a rash
man who predicted that he would see in his own lifetime
Delaware, Maryland, and Virginia free States.   Indeed, in the
First Congress a majority of the representatives from Maryland and Virginia inclined to anti-slavery views ; [1] and while
public sentiment in the three most southern States lagged
behind, a representative from Georgia stated in the House,
without contradiction, that not a man lived in Georgia who
did not wish there were no slaves, and everybody believed
that they were a curse to the country.[2]   But when the
Constitution was framed the cotton-gin had not been invented.   Eli Whitney's machine made possible the culture
of cotton on a large scale, and created a demand for negro
labor that could not have been foreseen.   The founders of
our government met to devise a more perfect union, to give
to a central authority enough power to create a nation, and
to make it respected and respectable in the eyes of the world.
To attain this supreme end, jarring interests and conflicting
ideas had to be reconciled, and it was indeed unfortunate
that slavery was one of those interests to mar an otherwise
perfect work.

The extraordinary political ability shown in that convention has led some European writers to judge its members
by ethical standards higher than those of the time; in other
words, to try the actors of the eighteenth century at the bar
of the nineteenth instead, and to criticise them, because,
having done what they did, they did not do more and set
operations in train whose result would have been the abolition of slavery.[3]   But this was what the majority of the
convention actually thought that they had done.   They believed, and not without apparent reason, that if the slave-

---

[1] History of the United States, Hildreth, vol. iv. p. 204.

[2] McMaster's United States, vol. ii. p. 359.

[3] "Europeans have a useful knack of forgetting their own shortcomings
when contemplating those of their neighbors."—American Commonwealth, Bryce, vol. ii. p. 121.

trade could be prohibited, the extinction of slavery would soon follow.

In its attitude towards this moral question, the convention was in advance of the world, as it confessedly was in progressive political ideas. No European country had at that time abolished the African slave-trade. Its maintenance was, as we have seen, an object of English commercial policy. Some of the ablest and purest men in Parliament worked earnestly to put a stop to it; yet, in 1791, a motion of Wilberforce for leave to bring in a bill to prevent the further importation of negroes into the West Indies, though supported by Pitt, Fox, and Burke, was defeated in the House of Commons by a vote of nearly two to one.[1] While ten of our States had prohibited the slave-trade and seven were abolishing slavery, serfdom and many feudal obligations still existed in Germany and France, and were only brought to an end by the French Revolution.[2] In England a species of white slavery was in force, almost as horrible in practice, if not in ethical theory, as the negro servitude in America.[3]

If we ask the question, Could a better organic instrument than our present Constitution be framed and adopted in the United States of to-day? we may not refuse to answer that it is "perhaps the most remarkable monument of political wisdom known to history."[4] If "human progress rarely

---

[1] Lecky's England in the Eighteenth Century, vol. vi. p. 293.

[2] Lecky's England, vol. v. p. 317. "Slavery or villeinage in France was only destroyed in that great revolution."—History of Civilization, Buckle, vol. i. p. 455.

[3] " It was one of the effects of the immense development of the cotton manufacture, that negro slavery in America, which at the time of Washington seemed likely to be extinguished by an easy and natural process, at once assumed gigantic dimensions. It was hardly more horrible, however, than the white slavery which for years after the establishment of the factory system prevailed both in England and on the Continent."— Lecky's England, vol. vi. p. 225.

[4] James R. Lowell in 1888, Political Essays, p. 311. " The framers of the Constitution" were " wiser than Justinian before them or Napoleon after them."—American Commonwealth, Bryce, vol. i. p. 364.

means more than a surplus of advantages over evils," [1] what amazing leaps in political affairs were made in America from 1776 to 1787!

If the convention was in advance of the world on this question, its leaders occupied a higher moral position than the body of which they in a great measure shaped the ends. Washington, although a slave-holder, was averse to buying or selling slaves, and on his plantation the family relation among the negroes was respected.[2]   He repeatedly urged upon the Legislature of his State the necessity of taking measures which would result in the gradual extinction of slavery.[3] The notion increased with his years and official experience, for while President, in a private letter, he emphatically expressed the opinion that at a period not far remote the system must be abolished in Virginia and Maryland ;[4] and by his last will he emancipated his own slaves.[5] Hamilton took the position of secretary of the New York Abolition Society, and was requested by Lafayette to propose him as a fellow-member of the same society.[6] Madison, in the constitutional convention, earnestly opposed the section which delayed the prohibition of the slave-trade until 1808, saying, "Twenty years will produce all the mischief that can be apprehended from the liberty to import slaves. So long a term will be more dishonorable to the American character than to say nothing about it in the Constitution ;"[7] and in the *Federalist* his warm advocacy of the Constitution did

---

[1] Lecky's England, vol. vi. p. 220.

[2] "It was once reported in the army that certain captured despatches from the General were found upon the person of a runaway slave belonging to him.   Somebody mustered courage to ask Washington if this was true. 'Sir,' said the Chief, coldly, 'I never had a slave run away from me.' "—*Century Magazine*, vol. xxxvii. p. 850; infra, Chap. III. p. 267.

[3] Bancroft, vol. vi. p. 179; Sparks, vol. ix. pp. 159, 164.

[4] Sparks, vol. xii. p. 326.

[5] Bancroft, vol. vi. p. 180; Sparks, vol. i. pp. 569, 570.

[6] Letter of Lafayette to Hamilton, quoted by Greeley, American Conflict, vol. i. p. 51.

[7] Life and Times of Madison, Rives, vol. ii. p. 449.

not forbid his saying that it would have been better to suffer the prohibition of the slave-trade to go into immediate operation.[1]   Franklin was President of the Pennsylvania Abolition Society, organized for promoting the abolition of slavery. Jefferson and John Adams had no part in framing the Constitution, for both were then serving their country at foreign courts; but, although soon to represent opposing political parties, they were at one on the question of negro servitude. Jefferson, in a letter written at about this time, expressing his ardent desire to see not only the slave-trade but also slavery abolished, laments that those whom he represents have not been able to give their voice against the practice.[2] John Adams, through his whole life, had held slavery in such abhorrence that he had never owned a slave, though he had lived for many years in times when the practice was not disgraceful, and when the best men in his vicinity thought it not inconsistent with their character.[3]

In 1790, during the second session of the First Congress, petitions from the Quakers of several States were presented, praying against the continuance of the slave-trade. The Pennsylvania Abolition Society, through its President, Franklin, earnestly entreated the serious attention of Congress to the subject of slavery; and further prayed "that you will be pleased to countenance the restoration of liberty to those unhappy men, who are degraded into perpetual bondage . . . and that you will step to the very verge of the power vested in you for discouraging every species of traffic in the persons of our fellow-men."[4]   These petitions gave rise in the House of Representatives to a warm and at times excited discussion on the question whether the memorials should be received and referred to a committee. The burden of the argument against their reception was borne by members from South Carolina and Georgia, and was to

---

[1] *Federalist*, No. 42.
[2] Jefferson's Works, vol. ii. p. 357.
[3] Adams's Works, quoted by Greeley, American Conflict, vol. i. p. 52.
[4] Benton's Abridgment of the Debates of Congress, vol. i. p. 208.

the effect that slavery, being commended by the Bible, could not be wrong; that the Southern States would not have entered into the Confederation unless their property had been guaranteed to them, and any action of the general government looking to the emancipation of the slaves would not be submitted to. South Carolina and Georgia, it was asserted, could only be cultivated by slaves, for the climate, the nature of the soil, and ancient habits forbade the whites from performing the labor; if the slaves were emancipated they would not remain in those States, and the whole of the low country, all the fertile rice and indigo swamps, must be deserted, and they would become a wilderness; furthermore, the prohibition of the slave-trade is at present unconstitutional.

After several days' debate, in which the opinions of the North and those of South Carolina and Georgia clashed, Madison poured oil upon the troubled waters, saying: " The debate has taken a serious turn, and it will be owing to this alone if an alarm is created. . . . If there was the slightest tendency by the commitment to break in upon the Constitution, he would object to it. The petition prayed in general terms for the interference of Congress so far as they were constitutionally authorized. . . . He admitted that Congress is restricted by the Constitution from taking measures to abolish the slave-trade. Yet there are a variety of ways by which it could countenance the abolition; and regulations might be made in relation to the introduction of them into the new States to be formed out of the Western territory."[1]

The memorials went through the usual legislative forms. It was finally resolved by the House that Congress could not prohibit the slave-trade until 1808, and that Congress had no authority to interfere in the emancipation of the slaves or in the treatment of them within any of the States.[2] This last resolution is of great historic importance. While it had not the binding force of law, it has always been considered as

---

[1] Annals of Congress, vol. i. p. 1246.   [2] Ibid., vol. ii. p. 1523.

an authoritative and just interpretation of the Constitution. The same principle was more than once afterwards reaffirmed by Congress, and no political party ever questioned the doctrine. The debate and resolution settled this point.[1] In all the slavery agitation, this principle stood out with the force of a fundamental truth; and in our consideration of the subsequent history, it can never too often be called to mind that the political parties of the Northern States, and their senators and representatives in Congress, scrupulously respected the constitutional protection given to the peculiar institution of the South, until, by her own action, secession dissolved the bonds of union.

In 1793 the first Fugitive Slave law was passed. The circumstance that led to its enactment deserves notice. Three white men had kidnapped a free negro in Pennsylvania and taken him to Virginia. The governor of Pennsylvania asked the rendition of the kidnappers, which Virginia refused on the ground that there was no law carrying into effect the constitutional provision for the surrender of fugitives from justice. The governor of Pennsylvania then submitted the facts to President Washington, who brought them before Congress. The result was the passage of the act known as the Fugitive Slave law of 1793, the two first sections of which related to the surrender of fugitives from justice, and the two last to the rendition of fugitive slaves. As the proceedings of the Senate were secret, neither the nature of the discussion nor the difference of opinion elicited in that body during the consideration of the bill is known. It passed the House, however, without debate: seven votes only are recorded against it, and two of these were from the slave States.[2]

---

[1] "The introduction of the Quaker memorial respecting slavery was, to be sure, not only ill-timed, but occasioned a great waste of time. The final decision thereon, however, was as favorable as the proprietors of this species of property could well have expected, considering the light in which slavery is viewed by a large part of the Union."—Washington to David Stuart, June, 1790, Sparks, vol. x. p. 98.

[2] See Fay House monograph, Fugitive Slaves, by Marion G. McDougall, and the authorities cited, especially State Papers, Annals of Congress,

The invention of the cotton-gin, in the year 1793, was of far greater importance to the landed proprietor of negroes than the statutory provision for the recovery of fugitive slaves. As already noted, it was destined to develop Southern industry and foster slave labor more effectually than extreme pro-slavery legislation could have done, and to a wider extent than the most earnest abolitionist could have feared. The cotton plant was indigenous to America, and the climate of the Southern States was peculiarly adapted to its culture. But the great obstacle in the way of cotton-production was the excessive labor necessary to clear the cotton fibres from the seed. The complete separation of a pound of fibre was an average day's work; hence the great cost of preparing it for the market limited the growth of cotton to countries like India, where labor is very cheap. Whitney's invention wholly changed these conditions. By the use of his gin, one man was able to separate fifty pounds of cotton from the seed in a day, and in this way the development of a great agricultural industry was made possible.[1] As cotton-cultivation depended more on climate than soil, a large portion of the land between 36° north latitude and the Gulf of Mexico was well adapted to it. Whitney's invention came into use at an opportune time, for complaints had been made that rice and indigo, the staple products of South Carolina and Georgia, were hardly worth growing, on account of their extremely low price.[2] Curiously enough, in this same year (1793) a protective duty of three cents per pound was placed upon cotton, the framers of the tariff little dreaming that this article was soon to become and long to remain our greatest article of export. Yet this is not more remarkable

---

and Senate journals; Benton's Abridgment of Debates, vol. i. p. 417. Hildreth says: This act "at the time of its passage and for many years after attracted little attention." At a later period the provisions were denounced as " exceedingly harsh and peremptory," vol. iv. p. 406.

[1] Whitney to Jefferson, Nov. 24th, 1793, Memoir of Eli Whitney, Olmsted. For an interesting account of Whitney and his invention, see Greeley's American Conflict, and McMaster's United States.

[2] Hildreth, vol. iv. p. 71.

than the seizure of eight bags of it in England, a few years before, on the ground that so great a quantity could not be supplied from the United States; and when Jay negotiated the treaty of 1794 with Great Britain, cotton was of so little significance that he did not know it was an article of export from his country.[1] The production of cotton from 1791 to 1860 increased more than a thousandfold,[2] and more than one half of the negro slaves were engaged in its culture.[3] What, asked Webster, created the new feeling in favor of slavery in the South, so that it became an institution—a cherished institution—" no evil, no scourge, but a great religious, social, and moral blessing? I suppose this is owing to the rapid growth and sudden extension of the cotton plantations of the South. It was the cotton interest that gave a new desire to promote slavery, to spread it, and to use its labor."[4]

Among the Fathers were men who had a correct notion of the possible future growth of the country, but no one could have dreamed that one of the very first of those splendid mechanical inventions, which are justly our boast and pride, would have the effect of riveting more strongly than ever the fetters of the slave. No one could have imagined that economic conditions were destined to prevail that would bring to naught the moral and humane expectations of the wisest statesmen of the time. It is more than probable that the invention of the cotton-gin prevented the peaceful abolition of slavery. Rice, sugar, and cotton were, apparently, the only products for which slave labor was necessary; and, compared with cotton, sugar and rice were in-

---

[1] Hildreth, vol. iv. p. 545; Webster's Works, vol. v. p. 338.

[2] Production, 1791, 2,000,000 pounds; 1860, 2,154,820,800 pounds.

[3] In 1850, according to De Bow, 1,800,000 of the 3,204,051 slaves were engaged in the cultivation of cotton. Compendium of Census, 1850; Olmsted's Cotton Kingdom, vol. i. p. 17. I have never seen any estimate for 1860, but the ratio, if changed, must have been greater, as the cotton crop of 1860 was more than double that of 1850: 1850, 2,445,793 bales; 1860, 5,387,052 bales.

[4] 7th of March, 1850, speech, Webster's Works, vol. v. p. 338.

significant products.[1] Tobacco and grain could be cultivated with greater economy by freemen. Had it not been for the new cotton-planters' demand for negroes, which made slave-breeding a profitable industry for the border States, Maryland, Virginia, and Kentucky would have been reclaimed from slavery, and Missouri would not have been admitted as a slave State. The moral and political force of so much free territory would have confined slavery below the latitude of 36° 30′, and the well-founded hopes of the framers of the Constitution might have been realized.

Cotton fostered slavery; slavery was the cause of the war between the States. That slavery is a blessing, and cotton is king, were associated ideas with which the Southern mind was imbued in the decade before the war. On the floor of the Senate it was declared that cotton had vanquished all powers, and that its supremacy could no longer be doubted. The leaders of the secession were confident that the influence of the great Southern staple would compel, if not acquiescence on the part of the North, at least recognition and open assistance from England.

The closing years of the eighteenth century need not detain us, although several warm debates on the slavery question took place in Congress, growing out of petitions that in different ways brought the national evil to the attention of Congress and the country.

In the beginning of the new century, President Jefferson effected the transfer of Louisiana.[2] The possession of the mouth of the Mississippi River was a commercial necessity, and Jefferson showed wisdom in promptly seizing the opportunity presented by a fortunate combination of circum-

---

[1] In 1860, value of cotton production, $244,256,368; of rice, $7,242,324; of sugar, $20,761,485.

[2] Louisiana comprised what is now the States of Louisiana, Arkansas, Missouri, Iowa, Nebraska, parts of Minnesota and Colorado, nearly all of Kansas and Montana, the Dakotas, Wyoming, part of Idaho, and the Indian Territory.

stances to secure the purchase of this magnificent domain
from the French government. During the negotiations and
the ratification of the treaty, the question of slavery did not
arise. The notion that this territory would be an accession
of strength to the slave-power seemed not to occur to Jefferson, to his advisers, or to the ardent advocates of Southern institutions; and although opposition to the purchase
was made by the Federalists, it was not on the ground that
it would lead to the extension of slavery. Nor was this
surprising. By this time all the States but South Carolina
had prohibited the slave-trade.[1] The year after the purchase of Louisiana (in 1804), New Jersey abolished slavery;
she was the seventh and last of the original thirteen States
to dedicate her soil to freedom. A conviction prevailed
that the power of slavery was rapidly diminishing. Even
John Adams, while President, had shared this belief.[2] It
might now have been possible to set apart to freedom, by
solemn legislative act, the whole of the new territory, ex-
cepting that portion which afterwards became the State of
Louisiana, where slavery existed and was protected by the
treaty of cession. The Quakers petitioned that Congress
would take measures to prevent the introduction of slavery
into any of the territories of the United States, but the opportune moment for legislation to that end was not seized.

The virtual understanding at the time the Constitution
was framed, in regard to the prohibition of the slave-trade,
was carried out. President Jefferson, in his annual message
to Congress, December, 1806, said : " I congratulate you, fellow-citizens, on the approach of the period at which you
may interpose your authority constitutionally to withdraw
the citizens of the United States from all further participation in those violations of human rights which have been
so long continued on the unoffending inhabitants of Africa,

---

[1] South Carolina had passed a law prohibiting the slave-trade, but
afterwards repealed the act.
[2] History of the United States, Schouler, vol. ii. p. 58.

and which the morality, the reputation, and the best interests of our country have long been eager to proscribe."[1]
Congress took prompt action.   A bill to prohibit the importation of slaves after January 1st, 1808, was passed by the
Senate, and, although its different provisions were the subject of considerable debate in the House, it was finally
passed with only five dissenting voices. This was practical unanimity, as the senators who voted against the bill
were from both free and slave States, and their objections
were not to the principle of the act, but to matters of detail.

In bringing about this devoutly wished-for consummation,
the abolition societies, which existed in all of the States as
far south as Virginia, played an important part. Their
meetings, their annual conventions, their memorials to Congress, their addresses to the country, were active agencies
to foster right thinking and to encourage effective action
respecting the slave-traffic. The first annual convention of
these societies had proclaimed that " freedom and slavery
cannot long exist together;" and, in the years that followed,
their influence did much to effect the abolition of slavery
in the States north of Mason and Dixon's line. With the
prohibition of the slave-trade, however, it seemed as if their
occupation was gone. The national conventions ceased,
meetings were no longer, or rarely, held, and most of the societies died out. The first anti-slavery movement in the
United States was no more. Virginia had by this time
(1807) given up any immediate hope of becoming a free
State; her interests, her sentiments, her social conditions,
were gradually drawing her into unison and sympathy with
her sister States farther south.

The question of the admission of Missouri made evident
to the country the influence that the profitable cultivation
of cotton had exercised on Southern opinion, and served as
a measure of the radically divergent ideas of the North and

----

[1] Jefferson's Works, vol. viii. p. 67.

the South. The opinion of the North on slavery was the same as at the adoption of the Constitution; that of the South had retrograded. Missouri was a part of the Louisiana purchase, and, having now a population of 56,000 freemen and 10,000 slaves, she desired recognition as a State of the Union. The usual form of bill was prepared; but when, during the winter session of 1819, it came to be considered in the House, Tallmadge, of New York, offered an amendment providing that the further introduction of slavery should be prohibited, and that all children born in the State after its admission into the Union should be free at the age of twenty-five. Since the organization of the government new States had been admitted from time to time, and by tacit agreement had entered in pairs, a free State and a slave State coming in at about the same time. Thus, Vermont and Kentucky, Tennessee and Ohio, Louisiana and Indiana, Mississippi and Illinois, had each been an offset to the other. Alabama was on the point of admission as a slave State, and the usage would require that another free State should be coincidently added to the Union. The North had been growing more rapidly than the South; in 1790 the two sections were nearly equal in population, but in 1820, in a total of less than ten millions, there was a difference of nearly 700,000 in favor of the North. Although the contest over Missouri took place in a House of Representatives based on the apportionment of the census of 1810, yet the Northern States, including Delaware, had a clear majority of twenty-nine members.[1]

Missouri had slavery, and was determined to keep it; and the supporters of the slave interest in Congress would not for one moment consent to a restriction which should create bars to the further increase of slaves within her borders. Tallmadge's proposed amendment, therefore, caused an exciting debate. Among the first to speak, vehemently opposing the restriction, was Henry Clay, Speaker of the

---

[1] There were 106 from the North, 2 of these from Delaware; and 77 from the South.

House, whose influence and power in the direction of affairs was great. None of his speeches on this subject have been reported; but from references made to them by his opponents we know that he denied the constitutional power of Congress to impose conditions on newly organized States in any way limiting their sovereign rights; that he contemptuously asserted that the anti-slavery men were troubled with negrophobia, and argued that by spreading slavery its evils might be cured, or at any rate palliated.[1] One historian relates that Clay, almost with tears in his eyes, pressed the argument that the restriction of slavery would be cruel to the slaves. While it would not lessen their numbers, it would expose them, crowded together "in the old, exhausted States, to destitution, and even to lean and haggard starvation, instead of allowing them to share the fat plenty of the new West."[2] This reasoning of Clay is the gist of the most weighty arguments relied upon by the opponents of the amendment; but they also urged that it was in violation of the treaty ceding Louisiana,[3] and the territorial delegate from Missouri protested against the restriction as a shameful discrimination against Missouri, which would eventually endanger the Union.

The Northern members in favor of the restriction met the constitutional objection by pointing to the fact that the restriction imposed by the Ordinance of 1787 was a condition made by Congress precedent to the admission of Ohio, Indiana, and Illinois; denied that the amendment in any way violated the treaty with France; averred that slavery was a moral and political evil, and directly opposed to the assertion of our Declaration of Independence that all men are

---

[1] See Life of Clay, Schurz, vol. i. p. 179; Taylor's and Fuller's Speeches, Benton's Abridgment of Debates, vol. vi.

[2] Hildreth, vol. vi. p. 664.

[3] This argument, which reappears in 1850-60, is with force refuted by Justice Curtis in his opinion in the Dred Scott case. Life and Writings of B. R. Curtis, vol. ii. p. 300.

created equal, while it had only through necessity been tolerated by the Constitution. Tallmadge, who closed the debate, met the assertion of a Georgia member, that if the North persisted in the restriction the Union would be dissolved, by a fierce note of defiance;[1] and he proceeded to delineate the evil of slavery with impassioned eloquence, calling it "this monstrous scourge of the human race," fraught with " dire calamities to us as individuals and to our nation." The speech produced a sensation, and under its influence the vote was taken. The Tallmadge amendment was passed by a vote of 87 to 76. The bill for the admission of Missouri as amended went to the Senate, which rejected the slavery restriction by the entire Southern vote, assisted by one senator from Massachusetts, one from Pennsylvania, two from Illinois, and two from Delaware.[2] If all the senators from the free States had voted for the amendment, it would have been carried. Each House held tenaciously to its own ideas; and when adjournment came, March 4th, 1819, no agreement had been reached.

Then began a discussion which engrossed the press of the country, and prompted many public meetings. The legislatures of Northern States adopted resolutions protesting against the admission of Missouri unless the further introduction of slavery should be prohibited. Illinois and New England were alone officially silent, but public meetings were held all over New England—Boston being impressed by the eloquence of Webster—and they proclaimed in strong language the same sentiment. Virginia and Kentucky were equally zealous for slavery; Maryland agreed with Virginia, but a meeting of citizens in Baltimore, over which the mayor presided, petitioned Congress against the further extension of slavery. The legislature of the slave State of Delaware was on the side of freedom, but her senators and

---

[1] A portion of this speech is given by Hildreth, vol. vi. p. 665.
[2] The vote was 22 against slavery-restriction, and 16 for it.

representatives did not by their votes give expression to the public will.

In January, 1820, the Senate resumed the consideration of the Missouri question, and for the first time in the history of the country its proceedings awakened more interest than those of the House. Hitherto it had been the debates of the representatives which had excited attention and educated public opinion. Indeed, during the first years of the government all the debates of the Senate were secret, and, though they had long since been open, sparkling contests did not take place in that dignified body, nor was that collision of mind with mind seen which is necessary to provoke general interest in legislative procedure. Madison never served in the Senate; he was an efficient worker in putting in motion the legislative machine of the new government, but his wise counsel and calm reasoning were heard in the House. In the House occurred the great debate on the Jay treaty, when Gallatin first appeared as a leader, and when Fisher Ames made the pathetic appeal in its favor that ranks among the remarkable efforts of American eloquence. John Randolph was in the House when he breathed out those invectives and gave free course to those sarcasms which have entitled him to a singular place in congressional history. Clay had been a senator for a portion of two terms, but he deemed it a welcome change to be elected to the House, and it was there that up to this time his public reputation had been made. Webster and Calhoun had been representatives, but it was after 1820 that Webster, Clay, and Calhoun were to make themselves and their Senate forever renowned. Nor was it surprising that the House should be the better arena for government by discussion. That body was not as large and unwieldy as it has since become, and its hall had not the vast proportions of the present chamber. The Senate had too small a number of members to be the almost ideal body of debate that it afterwards became; for at the organization of the government only twenty-two senators convened, and their deliberations

I.—3

savored rather of the cabinet than of the legislative body.[1] But in the Senate of 1820, consisting of forty-four members, began that series of parliamentary efforts which in eloquence have never been surpassed.

The oration of William Pinkney, of Maryland, was the masterpiece of the session. He had served his country abroad with ability and honor, but had won his greatest renown at the bar.[2] When Daniel Webster came to Washington to practise in the Supreme Court, Pinkney was the acknowledged leader of American lawyers, and this surpassing eminence he held to the day of his death, although his position began to be shaken after the Boston lawyer had made the great argument in the Dartmouth College case. Perhaps a perception of Webster's growing power and future rank led Pinkney to say to his friend and biographer that he " did not desire to live a moment after the standing he had acquired at the bar was lost, or even brought into doubt or question." [3] This great lawyer was as vain of a handsome face, accomplished manners, and an elegant dress as he was proud of his legal acumen. Clad in the extreme of fashion, he preferred to be regarded an idle and polished man of society rather than to be looked upon as what he really was, an unwearied student.[4] Always preparing his speeches with the utmost care, writing out the showy passages and learning them by heart, rehearsing in private the

---

[1] North Carolina and Rhode Island were not represented at the first session of the first Congress.

[2] " America never sent an abler representative to the Court of London."
—History of the United States, Henry Adams, vol. vi. p. 21. Chief Justice Marshall remarked shortly after the death of Pinkney that Pinkney " was the greatest man he had ever seen in a court of justice." Tyler's Taney, p. 141.

[3] Life of Pinkney, Wheaton, p. 179.

[4] "William Pinkney, a large, handsome man and remarkable for his somewhat foppish dress, wearing, when I saw him, a white waistcoat and white top-boots,"—Recollections of a Lifetime, S. G. Goodrich, vol. ii. p. 399.

appropriate gestures and rhetorical points, he sought to convey the notion that he spoke on the spur of the moment.

The speech of Pinkney, a labor of many weeks, was a reply to arguments that had been urged during the last session in favor of slavery restriction by the veteran Rufus
King. King was not only the head of the anti-slavery party in the Senate, but the leader in the agitation that had
spread throughout the country. He had made two speeches
at the previous session, neither of which had been reported,
but abstracts of them were published by the New York
committee, and widely circulated as campaign documents.
They had been potent agencies in arousing and educating
Northern sentiment. Pinkney's speech was never printed,[1]
but from contemporary accounts we know that it was regarded as the most remarkable oration of this Congress, and
by all odds the most effective reasoning on the Southern
side. Benton speaks of it as a magnificent exhibition, the
most gorgeous speech ever delivered in the Senate and the
most applauded, and Clay thought it "a display of astonish-
ing eloquence."[2] It was the master effort of Pinkney's life.
All of his auditors were impressed with a fine amplification
of a passage in Burke's speech on "Conciliation with America," which afforded the orator an opportunity to make an
adroit application of the warning of the English commoner,
that the spirit of liberty was more high and haughty in the
slave-holding colonies than in those to the northward. Pinkney
made two speeches against imposing the restriction of slavery
on Missouri as a condition for admission; the second speech,
made also in reply to King, has been reported, and it gives
us an idea of his florid eloquence and power of reasoning.

---

[1] For the first thirty-five years of the government, the debates of Congress were not reported verbatim, as they have been since. Pinkney
preferred to rest his reputation on the sensation produced by the delivery of the oration, and did not prepare it for publication. Benton's
Thirty Years' View, vol. i. p. 20.

[2] Thirty Years' View, vol. i. p. 20 ; Private Correspondence of H. Clay,
Colton, p. 61.

Having a fine command of language, acquired by the profound study of the accurate use of words, his oration is replete with classical and historical allusions, and the thought and language of it bear witness to hours spent with Milton.

With much force, Pinkney urged the Southern argument. States are sovereign, he maintained. If Missouri comes in with the restriction, it comes in shorn of its beams—crippled and disparaged beyond the original States—it is not into the original union that it comes. The original union was a union among equals; this would be a union between giants and a dwarf, between power and feebleness, between full-proportioned sovereignties and a miserable image of power. Under the Constitution you have a right to refuse to admit a State; but if you admit it, you must do so on full and complete equality with the other sovereign States of the union; you must receive it into the actual union and recognize it as a parcener in the common inheritance, without any other shackles than the rest have, by the Constitution, submitted to bear.

Meanwhile the question had assumed a new phase. Maine, recently separated from Massachusetts, had applied for admission as a State. Senator Thomas, of Illinois, had introduced a proviso which prohibited slavery in that part of the Louisiana purchase which lay north of the latitude of 36° 30′, except the portion included within the limits of the proposed State. This line was the southern boundary of Missouri, and the arrangement involved the admission of Missouri as a slave State. This was the famous Missouri Compromise. It was also understood that Maine should be admitted without opposition; and the parties to the bargain carried it through the Senate exactly as planned. Greater difficulty was encountered in getting the project through the House. But by the aid of eighteen Northern members, the slavery restriction was finally defeated; fifteen of them voted openly against it, while three absented themselves.[1]

---

[1] History of the United States, Schouler, vol. iii. p. 165.

The amendment prohibiting the introduction of slaves into Missouri was struck out by a majority of three,[1] and after this action it became easy to pass the compromise, although thirty-seven extreme Southerners, under the leadership of John Randolph, did not give the scheme their votes.[2]   This epigrammatic statesman denounced the compromise as a "dirty bargain," and called the eighteen Northern members "dough-faces," a term abiding in our political vocabulary as long as the slavery question remained in politics.[3]

Yet the compromise did not settle the Missouri question. The constitution adopted in June, 1820, by the convention of Missouri forbade her legislature to interfere with slavery, and required it to enact laws prohibiting the immigration of free colored persons into the State.   The House refused to admit her with these provisions in her constitution; but in the end the matter was compromised through the efforts of Clay, and Missouri became a State August 10th, 1821.[4]

Thirty-three years later, the provision of this act that prohibited slavery in the territory north of 36° 30′ was repealed; and the history of the Missouri Compromise was then so falsely related and its historical meaning so perverted by the advocates of the repeal that two facts need to be distinctly and emphatically stated.

First, the Missouri Compromise was a Southern measure. Its passage was considered at the time as in the interest of the South, for it gained immediately a slave State in Missouri, and by implication another in Arkansas, while the settlement of the northern portion of the territory was looked upon as remote.   The North regarded the Missouri Compromise as a surrender, and of the fifteen representatives

---

[1] The vote was 90 to 87.

[2] Schouler, vol. iii. p. 165.

[3] Besides authorities already quoted, I have consulted Curtis's Life of Webster, Harvey's Reminiscences, and Carr's Missouri.

[4] For a full account of this third Missouri controversy, see Schouler, vol. iii. p. 180; Life of Clay, Schurz, vol. i. p. 183; Benton's Thirty Years' View, vol. i. p. 8.

who voted against slavery-restriction, only three were returned to Congress.[1]

But the most important bearing of this controversy is that a very large majority of Congress, made up of Southern as well as Northern senators and representatives, went on record as averring that, by a true interpretation of the Constitution, Congress had power to prohibit slavery in the territories. Of greater significance even was the discussion of the question by the President and his cabinet. Monroe, a Virginian, before approving the act, asked his advisers "whether Congress had a constitutional right to prohibit slavery in a territory." John Quincy Adams, Crawford of Georgia, John C. Calhoun, Thompson of New York, McLean of Ohio, and William Wirt of Maryland, who composed the President's cabinet, "unanimously agreed that Congress have the power to prohibit slavery in the territories."[2] We have seen that one of the first interpretations of the Constitution which had the seal of the House of Representatives was that Congress had no power to interfere with slavery in the States, and it was remarked that this principle had the respect of the North until the outbreak of the civil war. The historian would write a grateful page could he add that the doctrine of 1820, solemnly agreed to by representative men of both sections, had received equal respect from the South.

Impartial historians have affirmed, with satisfying reasons, that the Missouri Compromise was a political necessity in order to preserve the fraternal relations that should

---

[1] The debate in Congress and analyses of the votes fully support these statements; see also Benton's Thirty Years' View, vol. i. pp. 5, 8. Benton's Abridgment of Debates, vol. vi., notes on pp. 333, 453; Hildreth, vol. vi. p. 694. A writer in the *North American Review* for April, 1820, said that the passing of the compromise was the first just cause of reproach on America for the toleration of slavery.

[2] Diary of John Q. Adams, Memoirs, vol. v. p. 5; Benton's Thirty Years' View, vol. ii. p. 141; Schouler, vol. iii. p. 167. On the action of Congress, see Benton's Abridgment, vol. vi., note on p. 367.

subsist between the members of a federal union.[1] That
harmony between the two sections was liable to be disturbed unless mutual concessions were made, cannot be denied. "This momentous question," wrote Jefferson from
Monticello, "like a fire-bell in the night, awakened and
filled me with terror. I considered it at once as the knell
of the Union."[2] "The words civil war and disunion," wrote
Clay, "are uttered almost without emotion;"[3] and Benton
says, "Compromise views prevailed, and enabled the Union
to be saved."[4]

A philosopher, admitting the compromise to be a political
necessity, might nevertheless have feared, if he looked into
the seeds of time, that this controversy began an irrepressible conflict. He must have noted that, since the adoption
of the Constitution, slavery had gained in power through
the development of the cotton-culture, the settlement of the
Gulf States, and the pecuniary interest which Virginia and
Maryland, having become slave-breeding States, now had in
the spread of slavery. The changed conditions in Virginia
had affected the opinions of the author of the Declaration

---

[1] Hildreth, vol. vi. p. 693; Schouler, vol. iii. p. 171; Life of H. Clay,
Schurz, vol. i. p. 199.

[2] Jefferson's Works, vol. vii. p. 159.

[3] Clay's Private Correspondence, p. 61.

[4] See also Senator Butler's remarks, Feb. 24th, 1854. "History tells us,
I know not how truly, that the Union reeled under the vehemence of
that great debate."—Seward, Feb., 1860. Niles, however, though earnestly
in favor of the compromise, "did not fear the dreadful things which
some silly folks talked of," Niles's Register, vol. xix. p. 265; see also
p. 371. Seward said, in September, 1860: "History says that the compromise of 1820 was necessary to save the Union from disruption. I do not
dispute history nor debate the settled moral questions of the past. I only
lament that it was necessary, if indeed it was so. History tells us that
the course then adopted was wise. I do not controvert it. I only
mourn the occurrence of even one case, most certainly the only one that
ever did happen, in which the way of wisdom has failed to be also the
way of pleasantness and the path of peace."—Seward's Works, vol. iv.
p. 311.

of Independence, for he eagerly grasped at Clay's theory
that the extension of slavery was far-seeing humanity.
Spreading the slaves, he wrote, " over a larger surface will
dilute the evil everywhere and facilitate the means of getting finally rid of it." [1]   Nor could Madison resist the entic-
ing logic of the rising statesman; beginning now to admire,
he came to revere Clay as the hope of the country. [2]   He
wrote to Monroe "that an uncontrolled dispersion of the
slaves now in the United States was not only best for the
nation, but most favorable for the slaves also." [3]   It is worthy of observation that Clay and Pinkney, who began their
political life with earnest efforts towards the abolition of
slavery in their respective States, now led the opposition to
the restriction of slavery; and that not a senator or Southern member of Congress had dared to vote on the side of
freedom. [4]

The nullification trouble of 1832–33, although caused by
the enactment of a high protective tariff, must claim our
attention, for the reason that, in this controversy, two constitutional theories were developed, one of which was hugged
to delusion by the South, while the other became the justification and incentive of the North to draw the sword.   The
obnoxious tariff, the " tariff of abominations," as its opponents called it, was enacted in 1828, and established a greater
degree of protection to manufactures than had any previous
revenue bill.   Calhoun and the people of his State had formerly been in favor of the protective principle.   But by this
time the belief had become fixed that, as England was the
largest purchaser of cotton, it was for the best interest of
South Carolina to have English goods brought in free ; or,
if that were impracticable, to have duties imposed upon

---

[1] Letter of Jefferson to Lafayette, Dec. 26th, 1820, Works, vol. vii. p. 193.
[2] See article of George Bancroft on Henry Clay, *Century Magazine*, vol.
viii. p. 479.
[3] Writings of James Madison, vol. iii. p. 169.
[4] Hildreth, vol. vi. p. 697.

thom for the sake of revenue only. The Palmetto State had
no manufactures, nor could she expect to build up any with
her system of labor. Her interest being to buy manufact-
ured articles as cheaply as possible, she could have no sympathy with legislation that had for its purpose the fostering
of home industries. The favorite idea was to exchange cotton for English goods, with no restrictions whatever on this
reciprocal trade. For the production of cotton slave labor
was then thought to be necessary; and free trade and negro
slavery, therefore, became associate and fundamental tenets
in the South Carolina political catechism.

The enactment of the tariff of 1828 created great excitement in South Carolina, and public meetings were held all
over the State, denouncing the law in unmeasured terms.[1]
Nullification was threatened, and, while the majority did
not seem ready to take that step, the sentiment in favor of
nullification simply needed a leader to give it shape and direction; and a leader was at hand in the person of the Vice-
President, John C. Calhoun. His opinions marked him out
for the guide of his native State. He had hitherto been intensely national in his feelings, and in favor of giving a liberal construction to the Constitution. "He is," wrote John
Quincy Adams in his diary, "above all sectional and factious
prejudices, more than any other statesman of this Union with
whom I have ever acted." He was then "a man of fair and
candid mind, of enlarged philosophical views, and of ardent
patriotism."[2] But, according to the same keen observer,
that was when Calhoun felt sanguine as to his prospects for
the presidency;[3] and this hope had a reasonable basis, for
the Northern States in 1824 voted almost in a body for him
for Vice-President. Even Webster at one time was strongly
inclined to support him for the highest office in the country.
In 1828 Calhoun had by no means renounced this ambition.

---

[1] See Niles's Register, vols. xxxiv. and xxxv.
[2] Memoirs of J. Q. Adams, vol. v. p. 361.
[3] Ibid., vol. vi. p. 7.

He was candidate for Vice-President on the same ticket with General Jackson; and for another term he hoped to have the influence of the great popular hero in favor of his own elevation to the higher place. He was now drawn in two directions—in one by the sentiment of his own State, in the other by his feeling of nationality and restless craving for the presidency. He would retain his support at the North, and yet he wished to lead the public sentiment of South Carolina. He was equal to the occasion. He did nothing until after election, when he had a handsome majority of the electoral votes for Vice-President; but in December the legislature printed a paper which he had prepared under the title of "The South Carolina Exposition and Protest on the Subject of the Tariff." This was a mild document, and merely a plain argument to show the great injury of a protective tariff to the "staple States;" and while the right of interposing the veto of the State is asserted, no threat is made, but, on the contrary, it is deemed advisable to allow time for further consideration and reflection, in the hope of a returning sense of justice on the part of the majority.[1] After this deliverance the excitement in South Carolina subsided.

The next act of the drama took place in the national theatre. Desiring to know how the country would receive the bare doctrine of nullification, Senator Hayne was put forward to deliver the prologue, but Calhoun was the prompter behind the scenes. Hayne asserted that, in case of a palpable violation of the Constitution by the general government, a State may interpose its veto; that this interposition is constitutional, and the State is to be the sole judge when the federal government transcends its constitutional limit. The senator's speeches were not remarkable, and would never have been remembered, had not his most labored effort given Webster the occasion for one of those rare bursts of eloquence that astonish and delight the

---

[1] For a good abstract of this document, see Von Holst's Calhoun, p. 76.

world.   On the morning of the day[1] when this masterpiece
of American oratory was delivered, a fellow-senator said to
Webster : "It is a critical moment, and it is time, it is high
time, that the people of this country should know what this
Constitution *is*." "Then," answered Webster, "by the blessing of Heaven, they shall learn this day before the sun goes
down what I understand it to be."[2]   An abstract of this
speech, which, as a literary production, has been compared
to the oration of Demosthenes on the Crown, need not detain us.   Webster's oration itself is familiar to students of
American history, to lovers of English literature, and to all
those whose admiration is kindled by eloquence in any
tongues.   Its famous peroration was soon declaimed from
every college and school platform, and it still retains its
place among such pieces of oratory by virtue of its earnest
feeling and classic style.   A large audience heard the speech,
but the interest in the question was so great that the brilliant crowd that gathered in the Senate chamber was but a
fraction of the people over whom his words were to have
lasting power.   He spoke to the whole country, and to the
American people of future ages.   The principles he laid
down are fundamental truths.   It took a long war to establish them ; but now, sealed in blood, they are questioned by
none save Southerners of the past generation.

That the argument crushed nullification was public opinion in the Northern, Western, and many of the Southern
States.[3]   It settled the question for the moment, and probably would have done so for a generation had not there occurred about this time a complete change in the political
fortunes of Calhoun.   General Jackson quarrelled with him,[4]
and this blasted his hopes for the presidency.   Adams
called him "a drowning man."   He no longer needed to
halt between two opinions.   He could abandon his national

---

[1] Jan. 26th, 1830.   [2] Life of Webster, Lodge, p. 178.
[3] Life of Webster, Curtis, vol. i. p. 366.
[4] Life of Jackson, Parton, vol. iii. chap. xxv.

ideas and devote himself to the seeming interests of his native State. His talents were well adapted to the work. The South had special interests based upon her peculiar system of labor. The North was growing much faster than the South, and the large immigration from Europe, just beginning, was being directed entirely to the free States. The South attracted none of this, for the reason that freemen would not work with slaves. The stubborn fact came home to every Southern politician that she was losing political power. A theory of the Constitution was therefore needed which should give the minority an absolute check on the majority. Calhoun was by nature and education as well fitted to construct a narrow and sectional hypothesis as Webster was adapted to elaborate a broad national one. After 1830, we look in vain to Calhoun for any exhibition of that pervasive patriotism that was so distinguishing a feature in the characters of Webster, Clay, and Jackson.

Calhoun now bent all his energies to the task, and worked out the fine-spun theory of nullification. He elaborated it in subtle language, and supported it by ingenious, metaphysical reasoning. Brave in the closet when developing his theories, on the stage of action he shrank from putting them in practice. He became a man of one idea; he lacked that commerce with the world which would have modified the opinions he elaborated in the study. "Calhoun is mind through and through," said Lieber;[1] and Harriet Martineau was struck by his "utter intellectual solitude," by his harangues at the fireside as if he were in the Senate, and, observing that he was full of his nullification doctrine, wrote, "I never saw any one who so completely gave me the idea of possession."[2] An impracticable theorist, he neglected the obvious application of his country's Constitution, of the constitutions of the different States, and of the English Con-

---

[1] Life and Letters of Francis Lieber, p. 123.

[2] This was in 1836. Retrospect of Western Travel, quoted by Sumner, Life of Jackson, p. 284.

stitution. In lieu thereof, he became such a student of Roman history and precedents that they became unconsciously
in his mind examples for us; and he had the utopian notion
that the divided powers of the Roman Republic might be
ingrafted on our own system. One of his admirers deplores
that he was not a sounder constitutional lawyer.[1]

In 1832, Congress revised the tariff. The revision, in the
opinion of Calhoun, caused " a small reduction in the amount
of duties, but a reduction of such a character that while it
diminished the amount of burden, it distributed that burden
more unequally than even the obnoxious act of 1828." [2] This
was the year of the presidential election; but the contest
between Jackson and Clay excited little interest in South
Carolina, for there the controversy turned on nullification,
and the struggle was for the control of the legislature. As
it was conceded that the nullifiers would get a majority,
the efforts of the Union men were directed to prevent their
gaining two thirds of the legislature, which was necessary
to authorize the calling of a convention. All agreed that
the legislature could not declare a law of the United States
unconstitutional and void; but this imposing act needed a
convention with a fresh mandate from the people. Calhoun
contributed powerfully to the success of the nullifiers, and
the election resulted in their favor.[3] A convention was
called, and met in November. In it the aristocracy of the
State was well represented ; no abler body of men ever came
together in South Carolina for a political purpose.[4] The
convention adopted the famous nullification ordinance,
which declared that the tariff acts of 1828 and 1832 were
"null, void, no law," and not binding on the officers or citizens of this State ; and that no duties enjoined by those acts
should be paid or permitted to be paid in the State of South

---

[1] Memoir of R. B. Taney, Tyler, pp. 185, 186.
[2] Speech of Calhoun in the Senate, Feb. 15th, 1833.
[3] Life of Calhoun, Jenkins, p. 243.
[4] Life of Jackson, Parton, vol. iii. p. 457.

Carolina after the first day of February, 1833. This action was immensely popular in the state. The nullifiers were blatant and aggressive, and the respectable minority of Unionists were silent. Warlike preparations began to be made, medals were struck bearing the impress "John C. Calhoun, first President of the Southern Confederacy." [1]

Here was a great opportunity for President Jackson, and he comprehended it fully. His honest and wise action in this trouble is his best title to fame, and it overshadows his arbitrary acts and injudicious measures. Apprehending nullification proceedings, he had already sent secret orders to the collector at Charleston, that in case there should be a refusal to pay any duties, the cargo in question should be seized forthwith, and sold to pay the duty charges. He had also ordered General Scott to Charleston. The President's answer to the nullification ordinance was a proclamation, in which were blended appeal, argument, and warning; in all respects it was a dignified state paper, worthy of the country, whose good fortune it was to have a fit executive at so important a crisis. The proclamation began by refuting the right to annul, and the right to secede as claimed by the nullifiers; any such rights were inconsistent with the main object of the Constitution, which was "to form a more perfect union." It was admitted that the tariff act complained of did act unequally; but so did every revenue law that ever had been or ever could be passed. "To say that any state may at pleasure secede from the Union, is to say that the United States are not a nation." In conclusion the people of South Carolina were plainly warned that in case any forcible resistance to the laws was tried by them, the attempt would meet the united power of the other states.[2] Every important idea in this proclamation may be found in Webster's reply to Hayne,[3] which shows

---

[1] Life of Jackson, Parton, vol. iii. p. 459.   [2] Ibid., p. 468.
[3] Everett's Memoir of Webster, prefixed to Webster's Works, p. cv.

what deep hold on General Jackson's mind this vigorous exposition of nationality had taken.

The North received the action of the President with great enthusiasm, and party lines were forgotten in the patriotic sentiment which it aroused. Even in all of the Southern States except three, his determination to resist any overt act was generally approved. But in South Carolina the proclamation caused great irritation. The Charleston *Mercury* called it "a declaration of war made by Andrew Jackson against the state of South Carolina." He was compared as a usurper to Cæsar, Cromwell, and Bonaparte. The editor hastened to add he had none of their genius. "If the Republic," says the fiery writer, "has found a master, let us not live his subjects." The proclamation was received by the legislature in session at Columbia with scorn and defiance. One member said, "the principles thus avowed . . . were not less new and startling than was the mode of announcing them. Who and whose are we? Are we Russian serfs or slaves of a divan?" Another member believed that "the contest would end in blood. The document of the President was none less than the edict of a tyrant."[1] These expressions were heard with undisguised approval, and the legislature asked the governor[2] to issue a counter-proclamation. He immediately complied with the request and published a pugnacious manifesto,[3] ending with the exhortation to resist at all hazards the employment of military force by the President. The governor, moreover, called out twelve thousand volunteers.[4]

Meanwhile Calhoun had been elected senator, had resigned the vice-presidency, and was on his way to Washington. His journey thither, says one of his biographers, "was like that of Luther to attend the diet at Worms.

---

[1] Niles's Register, vol. xliii.

[2] The governor was Hayne, the apologist of South Carolina in the celebrated debate with Webster.

[3] Parton, vol. iii. p. 470.   [4] Life of Calhoun, Jenkins, p. 245.

Out of South Carolina public opinion was certainly against him; and only here and there did he find a good Freundsberg to whisper in his ear, 'If you are sincere and sure of your cause, go on in God's name, and fear nothing.'"[1] Calhoun was in his seat in the Senate and heard the message from the President asking additional powers for the enforcement of the laws made necessary by the action of South Carolina and her governor. A bill, called by its enemies the Force bill, giving the President the authority he wished, was reported without delay. The action of the President thoroughly frightened Calhoun.[2] As Webster said of him, he had not seemed " conscious of the direction or the rapidity of his own course. The current of his opinion sweeps him along he knows not whither. To begin with nullification with the avowed intent, nevertheless, not to proceed to secession, dismemberment, and general revolution, is as if one were to take the plunge of Niagara and cry out that he would stop half-way down."[3] It was brought to the knowledge of Calhoun that General Jackson had determined to take at once a decided course with him, and that the matter of his arrest for high treason was under serious consideration.[4] If the logic of his closet found no place for compromise, the logic of events demanded one very imperatively. By whom could it be brought about? There was one man whose wide influence, winning address, and skill in party management might effect a compromise; that man was Henry Clay. To him, therefore, although they had not been on speaking terms, Calhoun repaired.[5] The result of one or more conferences and of mediation by mutual friends was a compromise tariff bill

---

[1] Life of Calhoun, Jenkins, p. 246.

[2] Parton, vol. iii. p. 474; Benton, vol. i. p. 343; Curtis's Webster, vol. i. p. 443.

[3] Speech, Feb. 16th, 1833. Works, vol. iii. p. 460.

[4] Benton, vol. i. p. 343; Parton, vol. iii. p. 474.

[5] Curtis, vol. i. p. 444; also see Benton, vol. i. p. 343.

which gradually reduced the tariff until, after a lapse of nine years, all duties should be diminished to the uniform rate of twenty per cent.[1] Clay's action is comprehensible. The next Congress, most of which had already been elected, would certainly be in favor of radical revenue reform, yet its action might now be forestalled by a moderate decrease. To our generation this argument is not unfamiliar, as it has served a like purpose. To Clay, moreover, occurred the obvious consideration that in nine years a Congress devoted to protection might be elected which could alter the tariff at will.[2] Besides, actuated by patriotic motives, he thought he was serving his country well in pouring oil into the inflamed wounds; his disposition to lead was mastering, and his animosity to Jackson was such that he did not wish the President to gain glory by the settlement of the trouble. Calhoun's course was a curious piece of inconsistency. The previous fall elections had decided that a better measure for South Carolina would pass at the next session, if the tariff were now left untouched. He had asserted in the strongest terms that a tariff for protection was unconstitutional and an inveterate and dangerous evil; yet Clay said of the compromise act, in open Senate, to Calhoun's face: "The main object of the bill is not revenue, but protection."[3] Calhoun and the nullifiers nevertheless voted for the bill in all its stages,[4] and before the close of the session it became a law. The reason for their action is apparent. Calhoun, his followers, and his State were in a predicament. Unless something should pass this Congress, they must retreat from their

---

[1] Tariff History of United States, Taussig, p. 110. The tariff of 1828 was equivalent to a 45 per cent. ad valorem tariff on dutiable articles, see Senate Report No. 2130, 51st Cong., 2d Sess., p. 306.

[2] See Taussig, note p. 112.

[3] Benton, vol. i. p. 321.

[4] "If this course does not prove that Calhoun was a 'coward and a conspirator,' it does prove, I think, that he was not a person of that exalted and Roman-toga cast which he set up to be, and which he enacted for some years with considerable applause."—Parton, vol. iii. p. 477.

I.—4

position ignominiously or come into collision with the federal power, for it was quite plain the country would sustain the President.   They were therefore ready to grasp at
anything having the semblance of compromise, and Clay's
project was now the best they could get.[1]

In the meantime the 1st of February had come, and the
South Carolina people had decided to defer practical nullification until, at any rate, after the adjournment of Congress.

Webster would have nothing to do with the compromise.
Clay had broached the matter to him, but he refused his
support.   " It would," he said, " be yielding great principles to faction ; the time has come to test the strength of
the Constitution and the government." [2]

A few days after the compromise tariff was introduced
occurred the debate on the Force bill in the Senate between
Calhoun and Webster, in which the opposite theories of the
nature of our government were maintained by their respective champions.   " The people of Carolina," said Calhoun, " believe that the Union is a union of States and not
of individuals ; that it was formed by the States, and that
the citizens of the several States were bound to it through
the acts of their several States ; that each State ratified the
Constitution for itself, and that it was only by such ratification of a State that any obligation was imposed upon its
citizens. . . . On this principle the people of the State
(South Carolina) . . . have declared by the ordinance that
the acts of Congress which imposed duties under the authority to lay imposts were acts not for revenue, as intended by the Constitution, but for protection, and therefore null
and void."   " The terms union, federal, united, all imply a
combination of sovereignties, a confederation of States. . . .
The sovereignty is in the several States, and our system is
a union of twenty-four sovereign powers, under a constitu-

---

[1] Benton, vol. i. p. 342.

[2] For the secret history of this compromise, see Benton, vol. i. p. 342.

tional compact, and not of a divided sovereignty between
the States severally and the United States."

Webster's answer was a piece of close and powerful reasoning,[1] but not a magnificent flight of eloquence like the
reply to Hayne. The speech contains hardly a classical allusion or historical illustration. Plain facts are dealt with,
and, while the argument is clear enough to commend itself
to an ordinary understanding, the chain of logic delights
the profound student of constitutional law. "His very statement was argument; his inference seemed demonstration."[2]
He begins this speech of February 16th, 1833, by saying
that he will endeavor to maintain the Constitution in its
plain sense and meaning against opinions and notions which
in his judgment threaten its subversion. "I admit, of
course," he said, "that the people may, if they choose, overthrow the government. But then that is revolution. The
doctrine now contended for is, that, by nullification or secession, the obligations and authority of the government may
be set aside or rejected without revolution. But that is
what I deny. . . . The Constitution does not provide for
events that must be preceded by its own destruction. Secession, therefore, since it must bring these consequences
with it, is revolutionary, and nullification is equally revolutionary. . . . I maintain—

"1. That the Constitution of the United States is not a
league, confederacy, or compact between the people of the
several States in their sovereign capacities, but a government
proper, founded on the adoption of the people, and creating
direct relations between itself and individuals.

"2. That no state authority has power to dissolve these
relations; that nothing can dissolve them but revolution;
and that consequently there can be no such thing as secession without revolution. . . .

---

[1] See Curtis, vol. i. p. 451.

[2] Webster's remark of a noted New England lawyer, in his reply to
Hayne.

" The truth is, and no ingenuity of argument, no subtlety of distinction, can evade it, that as to certain purposes the people of the United States are one people. . . . Sir, how can any man get over the words of the Constitution itself? —'We, the people of the United States, do ordain and establish this Constitution.' . . . Who is to construe finally the Constitution of the United States? . . . I think it is clear that the Constitution, by express provision, by definite and unequivocal words, as well as by necessary implication, has constituted the Supreme Court of the United States the appellate tribunal in all cases of a constitutional nature which assume the shape of a suit in law or equity." [1]

These citations only give Webster's bare positions, but the proofs are irrefragable. The detailed arguments are no longer necessary to carry conviction; the statements themselves command unquestioned assent; but it was not so when Webster made this speech. He had the majority of the South against him, and not every one at the North was prepared to adopt his strong national opinions.[2] But the greatest authority living, James Madison, in a letter congratulating Webster for his speech, agreed with the view he had taken of the nature of the government established by the Constitution.[3]

The justification alleged by the South for her secession in 1861 was based on the principles enunciated by Calhoun; the cause was slavery. Had there been no slavery, the Calhoun theory of the Constitution would never have been propounded, or, had it been, it would have been crushed beyond resurrection by Webster's speeches of 1830 and 1833,

---

[1] Webster's Works, vol. iii., speech entitled " The Constitution not a Compact between Sovereign States."

[2] See for example Memoirs of John Q. Adams, vol. viii. p. 526; *North American Review*, July, 1833. For comment on this debate from the Southern point of view, see War between the States, A. H. Stephens, vol. i. p. 387.

[3] Memoir of Webster by Edw. Everett, prefixed to Works, vol. i. p. cvii.

and by the prompt action of President Jackson.¹ The South could not in 1861 justify her right to revolution, for there was no oppression, no invalidation of rights. She could not, however, proclaim to the civilized world what was true, that she went to war to extend slavery. Her defence, therefore, is that she made the contest for her constitutional rights, and this attempted vindication is founded on the Calhoun theory. On the other hand, the ideas of Webster waxed strong with the years ; and the Northern people, thoroughly imbued with these sentiments, and holding them as sacred truths, could not do otherwise than resist the dismember-ment of the Union.

A few words will complete this notice of the nullification trouble. Clay's tariff act and the Force bill were passed almost simultaneously ; they were actually signed by the President on the same day, and thus the compromise of 1833 was complete. The nullification ordinance of South Caro-lina was repealed by the convention in less than a fortnight after the adjournment of Congress in March.²

While this controversy was going on, William Lloyd Gar-rison began the abolitionist movement by the establishment of the *Liberator* at Boston, January 1st, 1831.³ Although

---

¹ March 21st, 1833, Jackson wrote a private letter to Buchanan, who was representing this country at St. Petersburg, in which he said : The public "saw that although the tariff was made the ostensible object, a separa-tion of the Confederacy was the real purpose of its originators and sup-porters. The expression of public opinion elicited by the proclamation from Maine to Louisiana has so firmly repudiated the absurd doctrine of nullification and secession, that it is not probable that we shall be troubled with them again shortly." Life of Buchanan, Curtis, vol. i. p. 185.

² The repeal is dated March 15th. Statutes of South Carolina, edited, under the authority of the legislature, by Thomas Cooper, M.D., LL.D., vol. i.

³ Benjamin Lundy had been an apostle of abolition some years previ-ous to this, and his influence was powerful in the conversion of Garrison to the cause. There was, however, a lack of coherence in Lundy's ef-forts, so that for practical purposes the abolitionist movement may be said to date from the establishment of the *Liberator.*

he had for several years been advocating anti-slavery ideas, his denunciations of slavery had attracted as little attention at the national capital as Paul's preaching excited in the palace of the Cæsars. At this time, in the slave States, the opinion prevailed that slavery in the abstract was an evil. Miss Martineau conversed with many hundreds of persons in the South on the subject, but she met only one person who altogether defended the institution. Everybody justified its present existence, but did so on the ground of the impossibility of its abolition,[1] although forecasts were sometimes given of the position the South would in the future be forced to take. Senator Hayne, in the celebrated debate, argued that slavery in the abstract was no evil; but, in the course of the same discussion, Benton had addressed himself to the people of the North and with truthful emphasis assured them that "slavery in the abstract had but few advocates or defenders in the slave-holding states."[2] The sentiment at the North was well portrayed by Webster in his reply to Hayne. "The slavery of the South," he said, "has always been regarded as a matter of domestic policy left with the States themselves, and with which the federal government had nothing to do. . . . I regard domestic slavery as one of the greatest evils, both moral and political. But whether it be a malady and whether it be curable, and if so, by what means; or, on the other hand, whether it be the *vulnus immedicabile* of the social system, I leave it to those whose right and duty it is to inquire and decide. And this I believe is, and uniformly has been, the sentiment of the North."[3]

More than forty years had now passed since the establishment of the government. The hopes of its founders had not been realized, for the number of slaves was fast increasing; slavery had waxed strong and had become a source of great

[1] Society in America, Harriet Martineau, vol. i. p. 349. Miss Martineau was in the South in 1835.
[2] Thirty Years' View, vol. i. p. 136.   [3] Works, vol. iii. p. 279.

political and social power. While optimists, looking for a sign from heaven and a miracle, hoped that, by some occult process, the slaves would be freed voluntarily by the next generation, the abolitionists believed that reform from within the system could not be expected, but that its destruction must come from influences from the outside. The vital point was to bring home to the Northern people that negro slavery was a concern of theirs; that as long as it existed in the country without protest on their part, they were partners in the evil; and although debarred from legislative interference with the system, that was no reason why they should not think right on the subject, and bear testimony without ceasing against its hateful character.

The apostle who had especial fitness for the work, and who now came forward to embody this feeling and rouse the national conscience from the stupor of great material prosperity, was Garrison. Adopting the Stoic maxim, " My country is the world," he added its corollary, " My countrymen are all mankind," and with the change of *my* to *our* he made it the motto of the *Liberator*.[1] In his salutatory address he said : " I shall strenuously contend for the immediate enfranchisement of our slave population. . . . *I will be as harsh as truth and as uncompromising as justice*. . . . I am in earnest—I will not equivocate—I will not excuse—I will not retreat a single inch—and I will be heard." [2] In one of the succeeding issues he said : " Everybody is opposed to slavery, O, yes! there is an abundance of philanthropy among us. . . . I take it for granted slavery *is* a crime—a damning crime; therefore, my efforts shall be directed to the exposure of those who practise it." [3] Soon the *Liberator* appeared with a pictorial heading that displayed

---

[1] Garrison claimed originality for the motto. See Life of W. L. Garrison, vol. i. p. 219. Seneca had said, " I know that my country is the world;" and Marcus Aurelius had written, " An Antonine, my country is Rome ; as a man, it is the world." Quoted in Lecky's History of Morals, vol. i. p. 241.

[2] Life of W. L. Garrison, vol. i. p. 225.   [3] Ibid., p. 227.

the national capitol, floating from whose dome was a flag
inscribed " Liberty ;" in the foreground is seen a negro,
flogged at a whipping-post, and the misery of a slave auction.[1] This journal began in poverty ; but in the course of
the first year the subscription list reached five hundred.[2]
Garrison wrote the leading articles and then assisted to set
them up in type and did other work of the printer.

In August of this year (1831) occurred the Nat Turner insurrection in Virginia, which seemed to many Southerners a
legitimate fruit of the bold teaching of Garrison, although
there was indeed between the two events no real connection. But this negro rising struck terror through the South
and destroyed calm reason. The leader, Nat Turner, a
genuine African of exceptional capacity, knowing the Bible
by heart, prayed and preached to his fellow-slaves. He told
them of the voices he heard in the air, of the visions he saw,
and of his communion with the Holy Spirit. An eclipse of
the sun was a sign that they must rise and slay their enemies
who had deprived them of freedom. The massacre began
at night and continued for forty-eight hours ; women and
children were not spared, and before the bloody work was
checked sixty-one whites were victims of negro ferocity.
The retribution was terrible. Negroes were shot, hanged,
tortured, and burned to death, and all on whom suspicion
lighted met a cruel fate. In Southampton County, the
scene of the insurrection, there was a reign of terror, and
alarm spread throughout the slave States.[3]

This event, and the thought that it might be the precur-
sor of others of the same kind, account for much of the
Southern rage directed against Garrison and his crusade.
Nor, when we reflect on the sparsely settled country, the

[1] Life of W. L. Garrison, vol. i. p. 232.   [2] Ibid., p. 430.
[3] An interesting account of the massacre, by T. W. Higginson, may be
found in the *Atlantic Monthly*, vol. viii. p. 173. This article has been
reprinted in the volume entitled " Travellers and Outlaws," by T. W.
Higginson. See also History of the Negro Race in America, Williams,
vol. ii. p. 88.

wide distance between plantations—conditions that made a
negro insurrection possible—and when we consider what it
was for planters to have hanging over their heads the horrors of a servile war, will it seem surprising that judicial
poise of temper was impossible when Southerners discussed
the work of Garrison. They regarded it as an incitement
for their slaves to revolt. But they did injustice to Garrison, for Nat Turner had never seen a copy of the *Liberator*,
and the paper had not a single subscriber south of the Poto-
mac.[1] Nor did Garrison ever send a pamphlet or paper to
any slave, nor advocate the right of physical resistance on
the part of the oppressed.[2] He was a non-resistant, and did
not believe that force should be used to overturn legal authority, even when unjustly and oppressively exercised.
The assertion that slavery is a damning crime is one thing;
the actual incitement of slaves to insurrection is another.
The distinction between the two was not appreciated at the
South. Stringent laws were made against the circulation
of the *Liberator*, and vigilance committees sent their warnings to any who were supposed to have a part in spreading
its doctrines. In North Carolina Garrison was indicted for
a felony, and the legislature of Georgia offered a reward
of five thousand dollars for the arrest and conviction of the
editor or publisher.[3] One voice went abroad from public
officials, popular meetings, and from the press of the South,
demanding that the governor of Massachusetts or the
mayor of Boston should suppress the " infernal *Liberator*."

The people of Virginia had often struggled to free themselves from the coils of slavery, and the Nat Turner insurrection furnished the occasion for another attempt. At the
following session of the Legislature a proposition was made
to inquire into the expediency of some plan of gradual emancipation. In the debate that took place on the subject, the
evil of slavery was characterized in terms as strong as an

---

[1] Life of Garrison, vol. i. pp. 239, 251.   [2] Ibid., p. 489.
[3] Ibid., pp. 241, 247.

abolitionist could have used. The alarm excited all over
the South by the negro rising in Southampton County was
not, one member explained, from the fear of Nat Turner,
but it was on account of "the suspicion eternally attached
to the slave himself—a suspicion that a Nat Turner might
be in every family, that the same bloody deed might be
acted over at any time, and in any place; that the materials
for it were spread through the land, and were always ready
for a like explosion."[1]

But a majority of the House of Representatives, in which
the project was discussed, could not be had for ordering an
inquiry, and the further consideration of the subject was in-
definitely postponed. It has sometimes been asserted that
had not the abolitionist agitation begun, this Virginia movement would have resulted in the gradual emancipation of
slaves in that state; but there is, in truth, no reason for
thinking that anything more would have come of it than
from previous abortive attempts in the same direction. On
many pages of Virginia history may one read of noble efforts by noble men towards freeing their State from slavery.
But the story of the end is a repeated tale ; the seeds sown
fell among thorns, and the thorns sprung up and choked
them.

Meanwhile Garrison and his little band continued the up-
hill work of proselyting at the North, and especially in Boston. Merchants, manufacturers, and capitalists were against
the movement, for trade with the South was important, and
they regarded the propagation of abolition sentiments as in-
jurious to the commercial interests of Boston. Good society
turned the back upon the abolitionists. Garrison had no
college education to recommend him to an aristocracy based
partly upon wealth and partly upon culture.[2] The churches
were bitterly opposed to the movement. Oliver Johnson,

---

[1] For an abstract of this debate, see Rise and Fall of the Slave Power,
Wilson, vol. i. chap. xiv.
[2] Life of Garrison, vol. i. p. 515.

one of the early disciples of Garrison, relates that several times his efforts were in vain to persuade some one among a dozen white clergymen of Boston to open an anti-slavery meeting with prayer, and he was in each case forced at last to accept the services of a negro preacher from " Negro Hill." [1] The position of the church was well expressed by a noted clergyman, who attributed the sin of slavery to a past generation, and assigned the duty of emancipation to future generations.[2] The abolitionists, however, gradually gained ground.   The year 1833 was for them one of grateful memory.   Then, at Philadelphia, the American Anti-slavery Society was organized by delegates who made up in enthusiasm what they lacked in numbers.[3] The Declaration of Sentiments, drawn up by Garrison, was a paper worthy of the earnest and intelligent people who were its signers.   It referred to the immortal Declaration adopted in the same city fifty-seven years before, and, as the strongest abolition argument that could be made, quoted the phrase " that all men are created equal ; that they are endowed by their Creator with certain inalienable rights ; that among these are life, liberty, and the pursuit of happiness."   It denounced slavery in vigorous terms, yet conceded that Congress had no right to interfere with it in the States ; and while condemning the employment of material force in any way to promote abolition, the signers pledged themselves to use moral means, so far as lay in their power, to overthrow the execrable system of slavery.   This was not an inflammatory and seditious appeal; the delegates were men of good character, pure morals, and were law-abiding citizens ; yet it was necessary for the police to guard the convention hall against threatened mob violence.   The meeting was regarded by all Southern people, and by nearly all at the North, in much

---

[1] Garrison and his Times, Johnson, p. 71.

[2] Ibid., p. 109.

[3] The number was between fifty and sixty, mostly young men.   Life of Garrison, vol. i. p. 397.

the same way as we should now look upon an assemblage
of anarchists.[1]

This year (1833) is also noteworthy as furnishing a fresh
argument for the abolitionists. The British Parliament,
influenced by a long course of agitation, emancipated the
negro slaves in the West Indian colonies, so that henceforward freedom was the rule in all the vast colonial possessions of England, as it had been for years in the parent
state.

At the same time, ambitious Southern politicians began
to turn to their own advantage the anti-slavery agitation
at the North. This did not escape the keen observation of
Madison, who, though well stricken in years, was able to detect, from his country retreat, the reason of various moves
in the political sphere of his native state, which had for
their aim to make a unit of Southern opinion on the slavery
question. "It is painful," wrote Madison to Clay in June,
1833, "to observe the unceasing efforts to alarm the South
by imputations against the North of unconstitutional de-
signs on the subject of the slaves."[2] In a letter written
more than a year later, he said that one could see from the
Virginia newspapers and the proceedings of public meetings that aspiring popular leaders were inculcating the "impression of a permanent incompatibility of interests between
the South and the North."[3]

Excitement about the abolition movement characterized
the year 1835. Numerous public meetings and the press of
the South demanded almost with one voice that the abolitionists must be put down or they would destroy the Union.
A suspension of commercial intercourse with the North was

---

[1] A similar comparison suggested itself to Ampère in 1851 : " Les États
à esclaves," he writes, " défendent avec passion, avec fureur, ce qui est à
leurs yeux le droit de propriété : les abolitionistes sont pour eux ce que
sont les communistes pour les propriétaires français."—Promenade en
Amérique, vol. i. p. 48.

[2] Madison's Works, vol. iv. p. 301.   [3] Ibid., p. 358.

even suggested.[1] The Charleston post-office was forcibly
entered and a large number of tracts and papers sent there
by the American Anti-slavery Society were seized ; the next
night these papers and effigies of Garrison and other abolitionists were burned in the presence of a large number of
spectators.[2] On a false alarm of a projected slave rising in
Mississippi, several white men and negroes were hanged by
vigilance committees.[3] The wrath of the Southern people
against the abolitionists was reflected at the North, and the
feeling grew that the imputation of abolition ideas to the
whole Northern community must be repelled. As the *Liberator* could not be suppressed, nor anti-slavery meetings
prohibited by law, recourse was had to mob violence. Attacks upon abolitionists had previously been common, and
this sort of warfare culminated in the year 1835. A ferocious anti-negro riot took place at Philadelphia.[4] Rev. Samuel May, a devoted abolitionist and adherent of Garrison,
was mobbed at Haverhill, Mass., the home of Whittier, and
five times afterwards at different places in Vermont.[5] A
disgraceful anti-slavery riot occurred at Utica, N. Y. In
Boston, on the same day, a mob, variously estimated at
from two thousand to five thousand, including many gentlemen of property and influence,[6] broke up a meeting of the
Boston Female Anti-slavery Society. Garrison, one of the
men against whom the mob directed its fury,[7] had escaped
from the hall in which the ladies were assembled, but he
was seized and dragged bareheaded through the streets,

---

[1] Niles's Register, vol. xlix. pp. 73, 77.

[2] Life of Garrison, vol. i. p. 485 ; Niles's Register, vol. xlviii. p. 403.

[3] Niles, vol. xlix. p. 118.

[4] Life of Garrison, vol. i. p. 485.

[5] Recollections of the Anti-slavery Conflict, May, p. 152.

[6] Life of Garrison, vol. ii. p. 11. It was one of the surprises of Harriet
Martineau to learn that the mob was composed of gentlemen dressed in
fine broadcloth. Society in America, vol. i. p. 129.

[7] One great incitement to the mob was the supposed presence of George
Thompson, a zealous and imprudent anti-slavery agitator from England.

subjected to indignity and insult, and his life was threatened.
The mayor and police finally rescued him from the hands
of the rioters, and put him in jail as a protection against
further violence.

Yet the work of converting and creating Northern sentiment went on. In spite of misrepresentation, obloquy, and
derision, the abolitionists continued to apply moral ideas
and Christian principles to the institution of slavery. The
teachings of Christ and the Apostles actuated this crusade,[1]
and its latent power was great. If one looks for its results
merely to the numbers of congressmen chosen by the abolitionists, to the vote received by their distinctively presidential candidates, or even to the number of members enrolled
in the anti-slavery societies, only a faint idea of the force of
the movement will be had. The influence of the *Liberator*
cannot be measured by its subscribers, any more than the
French revolutionists of 1789 can be reckoned as of no
greater number than the readers of " The Social Contract."
If Rousseau had never lived, said Napoleon, there would
have been no French Revolution. It would be historical
dogmatism to say that if Garrison had not lived, the Republicans would not have succeeded in 1860. But if we wish to
estimate correctly the influence of Garrison and his disciples,
we must not stop with the enumeration of their avowed adherents. We must bear in mind the impelling power of
their positive dogmas, and of their never-ceasing inculcation
on those who were already voters and on thinking youths
who were to become voters, and who, in their turn, prevailed upon others. We must picture to ourselves this process of argument, of discussion, of persuasion, going on for
twenty-five years, with an ever-increasing momentum, and
we cannot resist the conviction that this anti-slavery agitation had its part, and a great part too, in the first election

[1] The anti-slavery agitation is " probably the last great reform that the
world is likely to see based upon the Bible and carried out with a millen-
nial fervor,"—Life of Garrison, vol. i, p. xiii.

of Lincoln.   It was due to Garrison and his associates that slavery became a topic of discussion at every Northern fireside.   Those who had heard the new doctrine gladly tried to convince their family and their friends; those who were but half convinced wished to vanquish their doubts or have put to rest the rising suspicion that they were partners in a great wrong; those who stubbornly refused to listen could not fail to feel that a new force had made its appearance, with which a reckoning must be made.   Slavery could not bear examination.   To describe it was to condemn it.   There was a certain fitness, therefore, in the demand of the Southerners that the discussion of slavery in any shape should be no longer permitted at the North.

But in what a state of turpitude the North would have been if it had not bred abolitionists!   If the abolitionists had not prepared the way, how would the political rising of 1854–60 against the slave power have been possible?   It is true that many ardent Republicans who voted for Lincoln would have repudiated the notion that they were in any way influenced by the arguments of Garrison and his associates.   And it is equally true that in 1835 the average Northern man satisfied himself by thinking slavery in the abstract a great evil, but that, as it existed in the South, it was none of his concern; he thought that " God hath made of one blood all nations of men " a good doctrine to be preached on Sunday, and " all men are created equal " a fit principle to be proclaimed on the Fourth of July; but he did not believe that these sentiments should be applied to the social condition of the South.   But that was exactly the ground on which the abolitionists planted themselves, and, by stirring the national conscience, they made possible the formation of a political party whose cardinal principle was opposition to the extension of slavery, and whose reason for existence lay in the belief of its adherents that slavery in the South was wrong.

A shining example of the change that was beginning to be wrought in Northern sentiment is seen in Dr. Channing.

In 1828 he wrote to Webster deprecating any agitation of
the question.   Our Southern brethren, he said, would "interpret every word from this region on the subject of slavery
as an expression of hostility."[1]   He feared the agitation
might harm the Union, and he loved the Union as Webster
loved it.   In 1835 he published a book on "Slavery," which,
with the exception of the *Liberator*, is the most remarkable
contribution of this decade to the cause of the abolitionists.
The appearance of Dr. Channing in this arena was for him
a notable sacrifice.   The effective work of his life had been
done.   He had led to triumph a liberal religious movement,
and he had a right to seek repose and shrink from another
contest.   He was now the pastor of a devoted and cultured
society in Boston, and the most eminent preacher in America.[2]   Emerson wrote that his sermons were sublime,[3] and
James Freeman Clarke says that Channing spoke "with the
tongues of men and of angels."[4]   He was one of the few
Americans who had a literary reputation in Europe; and,
while not as extensive as that of Washington Irving, it was,
in the opinion of Ticknor, "almost as much so, and deserv-
edly higher."[5]   A scholar and a student, he had projected
a work on "Man," for which he had been gathering materials many years.   The purpose of the book was an exposition of religion and philosophy, which he thought the world
needed, and he expected it would be his literary monument.

---

[1] Webster's Works, vol. v. p. 366.

[2] John Quincy Adams, on the death of Channing, wrote in his diary:
"Dr. Channing never flinched or quailed before the enemy.   But he was
deserted by many of his followers, and lost so many of his parishioners
that he had yielded to his colleague, E. S. Gannett, the whole care of his
pastoral office, giving up all claim to salary and reserving only the privilege of occasionally preaching to them at his convenience.   The loss of
Dr. Channing to the anti-slavery cause is irreparable."—Memoirs of J. Q.
Adams, vol. xi. p. 258.

[3] Memoir of R. W. Emerson, Cabot, vol. i. p. 105.

[4] Memorial and Biographical Sketches, p. 159.

[5] Life of George Ticknor, vol. i. p. 479.

The scholar who puts aside his cherished investigation to engage in a practical work of duty that is foreign to his taste is an unobtrusive martyr; he deserves a place among those who have given up their dearest hopes for the real or fancied good of humanity. Dr. Channing made such a sacrifice when he gave the services and the high influence of his pen to the anti-slavery cause.

With a disposition to look upon the bright side of human nature, he was loath to admit to himself the graveness of the evil that afflicted the country he loved so well. His conversion was slow, but a winter spent in the West Indies revived his youthful antipathy to slavery. The influence of the *Liberator*, although the harsh manner of Garrison was a shock to his delicate nature, completed the change in his ideas that his own observations had begun. The final bent was given by a conversation with the Rev. Samuel J. May, a Garrison abolitionist and a Unitarian minister, who looked up to Channing as his spiritual leader.[1]

Dr. Channing's work on "Slavery" attracted wide attention, and might be found on many a parlor-table from which the *Liberator* was excluded with scorn. Many Southerners and nearly every prominent man in public life read it. A slave-holder in Congress declared that the slaves in the South knew that Dr. Channing had written a book on their behalf, and it was not long before the Southern aristocracy and their Northern partisans considered Channing a more dangerous man than even Garrison.

The justification of this little book of one hundred and fifty-nine pages may be summed up in the averment that "Slavery ought to be discussed. We ought to think, feel, speak, and write about it. But whatever we do in regard to it should be done with a deep feeling of responsibility, and so done as not to put in jeopardy the peace of the slave-

---

[1] For this conversation, see Anti-slavery Conflict, May, p. 173; Life of Channing, p. 529.

I.—5

holding states." The argument is an elaboration of the thesis: No "right of man in man can exist. A human being cannot be justly owned;" and the duty then incumbent upon Northern people is thus formulated: "Our proper and only means of action is to spread the truth on the subject of slavery."

If slavery were wrong, the only valid objection to discussing it lay in the possibility that the agitation might excite servile insurrection. This argument appears and reappears in Congress, in the press and the pulpit of the time. Dr. Channing addressed himself with success to the refutation of this reasoning, and the course of events proved that his position was well taken. From Nat Turner's to John Brown's, a period of twenty-eight years, no slave insurrection gathered to a head; and both of these were, in their immediate physical results, insignificant. The first revolt was, as we have seen, contemporaneous with the inception of the abolition movement. The John Brown invasion, in no way a rising of slaves, occurred after the moral agitation had accomplished its work, and when the cause had been consigned to a political party that brought to a successful issue the movement begun by the moral sentiment of the country. A potent influence of Dr. Channing's book lay in the fact that he had little sympathy with Garrison's methods, and represented a different range of sentiment; and he was apparently not aware how much he had been influenced by the abolitionist agitation. Channing, like Emerson, would never have initiated a movement of this kind. They were apostles of an advanced religion and philosophy, but they loved the tranquillity of culture, and could not play the part of violent iconoclasts. They were optimists; they were not aggressive natures; they were not the sort of men to whom would come, as a call from on high, the burning conviction that the times were out of joint, and they must go to work and set them right. Emerson, with the abolitionists in his mind, said that " the professed philanthropists are an altogether odious set of people, whom one would shun as the worst of bores and canters." [1]   But his respect for Garrison grew with his knowledge, and he wittily said of this chief agitator and of the men who threw themselves unhesitatingly into the contest, that " they might be wrong-headed, but they were wrong-headed in the right direction." [2]

We must now turn our eyes towards the national capital.   There the abolitionists had made themselves felt. Since the settlement of the Missouri controversy the subject of slavery had hardly been alluded to in Congress, but in 1835 it was brought before that body by the first reference made in a President's message to abolitionism.   General Jackson called attention to the transmission through the mails of "inflammatory appeals addressed to the passions of the slaves, in prints and in various sorts of publications, calculated to stimulate them to insurrection, and to produce all the horrors of a servile war;" and he suggested the propriety of passing such a law as would prohibit, under severe penalties, this practice.   The result of the consideration of this part of the message was a bill, reported by Calhoun from a special committee of which he had been made the chairman, subjecting to penalties any postmaster who should knowingly receive and put into the mail any publication or picture touching the subject of slavery, to go into a state or territory in which the circulation of such documents should be forbidden by the state or territorial laws.   Benton, in a speech in the Senate, described a print that had been sent to him, and which was a sample of what were in circulation.   It represented " a large and spreading tree of liberty, beneath whose ample shade a slave-owner was at one time luxuriously reposing, with slaves fanning him ; at another, carried forth in a palanquin, to view the half - naked laborers in the cotton-field, whom drivers with whips were scourging to the task." [3]   Calhoun supported his bill by the argument that

---

[1] Memoir of R. W. Emerson, Cabot, vol. ii. p. 427.
[2] Ibid., p. 430.   [3] Thirty Years' View, Benton, vol. i. p. 577.

had now become usual with him : If Congress would not do what it lawfully could to stop the work of the abolitionists, the Union would be in danger, and the South would have recourse to nullification, which, he asserted, had been carried into practice successfully on a recent occasion by the gallant state he had the honor to represent. Clay opposed the bill, and Webster made a strong argument against it, taking the broad ground that it would conflict with the liberty of the press. After three tie votes in different parliamentary stages of the bill, it was defeated by a majority of six.

The important consideration now to be observed is the great change in Southern sentiment regarding slavery. Silent and unseen forces had been at work revolutionizing public opinion,[1] and their result was now manifest. Governor McDuffie, in his message to the South Carolina legislature, said, " Domestic slavery is the corner-stone of our republican edifice ;" and Calhoun, two years later, averred in open Senate that slavery is a good, a positive good.[2] William Gilmore Simms, the poet and novelist, whom the Southern people delighted to read and honor, could not in 1852 felicitate himself too highly that he had fifteen years previously been one of the first to advocate that slavery was " a great good and blessing."[3] At the birth of the nation, as we have seen, the difference of opinion on the subject between the North and the South was not great, but opinions had moved on divergent lines. If we seek to apportion the blame for this increasing irritation, we have an impartial witness, Senator Thomas Benton, of Missouri. A student of books, but pedantic, ostentatious, and inapt in the use of learning, Benton was still a profound observer of men, an honest man, and a loyal citizen. He loved the

---

[1] See Memoirs of J. Q. Adams, vol. v. p. 10 et seq.

[2] Calhoun's Works, vol. ii. p. 631.

[3] Pro-slavery Argument, Charleston, Walker, Richards & Co., 1852, p. 178.

Union, he hated nullifiers and abolitionists. He approved of the Northern mobs that had " silenced the gabbling tongues of female dupes and dispersed the assemblages, whether fanatical, visionary, or incendiary." [1] He was withal a slave-holder, and represented a slave-holding state. " From the beginning of the Missouri controversy up to the year 1835," he writes, " the author of this view looked to the North as the point of danger from the slavery agitation ; since that time he has looked to the South for that danger, as Mr. Madison did two years earlier." [2]

Meanwhile, a champion for the abolition cause appeared in the House of Representatives in one who had gained reputation in the field of diplomacy, whose many years as Secretary of State had caused to shine more brightly the lustre he had acquired abroad, who had served with honor one term as President, but to whose destiny it fell to win his greatest renown and to render the country his greatest service in the popular branch of Congress. This was John Quincy Adams. He had from time to time presented petitions for the abolition of slavery and the slave-trade in the District of Columbia, and they had gone through the usual parliamentary forms without remark. But they were coming too thick and fast for Southern sentiments, and in January, 1836, when Adams presented a petition in the usual language, a member from Georgia moved that it be not received. A heated discussion of some days followed, and months were spent in the concoction of a scheme by which these abolition ideas might be excluded from the halls of Congress. The result was the adoption of the famous gag rule. This provided that whereas the agitation of the subject was disquieting and objectionable, " all petitions, memorials, resolutions, or papers relating in any way, or to any extent whatsoever, to the subject of slavery or the abolition of slavery, shall, without being either printed or referred,

---

[1] Thirty Years' View, vol. i. p. 579.   [2] Ibid., vol. i. p. 623.

be laid upon the table, and that no further action whatever shall be had thereon." [1]

This, for the Southern leaders, was the beginning of the madness that the gods send upon men whom they wish to destroy; for, instead of making the fight on the merits of the question, they shifted the ground. Had they simply resisted the abolition of slavery in the District, the vast preponderance of Northern sentiment would have been with them; but, with a fatuitous lack of foresight, they put Adams in a position where his efforts in the anti-slavery cause were completely overshadowed in his contest for the right of petition. At each session of Congress, "the old man eloquent," [2] for he had gained this name, presented petition after petition for the abolition of slavery and the slave-trade in the District of Columbia, and each time they were disposed of under the gag rule. [3] The anti-slavery people of the country, fully alive to the fact that a representative had appeared who would present such prayers, busied themselves in getting up and forwarding to him petitions, and those he presented must be numbered by thousands, and they were signed by 300,000 petitioners. [4] Never had there been such a contest on the floors of Congress. One man, with no followers and no adherents, was pitted against all the representatives from the South. It was a contest that set people to thinking. The question could not fail to be asked, If the slave power now demands that the right of petition must be sacrificed, what will be the next sacred republican principle that must be given up in obedience to its behests? Yet the merchants and manufacturers of Boston had no sympathy with the efforts of Adams; they did not approve of his stirring up the question. But the district

---

[1] Life of John Quincy Adams, Morse, p. 251.

[2] "That grand old man," W. H. Seward called him. Life of Seward, vol. i. p. 713.

[3] This rule was not repealed until Dec. 3d, 1844.

[4] Schouler, vol. iv. p. 302.

he represented was the Plymouth, and, true to the sacred memories of freedom its name suggests, its voters sent him for eight successive terms to the House, and he died there with the harness on his back.[1]

Adams was a master of sarcasm and invective, and his use of these weapons of argument was unsparing and effective. A man without friends, his enemies were many. While not an orator in the highest sense of the term, he was ever ready to speak, and kept a cool head in the midst of the heat and excitement that his efforts always aroused. His is a character on whom the historian would fain linger. His honesty of purpose and fearless bearing atone manifold for his cold heart and repellent exterior. It is not given to us to see many public men as we see John Quincy Adams. In his famous diary he jots down his impressions of men and events, and discloses his inmost thoughts and feelings. His record is a crucial test of character. No one can rise from a perusal of that diary without an increased feeling of admiration for the man. We may discern foibles we had not looked for, but we see with greater force the virtues. The honesty, the sincerity and strength of character give us a feeling of pride that such a man was an American.

While Adams appeared with a bold front in public, he was in reality torn by conflicting emotions. He confides to his diary: "The abolitionists generally are constantly urging me to indiscreet movements which would ruin me, and weaken and not strengthen their cause. My own family, on the other hand, exercise all the influence they possess to restrain and divert me from all connection with the abolitionists and their cause. Between these adverse impulses my mind is agitated almost to distraction. The public mind in my own district and State is convulsed between the slavery and abolition questions, and I walk on the edge of a precipice in every step that I take."[2] Another entry

---

[1] An interesting account of this work of Adams may be found in chap. iii. of Life of J. Q. Adams, by Morse, which I have freely used.

[2] Entry in diary, Sept. 1st, 1837, Memoirs, vol. ix. p. 365.

made in the diary in the same year is a faithful representation of the state of public opinion on what had now become the all-absorbing question. " It is also to be considered," he wrote, " that at this time the most dangerous
of all the subjects for public contention is the slavery question. In the South it is a perpetual agony of conscious
guilt and terror, attempting to disguise itself under sophis-
tical argumentation and braggart menaces. In the North
the people favor the whites and fear the blacks of the
South. The politicians court the South because they want
their votes. The abolitionists are gathering themselves
into societies, increasing their numbers, and in zeal they
kindle the opposition against themselves into a flame ; and
the passions of the populace are all engaged against them." [1]

In 1837, Webster, in a speech at New York, described
the anti-slavery sentiment of the country in felicitous words.
" The subject" (of slavery), said he, " has not only attracted
attention as a question of politics, but it has struck a far
deeper-toned chord. It has arrested the religious feeling
of the country ; it has taken strong hold on the consciences
of men. He is a rash man indeed, and little conversant
with human nature, and especially has he a very erroneous
estimate of the character of the people of this country, who
supposes that a feeling of this kind is to be trifled with or
despised." [2] It no longer required the martyr spirit to be
an abolitionist in the eastern part of the country, and yet
there were few accessions from the influential part of the
community. It was an affair of great moment, when Wendell Phillips and Edmund Quincy, representatives of the
wealth, culture, and highest social position of Boston, joined
the anti-slavery society. Wendell Phillips became an abolitionist from seeing Garrison dragged through the streets
of Boston by a mob ; and Quincy's action was decided by
the martyrdom of Lovejoy, who persisted in publishing an

---

[1] Entry, April 19th, 1837, Memoirs, vol. ix. p. 349.
[2] Life of Webster, Curtis, vol. i. p. 560.

anti-slavery paper at Alton, Ill., and was shot down by a pro-slavery mob.

In 1838, Calhoun averred that the abolition "spirit was growing, and the rising generation was becoming more strongly imbued with it."[1]   His colleague, Senator Preston, alarmed at the increasing power of the movement, declared from his seat in the Senate that if they could catch an abolitionist in South Carolina, they would try him and hang him.[2] Yet the road to political preferment was not through sympathy with the abolitionists.   Clay, anxious for the presidential nomination of 1840, took occasion to place upon record his opinion of these agitators.[3] He abused them roundly, denounced their methods, and said that a single idea had taken possession of their minds, which they pursued, "reckless and regardless of all consequences." They were ready to hurry us down "that dreadful precipice" to "civil war, a dissolution of the Union, and the overthrow of a government in which are concentrated the fondest hopes of the civilized world."[4]   When Clay had finished, Calhoun rose and commended highly the Kentucky senator for his change of opinion on slavery.   A biographer of Clay considers it probable that this speech was carefully prepared, and submitted before delivery to Senator Preston for approval, and it was in reference to the thoughts he therein formulated that Clay gave utterance to the well-known saying, "I trust the sentiments and opinions are correct; I had rather be right than be President."[5]

"The most angry and portentous debate which had yet taken place in Congress" on slavery occurred in 1839, in the House of Representatives.[6] The slavery question could

---

[1] Thirty Years' View, Benton, vol. ii. p. 135.
[2] Life of Garrison, vol. ii. p. 247.
[3] In the Senate, Feb., 1839.
[4] Thirty Years' View, Benton, vol. ii. p. 155.
[5] Life of Clay, Schurz, vol. ii. p. 169 *et ante.*
[6] Thirty Years' View, Benton, vol. ii. p. 150.

no longer be shut out from the halls of the national legislature. The abolitionists had now begun to take political
action; this was the reason why Clay spoke with such vehemence against them, and it tended to intensify the excitement each time that the subject was broached in either
the House or the Senate. For more than a year they had
adopted the system of putting questions to candidates, congressional and local, demanding an expression of opinion
on the vital question; and, guided by these declarations of
sentiments, the abolitionist vote was beginning to have in
some states an important influence on the result of elections. In 1840 a division in the ranks of the abolitionists
took place, arising out of a difference of opinion regarding
political action. Many of them thought they should take
a part in active political life, and even form a political party,
while others, headed by Garrison and Phillips, held that the
movement ought to remain purely moral, and they should
only use moral means for the accomplishment of their ends.
Garrison never voted but once, and Wendell Phillips never
voted.[1] The separation into two factions is a proof of the
growing power of the abolitionists, for as long as all hands
were raised against them, perfect harmony existed in their
ranks. Dissension, or rather division, came with prosperity;
there were now two thousand anti-slavery societies with a
membership of 200,000.[2] This was the acme of the moral
movement. The *Liberator*, indeed, continued to appear
weekly, but its denunciations of the slave power were accompanied by criticisms of the opposing faction. In the
next decade the Garrison abolitionists suffered loss of influence by advocating disunion as a remedy. Failing to
appreciate the love for the Union and reverence for the
Constitution that prevailed among the mass of the Northern
people, they adopted the motto, " No union with slave-
holders," and proclaimed the Constitution " a covenant with

[1] Life of Garrison, vol. i. p. 455; Life of Wendell Phillips, Austin, p. 5.
[2] Rise and Fall of the Slave Power, Wilson, vol. i. p. 186.

death and agreement with hell." [1] Many years afterwards Garrison virtually admitted his mistake, saying that " when he pledged himself to fight against the covenant with death and agreement with hell, he did not think that he should live to see death and hell secede from the Union." [2]

The muse of history has done full justice to the abolitionists. Among them were literary men, who have known how to present their cause with power, and the noble spirit of truthfulness pervades the abolition literature. One may search in vain for intentional misrepresentation. Abuse of opponents and criticism of motives are common enough, but the historians of the abolition movement have endeavored to relate a plain, honest tale; and the country has accepted them and their work at their true value. Moreover, a cause and its promoters that have been celebrated in the vigorous lines of Lowell, and sung in the impassioned verse of Whittier, will be of perennial memory. Lowell's tribute to Garrison, as the " poor, unlearned young man," toiling over his types, "friendless and unseen," while yet through his efforts "the freedom of a race began," fixes his place in history. Whittier repels the charge against Garrison that he is "rash and vain," "a searcher after fame;" the poet has known the agitator well, has read " his mighty purpose long," and nothing can " dim the sunshine of my faith and earnest trust in thee." Praise like this is more than mere poetry for the moment; it is the deep, earnest conviction of men of high character. [3]

The story of the annexation of Texas and the conquest of New Mexico and California is not a fair page in our history. The extension of our boundary to the Rio Grande, and the rounding of our Pacific possessions by the acquisition of California, gave symmetrical proportions to our territory, and

---

[1] Garrison and his Times, Johnson, pp. 340–342.   [2] Ibid., p. 347.
[3] " Garrison was the courageous and single-minded apostle of the noble body of abolitionists."—Autobiography of John Stuart Mill, p. 268.

this consideration has induced many writers to justify the winning of this domain.[1] But in pondering the plain narrative of these events, more reason for humiliation than pride will be found.

Texas, a part of the Mexican republic, was settled by hardy adventurers from our southwestern States, who, despite the fact that Mexico had abolished slavery by presidential decree, took with them to the new country their slaves. The Americans, after their arrival, paid no attention to the prohibition of slavery, and the Mexican government, in the interest of peace, allowed an interpretation of the edict that excluded Texas from its operation. But there were no sympathetic relations between the Texans and Mexicans. The difference between the Spanish and English nationalities, between Continental and English institutions, between the Catholic and Protestant religions, was too great for the hope that any union could exist between the two peoples. Texas had with the province of Coahuila been constituted one state by the Mexican Constitution of 1827. This was not satisfactory to the Texans, who demanded autonomy. This demand caused constant friction between them and the central government, and finally resulted in an attempt of the President, Santa Anna, to enforce obedience by military authority, and Texas rebelled. The Texans were victorious in the decisive battle of San Jacinto in 1836, and gave the world evidence that they were able to establish a government *de facto*.[2] The independence of Texas

---

[1] Emerson had remarkable foresight. In 1844 he wrote in his diary: "The question of the annexation of Texas is one of those which look very differently to the centuries and to the years. It is very certain that the strong British race, which have now overrun so much of this continent, must also overrun that tract and Mexico and Oregon also; and it will in the course of ages be of small import by what particular occasions and methods it was done."—Memoir of R. W. Emerson, Cabot, vol. ii. p. 576.

[2] President Jackson had tried to buy Texas, and, failing in that, had, according to John Q. Adams, engaged in a plot with his friend Houston

was recognized by the United States in 1837, and soon after by England, France, and Belgium. In the Senate debate on the subject, Calhoun avowed that he was not only in favor of the recognition of the new republic as an independent nation, but he desired the admission of Texas into the Union. This project soon came to have warm advocates, and attracted so much attention that Webster deemed it incumbent on him to express an opinion on the matter in a set speech delivered in New York City. " Texas," said he, " is likely to be a slave-holding country, and I frankly avow my entire unwillingness to do anything that shall extend the slavery of the African race on this continent or add other slave-holding states to the Union. When I say I regard slavery in itself as a great moral, social, and political evil, I only use language which has been adopted by distinguished men, themselves citizens of slave-holding states. I shall do nothing, therefore, to favor or encourage its further extension. . . . In my opinion, the people of the United States will not consent to bring into the Union a new, vastly extensive, slave-holding country. . . . In my opinion, they ought not to consent to it." [1]

This was the general feeling at the North. Webster was an exponent of the principles of the Whig party, and the action of President Van Buren later in the same year makes it apparent that the Northern Democrats were opposed to annexation. The Texan envoy at Washington broached the project to the President, but after careful consideration he declined the proffer, giving for an ostensible reason that as Mexico and Texas were at war, the incorporation of Texas into the Union would imply a disposition on our part to espouse her quarrel with Mexico. In the next year, the Senate was applied to, but that body, by a decisive majority, refused to take any step towards annexation.

---

for the revolt of Texas and for bringing her into the Union. See Schouler, vol. iv. p. 251.

[1] Speech at Niblo's Saloon, New York City, March, 1837, Webster's Works, vol. i. p. 356.

Owing to these rebuffs, the question slept until 1843. Meanwhile Harrison had been elected President, had died, and had been succeeded by John Tyler, who, though formerly a Democrat, had become a Whig and was chosen Vice-President. He had not been long in the presidential chair when it was evident that he leaned towards the party of his first love ; and when he came into conflict with the Whig party, where its fundamental principles were involved, all the members of the original cabinet resigned except Webster, who retained the portfolio of State for the reason that he was engaged in the negotiation of an important treaty with England. He remained in the cabinet until he and Lord Ashburton had agreed upon the treaty of Washington ; and he still lingered until it had been ratified by both governments, and Congress had passed laws carrying it into effect.[1] The position, however, became distasteful to him, owing to the quarrel between the President and the Whigs, and in the spring of 1843 he resigned. By this time Tyler had become committed to Texas annexation, and, as he knew Webster was opposed to it, he gladly accepted the resignation.[2] A short time afterwards Upshur, of Virginia, who was ardently in favor of the Texas project, became Secretary of State. In the summer of 1843 the intrigue began. Congress was not in session. The President, Upshur, and the Southern schemers could pursue their machinations almost unnoticed.

On the assembling of Congress, in December, 1843, the scheme began to develop. As Benton had strong national sentiments, as he had been opposed to the retrocession of Texas,[3] and was a true embodiment of the boundless spirit

---

[1] Life of Webster, Lodge, p. 259 ; Life of Crittenden, Coleman, vol. i. p. 205.

[2] The President had broached the subject tentatively to Webster in a letter dated Oct. 11th, 1841. Letters and Times of the Tylers, vol. ii. p. 126. I do not know what reply, if any, was made to this communication. See Memoirs of J. Q. Adams, vol. xi. p. 347; also Schouler, vol. iv. pp. 437, 447, note.

[3] Texas had generally been considered as included in the Louisiana

of the West, the project was opened to him. But the intriguers had not reckoned wisely on the man, for Benton told them he believed their scheme was, on the part of some, a presidential intrigue against Van Buren and a plot to dissolve the Union, and on the part of others a Texas scrip and land speculation, and he was against it.[1] These motives had their share, but the consideration above all others that prompted the Southern faction was the desire to restore, by an accession of slave territory, the balance of power lost by the gain in population at the North. If four slave states could be carved out of Texas, the South might retain her control of the Senate, although she had lost the House.

In this same winter, Webster, though not at that time in public life, got an inkling, while at Washington attending the Supreme Court, of the negotiations the administration were carrying on with Texas. "I was astounded," he said, "at the boldness of the government."[2] Tyler was a liberally educated gentleman, of good birth, fine breeding, and graceful manners, but of moderate capacity and narrow ideas; yet he had a certain dogged persistence and audacity that sometimes take the place of ability. The President did not advocate the annexation of Texas, however, for the reason that it would augment the slave power. He thought that he took a broad national view of the subject, and not a narrow sectional one. "The monopoly of the cotton plant," he afterwards wrote, "was the great and important concern;" and he said that Calhoun could only see the extension of slavery in connection with the Texas project. "That idea," he wrote, "seemed to possess him and Upshur *as a single idea*."[3]

On February 28th, 1844, occurred a distressing accident,

---

purchase, but in the treaty with Spain for the acquisition of Florida it had been ceded to Mexico, then belonging to Spain, by the administration of Monroe.

[1] Thirty Years' View, vol. ii. p. 583.

[2] Curtis, vol. ii. p. 232.

[3] Letters and Times of the Tylers, vol. ii. p. 483. See also p. 126.

the results of which were to hasten the execution of the annexation treaty with Texas that had already been prepared.[1] The President, a party of officials, and friends were assisting as spectators at the trial of a new piece of ordnance on board of the man-of-war *Princeton*, when the bursting of the big gun "Peacemaker" killed several persons, among whom was Upshur, the Secretary of State. Passing the night after the accident in deep reflection, Henry A. Wise, of Virginia, a confidential friend of the President, whose eagerness for the annexation of Texas went beyond bounds, came to the conclusion that the man of all others to drive the project forward was Calhoun. Repairing to the White House in the early morning, and while the President was still a prey to the painful emotions excited by the previous day's occurrence, Wise actually browbeat Tyler into the appointment of Calhoun as Secretary of State.[2] Calhoun became the master spirit of the cabinet. The man of one idea, and that idea the extension of slavery, had a large share of executive direction. The annexation project no longer lagged; it galloped towards consummation. Calhoun was appointed and confirmed March 6th (1844). On April 11th, although Mexico was at peace with us, he complied with a request, made some months previously, and promised to lend our army and navy to the President of Texas to be used in her war against Mexico. On the following day, the treaty of annexation of Texas to the United States was signed. What Texas had vainly sought, and what the extreme Southern party had ardently desired for eight years, was accomplished, so far as it lay in the power of the executive department of the government.

Ten days went by before the treaty was sent to the Senate,[3] for Calhoun wished to submit with it his reply to a

[1] "The treaty as signed was the work of Abel P. Upshur."—Letters and Times of the Tylers, vol. ii. p. 297.

[2] See Seven Decades of the Union, Henry A. Wise, chap. xi.; Letters and Times of the Tylers, vol. ii. p. 294.

[3] "The treaty for the annexation of Texas to this Union was this day

letter of Lord Aberdeen, the British Minister of Foreign Affairs, which he esteemed a powerful argument in favor of annexation. A despatch of Aberdeen had been communicated to Upshur in the usual diplomatic manner, in which was expressed the desire to see slavery abolished in Texas, for Great Britain exerted herself to procure the abolition of slavery everywhere; but any thought of acting directly or indirectly on the United States through Texas was plainly disclaimed, and the minister avowed for his government that nothing but open and honest efforts would be made. Calhoun asserted that this policy of Great Britain made it necessary for the United States to annex Texas as a measure of self-defence.[1] This letter that he sent to the Senate with the treaty began with a false assumption[2] and unfair reasoning, and ended with the humiliating argument showing the wisdom and humanity of African slavery by a statistical contrast of the comfort, intelligence, and morals of slaves as compared with the free colored people in the United States.[3]

But the letter failed to convince the Senate, and it refused to ratify the treaty by a vote of 35 to 16.[4] The President and his Secretary were grievously disappointed. In addition to the chagrin at the failure of a cherished state plan, Calhoun felt keenly the loss of opportunity further to air

---

(April 22d) sent in to the Senate; and with it went the freedom of the human race."—Diary of J. Q. Adams, Memoirs, vol. xii. p. 13.

[1] Life of Calhoun, Von Holst, p. 231.

[2] "However flexible political morality may be, a lie is a lie, and Calhoun knew that there was not one particle of truth in these assertions."—Life of Calhoun, Von Holst, p. 233.

[3] This letter was published in Niles's Register, vol. lxvi. p. 172; see defence of Calhoun, Life by Jenkins, p. 403.

[4] "During the whole continuance of these debates in the Senate, the lobbies of the chamber were crowded with speculators in Texas scrip and lands, and with holders of Mexican claims—all working for the ratification of the treaty, which would bring with it an increase of value to their property."—Thirty Years' View, Benton, vol. ii. p. 623.

his closet dialectics. A letter of his written at this time [1] shows that in the event of annexation he expected a reply from Aberdeen, to which he hoped to return a crushing rejoinder. Happily the country was spared the humiliation of maintaining the affirmative in a diplomatic controversy on the question, Is slavery right? Calhoun was disappointed not to have the occasion to lecture England again on the advantage of slavery. But he astonished the humane King Louis Philippe by a despatch, forwarded by the American minister at Paris, in which he attempted to make clear the community of interest between France and the United States in maintaining slavery on the American continent. [2]

Although signally defeated in the Senate, the administration by no means abandoned its project. The President appealed from the Senate to the House of Representatives. He sent all the documents to the House, with an explanatory message suggesting that Congress had the power to acquire Texas in another way than by the formal ratification of the treaty. This was an obvious hint for annexation by joint resolution of Congress.

Meanwhile the friends of the Texas scheme did not confine themselves to the advocacy of it before Congress. They proposed to submit the question to the people in the presidential election taking place this year (1844). Clay received by acclamation the nomination from the enthusiastic Whigs. The adroit management of the annexationists was shown in the manipulation of the Democratic convention, which met some weeks later. A majority of the convention was in favor of the nomination of Van Buren, and his choice would have given satisfaction to Northern Democrats, but his opposition to immediate annexation caused his defeat. The old rule requiring two-thirds of the convention to nominate was adopted, and this resulted in the choice, on the

---

[1] It was not published until sixteen years later, see Life of Calhoun, Von Holst, p. 241.

[2] This letter may be found in Greeley's American Conflict, vol i. p. 169.

ninth ballot, of James K. Polk.   Had ability constituted the
test, Polk would not have been selected, nor had a long service in the House of Representatives given him a claim to
distinction;[1] but he had written, "I am in favor of the *immediate re-annexation* of Texas to the territory and government of the United States,"[2] and this was the reason of his
nomination.

The election of Polk was due to a clever letter written
by himself and to foolish letters by Clay.   Polk satisfied
the Pennsylvania protectionists, and the campaign in that
state was successfully conducted with the watchword "Polk,
Dallas, and the tariff of 1842."   Texas annexation was the
rock on which Clay made shipwreck.   In April, before his
nomination, he wrote a letter against annexation.   Then it
was represented that the close Southern States were in
danger, and in July came from his pen the expression of
a wish to see Texas added to the Union "upon just and fair
terms," and the opinion that "the subject of slavery ought
not to affect the question one way or the other."[3]   But
now his anti-slavery supporters made clamor, and in September Clay declared against immediate annexation.   This
expression, however, did not counteract the mischief done
by the July letter, and was inadequate to retain him the
favor of many strong anti-slavery men.   The Liberty party,
made up of abolitionists who had separated from the anti-
slavery society of Garrison, had nominated for the presidency James G. Birney.   Birney, of Southern birth but

---

[1] The question "Who is Polk?" was frequent during the campaign.

[2] On the use of the word re-annexation, see Niles's Register, vol. lxvi.
p. 250.   "General Cass has proved, out of *Fraser's Magazine*, that the
United States should never buy nor sell out the word *re-annexation*.   Ill-
natured people there are, who will call this a violent occupation of foreign domain.   But they have a humor of giving ill names to everything.
We should regard it no more than Ancient Pistol the word *steal*: '*Convey*, the wise it call.   Steal? foh! a fico for the phrase!'"   Cited from
the Newark *Daily Advertiser*.

[3] Niles's Register, vol. lxvi. p. 439.

Northern education, was a gentleman of high character and a practical abolitionist, for, becoming convinced of the wrong of slavery, he had emancipated his own slaves and thenceforward devoted himself to the anti-slavery cause. He had gained note by a tract he had written entitled " The American Churches the Bulwarks of American Slavery." He had been the candidate of the Liberty party four years previously, but in the whole country had only received seven thousand votes. His candidacy in 1844 would probably have been of no greater moment had it not been for the unfortunate July letter of Clay, which alienated enough Whigs to lose him the State of New York, and therefore the election. Polk carried New York State by a plurality of little more than five thousand, while Birney polled in the same state nearly sixteen thousand votes. The feeling against the annexation of Texas gave Birney this important support, and, while well-meaning, it was ill-considered action. Polk or Clay was certain to be elected President. The success of Polk would register the desire of the country to have Texas, regardless of consequences, while the election of Clay would certainly postpone, and might defeat, the project of annexation ; and a vote for Birney was indirectly a vote for Polk. Thus argued Adams, Seward, Greeley, and Giddings, all strong anti-slavery men. But the abolitionists rejoiced at the defeat of Clay ; their high-toned exultation mingled with the boisterous demonstrations of the New York Democrats ;[1] while never before or since has the defeat of any man in this country brought forth such an exhibition of heart-felt grief from the educated and respectable classes of society as did this defeat of Clay. Men were frequently heard to say that they now " had no more interest in politics." [2]

The real meaning of the election of Polk was proclaimed by President Tyler in his annual message. A controlling

---

[1] Life of Seward, p. 731.

[2] Ibid., p. 732; Life of Lincoln, Herndon, p. 270; Life of Wade, Riddle, p. 192.

majority of the people, he said, and a large majority of the states have declared in favor of immediate annexation. The House of Representatives now entered into the plan with zeal, and near the close of January, 1845, passed a resolution providing for the admission of Texas, and, with her consent, the formation of four additional states out of the territory; in states formed north of the line of 36° 30′ north latitude, slavery was prohibited. The Senate did not incline so favorably to the project. Several Democratic senators were opposed to accomplishing the object in this manner, and Benton tells how their support was gained. In the Senate, the House resolution was amended by giving the President the option of negotiating another treaty of annexation or of submitting the joint resolution to Texas for her acceptance of its prescribed conditions. Benton and his fellow-senators, who were of like mind, had assurances directly and indirectly from the President-elect that he would take the option of treaty negotiation;[1] and they had the assertion in open Senate of McDuffie, the close friend of Calhoun, that the actual administration would take no steps in the matter in its few remaining days of power. The bill, as amended, passed the Senate by a majority of two votes; it went through the House on the last day of February, 1845, and twenty-four hours later it received the signature of the President. No sooner was the bill signed than Tyler and Calhoun, although they had but three days more of office, despatched a special agent to Texas to offer the terms of annexation as provided in the joint resolution. It is true that the instructions to their envoy were courteously submitted to Polk, who, however, declined any interference in the matter.[2] Texas accepted the terms, and at the next session of Congress was formally admitted as one of the states of the Union.[3]

---

[1] Thirty Years' View, Benton, vol. ii. pp. 636–638. This is denied in Letters and Times of the Tylers, vol. ii. pp. 405, 409.

[2] Letters and Times of the Tylers, vol. ii. p. 363.

[3] A few years afterwards a controversy between Calhoun and Tyler

Although now a foregone conclusion, Webster, who had been sent again to the Senate, gave voice to his opposition to the scheme. He objected to the admission of Texas because it was newly acquired slave territory, and he had, moreover, another reason, which he put into words of wisdom. " It is," said he, " of very dangerous tendency and doubtful consequences to enlarge the boundaries of this country. . . . There must be some limit to the extent of our territory, if we would make our institutions permanent. . . . I have always wished that this country should exhibit to the nations of the earth the example of a great, rich, powerful republic which is not possessed by a spirit of aggrandizement. It is an example, I think, due from us to the world in favor of the character of republican government." [1]

The diplomacy of the Polk administration, though not as secret as that of Tyler, was fully as tortuous. Polk, in his inaugural address, declared that our title to the whole of Oregon was clear and unquestionable,[2] and that he intended to maintain that title. The whole of Oregon then meant as far north as 54° 40' north latitude, now the southern boundary of Alaska. The northwestern boundary had long been in dispute between Great Britain and the United States ; but the assertion of the President was extravagant, and savored rather of party pressure than of wise diplomacy, for the claim had not a good foundation. Both Webster and Calhoun, whose experience in the State department gave weight to their judgment, were of the opinion that to adopt the parallel of 49° would be a fair settlement of the dispute. After a certain amount of diplomatic fencing between the

---

arose as to who should have the credit of the annexation. See Benton's Thirty Years' View, and Letters and Times of the Tylers.

[1] Speech in the Senate, Dec., 1845, Works, vol. v. p. 56.   President Tyler said, in one of his messages advocating annexation, that no civilized government on earth would reject the offer of such a rich and fertile domain as Texas.   Letters and Times of the Tylers, vol. ii. p. 300.

[2] This was resolved by the Democratic convention which nominated Polk.

two countries, the Senate, on request, by a large majority, advised the President to conclude a treaty on that basis.

Very differently did the administration act regarding the disputed boundary question with Mexico. Although that unfortunate country had officially notified the United States that the annexation of Texas would be treated as a cause of war, so constant were the internal quarrels in Mexico that open hostilities would have been avoided had the conduct of the administration been honorable. That was the opinion of Webster, Clay, Calhoun, Benton, and Tyler. But as the satirist expressed it, the Southerners were after "bigger pens to cram with slaves."[1] Having acquired Texas, they longed for New Mexico and California. A dispute arose whether the southwestern boundary was the river Nueces or the Rio Grande. Negotiation in the same spirit as that had with Great Britain would undoubtedly have settled the difficulty, but the President arrogated the right of deciding the question. Mexico was actually goaded on to the war. The principle of the manifest destiny of this country was invoked as a reason for the attempt to add to our territory at the expense of Mexico.[2] General Taylor, who had command of the United States troops in Mexico, was ordered to advance to the Rio Grande. "Why not," Benton had thundered, "march up to fifty-four forty as courageously as we march upon the Rio Grande? Because Great Britain is powerful and Mexico weak."[3] On General Taylor's arrival at the Rio Grande, he planted a battery which commanded the public square of Matamoras, a Mexican town on the opposite side of the river, and blockaded the river in order to cut off supplies from the town. The Mexican general main-

---

[1] Biglow Papers.
[2] "Parson Wilbur sez

thet all this big talk of our destinies
Is half on it ig'rance an' t'other half rum."

—Biglow Papers.

[3] Thirty Years' View, vol. ii. p. 610.

tained that this began hostilities; he crossed over to the east bank of the Rio Grande, and had a skirmish with a smaller American force, in which sixteen of our dragoons were killed.

When this news arrived in Washington, early in May, 1846, the President sent a message to both houses of Congress, stating that American blood had been spilled on American soil, and asked that the existence of the war might be recognized, and energetic measures taken for its prosecution. Congress, with only two dissenting voices in the Senate and fourteen in the House, immediately declared war. This unanimity of feeling is not remarkable; for as long as love of country shall remain a cardinal virtue, the effort will be made to avenge an attack on one's countrymen. The national feeling had such root that the doctrine "Our country, right or wrong," was proclaimed to justify the sympathies of those who believed the war in its inception to have been an outrage. The Mexicans thought that the war was the result of a deliberately calculated scheme of robbery on the part of the superior power.[1] As Birdofredom Sawin, a private in the Mexican war, was told, "Our nation's bigger 'n theirn, an' so its rights air bigger."[2] While some quiet opposition at the North existed,[3] the war in the main was very popular. It needed no draft to fill the army; more volunteers offered than could be used. The war lasted nearly two years,[4] and was an unbroken series of victories. Our people would have

---

[1] H. H. Bancroft, cited in Winsor's Narrative and Critical History, vol. vii. p. 356. "For myself, I was bitterly opposed to the measure [the annexation of Texas], and to this day regard the war which resulted as one of the most unjust ever waged by a stronger against a weaker nation."— General Grant, Personal Memoirs, vol. i. p. 53.

[2] Biglow Papers.

[3] "I met with no one person in society who defended the aggression on Mexican territory." The dissatisfaction of many with the war "is unbounded."—Sir Charles Lyell, 1846, Second Visit, vol. ii. p. 256.

[4] It virtually ended, however, in Sept., 1847, having begun in May, 1846.

been more than human had they not exulted over our successes, due, as they were, to the genius of our generals and
bravery of our troops.   The Polk administration was de-
servedly unpopular; it declined in public estimation for the
reason that the victories in the field were won by two Whig
generals whom Polk and his cabinet fettered, but did not
dare to displace.[1]   The war gave Taylor his military reputation and made him President ; it added to Scott's fame and
made him a presidential candidate.

This administration, said Benton, "wanted a small war
just large enough to require a treaty of peace, and not large
enough to make military reputations dangerous for the presidency."[2]   It waged war with the sword in one hand and
the olive branch in the other; but the olive branch was to
be backed with money.   In August of this year (1846), and
after liberal appropriations had been made for the vigorous
prosecution of the war, the President, in addition, asked
Congress for two million dollars for the purpose of settling
our difficulties with Mexico.   It was no secret that this
money would be used to aid negotiations that had in view
the cession of considerable territory to this country, but
now the discussion took an unforeseen course, and one far
from welcome to the administration.   David Wilmot, a
Democratic representative from Pennsylvania, was selected
to propose a vital condition to this appropriation of money.
He had advocated Texas annexation.   He now asserted the
necessity of the war, and avowed himself in favor of the
acquisition of New Mexico and California; but he offered
an amendment to the two-million bill, which provided that
slavery should be forever prohibited in all the territory to

---

[1] " Mr. Polk's mode of viewing the case seems to have been this: Scott
is a Whig; therefore the Democracy is not bound to observe good faith
with him.   Scott is a Whig, therefore his successes may be turned to the
prejudice of the Democratic party."—Autobiography of Lieut.-General
Scott, p. 400.

[2] Thirty Years' View, vol. ii. p. 680.

be acquired from Mexico. This was the famous Wilmot proviso; it received a majority of nineteen in the House, but failed in the Senate, as did likewise the original bill. It was charged at the time, but probably with injustice, that the defeat of the proviso was due to the loquacity of one of its strong supporters, "honest John Davis," senator from Massachusetts.[1]

At the next session of Congress, in the following February (1847), the Wilmot proviso again came up. The President asked for an appropriation of three million dollars, secret service money, to be employed at his discretion in negotiating a treaty with Mexico. A bill was brought into the House with the desired stipulation, and to it was tacked the anti-slavery proviso, but only by a majority of nine. The Senate struck out the amendment, and passed the three-million bill, pure and simple, in accordance with the wish of the administration. The matter now went back to the House, and, by a majority of five, it receded from the Wilmot proviso. The House then passed the bill as it came from the Senate. All of the Whigs and many of the Democrats from the free States voted for the anti-slavery amendment, but every member from the slave States, except the one from Delaware, voted against it. Popular sentiment at the South was very strongly aroused in opposition to the Wilmot proviso, while the North was equally zealous in its favor.

During the year 1847 the vigorous prosecution of the war went on. From March to September Scott gained marvellous victories;[2] at last he took the city of Mexico, and dis-

---

[1] See defence of Davis, Senate speech, March, 1847; speech of Wilmot, Feb., 1847; Wilson's Rise and Fall of the Slave Power, vol. ii. p. 17; per contra, see Von Holst, vol. iii. p. 287; *Congressional Globe*, vol. xxviii. p. 1251; Life and Speeches of A. Lincoln, Bartlett, p. 64. Davis was one of the two senators who voted against the declaration of war against Mexico.

[2] "If 'Waverley' and 'Guy Mannering' had made the name of Scott immortal on one side of the Atlantic, Cerro Gordo and Churubusco had

persed the Mexican army. Meanwhile, we had obtained
possession by military power of the territories of New
Mexico and California. The new House of Representatives
that met in December differed widely in sentiment from the
preceding House towards the administration. Then there
had been a Democratic majority of sixty; in the present
House the Democrats were in a minority of eight. This
showed a strange revulsion of political feeling, for the elections took place while the country was resounding with the
victories of Taylor and Scott. It is amazing that an administration should have been condemned by the voice of the
people when the operations in the field had been so signally
successful; but this was due to the deep-seated conviction
that the war had been unjustly begun, and that the paramount object of Polk and his advisers was to add more
slave territory to the Union.

This feeling soon found expression in a House resolution
that the war with Mexico was "unnecessarily and uncon-
stitutionally begun by the President of the United States,"
and this opinion was heartily endorsed by Webster in a
Senate speech. "I concur in that sentiment," he said; "I
hold that to be the most recent and authentic expression of
the will and opinion of the majority of the people of the
United States."[1] This speech set forth ably and with much
feeling the dangers that were liable to accrue from an accession of new territory. It was an amplification of his
remarks at the preceding session when he stated: "We
want no extension of territory. We want no accession of
new States. The country is already large enough."[2] With
a premonition of the evils in store for his beloved country,
and with perhaps a dim presage of how his own great rep-

---

equally immortalized it on the other. If the novelist had given the
garb of truth to fiction, had not the warrior given to truth the air of
romance ?"—Sir Henry Bulwer at New York, 1850, Scott's Autobiography, p. 539.

[1] Speech, March 23d, 1848, Works, vol. v. p. 274.
[2] Remarks in the Senate, Feb., 1847, Curtis, vol. ii. p. 305.

utation was to suffer in the effort to grapple with them, he had said: "I pretend to see but little of the future, and that little affords no gratification. All I can scan is contention, strife, and agitation."[1]

The opinion of an unimportant member of the House has an interest for us inspired by his after-career. Abraham Lincoln, serving his first and only term in Congress, eager for distinction and stimulated by the expectations of his Illinois comrades, was an industrious member, ready in speech and prompt in action.[2] He voted for the House resolution to which reference has been made, and delivered a set speech on the Mexican war, which had the merit of using plain words to express opinions shared by many of his fellow-Whigs, though not by the constituents of his prairie district. His course on this question is best described in his own words of some years later. "I was an old Whig," said he, "and whenever the Democratic party tried to get me to vote that the war had been righteously begun by the President, I would not do it. But when they asked money or land warrants, or anything to pay the soldiers, I gave the same vote that Douglas did."[3]

In the early part of February, 1848, a treaty of peace was negotiated by a United States Commissioner in Mexico, and this afterwards received the ratification of the President and the Senate. By its provisions, New Mexico and Upper California[4] were ceded to the United States, and the lower Rio Grande, from its mouth to El Paso, was taken as the boundary of Texas. In consideration of these ac-

---

[1] Curtis, vol. ii. p. 307.

[2] Life of Lincoln, Lamon, p. 280.

[3] Lincoln-Douglas debates, Life of Lincoln, Arnold, p. 78.

[4] New Mexico included part of the present territory of the same name, all of Arizona except the southern part (which was purchased in 1853), practically all of Utah and Nevada, and part of Colorado. Upper California was substantially the present State of California. See Narrative and Critical History of North America, Winsor, vol. vii. p. 552, for map showing exactly the territory acquired.

quisitions, we agreed to pay Mexico fifteen million dollars. The significant remark was made that we obtained Louisiana for the same amount of money and without a war.

An incident in the negotiation of the treaty displayed whither was our drift in obedience to the behest of the slave power. The reader will remember that slavery did not exist under Mexican law, and that New Mexico and California were free territory. During the progress of the negotiations, Mexico begged for the insertion of an article providing that slavery should not be permitted in any of the territories ceded. Our commissioner replied that the bare mention of the subject in a treaty was an utter impossibility; that if the territory should be increased tenfold in value, and, besides, covered all over a foot thick with pure gold, on the single condition that slavery should be excluded therefrom, he could not then even entertain the proposition, nor think for a moment of communicating it to the President.[1] The "invincible Anglo-Saxon race" could not listen to the prayer of "superstitious Catholicism, goaded on by a miserable priesthood,"[2] even though the prayer was on the side of justice, progress, and humanity.

New Mexico and California were ours, and some measure of government for them must be devised; Oregon likewise demanded attention; and it would all have been a simple matter had not the question of slavery existed. Early in the year 1848, Douglas brought into the Senate a bill providing a territorial government for Oregon.[3] It excited no discussion until May, when John P. Hale, of New Hampshire, a Free-soil Democrat, offered an amendment, of which

---

[1] Letter of N. P. Trist to James Buchanan, Secretary of State, quoted by Von Holst, vol. iii. p. 334; see also Rise and Fall of the Slave Power, Wilson, vol. ii. p. 26.

[2] These expressions were used by Senator Preston in an enthusiastic speech made in 1836 on the news of the Texan victory at San Jacinto. Thirty Years' View, vol. i. p. 665.

[3] The Territory of Oregon comprised the present States of Oregon and Washington.

the intent was that slavery should be prohibited in Oregon. This gave rise to a long and earnest debate, in which the amendment was opposed with great pertinacity. The slavery extensionists, however, had no idea of introducing their system of labor into Oregon, and the discussion did not so much hinge on the actual project as on the principle involved and its application to New Mexico and California; for they determined to have the territory which had been acquired from Mexico dedicated to slavery. But at the threshold of their desire they found an inherent obstacle. California and New Mexico were free; and, as was pointed out during the senatorial debate, "by the laws of nations, the laws of all conquered countries remain until changed by the conqueror. There is an express law containing the prohibition of slavery [in California and New Mexico] and this will continue until we shall change it."[1] Yet the closet theorist, Calhoun, was equal to the emergency, and he had a political doctrine to fit the occasion. Benton called it the new dogma "of the transmigratory function of the Constitution, and the instantaneous transportation of itself in its slavery attributes into all acquired territories." Calhoun denied that the laws of Mexico could keep slavery out of New Mexico and California. "As soon as the treaty between the two countries is ratified," said he, "the sovereignty and authority of Mexico in the territory acquired by it become extinct, and that of the United States is substituted in its place, carrying with it the Constitution, with its overriding control over all the laws and institutions of Mexico inconsistent with it."[2] The Constitution by implication recognized slavery; therefore it permitted slave-owners to take their slaves into this new territory, or, in other words, it legalized slavery.[3] As a necessary deduction, the

---

[1] Senator Phelps, of Vermont.

[2] Niles's Register, vol. lxxiv. p. 61; Thirty Years' View, vol. ii. p. 713.

[3] "It is useless to prove what indeed is known to every one who has bestowed the slightest attention to it, namely, that slavery is considered

senator asserted that neither Congress, nor the inhabitants
of the territories, nor the territorial legislature have the
right to exclude slavery from the territories. This doctrine was completely refuted by Webster at the next session of Congress. For the present he contented himself with
a passing allusion; "I am not going into metaphysics,"
said he, "for therein I should encounter the honorable senator from South Carolina, and we should find 'no end, in
wand'ring mazes lost.' "[1]

It is indeed wondrous pitiful to contemplate Calhoun,
who had fine ability and sterling morality in private life,
thus held captive by one idea, and that idea totally at variance with the moral sentiment of the nineteenth century.[2]
In other service he would have been a useful statesman, but
he must be judged by the fruits of his two favorite dogmas,
the extreme states-rights theory of 1832, and the slavery-
extension doctrine of 1848. The two, thoroughly dissem-
inated throughout the South, became prime elements of
political faith. Their working forced her onward to secession, and induced a proud, high-spirited people to battle
for an idea utterly condemned at the tribunal of modern
civilization.

The debate went on in the Senate for some weeks, and as
the prospect of a satisfactory conclusion seemed remote, the
whole matter was referred to a special committee. They
soon reported a bill through their chairman, Clayton, of
Delaware, which provided territorial governments for Oregon, New Mexico, and California. The legitimate result of
the bill would be the prohibition of slavery in Oregon, but

emphatically and exclusively a municipal institution by all countries and
jurists, as well as publicists, European and American, Northern and
Southern; a truth—I add it in sorrow and deep concern—which you are
the first that has ever denied."—Letter of Francis Lieber to Calhoun,
Life and Letters of Lieber, p. 232.

[1] Webster's Works, vol. v. p. 308.

[2] So confessed by his eulogist, Lamar, in an address at Charleston,
April, 1887.

the question whether the Constitution permitted slavery in New Mexico and California was to be referred to the territorial courts, with the right of appeal to the United States Supreme Court. As Thomas Corwin, in a caustic speech opposing the measure, said, " It does not enact a law; it only enacts a lawsuit." [1] The bill passed the Senate, but was immediately laid upon the table in the House.

Meanwhile the House had been at work on a plan for Oregon. In the early part of August, its bill providing a territorial government for Oregon, with the prohibition of slavery, passed. In the Senate, an amendment was tacked to it, extending the Missouri Compromise line to the Pacific Ocean.[2] It must be called to mind that the Missouri Compromise, which prohibited slavery north of 36° 30' north latitude and permitted it south of that line, only applied to the Louisiana purchase, of which Oregon was not a part. The purpose in view Webster well expressed: " The truth is," said he, " that it is an amendment by which the Senate wishes to have now a public legal declaration, not respecting Oregon, but respecting the newly acquired territories of California and New Mexico. It wishes now to make a line of slavery which shall include those new territories." [3] On a previous day he had stated that " his objection to slavery was irrespective of lines and points of latitude; it took in the whole country and the whole question. He was opposed to it in every shape and every qualification; and was against any compromise of the question." [4] The bill with the amendment passed the Senate; the amendment was disagreed to by the House; finally, on the last day of the session, the Senate receded from its amendment and enacted the measure establishing a territorial government for Oregon, with the express prohibition of slavery.

---

[1] Speeches, p. 439.

[2] This would have permitted slavery in what is now New Mexico and Arizona, and in almost the southern half of California.

[3] Works, vol. v. p. 303.

[4] *Congressional Globe*, 1st Sess., 30th Cong., p. 1060.

While Congress was wrangling over the question, the two great political parties made their nominations for President; but their conventions completely ignored the vital issue of the day. The Democratic party chose General Cass as its candidate, and adopted a long series of resolutions, touching upon every conceivable subject save only the question of slavery in the territories. The Whig convention nominated General Taylor, but adopted no resolutions and issued no address. The candidate was the platform. Later, a convention was held at Buffalo, composed of those dissatisfied with the action of both of the great parties and who were opposed to the extension of slavery. Van Buren was nominated for President. The resolutions declared it to be the duty of the federal government to abolish slavery wherever it had the constitutional power; and that the true and only safe means of preventing the existence of slavery in territory still free was by congressional action. The selection of Martin Van Buren to head an anti-slavery movement partook of the grotesque. The enthusiasm with which sincere anti-slavery men rallied to his support was singular, when we call to mind that some years previously he had been denounced as a "Northern man with Southern principles." Van Buren's candidature did the Democrats more harm than the Whigs, and particularly in the State of New York. That state decided the election, as it had done four years previously. Van Buren polled more votes than Cass, and the two together sixteen thousand more than Taylor. Taylor had, however, the electoral vote of the state by a handsome plurality, and was chosen President.

On the assembling of Congress in December of this year (1848), President Polk strongly urged the necessity of providing territorial governments for New Mexico and California. He favored as a fair settlement the extension of the Missouri Compromise line to the Pacific. More than one attempt was made by Congress to dispose of the matter, but the only measure which passed the Senate was an amendment to the general appropriation bill providing for the extension of the

I.—7

Constitution to the territories. The consideration of this amendment gave rise to an important debate in which Webster and Calhoun were prominent.[1] Calhoun elaborated and explained the theory he had set forth at the previous session; but Webster, by a few trenchant questions and the assertion of some patent truths, showed plainly that the idea was impracticable, and completely at variance with our legislative precedents and judicial decisions. The House would not agree with the Senate; and as the amendment was tacked to the general appropriation bill, scenes of great excitement were common during the closing days of the session. Horace Mann, then a representative, wrote that blows were exchanged in the Senate, and two fist-fights took place in the House, in one of which blood flowed freely; and he expressed the opinion that "had the North been as ferocious as the South, it is probable there would have been a general mêlée."[2] Finally, however, the Senate receded from its amendment and passed the appropriation bill. The session came to an end, but nothing had been done towards the organization of governments for the territories. This and the allied question of slavery were left as a legacy to the new Congress. The necessary executive measures meanwhile devolved upon the new President, a man who came to the highest office of the state unversed in civil affairs, and untried in their orderly administration.

---

[1] This debate may be found in Curtis, vol. ii. p. 364.
[2] Quoted by Von Holst, vol. iii. p. 454.

CHAPTER II

Zachary Taylor was inaugurated March 5th, 1849. He was sincerely honest, a man of good judgment, pure morals, great energy, of independent and manly character, and possessed rare moral as well as physical courage. He had little education and many prejudices. But he was in every sense of the word a patriot and nothing of a partisan. Doubt had for a time, indeed, prevailed regarding his political opinions, for he had never voted. The party managers induced him to say, finally, that he was a Whig; but General Taylor at the same time insisted that if elected " he would not be the President of a party, but the President of the whole people."

He was, as we have seen, nominated by the regular Whig convention; but while the campaign was in progress he had discomfited his Northern adherents by accepting the nomination of a Democratic meeting at Charleston, which preferred him to Cass, as he was deemed safer on the slavery question. Taylor was from Louisiana, and owned a large sugar plantation there, with several hundred slaves. As the Whig convention had adopted no declaration of principles, what course the newly-elected President would take on the question of slavery in the territories was problematical. It had, however, been asserted with confidence at the North during the campaign that he would not veto any anti-slavery legislation which should receive the assent of Congress. While the President, in his inaugural address, did not touch upon the question which had distracted the legislature of the country, nevertheless its guarded expressions seemed to indicate that his Northern supporters had fairly outlined his policy.

But his cabinet appointments were favorable to the Southern section of his party; four of them were from the slave and three from the free States. The prominent members were John M. Clayton, of Delaware, Secretary of State; Thomas Ewing, of Ohio, Secretary of the Interior; Reverdy Johnson, of Maryland, Attorney-General; and Jacob Collamer, of Vermont, Postmaster-General. Collamer was the only man of marked anti-slavery sentiments.[1]

The problem which the country had to solve called for its wisest statesmanship. It demanded the full measure of the time and ability of the President and his advisers, but they were not able to devote their attention immediately to the exigency of the State. The executive power had passed from one political party to the other; the Democrats, therefore, must be turned out of the offices to make room for the faithful Whigs. "To the victors belong the spoils" was a doctrine first put in practice by the Democratic party. But the Whigs were apt pupils, and as there were about fifty thousand places in the civil service,[2] a horde of hungry office-seekers flocked to Washington. General Taylor was a man of business habits. His long service in the army, and his experience in the management of a large plantation, had taught him that merit and fitness were the proper and only tests that should be required of subordinates, and his mind was still filled with this notion when he delivered his inaugural address. He said: "I shall make honesty, capacity, and fidelity indispensable prerequisites to the bestowal of office."[3] Although the President had good business ideas, he was ignorant of party management, and soon allowed himself to be guided by those who had all their lives wrought in the sphere of practical poli-

---

[1] The other members of the cabinet were Meredith of Pennsylvania, Secretary of the Treasury; Crawford of Georgia, Secretary of War; and Preston of Virginia, Secretary of the Navy.

[2] New York *Tribune*, April, 1849.

[3] Niles, vol. lxxv. p. 150.

tics. General Taylor had a high respect for the Vice-President, Millard Fillmore, of New York, and, until unde-ceived a short time before his arrival at Washington, he thought that the Vice-President could be *ex officio* a member of his cabinet.[1] He was nevertheless disposed to rely upon the experience of Fillmore in all important matters, and nothing at first seemed so important as the New York pat-ronage. But in this State there were two divisions of the Whig party, one headed by Fillmore and the other by Will-iam H. Seward, who had recently been elected to the Sen-ate ; and, to forestall differences that might naturally arise, Thurlow Weed, a common friend, had them both dine with him at Albany when they were on their way to Washing-ton. " Here," as Weed himself relates, " everything was pleasantly arranged. The Vice-President and the Senator were to consult from time to time, as should become nec-essary, and agree upon the important appointments to be made in our State."[2]   Fillmore, however, seems to have had the better of the arrangement ; for the first knowledge that came to Seward of the New York custom-house appoint-ments was when their names were read in executive session of the Senate.[3]

The President also appointed anti-Seward Whigs to other lucrative offices in the State. Seward, as Lincoln afterwards said, " was a man without gall,"[4] and did not openly resent the infraction of the agreement. He did not retire to his tent, but patiently bided his time. He voted for the con-firmation of his adversaries, and then went to work with serenity to supplant his rival in the favor of the President.[5]

---

[1] Thurlow Weed's Autobiography, p. 586.

[2] Ibid., p. 586.

[3] Ibid., p. 587 ; see also letters of Seward to Weed, March 1st and 10th, Life of Seward, F. W. Seward, vol. ii. pp. 101, 107.

[4] Life, by Nicolay and Hay, *Century Magazine*, vol. xxxii. p. 562.

[5] See letter of Seward to Weed, March 24th, Life of Seward, F. W. Sew-ard, vol. ii. p. 107.

In this he was much assisted by his friend Weed, who had great influence, for he was one of the first to look to General Taylor as a presidential candidate. Their efforts were successful, and soon Seward became the directing spirit of the administration.

Thurlow Weed relates with great satisfaction that the President "became convinced that the significance of a zealous and patriotic movement of the people, which overthrew Democratic supremacy, meant something more than the election of a Whig President and the appointment of a Whig cabinet." "I did not think it wise or just," the President himself remarked, "to kick away the ladder by which I ascended to the presidency; colonels, majors, captains, lieutenants, sergeants, and corporals are just as necessary to success in politics as they are to the discipline and efficiency of an army." On another occasion the President inquired of the Secretary of the Treasury "whether you think our friends are getting their share of the offices." The Secretary answered that he "had not thought of the matter in that light." "Nor," rejoined the President, "have I until recently. But if the country is to be benefited by our services, it seems to me that you and I ought to remember those to whose zeal, activity, and influence we are indebted for our places. There are plenty of Whigs, just as capable and honest, and quite as deserving of office, as the Democrats who have held them through two or three presidential terms. Rotation in office, provided good men are appointed, is sound Republican doctrine."[1]

The Democratic newspapers of the day are full of derisive taunts at the wholesale removals from office. The Whigs either defended them as the work of reform,[2] or else retorted by recriminations. Yet many of the leading Whigs were far from being satisfied. Clay complained that the good positions went to those who had been instrumental in bring-

---

[1] Life of Thurlow Weed, vol. ii. pp. 175, 176.
[2] This is the expression of the New York *Tribune*, April 17th, 1849.

ing about the nomination of General Taylor,[1] and Webster grieved bitterly over the refusal of the administration to grant his request for an office of "small pecuniary consideration" for his only son.[2]   Abraham Lincoln was an urgent applicant for the office of Commissioner of the General Land Office.   He solicited support from his late friends in Congress, and endeavored to have his claim advocated in the party newspapers, but his efforts were without fruit.[3]   The Postmaster-General Collamer, in a letter to his friend John J. Crittenden, laments not having been able to carry out Crittenden's wishes in reference to the appointment of the local mail agent at Louisville.   But the President had taken the matter out of his hands, and as he was "but a subaltern," he had to obey.[4]   The Secretary of State found fault with Collamer, and wrote : " Our friend Collamer is behind ; he is a glorious fellow, but *too tender* for progress.   He has been often, indeed, at his wits' end, frightened about removals and appointments, but I cry courage to them all, and they will go ahead *all*, by and by !   Taylor has all the moral as well as physical courage needed for the emergency."[5]   Yet the President, whose knowledge of literature went not " much beyond good old Dilworth's spelling-book,"[6] unwittingly did the cause of letters a great service in the removal of Nathaniel Hawthorne from the surveyorship of the Salem custom-house, for on the afternoon of the day on which the gifted author was deprived of his

---

[1] Clay's Private Correspondence, p. 587.   "It is undeniable that the public patronage has been too exclusively confined to the original supporters of General Taylor, without sufficient regard to the merits and just claims of the great body of the Whig party."

[2] Harvey's Reminiscences, p. 178.   The President later gave Webster's son, "though after delay and hesitation," "a lucrative office," Schouler, vol. v. p. 150.

[3] Lamon, p. 333.

[4] Life of Crittenden, Coleman, vol. i. p. 346.

[5] Ibid., p. 344.

[6] Autobiography of Lieutenant-General Scott, vol. ii. p. 383.

place he began to write "The Scarlet Letter."[1]   He lost
his salary of twelve hundred dollars a year, but he gave to
his country its greatest romance.[2]

While Congress was still in session Calhoun was busy in
working up a sentiment that should fire the Southern heart
with zeal to defend the rights which were in supposed jeopardy.   A convention of Southern members of Congress issued an address drawn up by Calhoun.   In this declaration
they complained of the difficulties in recovering fugitive
slaves; they found fault with the systematic agitation of

---

[1] Hawthorne and his Wife, Julian Hawthorne, vol. i. p. 340.

[2] Hawthorne describes the enormous specimen of the American eagle
"which hovers over the entrance of the custom-house," and which "appears by the fierceness of her beak and eye, and the general tendency of
her attitude, to threaten mischief to the unoffensive commûnity."   "Nevertheless, vixenly as she looks, many people are seeking, at this very moment, to shelter themselves under the wing of the Federal eagle; imagin-
ing, I presume, that her bosom has all the softness and snugness of an
eider-down pillow.   But she has no great tenderness, even in her best
of moods, and, sooner or later—oftener soon than late—is apt to fling off
her nestlings, with a scratch of her claw, a dab of her beak, or a rankling wound from her barbed arrows. . . . But now, should you go thither
to seek him, you would inquire in vain for the Locofoco surveyor.   The
besom of reform has swept him out of office; and a worthier successor
wears his dignity and pockets his emoluments. . . . A remarkable event
of the third year of my surveyorship was the election of General Taylor
to the presidency.   It is essential, in order to a complete estimate of the
advantages of official life, to view the incumbent at the incoming of a
hostile administration.   His position is then one of the most singularly
irksome, and, in every contingency, disagreeable, that a wretched mortal
can possibly occupy; with seldom an alternative of good on either hand,
although what presents itself to him as the worst event may very probably be the best."   Hawthorne wrote more truly than he then knew.   He
felt his removal from office keenly.   The letter pleading for Hillard's influence in favor of the retention of his office, his lamentation at being
turned out, his appeal for re-appointment, with the assignment of categorical reasons why he should not have been proscribed by the Whig
administration, are pathetic, and make an exquisitely phrased condemnation of the spoils system.   See letters to Hillard, Life of Hawthorne,
Conway, p. 111.

the slavery question by the abolitionists; they demanded the right of emigrating into the territories with their slaves; and they inveighed bitterly against the House for its action in regard to New Mexico and California. More than eighty members participated in the meeting when this address was adopted, but only about half of that number affixed their signatures to the instrument. It was published throughout the South with a flourish of trumpets; and soon it was hailed by its authors as the second declaration of independence.[1] Except in South Carolina, however, the address did not make a deep impression.[2] For the moment Calhoun seemed to have lost influence. His intellectual vagaries had become tiresome, and his over-refinement of phrase proved tedious even to those whose sympathy was ardent with the Southern cause.

Of greater moment were the resolutions of the Virginia legislature. They affirmed that "the adoption and attempted enforcement of the Wilmot proviso" would present two alternatives to the people of Virginia; one of "abject submission to aggression and outrage," and the other "of determined resistance at all hazards and to the last extremity."[3] The sovereign people of Virginia, as they valued their rights of property and dearest privileges, could have no difficulty in making a choice between the two alternatives. It was likewise resolved that the abolition of slavery or of the slave-trade in the District of Columbia would be a direct attack upon the institution of the Southern States. These resolutions were carried by a large majority; and this official utterance of the most powerful State in the South was an incitement to Southern feeling and a guide to the way of evincing it. The resolutions were approved at many public meetings held all over the South; they were endorsed by several Democratic state conventions; and they

---

[1] Benton's Thirty Years' View, vol. ii. p. 734.
[2] *New-Englander*, Aug., 1849.
[3] Niles, vol. lxxv. p. 73.

formed the basis of similar expressions from other legislatures.

The excitement was especially great in Missouri. The legislature of this State had passed resolutions protesting against the principle of the Wilmot proviso, and instructing her senators and representatives to act in hearty co-operation with the members from the slave-holding States.[1] This was a shaft aimed at Senator Benton, who was opposed to the extension of slavery. He accepted the challenge, repaired to Missouri when the Senate adjourned, and made a noble fight against the slavery extensionists. He spoke at meeting after meeting, defending his own course and making an aggressive warfare on Calhoun and his Missouri disciples.

The feeling was at fever heat in Tennessee. The address of the Democratic State Central Committee to the voters said, " The encroachments of our Northern brethren have reached a point where forbearance on our part ceases to be a virtue." [2] In Kentucky, Clay had written a letter intended to influence the constitutional convention about to assemble, in which he favored a plan of gradual emancipation of the slaves in his State. A people's meeting held in Trimble County, Ky., requested him to resign his place as senator in consequence of the sentiments avouched in this letter.[3] The question of freeing the slaves was made an issue and discussed in every county of the State, but not one avowed emancipationist was elected to the convention. The convention itself not only failed to adopt any plan of gradual emancipation, but, on the contrary, the new constitution asserted, in the strongest terms, the right of property in slaves and their increase.

In the cotton States the feeling was more intense than in the border States. The Virginia resolutions were everywhere endorsed. The prevailing sentiment of South Carolina was shown at a dinner to Senator Butler, when " Slav-

---

[1] Niles, vol. lxxv. p. 270.   [2] Ibid., p. 373.   [3] Ibid., p. 384.

ery," " Our territorial acquisitions from Mexico," and " A
Southern Confederacy " were toasted amid great enthusiasm.[1] The Democrats were more outspoken than the Whigs,
but party lines were beginning to be merged and swallowed
up in the community of sectional interest.   Yet the Northern Whigs tried to think that they and the Southern members of their party could meet on common ground.   The
New York *Tribune* maintained that "the Southern Whigs
want the great question settled in such a manner as shall
not humble and exasperate the South ; the Southern Loco-
focos [i. e. Democrats] want it so settled as to conduce to
the extension of the power and influence of slavery."[2]   But,
in truth, when a question of practical legislation arose, the
interest of section was stronger than the hold of party.

The feeling in the North was as deeply stirred as in the
South.   The conflict of sentiment was well shown in the
reception given to the letter of Clay which favored the gradual emancipation of the slaves in Kentucky.   In the North
it was universally approved ; in the South, outside of his
own State, it was just as emphatically condemned.   Every
one of the legislatures of the free States, except Iowa,[3]
passed resolutions to the effect that Congress had the power,
and that it was its duty, to prohibit slavery in the territories.[4]
Many States also requested their senators and representatives to use their utmost influence to abolish slavery and
the slave-trade in the District of Columbia.   Party lines
were not considered ; they had no influence upon this action.
Some of the legislatures were strongly Whig ; in others the
Democrats were greatly in the ascendant.   But the parties
seemed to vie with each other in taking advanced anti-slav-

---

[1] New York *Tribune*, April 25th, 1849.

[2] Ibid., Oct. 24th, 1849.

[3] In Iowa instructions to her senators and representatives to vote for
the Wilmot proviso passed the State Senate, but were laid upon the table
in the House.—Niles, vol. lxxv. p. 113.

[4] New York *Tribune*, July 23d, 1849.

ery ground, and in some of the legislatures the resolutions were passed by a nearly unanimous vote.[1]   As a body, the Whigs were more pronounced in their views than were the regular Democrats.   Greeley maintained that the Whigs of New York State recognized "the restriction of slavery within its present limits as one of the cardinal principles of our political faith;"[2] but the Free-soilers, comprising for the most part those who had supported Van Buren the previous year, were strenuous in their demands that the general government should forbid slavery where it had the power. Charles Sumner came to the front in a Free-soil convention at Worcester, Mass., and wrote the vigorous address which proclaimed "opposition to slavery wherever we are responsible for it," demanded its prohibition in the new territories, and its abolition in the District of Columbia.[3]   The Democrats of Ohio felt very powerfully the impulse of the anti-slavery movement, and in February the legislature, by a combination of two Free-soilers, who held the balance of power, with the Democrats, elected Salmon P. Chase to the United States Senate.   He was a strong opposer of slavery ; was of partially Democratic antecedents, and had presided over the Free-soil convention which nominated Van Buren for the presidency.   At Cleveland an enthusiastic convention of Free-soilers was held on the 13th of July to celebrate the passage of the Ordinance of 1787.   Clay was invited to be present, but declined on account of other engagements ; he seemed to think, however, that the commemoration was ill-timed as being liable "to increase the prevailing excitement."[4]

General Cass tried to stem the current of popular opinion in the West.   He held that Congress had no right to legislate upon slavery in the territories; and, while the legislat-

[1] Niles, vol. lxxv. pp. 190, 239, 399.
[2] New York *Tribune*, Oct. 3d, 1849.
[3] Life and Public Services of Charles Sumner, Lester, p. 67.
[4] Washington *National Intelligencer*, July 21st, 1849.

ure of Michigan elected him to the Senate—for they could
not forget the part he had played in the material development and civil organization of their State—yet the same
body of men resolved that Congress ought to prohibit slavery in New Mexico and California. The Cleveland *Plain
Dealer*, which had loyally supported Cass for President, expressed the opinion of the majority of Ohio Democrats
when it declared that "the institution of slavery is bound
to be the death of Democracy in this country, unless the
Democratic party as a body eschew its requirements."[1]

The position which President Taylor was gradually taking proved a source of gratification to the anti-slavery people. When he came to Washington his Southern sympathies were strong, and he had the notion that the Northerners were encroaching on the rights of the South. A short
experience in the executive office served to convince him
that the encroachment was from the opposite direction, and
he had the manliness to act contrary to the supposed interests of his own section. The influence of Seward, moreover,
was a potent factor in the President's actual envisagement
of the situation. Complaint had been made at the South
that a majority of the cabinet were in favor of the principle of the Wilmot proviso; and this notion was heightened
by a speech of the President at Mercer, Pa., in August,
when he said : "The people of the North need have no apprehension of the further extension of slavery; the necessity of a third party organization on this score would soon
be obviated."[2] State and congressional elections took place
during the spring, summer, and fall, but they afforded no
guide to the direction of popular sentiment. On the whole,
the Whigs lost some advantages as compared with the Presidential election. Party divisions were rigidly observed,
but the slavery question was nowhere at issue in any of the
States at the North. The Van Buren and the Cass Demo-

---

[1] Cleveland *Plain Dealer*, May 16th, 1849.
[2] New York *Tribune*, Sept. 10th, 1849.

crats had generally united on the State tickets—in some
States on an anti-slavery platform, in others by ignoring the
national question. The New York *Tribune,* however, explained that the result of the elections in Tennessee and
Kentucky was due to the fact that the Whigs " were cried
down in those States as an anti-slavery party." [1] It is indubi-
table that the Northern sentiment was wholesome and thoroughly imbued with the desire to check the extension of
slavery.

Towards the latter part of the year speculations as to the
action of Congress began to be made ; the opinion prevailed
that at the next session the question would be settled, and
there was little doubt of its settlement in a manner that
would satisfy Northern sentiment. It seemed as if this feeling needed only discretion in its guidance, and nerve in the
assertion of its claims, to become embodied in legislative acts
that should fix the vital principle at issue.

Meanwhile, from action which was taking place in California, one bone of contention seemed liable to be removed.
After this territory had been taken possession of by the
Americans, it was placed under a quasi-military government,
and this was continued after the treaty of peace was proclaimed. [2] Before his inauguration General Taylor had
been anxious that Congress should settle on some plan of
government for California ; he said that " he desired to substitute the rule of law and order there for the bowie-knife
and revolvers." [3] A month after his inauguration he sent T.
Butler King, a Whig congressman from Georgia, to California, as a confidential agent of the administration, to assist the
growing movement towards the formation of a State government, and to work in conjunction with the military governor.
California, which, when acquired, had been deemed an insignificant province, had now become the El Dorado of the

---

[1] New York *Tribune,* Sept., 1849.

[2] History of the Pacific States, H. H. Bancroft, vol. xviii. p. 262.

[3] Seward's Works, vol. iii. p. 444.

world.   Nine days before the treaty of peace between the
United States and Mexico was signed,[1] gold was discovered
in the foot-hills of the Sierras.   Only a few persons in California were aware of the find, and none in the United States
or Mexico knew of it when the treaty was ratified.   "The
accursed thirst of gold" was to work out the destiny of this
territory; but it was not until well into May, 1848, that
scepticism in San Francisco gave way to faith in this discovery.   By the middle of the summer the news was believed everywhere, and from all parts people flocked to
the gold diggings.   When it became known at Monterey,
Colton relates that every one began to make preparations to
go to the mines.   Blacksmiths, carpenters, masons, farmers,
bakers, tapsters, boarding-house keepers, soldiers, and do-
mestics—all left their occupations.   That writer, who was
the alcalde of Monterey, reports that he only had a community of women left, a gang of prisoners, and a few soldiers.[2] So it was everywhere in the territory.   The country was in a state of frenzy.   The hunger of wealth had
taken hold of the whole population.   Laborers demanded
ten dollars a day and carpenters sixteen dollars.[3]   Privates
from the army and sailors from the naval ships deserted and
repaired to the gold diggings.   A private could make more
money in the mines in a day than he received in the service
in a month.[4]

At that time it required about forty days for the transmission of the mails from San Francisco to New York. The
fabulous stories were at first doubted in the eastern part of
the country, but were soon accepted with fervid belief. The
news had soon reached all parts of the civilized world, and

---

[1] Jan. 24th, 1848.

[2] Three years in California, Colton, p. 247.   "A general of the U. S.
Army, the commander of a man-of-war, and Alcalde of Monterey, in a
smoking kitchen, grinding coffee, toasting a herring, and peeling onions!"
—Ibid., p. 248.

[3] Memoirs of General W. T. Sherman, pp. 53, 78.

[4] Ibid., p. 72.

then began an emigration to California for which nowhere could there be found a likeness save in a tale of legendary Greece. The thirsters after gold, the seekers of El Dorado, were Argonauts in search of the golden fleece. Yet the resemblance fails when we come to consider the character of the California emigrants. While they numbered many good men, especially from the Western States,[1] there were many outlaws and criminals among them. From all parts of the world outcasts and vagrants swelled the crowd that undertook the hardships of the dangerous journey for the sake of bettering their condition and their fortunes. In truth, the journey was one that only the hardy could endure. If the emigrant chose to go by sailing vessel from New York around Cape Horn, he had to brave the perils and discomforts of the most dangerous of ocean voyages. He could, indeed, go by the Isthmus of Panama, but, as the railroad was not then built, the crossing of the isthmus was attended with great hazard. Arriving at Panama, on the Pacific side, the travellers had to wait for days, and even weeks, in an atmosphere whose every breath was laden with pestilential spores. On more than one occasion, when the steamship arrived which was to take them to the Golden Gate, it was found that the expectant passengers largely exceeded the capacity of the boat, and men scrambled and fought to get on board to secure their paid-for passage.

There was still left the overland route. This was a wagon journey of more than two thousand miles, through a country of great variety in its physical features. Warm, pleasant valleys were succeeded by bleak and almost impassable mountains ; thence the route proceeded down into miasmatic swamps, then across forbidding alkali wastes and salt flats, baked and cracked by the sun. The travellers were stifled with heat and dust, yet were likewise sure to encounter drenching rains. It was often necessary to cross flooded lowlands and sweeping river currents ; as if the misery were

---

[1] H. T. Davis, Solitary Places Made Glad, p. 47.

not complete, they met with occasional chilling blasts and suffocating simoons. They were not only subject to these changes of climate and altitude, but they were in constant fear of the savages.[1] Whether by starvation, disease, or violence, many of the overland emigrants perished on the way. Nevertheless, in spite of all these obstacles, there arrived in California, in the year 1849, 39,000 souls by sea and 42,000 overland.[2] These were the "inflowing Argonauts," known to this day as "forty-niners," from the year in which they made their journey. Discouraging and conflicting reports came home from the emigrants, but the rush continued; and some years later, in England, the telling pen of De Quincey was enlisted to decry California. "She," said the brilliant Englishman, "is going ahead at a rate that beats Sindbad and Gulliver." Its story reads "to the exchanges of Europe like a page from the 'Arabian Nights.'"[3]

What was the government of this community? How was law administered? There was the military governor, who had no authority save such as he might choose to assume; and there were the alcaldes, a survival of the Mexican officials, with duties that were partly judicial and partly executive; their business was to maintain order, punish crime, and redress injuries.[4] Some of the old Mexican alcaldes still held their sway, and others were chosen by the communities over which they presided. Walter Colton was appointed alcalde

---

[1] This description of the overland route is partly quoted and partly paraphrased from H. H. Bancroft, vol. xviii. p. 148.

[2] Ibid., p. 159.

[3] De Quincey's Essay on California. The romantic side of the California fever did not escape the notice of George Ticknor. He writes to Sir Charles Lyell, in 1849, that it is evidence that there is "in our Anglo-Saxon blood more of a spirit of adventure and romance than belongs to the age."—Life of George Ticknor, vol. ii. p. 241. Only three years previously American fellow-travellers of Lyell had told him in their journey from New York to Boston that they hoped to see in their lifetime a population of fifteen thousand souls in California and Oregon. Sir Charles Lyell's Second Visit, vol. ii. p. 265.

[4] Colton, p. 19.

I.—8

of Monterey by the commodore of the naval ship which was stationed at that port.[1] But on the whole the territory was bordering on a state of anarchy. There were no land laws; mining titles were disputed and sometimes fought over.[2] A deserted wife at San Francisco complained that there was no power to give her a legal divorce. The habit of carrying weapons was universal; drunken brawls were common; the Indians made raids on the settled communities and stole horses and cattle; the vineyards and orchards of San José and Santa Clara were destroyed by immigrants; it was complained that San Luis Obispo had become "a complete sink of drunkenness and debauchery;" ruffians united themselves in bands to rob, and the convoys from the mines were their especial prey; murders were common, and lynch law was put into execution not infrequently; yet murder was deemed a lesser crime than theft; and when law-breakers were put in prison, the alcalde was in constant fear that a mob would break in and release the prisoners.[3] The cry that went out of Macedonia for help was no louder than that which went from the majority of Californians to Congress to give them a territorial government. Yet, if Congress would not help them, they determined to help themselves. The first immigration was largely from Mexico, Peru, Chili, China, and the Hawaiian Islands,[4] and the food-supply of the miners came in considerable portion from this group.[5] But as the American population increased, and as men of better antecedents joined the fortune-seekers, that knack at political organization which is so prominent a trait of our national character,

---

[1] Colton, p. 17.

[2] California Inter Pocula, H. H. Bancroft, chap. ix.

[3] H. H. Bancroft, vol. xviii. pp. 229, 268. Bayard Taylor's account is different, but there is no question as to which authority should be followed. Bret Harte has exquisitely given us the flavor of those rough times in "Tales of the Argonauts," "Luck of Roaring Camp," "Outcasts of Poker Flat," etc.

[4] Eldorado, Taylor, p. 100; also Bancroft.

[5] Alexander's History of the Hawaiian Islands, p. 273.

appeared, and it was determined to establish a civil government.[1] Meetings were held at many places in the territory,
and a convention to frame a government was called to meet
May 6th, 1849 ; so that in case Congress adjourned March
4th without making any provision for them, they could go
ahead and institute a government of their own. They were
assisted in this movement by the military governor and the
confidential agent of the administration. Forty-eight members were chosen for the convention, of whom twenty-two
were from the Northern States, fifteen from the slave States,
seven were native Californians, and four foreign - born.[2]
Party or sectional opinions had not entered into the choice
of the delegates, but it was supposed that their action would
be controlled by Southern men.[3] The meeting of the convention was postponed from time to time ; but at last it met
at Monterey on the 3d of September, with the object of
forming a State. The convention was by no means destitute of ability, although an assemblage of young men.
Scarcely a gray head could be seen.[4] There were fourteen
lawyers, twelve farmers, seven merchants ; the remainder
were engineers, bankers, physicians, and printers.[5] The idea
of forming an original constitution did not enter into their
heads. There were men from various states who were familiar with the provisions of their own organic law ; but
the Constitution was largely modelled after those of New
York and Iowa. To the astonishment of Northern men, no
objection whatever was made to the clause in the bill of
rights which forever prohibited slavery in the state.[6] The

[1] "The Americans surpass all other nations in their power of making
the best out of bad conditions, getting the largest results out of scanty
materials or rough methods."—American Commonwealth, Bryce, vol. i.
p. 169.
[2] Bancroft, vol. xviii. p. 282.
[3] Ibid., p. 286.
[4] There were three members over fifty, and but ten over forty.
[5] Bancroft, vol. xviii. p. 288.
[6] Bancroft, vol. xviii. p. 290. At first sight this unanimity may seem

members of the convention worked diligently day and night; on the 13th of October their labors were at an end and they affixed their signatures to the Constitution.¹ One month later it was adopted by the vote of the people. The legislature which it constituted met in December, and, by a compromise arrangement, elected John C. Frémont and William M. Gwin senators; Frémont held anti-slavery and Gwin pro-slavery opinions.

When Congress met on the first Monday of December, 1849, the vastly preponderating sentiment in the free States was that California and New Mexico should remain free territory. On the other hand, the sentiment was equally strong in the South against any congressional legislation that should interfere with their supposed right of taking their slaves into the new territories. In other words, a population of thirteen millions demanded that the common possession should be dedicated to freedom; a population of eight millions demanded the privilege of devoting it to slavery.² California, by the unanimous vote of a convention regularly chosen, whose action was ratified by an honest vote of her people, had cast her lot on the side of the free States.

Congress met December 3d. The House was made up

---

strange, as where labor was scarce and high and gold plenty it might seem desirable to have slaves. But I think the gist of the whole matter is contained in the following statement of a voting citizen: " One of the prominent questions in the election was an expression as to whether slavery shall be allowed in California; the candidate, though a Louisianian, was opposed out and out to the introduction of slavery here, and so we all voted for him. For myself, I was of the opinion of an old mountaineer, who, leaning against the tent-pole, harangued the crowd, that in a country where every white man made a slave of himself there was no use in keeping niggers."—Correspondence of the Boston *Times*, copied into the New York *Tribune* of Oct. 22d, 1849.

¹ "The most magnificent illustration of the wonderful capacity of this people for self-government."—Von Holst, vol. iii. p. 463.

² These figures are simply round numbers, as shown by the census of 1850; three-fifths of the slaves are included in the slave-State population.

of 112 Democrats, 105 Whigs, and 13 Free-soilers,[1] and its
organization first demanded attention. The candidate of
the Whigs for speaker was Winthrop, of Boston, an able
and honorable gentleman, of fine birth and breeding, who
had been speaker of the previous Congress. Eight of the
Free-soilers, however, under the lead of Joshua R. Giddings,
refused their support on the ground that he had not during
his term as speaker recognized the anti-slavery sentiment in
the appointment of the committees, nor would he pledge
himself to do so should he be chosen at this session. Giddings represented a district of northeastern Ohio composed
of several of the counties of the Western Reserve; with the
exception of the Plymouth, it was the most liberty-loving
district in the country. He had served many terms in the
House, and had distinguished himself, battling by the side
of John Quincy Adams for the right of petition and for the
anti-slavery cause. Although not a man of great ability,
he had great zeal; and as he felt himself untrammelled by
the shackles of party, he served his district to its full satisfaction, and made an enviable record as an advocate of freedom. Yet eleven years of legislative experience had failed
to teach him that, while it is true there are now and then
political principles that must not be bated a jot, even though
the heavens fall, it is equally true that for the most part in
public life one should sacrifice his ideal good for the best attainable. It was so in this case. If Giddings and his associates had voted for Winthrop, he would have been chosen
speaker. They did not choose to do so, and finally Howell
Cobb, of Georgia, was elected. His devotion to slavery and
Southern interests was the distinguishing feature of his character, and he made up the committees in a way extremely

---

[1] I follow the classification of the *Congressional Globe*. Giddings
states the number of Free-soilers as eight (History of the Rebellion, p.
300); while Julian, who was one of them, says they were nine (Political
Recollections, p. 73). Giddings and Julian classify them according to the
vote for speaker, while the *Globe* ranges them with regard to their vital
principles.

favorable to the South and the slave interest.[1] "He loves slavery," said Horace Mann; "it is his politics, his political economy, and his religion."[2]   Horace Mann had gained a wide and well-deserved reputation as an educator; but on the death of John Quincy Adams he was prevailed upon to fill the vacant place of representative of the Plymouth district.   He was wiser than his Ohio colleague, for he voted steadily for Winthrop "as the best man we could possibly elect."[3]   The acme of logical adherence to a fixed idea, in spite of surrounding circumstances, was reached when Giddings and his followers voted for Brown, of Indiana, for speaker, a Democrat of the straitest sect, because he agreed to make the constitution of certain committees satisfactory to them; and that, too, while, as Giddings himself said, "Neither the moral nor political character of Mr. Brown recommended him to the favor of just and honorable men."[4] The balloting for speaker lasted nearly three weeks, and the excitement occasioned by the protracted organization of the House boded no good for the Northern cause.   Between the ballots animated discussions sometimes took place, and the Southern bluster was loud and menacing.   Disunion was emphatically threatened in case the principle of the Wilmot proviso was insisted upon, or if the attempt were made to abolish slavery in the District of Columbia.   Robert Toombs and Alexander Stephens, both Whigs from Georgia, were the most vehement in their threats to the North and their

---

[1] "Although the Whigs and Free-soilers are a majority, yet only one from their number is a chairman of any one of the thirty-seven committees.   Of the other thirty-six chairmen, nineteen are Locos from the slave States, and seventeen Locos from the free States.   Texas, Alabama, and South Carolina afford five chairmen; the three millions of New York only one."—New York *Tribune*, Jan. 23d.

[2] Life of Horace Mann, p. 283.

[3] Ibid., p. 285.

[4] History of the Rebellion, p. 302.   Julian, of Indiana, was not concerned in this intrigue.   He was ill, and was not at Washington at this time.   Root, of Ohio, likewise would not vote for Brown.

appeals to the South. Contemptuous epithets were bandied to and fro; at one time the lie was given, and only the interference of the sergeant-at-arms with his mace of office prevented a fist-fight on the floor of the House.[1]

As soon as the House was organized, the President sent his message to Congress. He touched briefly on the important question, but his words were carefully weighed. The latest advices from California gave him reason to believe that she had framed a Constitution, established a state government, and would shortly apply for admission into the Union. This application was recommended to the favorable consideration of Congress. It was likewise believed that at a time not far distant the people of New Mexico would present themselves for admission into the Union. He counselled Congress to await their action, for that would avert all causes of uneasiness, and good feeling would be preserved. It was his opinion, moreover, that "we should abstain from the introduction of those exciting topics of sectional character which have hitherto produced painful apprehensions in the public mind."

The great intellectual contest was to take place in the Senate. There Webster, Clay, and Calhoun appeared together for the last time. They were all of them born during the Revolutionary War,[2] and were of that school of statesmen who had the privilege of learning their lessons in constitutional law from the lips of many of the fathers of the government themselves. It was the last scene they were to play upon the political stage; but before they made their exit they saw the entrance of the rising class of statesmen whose mission was to proclaim that slavery was sectional, that freedom was national, and who were more imbued with the sacred notions of liberty that the founders of the republic at first maintained than were Webster and Clay, whose contact had been actual with Jefferson and

---

[1] Public Men and Events, Sargent, vol. ii. p. 851.
[2] Clay in 1777, Webster and Calhoun in 1782.

Adams, with Madison and Marshall. Seward and Chase now appeared in the Senate for the first time, while Hale entered upon his third year of service.

It is now time to describe Clay more fully. He was a man of large natural ability, but he lacked the training of a systematic education. He learned early to appreciate his heaven-born endowments, and to rely upon them for success in his chosen career. Of sanguine temperament, quick perception, irresistible energy, and enthusiastic disposition, he was well fitted to be a party advocate, and was the greatest parliamentary leader in our history.[1] He was, however, inclined to "crack the whip" over those of his supporters who exhibited a desire to hang back and question whither his impetuous lead would tend.[2] He knew men well, but he had no knowledge of books. The gaming-table had for him allurements that he could not find in the library. According to the manners of his time, he drank to excess. His warm heart made him a multitude of friends; his impulsive action and positive bearing raised up enemies; yet at his death he left not an enemy behind him.[3] He was withal a man of inflexible integrity. Straitened in pecuniary circumstances during a large part of his Congressional career, he nevertheless held himself aloof from all corruption. Other Americans have been intellectually greater, others have been more painstaking, others still have been greater benefactors to their country; yet no man has been loved as the people of the United States loved Henry Clay.

In his declining years his thoughts took on a serious cast, and he embraced the Christian religion. It is noteworthy that he began his speech on the compromise resolutions with words not only solemn, but tinctured with religious fervor. He had not been consistent on the slavery question; yet when we consider that he was a slave-holder and that he represented a slave State, his impulsive outbursts

---

[1] See Blaine's Eulogy of Garfield.
[2] George Bancroft, *Century Magazine*, vol. viii. p. 479.   [3] Ibid.

for the cause of freedom are more to be admired than his
occasional truckling to the slave power is to be condemned.
At this time, he was keenly alive to his own importance.
His forty years of public life, in which his name had been
identified with measures of the utmost significance, impelled him to think that no legislative act of far-reaching
moment would be complete unless he had a hand in its
framework. Nearly eight years of retirement had only
made him more anxious to act a leading part when he
came again upon the scene of action. Before going to
Washington, he had been flattered by hearing indirectly
that the administration was counting much on his exertions at the approaching session.[1] On his arrival at the
capital he was unquestionably disappointed that President
Taylor did not receive him with open arms and ask and
take his advice regarding the policy of the administration.
" My relations," writes Clay, " to the President are civil and
amicable, but they do not extend to any confidential con-
sultations in regard to public measures."[2] It is possible
that had General Taylor put himself under the guidance
of Clay he might have adopted the President's plan with
some elaboration and extension,[3] but it was contrary to his
nature and to the whole course of his life to give unre-
served adherence to the scheme of another. He could lead,
but he could not follow. Especially was it impossible for
him to follow the President, whose political ability he despised; nor could he rid his inmost heart of the notion that
Taylor occupied the place which rightfully belonged to himself.[4] A feeling of pique influenced him as he went to work
to concoct his scheme; but as he became more deeply engaged in the labor, the overmastering sentiment of his mind

---

[1] Clay's Private Correspondence, p. 590.
[2] Letter of Jan. 24th, 1850, Private Correspondence, p. 600.
[3] See his speech in the Senate of May 13th, 1850.
[4] See letter on p. 615, Private Correspondence.

was certainly that of sincere patriotism. He believed that the Union was in danger. Such was the constitution of his mind that, while he was blind to the merits of the plan of another, the benefits of his own dazzled him to the sight of all objections. He honestly felt that he was the man of all others to devise a scheme which should save the Union. It is true that his talents as a constructive statesman were of high rank. His hope was that this compromise would give peace to the country for thirty years, even as the Missouri Compromise had done.[1] The plan was perfected by the last of January, and on the 29th Clay introduced it into the Senate in the form of a series of resolutions which were intended to be a basis of compromise, and whose object was to secure " the peace, concord, and harmony of the Union." Their provisions were as follows :

1. The admission of California with her free Constitution.

2. As slavery does not exist by law and is not likely to be introduced into any of the territory acquired from Mexico, territorial governments should be established by Congress without any restriction as to slavery.

3. The boundary between Texas and New Mexico, which was in dispute, was determined.

4. Directs the payment of the *bona fide* public debt of Texas contracted prior to the annexation, for which the duties on foreign imports were pledged, upon the condition that Texas relinquish her claim to any part of New Mexico.

5. Declares that it is inexpedient to abolish slavery in the District of Columbia without the consent of Maryland, of the people of the district, and without just compensation to the owners of slaves.

6. Declares for the prohibition of the slave-trade in the District of Columbia.

7. More effectual provision should be made for the rendition of fugitive slaves.

---

[1] Rise and Fall of the Confederate Government, Jefferson Davis, vol. i. p. 17. See also Clay's speech of Feb. 6th, 1850.

8. Declares that Congress has no power to interfere with the slave-trade between the States.

Several days after the introduction of the resolutions, Clay obtained the floor of the Senate and made a set speech in their favor. He was a persuasive speaker, his magnetism was great; the impassioned utterance and the action suited to the word aroused the enthusiasm of the moment, and carried everything resistlessly before him, whether he addressed the tumultuous mass-meeting or his cultured audience of the Senate. Yet he can hardly be ranked as among the half-dozen great orators of the world. It is true that his speeches in print convey no idea of the effect of their delivery, and, in the reading, one loses the whole force of his fine physical presence, and fails to appreciate the strength derived from his supremely nervous temperament. He began in an egotistical vein, referring in the most natural way to his long absence from the Senate, explained that his return was simply " in obedience to a stern sense of duty," [1] and disclaimed any higher object of personal ambition than the position he now occupied. None could doubt his sincerity. He had given up all hope of attaining the presidency, which he had so long and so ardently desired. Age [2] and ill-health, for his body was racked by a cruel cough, served to remind him that the sands of his earthly career were almost run. On this day that he was to speak for the cause of the Union, he was so weak that he could not mount the steps of the Capitol without leaning on the arm of his companion and stopping to rest. [3] Although the floor of the Senate was crowded and the galleries were filled with a brilliant audience of grace, beauty, and intelligence, [4] his expression of opinion was as honest

---

[1] Speech of Henry Clay, Feb. 5th, 1850.

[2] He was now in his seventy-third year.

[3] Last Seven Years of Henry Clay, Colton, p. 131.

[4] " Mr. Clay's unrivalled popularity has again secured him an audience such as no other statesman, no matter however able and respected, has

and frank as if he were talking to a confidential friend. He
was thoroughly impressed with the dangers that beset the
country. He speaks of never before having been "so ap-
palled and so anxious;" he calls his theme "the awful subject." As an evidence of the intense party feeling, he alluded to the fact that the House had spent one whole week in
the vain attempt to elect a doorkeeper because the point
at issue was "whether the doorkeeper entertained opinions
upon certain national measures coincident with this or that
side of the House." He thus described the manifestations
of the excitement prevalent in the country: "At this moment we have in the legislative bodies of this capitol and
in the States twenty odd furnaces in full blast, emitting
heat and passion and intemperance, and diffusing them
throughout the whole extent of this broad land." His endeavor had been to "form such a scheme of accommoda-
tion" as would obviate "the sacrifice of any great principle" by either section of the country, and he believed that
the series of resolutions which he presented accomplished
the object. Concession by each side was necessary, "not
of principle, but of feeling, of opinion in relation to matters in controversy between them." The admission of California as a State would, under the circumstances, be simply
the recognition of a time-honored precedent of the government. The North insisted on the application of the Wilmot proviso to the rest of the territory acquired from Mexico; yet slavery did not exist there by law, and the orator
in a few pregnant questions stated the case in the most
powerful manner: "What do you want who reside in the
free States? You want that there shall be no slavery introduced into the territories acquired from Mexico. Well,
have you not got it in California already, if admitted as a
State? Have you not got it in New Mexico, in all human
probability, also? What more do you want? You have

---

ever before obtained here. To get within hearing of his voice I found
to be impossible."—Washington correspondence of New York *Tribune*.

got what is worth a thousand Wilmot provisos. You have got nature itself on your side. You have the fact itself on your side." It was, however, necessary to institute a territorial government for New Mexico. It was not right to allow matters to run along without interference from Congress, to establish a regular system. The orator referred to the fact that in the previous September the people of New Mexico had held a convention, had chosen a delegate to Congress, and had instructed him to represent to that body that their actual government was "temporary, doubtful, uncertain, and inefficient in character and operation," that they were "surrounded and despoiled by barbarous foes, and ruin appears inevitably before us, unless speedy and effectual protection be extended to us by the United States."

Of only one other item of the compromise resolutions is it necessary to speak in detail. The settlement of the Texas boundary may be regarded as an eminently proper one, although the payment of the Texan debt was open to objection as being a measure not free from corruption. As there "was money in it," that feature might be looked upon as intending to win support for the entire project. In the provisions regarding the District of Columbia, a concession was made to the demands of each side.

There remained, then, the declaration in favor of a provision for the more effectual rendition of fugitive slaves. Until he reached this point, Clay's leaning had evidently been more to the Northern than to the Southern side of the controversy, although he tried to hold the balance level between them, and endeavored to blend appeal and argument equally to each section. But on this point he took extreme Southern ground. The Fugitive Slave law, passed in the first years of the government,[1] required the aid and countenance of the State magistrates as well as judges of the United States for its execution ; but, as the sentiment on the slavery question diverged more widely between the two sections,

---

[1] See p. 24.

there arose a strong feeling in the Northern States against
lending their assistance to restore fugitive slaves. The legislature of Massachusetts enacted a law, making it penal for
her officers to perform any duties under the act of Congress
of 1793 for their surrender. Pennsylvania passed an act forbidding her judicial authorities to take cognizance of any
fugitive-slave case.[1] The border States especially complained
of the difficulties encountered in reclaiming their runaway
negroes. And as it had been decided by the United States
Supreme Court that the Constitution had conferred on Congress an exclusive power to legislate concerning their extradition, it was demanded by those Southerners who were
willing to compromise the matters in dispute that a more
effectual law for the recovery of fugitive slaves should be a
part of the arrangement. So much explanation is necessary
to understand Clay's very positive expressions. "Upon this
subject," he said, "I do think that we have just and serious
cause of complaint against the free States. . . . It is our
duty to make the law more effective; and I shall go with
the senator from the South who goes furthest in making
penal laws and imposing the heaviest sanctions for the recovery of fugitive slaves and the restoration of them to their
owners."

After touching upon each one of his resolutions in order,
Clay offered some general considerations: "There have
been, unhappily, mutual causes of agitation furnished by
one class of the States as well as by the other, though, I admit, not in the same degree by the slave States as by the free
States." Yet he had "an earnest and anxious desire to present the olive branch to both parts of this distracted and at
the present moment unhappy country." He made an appeal to both sides to do something to quiet the clamors of
the nation; depicting, in lively colors, the vast extent of the

[1] Thirty Years' View, Benton, vol. ii. p. 774; Massachusetts, Acts and
Resolves, 1843–45, chap. xlix.; Laws of Pennsylvania, Session of 1847,
p. 207, Act No. 159.

country, its present prosperity and wealth, the success of
the government, as having proceeded from the Union. If
these great blessings were worth conserving, mutual concessions should certainly be made to save the Union from dissolution. "War and dissolution of the Union are identical,"
he exclaimed. The orator closed with a prophecy that
events have completely falsified. Should the Union be dissolved and war follow, he declared, it would be a war more
ferocious and bloody, more implacable and exterminating,
than were the wars of Greece, the wars of the Commoners
of England, or the revolutions of France. And after a war
—"not of two or three years' duration, but a war of inter-
minable duration . . . some Philip or Alexander, some Cæsar or Napoleon, would arise and cut the Gordian knot and
solve the problem of the capacity of man for self-government, and crush the liberties of both the severed portions
of this common empire." [1]

The floor of the Senate was assigned to Calhoun for
the 4th of March, to speak on the compromise resolutions.
Long battle with disease had wasted his frame, but, swathed
in flannels, he crawled to the Senate chamber to utter his
last words of warning to the North, and to make his last
appeal for what he considered justice to his own beloved
South. He was too weak to deliver his carefully written
speech. At his request, it was read by Senator Mason. Calhoun sat, with head erect and eyes partly closed, immovable
in front of the reader; and he did not betray a sense of the
deep interest with which his friends and followers listened
to the well-matured words of their leader and political
guide.[2] This was Calhoun's last formal speech; before the
end of the month he had passed away from the scene of
earthly contention. The speech is mainly interesting as
stating with precision the numerical preponderance of the

---

[1] The quotations are from Clay's speech made Feb. 5th and 6th, 1850,
and taken from Last Seven Years of Henry Clay, Calvin Colton.

[2] C. A. Dana, Washington correspondent of New York *Tribune.*

North, the reasons of Southern discontent, and the forebodings of his prophetic soul in reference to the future. He
admitted that universal discontent pervaded the South. Its
"great and primary cause is that the equilibrium between
the two sections has been destroyed." It was the old story
that the North had grown faster in population than the
South. Every one knows that it was slavery which kept
back the South in the race; but this Calhoun could not see,
and he sought the cause in remote and unsubstantial reasons.
When Calhoun said the South, he meant the slave power,
and the South had not held pace with the North because,
first, in his opinion, the Ordinance of 1787 and the Missouri
Compromise had excluded her from territory that should
have been left "open to the emigration of masters with their
slaves;" second, the tariff and internal-improvements system
had worked decidedly against her interests ; and, third, the
gradual yet steady assumption of greater powers by the
federal government at the expense of the rights of the States
had proved an inestimable injury to the South. " The cords
that bind the States together," said the senator, "are not
only many, but various in character. Some are spiritual or
ecclesiastical ; some political, others social." The strongest
are those of a religious nature, but they have begun to
snap. The great Methodist Episcopal Church has divided;
there is a Methodist Church North and a Methodist Church
South, and they are hostile. The Protestant organization
next in size, the Baptist Church, has likewise fallen asunder.
The cord which binds the Presbyterian Church " is not entirely snapped, but some of its strands have given way.
That of the Episcopal Church is the only one of the four
great Protestant denominations which remains unbroken
and entire. . . . If the agitation goes on, the same force,
acting with increased intensity, will finally snap every cord "
—political and social as well as ecclesiastical—" when nothing will be left to hold the States together except force." It
is undeniable that the Union is in danger. How can it be
saved? Neither the plan of the distinguished senator of

Kentucky nor that of the administration will save the Union.
It rests with the North, the stronger party, whether or not
she will take the course which will effect this devoutly to
be-wished-for consummation.   The North must give us
equal rights in the acquired territory; she must return
our fugitive slaves; she must cease the agitation of the
slave question; and she must consent to an amendment
to the Constitution "which will restore to the South, in
substance, the power she possessed of protecting herself
before the equilibrium between the two sections was destroyed by the action of this government."   The admission of California will be the test question.   If you admit
her, it will be notice to us that you propose to use your
present strength and to add to it "with the intention of
destroying irretrievably the equilibrium between the two
sections."[1]

The latter part of Calhoun's speech is important solely
because it defines the position of the extreme Southern party.   The mildness of his language, and the almost pathetic
appeal to Northern senators, did not veil the arrogance of
his demands.   He did not now explain the nature of the
constitutional amendment which in his judgment was required, but in a posthumous essay,[2] which was designed as
his political testament, he entered upon the matter fully.
The amendment was to provide for the election of two
Presidents, one from the free States and one from the slave
States; either was to have a veto on all congressional legislation.   He held until the end to the fanciful Roman anal-
ogy.[3]   He saw in his mind's eye the Southern tribune check-
ing the power of the Northern consul and of Congress; and
while he remembered that the tribunes of Rome became as

---

[1] For the whole speech of Calhoun see *Congressional Globe*, vol. xxi.
part i. p. 451.   A very good abridgment may be found in American Orations, vol. ii. p. 46.

[2] Discourse on the Constitution and Government of the United States.

[3] See p. 44.

I.—9

despots with absolute power, this did not lessen his wish for
a like authority as a safeguard of Southern interests.   Intellectual vagary can go to no extremer length in politics
than to propound a scheme which is alike impossible of
adoption, and would be utterly impracticable in operation.
The constitutional amendment suggested by Calhoun was
generally regarded at the South as a utopian scheme; yet
he had a following of something like fifty members[1] of Congress, who, even if they did not subscribe to his vague ideas
in the science of government, were willing to follow him to
the extreme length of secession from the Union, if the dispute could not be settled to their liking.   These members
represented fairly the feeling of their slave-holding constituents.

Before proceeding to the further consideration of the
debate on the compromise resolutions, we should satisfy
ourselves whether the Union was indeed in danger.   The
proceedings of Congress had certainly intensified the excitement.   The contest for speaker, the clashes between the
representatives of the opposing views, the threats on one
side and defiance on the other, had added to the gravity of
a situation already grave.   " Two months ago," said Clay,
" all was calm in comparison to the present moment.   All
now is uproar, confusion, and menace to the existence of the
Union and to the happiness and safety of the people."[2]
Yet Clay had great difficulty in making up his mind as to
how much of the danger was real, and how much only apparent.   He writes, " My hopes and fears alternate."[3]   Calhoun's speech was as sincere as a death-bed utterance, and
leaves no doubt that he believed the country on the eve of
disunion.   Webster was as much perplexed as Clay.   In

---

[1] Nine senators and forty representatives, according to the New York
Tribune of March 5th.

[2] Speech of Henry Clay, Feb. 5th.

[3] Letter to T. B. Stevenson, Jan. 26th, Last Seven Years of Henry Clay,
p. 497.

the middle of February he did not fear dissolution of the
Union or the breaking-up of the government.[1]   He writes:
"I think that the clamor about disunion rather abates.   I
trust that if on our side we keep cool, things will come to
no dangerous pass.   California will probably be admitted
just as she presents herself."[2]   Three weeks later he had
materially modified his opinion.   Still, there was not so
much change in the actual situation as in one's apprehension of it.   For it was a time of seething commotion; the
political atmosphere was highly charged; one's settled
opinions of to-day were liable to be disturbed by violent collision of opposing notions to-morrow; and the impetuous
speech of some Southern Hotspur might shake the resolution of timorous Northern men.[3]   Yet the fears were not
all confined to the national capital.   Scott, the general
of the army, who was stationed at New York, thought
that "our country was on the eve of a terrible civil war."[4]
Senator Benton, however, ridiculed the idea of danger.[5]
Seward thought the threats of disunion "too trivial for
serious notice."[6]   Chase was not in the least alarmed at

---

[1] Letter to P. Harvey, Feb. 14th, Curtis, vol. ii. p. 398.

[2] Letter to Edward Everett, Feb. 16th, Private Correspondence, vol. ii.
p. 355.

[3] "It is undeniable that there exists no small degree of violent feeling
among a small portion of the Southern members.   And so peculiar is the
state of society in the South, so morbid is the sensitiveness caused by the
influence of slavery, that it is only at the utmost peril that a Southern
man can allow any other man to outstrip him in apparent zeal and violence for the defence of that institution.   When one roars, therefore all
must roar; when one whines, all must whine.   Hence there is an apparent combustibleness on all occasions, which superficial observers are apt
to take for a deep-seated and durable determination to break from the
Union."—Washington correspondence, New York *Independent*, Feb. 23d,
1850.

[4] Remark made to General Sherman, Memoirs of General Sherman,
vol. i. p. 82.

[5] Thirty Years' View, vol. ii. p. 749.

[6] Life of Seward, Baker, p. 145; Seward's Works, vol. i. p. 81.

"the stale cry of disunion."[1] Giddings thought the "cry
of dissolution was gasconade. . . . It has been the *dernier
ressort* of Southern men for fifty years whenever they desired
to frighten dough-faces into a compliance with their measures.[2] In general, the Northern anti-slavery men treated the
Southern threats as bravado and as hardly worth serious
notice.[3] Yet there was one notable exception to this universal opinion. Horace Mann believed that if the North
insisted upon passing the Wilmot proviso for the territories,
some of the Southern States would rebel.[4] Still, there was
an earnest feeling at the North, and especially in New England, that if there were a risk in insisting that slavery should
go no further, it was a risk well worth taking.[5]

---

[1] Senate speech, March 27th.

[2] Giddings's Speeches, p. 409.

[3] "Our Northern friends are blind, absolutely blind, to the real dangers
by which we are surrounded."—Letter of C. S. Morehead, Whig representative from Kentucky, to John J. Crittenden, March 30th, Life of Crittenden, vol. i. p. 363. The opinion at that time of the extreme abolitionist
was well stated by Theodore Parker in a sermon delivered in 1852. He
combated strenuously the idea that there was any danger of dissolution
of the Union in 1850. "We have," he said, "the most delicate test of
public opinion—the state of the public funds, the barometer which indi-
cates any change in the political weather;" but during all this discussion
"the funds of the United States did not go down one mill." "The Southern men know well that if the Union were dissolved their riches would
take to itself legs and run away—or firebrands, and make a St. Domingo
out of South Carolina! They cast off the North! They set up for themselves! Tush! tush! Fear boys with bugs!"

[4] "I really think if we insist upon passing the Wilmot proviso for the
territories that the South—a part of them—will rebel; but I would pass
it, rebellion or not. I consider no evil so great as that of the extension
of slavery."—Letter of Horace Mann, Feb. 6th, Life, p. 288.

[5] "Rather than consent voluntarily to the extension of the slave institution to one foot of free territory—rather than surrender their principles
—they [the Northern people] would submit to have the Union severed.
This, we believe, is the true feeling of the North."—Springfield *Republican*, Feb., 1850, cited by the *Liberator*. See also Life of Samuel
Bowles, vol. i. p. 77. "Let the Union be a thousand times shivered rather

Carefully weighing the contemporary evidence, and looking on it in the light of subsequent history, I think that little danger of an overt act of secession existed while General Taylor was in the presidential chair. The power of a determined executive to resist the initial steps towards casting off allegiance to the general government was great. While diverse constitutional interpretations and different views as to the force of various precedents might puzzle the President, he was certain to discern betimes any move towards rebellion; and that he was resolved to put down with all the force at his command.[1]

An incident occurring at this time shows to what stern determination General Taylor had come. The extreme pro-slavery Whigs from the Southern States took the position that they were willing to admit California, provided that in the rest of the territory in question the government would protect and recognize property in slaves, even as other property was protected and recognized. But until this point was formally acknowledged they were utterly opposed to the admission of California with her free constitution, and, with the assistance of the Southern Democrats, they prevented by filibustering the consideration of a bill in the House which had that for its object. While this obstruction was in progress, Alexander H. Stephens and Robert Toombs, both Southern Whig representatives, called to see the President to discuss his policy and to demand that he, as their party's chief, should use his influence and power to favor the end which they had in view. The President plainly informed them that he would sign any constitutional law which Congress might pass. The direct intimation was that he would sign a bill which provided

---

than we should aid you [the South] to plant slavery on free soil."—New York *Tribune*, Feb. 20th.

[1] "The malcontents of the South mean to be factious; and they expect to compel compromise. I think the President as willing to try conclusions with them as General Jackson was with the nullifiers."—Seward to Weed, Nov. 30th, 1849, Life of Seward, vol. ii. p. 112.

unconditionally for the admission of California; and they
were indirectly given to understand that he would approve
the application of the Wilmot proviso to the territories.[1]
As a reply to this outline of future action, the Southern
congressmen threatened dissolution of the Union, when
the President got angry and said that, if it were necessary,
he would take the field himself to enforce the laws of his
country; and if these gentlemen were taken in rebellion
against the Union, he would hang them with as little mercy
as he had hanged deserters and spies in Mexico.[2]

In the midst of the mutual recrimination accompanying
this inevitable sectional controversy, there can be no better
evidence as to whence came the aggression than the complete change that had taken place in the sentiments of General Taylor since he had occupied the executive office. Before he was nominated for President, he had written an

---

[1] See letter of R. Toombs to J. J. Crittenden, Life of Crittenden, Coleman, vol. i. p. 365. Toombs wrote, April 25th: "I saw General Taylor
and talked fully with him, and, while he stated he had given and *would
give* no pledges either way about the proviso, he gave me clearly to understand that if it was passed he would sign it. My course became instantly fixed. I would not hesitate to oppose the proviso, even to the
extent of a dissolution of the Union."

[2] Memoir of Thurlow Weed, p. 177; see also New York *Tribune* of
Feb. 23d; Wilson's Rise and Fall of the Slave Power, vol. ii. p. 259. Hannibal Hamlin wrote me, Aug. 23d, 1889: "In answer to your inquiry, I can
inform you that the statement made by Mr. Wilson to which you refer is
correct and accurate. You will find a corroboration of it in the Life or
Memoirs of Thurlow Weed." Wilson said in the Senate, July 9th, 1856:
"It is said that the Senator from Georgia [Toombs] and others talked very
plain to General Taylor in 1850 about a dissolution of the Union, and that
General Taylor intimated to them pretty distinctly that the Union was to
be preserved and the laws of the country executed." Toombs was present
and made an immediate reply to a portion of Wilson's speech, but did not
in any way contradict this statement. *Congressional Globe*, vol. xxxiii. p.
857. Stephens and Toombs, in letters to the New York *Herald* in 1876,
denied this story. See New York *Herald*, June 13th and Aug. 8th, 1876.
In this connection see letter of Stephens written directly after the death
of General Taylor, Life of Stephens, Johnston and Browne, p. 258.

emphatic letter to his son-in-law, Jefferson Davis, in which
he had maintained that the South must resist boldly and
decisively the encroachments of the North; and the Southerners had counted much on his assistance. He now, however, looked upon several Southern members as conspirators,
and Jefferson Davis as their chief.[1] If we lay aside the
speeches in Congress as merely threats of irate Southerners,
and get at Southern sentiment from legislative resolutions,
from expressions of the press, and from public meetings, it
is undeniable that had the Wilmot proviso passed Congress,
or had slavery been abolished in the District of Columbia,
the Southern convention for which arrangements were
making would have been a very different affair from the
one that actually did assemble at Nashville. Steps would
undoubtedly have been taken towards disunion; and while
resolute action of the President was certain to arouse the
dormant Union feeling in the South, his task would have
been more difficult than was that of General Jackson, for
he would have to contend with more States than South
Carolina.

A change in Southern sentiment is, however, noticeable
shortly after the introduction of Clay's compromise resolutions. This was assisted by a vote in the House of Representatives, laying on the table a resolution which provided
for the application of the Wilmot proviso to the territory
east of California.[2] Clay's speech influenced powerfully the
opinion of Southern Whigs. From the beginning of February, it is easy to trace the growth of a Southern sentiment
favorable to the admission of California, if only the Wilmot

---

[1] Memoir of Thurlow Weed, p. 177. " We firmly believe that there are
sixty members of Congress who this day desire a dissolution of the Union,
and are plotting to effect it."—New York *Tribune*, editorial, Feb. 23d.

[2] The resolution was that of Root, of Ohio. The vote to table was 105
yeas, 75 nays. Thirty-two Northern members voted to defeat the Wilmot
proviso, eighteen of whom were Democrats and fourteen Whigs. There
were twenty-seven absentees from the free States. Wilson, Rise and Fall
of the Slave Power, vol. ii. p. 222.

proviso were not insisted upon for New Mexico, and slavery were allowed to remain in the District of Columbia. This by no means pleased the knot of Southern disunionists, who desired nothing better than the passage by Congress of the Wilmot proviso.[1] In that event they had well-grounded hopes that they could unite the South in their views; then they would give their ultimatum, and, if it were rejected, they would dissolve the Union. Efforts, indeed, were made by the extreme Southern Democrats to check the slowly rising Union sentiment. Their aim was to resist the admission of California, and to make the resistance a sectional shibboleth in place of opposition to the Wilmot proviso.[2]

While, thus, the fear of a formal secession from the Union, such as took place eleven years later, had not at this time sufficient foundation, there was danger in the adjournment of Congress without provision for the matters in dispute.[3] The war of legislative declarations, of resolutions, of public meetings, would continue, and inflammatory writing in the press would not cease. Northern legislative action, supported by public sentiment, would not only make it difficult, but impossible, to recover a fugitive slave. On the other hand, it was probable that most of the Southern states as retaliatory legislation would pass laws to prevent the sale of Northern products by retail in their limits.[4] The governor of Virginia, John B. Floyd, proposed to his legislature a sys-

---

[1] New York *Tribune*, Feb. 4th. See also Benton's Thirty Years' View. "I am pained to say that I fear that there are some Southern men who do not wish a settlement."—Letter of C. S. Morehead, M.C. from Kentucky, to J. J. Crittenden, Life of Crittenden, Coleman, vol. i. p. 362.

[2] See New York *Tribune*, Feb. 25th and March 13th; also the Mobile *Advertiser*, the Richmond *Enquirer*, Columbia (S. C.) *Telegraph*, Charleston (S. C.) *Courier*, Richmond *Whig*, for February.

[3] "In the Senate there are eight Southern senators and in the House thirty members from the same section who are organized as disunionists and are opposed to any compromise whatever looking to the perpetuity of the Union."—Washington correspondence New York *Tribune*, Feb. 2d.

[4] Life of Crittenden, Coleman, vol. i. p. 363.

tem of taxation of the products of those states which would not deliver up fugitive slaves.[1] A suspension of intercourse between the two sections would follow, and the situation would be strained to the utmost. If, indeed, armed conflicts at various points did not result from the excited feeling, it was certain that the harmony which should subsist between the parts of a federal Union would be utterly destroyed; and after months or even years of such a state of mutual repulsion, it could only end in compromise, peaceable separation, or war.[2]

Two of the great senatorial triumvirate had spoken; the Senate and the country had yet to hear the greatest of them all. Daniel Webster spoke on the compromise resolutions the 7th of March. In the course of this work, whenever possible, his precise words have been used, in narration and illustration; for in intellectual endowment Webster surpassed all of our public men. No one understood the fundamental principles of our polity better; no one approached his wonderful power of expression. It seemed that the language of the constitutional lawyer who laid down principles of law that the profound legal mind of Marshall fixed in an immutable judicial decision, and who, at the same time, could make clear abstruse points and carry conviction to the understanding of men who were untrained in logic or in law, was best fitted to guide us through the maze of constitutional interpretation in which our history abounds. Indeed, the political history of the country for twenty-seven years preceding 1850 might be written as well and fully from the speeches, state papers, and letters of Webster as the story of

---

[1] The *Liberator*, April.

[2] "I am not one of those who, either at the commencement of the session or at any time during its progress, have believed that there was present any actual danger to the existence of the Union. But I am one of those who believe that, if this agitation is continued for one or two years longer, no man can foresee the dreadful consequences."—Clay, Senate, May 21st.

the latter days of the Roman republic from the like material of Cicero which has come down to us.[1]

As an orator, Webster has been compared in simplicity to Demosthenes and in profundity to Burke.[2] This is the highest praise. The wonderful effect of his oratory is strikingly told by George Ticknor, who, fresh from a long intercourse with the most distinguished men in England and on the Continent, went to hear Webster deliver his Plymouth oration. Ticknor writes: "I was never so excited by public speaking before in my life. Three or four times I thought my temples would burst with the gush of blood;" and, though from his youth an intimate friend of Webster's, he was so impressed that " when I came out I was almost afraid to come near him. It seemed to me as if he was like the mount that might not be touched, and that burned with fire."[3] Thomas Marshall, of Kentucky, heard the reply to Hayne, and when Webster came to the peroration he "listened as to one inspired, and finally thought he could see a halo around the orator's head like what one sees in the old pictures of saints and martyrs."[4]

The diction of Webster was formed by a grateful study of Shakespeare and Milton; through his communion with these masters, his whole soul was thoroughly attuned to the high-

---

[1] " His ideas, his thoughts [are] spread over every page of your annals for near half a century. His ideas, his thoughts [are] impressed upon and inseparable from the mind of his country and the spirit of the age." —Senate speech of W. H. Seward, Aug. 14th, 1852. " Whoever in after-times shall write the history of the United States for the last forty years will write the life of Daniel Webster."—Edward Everett, Oct. 27th, 1852.

[2] John Adams, who was present at the trial of Warren Hastings, and had heard Pitt and Fox, Burke and Sheridan, wrote to Webster, after reading his Plymouth oration: " Mr. Burke is no longer entitled to the praise—the most consummate orator of modern times." Lodge, p. 123.

[3] Letter of Ticknor from Plymouth, Dec. 21st, 1820, Life of Ticknor, vol. i. p. 330.

[4] William Schouler, Personal and Political Recollections, Boston *Journal*, Dec. 10th, 1870.

est thinking and purest harmonies of our literature. He is
one of the few orators whose speeches are read as literature.
He was our greatest lawyer,[1] yet in a bad cause he was
not a good advocate, for he had not the flexibility of mind
which made the worse appear the better reason ; but in cases
apparently hopeless, with the right on his side, he won imposing triumphs.[2] He was our greatest Secretary of State. He
had, said Sumner, " by the successful and masterly negotiation of the treaty of Washington" earned the title of "Defender of Peace."[3]

The Graces presided at his birth. His growth developed
the strong physical constitution with which nature had endowed him equally with a massive brain. His was a sound
mind in a sound body. His physical structure was magnificent, his face handsome; he had the front of Jove himself.[4] "He is," said Carlyle, "a magnificent specimen. . . .
As a logic-fencer, or parliamentary Hercules, one would incline to back him at first sight against all the extant world."[5]
"Webster," said Henry Hallam, "approaches as nearly to
the beau ideal of a republican senator as any man that I
have ever seen in the course of my life."[6] Josiah Quincy
speaks of him as a "figure cast in heroic mould, and
which represented the ideal of American manhood."[7] He
was well described by the bard he loved so well: "How
noble in reason! how infinite in faculties! in form and
moving, how express and admirable! in action, how like
an angel! in apprehension, how like a god!" On the
basis of this extraordinary natural ability was built the

[1] "Whatever else concerning him has been controverted by anybody,
the fifty thousand lawyers of the United States conceded to him an un-
approachable supremacy at the bar."—Seward's eulogy in the Senate.

[2] This is remarked by the *Westminster Review*, Jan., 1853.

[3] Speech before the Whig Convention at Boston, Sept., 1846, Rise and
Fall of the Slave Power, Wilson, vol. ii. p. 119.

[4] See Lodge, p. 195.   [5] Curtis, vol. ii. p. 21.

[6] Ibid., p. 27.   [7] Figures of the Past, p. 267.

superstructure of a systematic education. His devoted father mortgaged the New Hampshire farm to send him to college, and three years of laborious study of law followed the regular course at Dartmouth. Years afterwards he repaid his Alma Mater for her gifts when he pleaded, and not in vain, for her chartered rights in invincible logic before the most solemn tribunal of the country. Intellectually, Webster was a man of slow growth. The zenith of his power was not reached until he made the celebrated reply to Hayne, and he was then forty-eight years old.

In union with this grand intellect were social qualities of a high order. His manners were charming, his nature was genial, and he had a quick sense of seemly humor. Carlyle speaks of him as "a dignified, perfectly bred man."[1] Harriet Martineau says "he would illuminate an evening by telling stories, cracking jokes, or smoothly discoursing to the perfect felicity of the logical part of one's constitution."[2] Ticknor, who was so impressed with the majestic delivery of the orator, speaks of his being "as gay and playful as a kitten."[3] The social intercourse between Webster and Lord Ashburton, while they were at work on the Washington treaty, is one of those international amenities that grace the history of diplomacy. This treaty, by which we gained substantial advantages and England made honorable concessions, was not negotiated through stately protocols, but was concluded through a friendly correspondence and during the interchange of refined social civilities. During this transaction Ashburton was impressed with "the upright and honorable character" of Webster.[4] As late as 1845 there might be seen engravings which were an indication of the popular notion that honesty was his cardinal virtue.[5]

[1] Curtis, vol. ii. p. 21.
[2] Retrospect of American Travel, vol. i. p. 147.
[3] Letter, Dec. 23d, 1820, Life of Ticknor, vol. i. pp. 331 and 379.
[4] Memoir of Everett, Webster's Works, vol. i. p. cxxiv.
[5] Sir Charles Lyell saw "a most formidable likeness of Daniel Web-

He had strong domestic feelings. He honored his father, loved his brother, and was devoted to his wife and children; his affection for his many friends was pure and disinterested. He had during his life a large share of domestic affliction, and his deep and sincere grief shows that he had a large heart as well as a great head. He had a constant belief in revealed as well as natural religion.[1]

His healthy disposition was displayed even in his recreations. He was a true disciple of Izaak Walton, and he also delighted in the chase. Few men have loved nature more. Those grand periods that will never cease to delight lovers of oratory were many of them conned at his Marshfield retreat, where he worshipped the sea and did reverence to the rising sun. After a winter of severe work in his declining years, he gets to Marshfield in May, and writes: "I grow strong every hour. The giants grew strong again by touching the earth; the same effect is produced on me by touching the salt sea-shore."[2]

The distinctive virtue of Webster was his patriotism. He loved his country as few men have loved it; he had a profound reverence for the Constitution and its makers. He spoke truly when he said: "I am an American, and I know no locality but America; that is my country;"[3] and he was deeply in earnest when he gave utterance to the sentiment, "I was bred, indeed I might almost say I was born, in admiration of our political institutions."[4] Webster's great work was to inspire the country with a strong and enduring

---

ster, being an engraving published in Connecticut. Leaning over the portrait of the great statesman is represented an aged man holding a lantern in his hand, and, lest the meaning of so classical an allusion should be lost, we read below:

> "'Diogenes his lantern needs no more—
> An honest man is found, the search is o'er.'"

Second Visit to United States, vol. i. p. 55.

[1] Curtis, vol. ii. p. 333.   [2] Ibid., p. 377.
[3] Ibid., p. 448.   [4] Ibid., p. 513.

national feeling; and he impressed upon the people every-where, except in the cotton States, a sacred love for the Union. How well his life-work was done was seen, less than nine years after he died, in the zealous appeal to arms for the defence of the nation. In the sleepless nights before his death, no sight was so welcome to his eyes as the lantern he saw through the windows placed at the mast-head of the little shallop, in order that he might discern, fluttering at the mast, the national flag, the emblem of that Union to which he had consecrated the best thoughts and purest efforts of his life.

During the last twenty years of his career Webster had a great desire to be President. Three times he was exceedingly anxious for the Whig nomination, and thought his chances were good for getting it; but the nomination even never came to him. Indeed, he always overrated the probabilities of his success. He was of that class of statesmen who were stronger before the country than before the political convention. Had he ever been named as his party's choice, he would unquestionably have been a strong candidate; but he never had the knack of arousing the enthusiasm of the party, which Clay possessed in so eminent degree. Nor did his frequent action independent of political considerations commend him to the men who shaped the action of the party convention. George Ticknor said, in 1831, Webster "belongs to no party; but he has uniformly contended for the great and essential principles of our government on all occasions;"[1] and this was to a large extent true of him during his whole life. His tendency to break away from party trammels was shown more than once during his long career. In 1833, as we have seen,[2] he supported with enthusiasm the Democratic President, and would not assent to the compromise devised by the leader of his party. But the crowning act of independence was when he remained in the

---

[1] Life of George Ticknor, vol. i. p. 393.   [2] See p. 50.

cabinet of President Tyler, when all his colleagues resigned. The motive for this action was the desire to complete the negotiation of the Ashburton treaty, for Webster felt that he of all men was best fitted for that work ; and his heart was earnestly enlisted in the effort to remove the difficulties in the way of a peaceful settlement, and to avert a war between England and the United States. His course, although eminently patriotic, was certain to interfere with his political advancement. For he resisted the imperious dictation of Clay, he breasted the popular clamor of his party, and he pursued his own ideas of right despite the fact that he had to encounter the tyranny of public opinion which De Tocqueville has so well described.

The French, who make excuses for men of genius as the Athenians were wont to do, have a proverb, " It belongs to great men to have great defects." Webster exemplified this maxim. He was fond of wine and brandy, and at times drank deep ; he was not scrupulous in observing the seventh commandment. Though born and reared in poverty, he had little idea of the value of money and of the sacredness of money obligations. He had no conception of the duty of living within his means, and he was habitually careless in regard to the payment of his debts. His friends more than once discharged his obligations ; besides such assistance, he accepted from them at other times presents of money, but he would have rejected their bounty with scorn had there gone with it an expectation of influencing his public action. This failing was the cause of serious charges being preferred against him. He was accused of being in the pay of the United States Bank, but this was not true ;[1] and he was charged with a corrupt misuse of the secret service fund while Secretary of State under Tyler, but from this accusation he was fully and fairly exonerated.[2]

---

[1] Curtis, vol. i. p. 498.

[2] Ibid., vol. ii. p. 267; Memoirs of John Quincy Adams, vol. xii. pp. 260, 263; Life of Jefferson Davis by his Wife, vol. i. pp. 248 and 634.

Considering that it was only by strenuous effort that the son of the New Hampshire farmer obtained the highest rank in political and social life,[1] it is hard to believe that he was constitutionally indolent, as one of his biographers states. When sixty-seven years old it was his practice to study from five to eleven in the morning; he was in the Supreme Court from eleven to three, and the rest of the day in the Senate until ten in the evening. When he had the time to devote himself to his legal practice, his professional income was large.

Such, in the main, if Daniel Webster had died on the morning of the seventh day of March, 1850, would have been the estimate of his character that would have come down to this generation. But his speech in the Senate on that day placed a wide gulf between him and most of the men who were best fitted to transmit his name to posterity. Partisan malignity has magnified his vices, depreciated his virtues, and distorted his motives.

It is now time to consider this speech, which the orator himself thought the most important effort of his life.[2] The most important event in the long session of Congress we are at present considering, it was almost as momentous in the history of the country as it was in the life of Webster. It is the only speech in our history which is named by the date of its delivery, and the general acquiescence in this designation goes to show that it was a turning-point in the action of Congress, in popular sentiment, and in the history of the country.

Webster began: " I wish to speak to-day, not as a Massachusetts man, nor as a Northern man, but as an American. . . . It is not to be denied that we live in the midst of strong agitations, and are surrounded by very considerable dangers to our institutions and government. The imprisoned winds are let loose. The East, the North, and the stormy

---

[1] E. P. Whipple, *North American Review*, July, 1844.
[2] Curtis, vol. ii, p. 529.

South combine to throw the whole sea into commotion, to toss its billows to the skies, and disclose its profoundest depths. . . . I speak to-day for the preservation of the Union. 'Hear me for my cause.'" He spoke of the Mexican war as having been " prosecuted for the purpose of the acquisition of territory. . . . As the acquisition was to be south of the line of the United States, in warm climates and countries, it was naturally, I suppose, expected by the South that whatever acquisitions were made in that region would be added to the slave-holding portion of the United States. Very little of accurate information was possessed of the real physical character either of California or New Mexico, and events have not turned out as was expected. Both California and New Mexico are likely to come in as free States, and therefore some degree of disappointment and surprise has resulted. . . . It is . . . the prohibition of slavery which has contributed to raise . . . the dispute as to the propriety of the admission of California into the Union under this Constitution."

The orator then proceeded to discuss slavery from a general historical standpoint, whence an allusion followed naturally to the different view taken of the institution at the North and at the South. It is too long to quote, but it is a fair, dispassionate statement, and rises to the level of a judgment by a philosophical historian.[1] He regrets the separation of the Methodist Episcopal Church. Speaking with the utmost feeling on the subject, he expresses the opinion that the schism might have been prevented ; and he then comments upon the matter in words pregnant with wisdom that not only applied with force to the slavery question in 1850, but have a meaning for all controversies to all time.

At the time the Constitution was adopted, there was, he said, " no diversity of opinion between the North and the South upon the subject of slavery. It will be found that

---

[1] See Webster's Works, vol. v. p. 330.

I.—10

both parts of the country held it equally an evil, a moral
and political evil. . . . The eminent men, the most eminent
men, and nearly all the conspicuous politicians of the South
held the same sentiments—that slavery was an evil, a blight,
a scourge, and a curse. . . . There was, if not an entire unanimity, a general concurrence of sentiment running through
the whole community, and especially entertained by the
eminent men of all parts of the country. But soon a change
began at the North and the South, and a difference of opinion showed itself ; the North growing much more warm and
strong against slavery, and the South growing much more
warm and strong in its support." The reason that the South
ceased to think it an evil and a scourge, but, on the other
hand, maintained that it was "a great religious, social, and
moral blessing," was " owing to the rapid growth and sudden extension of the cotton plantations of the South."[1]

In reply to Calhoun's statement that "there has been a
majority all along in favor of the North," Webster averred
that " no man acquainted with the history of the Union can
deny that the general lead in the politics of the country, for
three-fourths of the period that has elapsed since the adoption of the Constitution, has been a Southern lead." He directed attention to the events that brought about the annexation of Texas, referred at length to the joint resolution
which allowed four more States to be formed out of her territory ; and laid great stress upon the stipulation that the
States which would be created south of the line of 36° 30'—
and this embraced nearly the whole of Texas—were permitted to have slavery, and would without question be slave
States. To that "this government is solemnly pledged by
law and contract . . . and I for one mean to fulfil it, because I will not violate the faith of the government. . . . Now
as to California and New Mexico, I hold slavery to be excluded from those territories by a law even superior to that
which admits and sanctions it in Texas. I mean the law of

---

[1] See p. 26.

nature, of physical geography, the law of the formation of
the earth. That law settles forever, with a strength beyond
all terms of human enactment, that slavery cannot exist in
California or New Mexico. . . . What is there in New Mexico that could by any possibility induce anybody to go there
with slaves ? There are some narrow strips of tillable land
on the borders of the rivers ; but the rivers themselves dry
up before midsummer is gone. . . . And who expects to see
a hundred black men cultivating tobacco, corn, cotton, rice,
or anything else, on lands in New Mexico, made fertile only
by irrigation ?" Considering that " both California and New
Mexico are destined to be free, . . . I would not take pains
uselessly to reaffirm an ordinance of nature, nor to re-enact
the will of God. I would put in no Wilmot proviso for the
mere purpose of a taunt or reproach. . . . Wherever there
is a substantive good to be done, wherever there is a foot
of land to be prevented from becoming slave territory, I am
ready to assert the principle of the exclusion of slavery.   I
am pledged to it from the year 1837 ; I have been pledged
to it again and again ; and I will perform those pledges ;
but I will not do a thing unnecessarily that wounds the feelings of others, or that does discredit to my own understanding."

As regards the non-rendition of fugitive slaves, Webster
thought that the complaints of the South were just, and that
the North had lacked in her duty ; and he proposed, with
some amendments, to support the fugitive slave bill which
had been drawn up and introduced by Senator Mason of
Virginia. He referred to the abolition societies at the North,
and did not "think them useful. I think their operations for
the last twenty years have produced nothing good or valuable. . . . The violence of the Northern press is complained
of." But " the press is violent everywhere. There are out-
rageous reproaches in the North against the South, and there
are reproaches as vehement in the South against the North."
There is, however, " no solid grievance presented by the South
within the redress of the government . . . but the want of

a proper regard to the injunction of the Constitution for the delivery of fugitive slaves."

It is near the close of this speech that occurs the fine passage depicting the utter impossibility of peaceable secession. "Sir, he who sees these States, now revolving in harmony around a common centre, and expects them to quit their places and fly off without convulsion, may look the next hour to see the heavenly bodies rush from their spheres, and jostle against each other in the realms of space, without causing the wreck of the universe." And in his peroration, which in eloquence almost equals that of his reply to Hayne, he adjured the Senate and the country, " instead of speaking of the possibility or utility of secession, instead of dwelling in those caverns of darkness, instead of groping with those ideas so full of all that is horrid and horrible, let us come out into the light of day; let us enjoy the fresh air of liberty and union. Never did there devolve on any generation of men higher trusts than now devolve upon us for the preservation of this Constitution, and the harmony and peace of all who are destined to live under it. Let us make our generation one of the strongest and brightest links in that golden chain which is destined, I fondly believe, to grapple the people of all the States to this Constitution for ages to come."[1]

This speech of Webster had been long and anxiously awaited. The desire was great to know what position he would take; the curiosity was intense to know whether he would support the compromise or would join the anti-slavery Whigs and approve the plan of the President. It had been rumored that he, in connection with some Southern senators, was intending to prepare a scheme of adjustment;[2] on

---

[1] The quotations are taken from the speech as printed in vol. v. of Webster's Works. The whole speech is well worth reading.

[2] *National Era*, March 7th, 1850; Rise and Fall of the Slave Power, vol. ii. p. 149; New York *Herald* and New York *Journal of Commerce*, Feb. 28th; New York *Tribune*, March 1st; Correspondence of C. A. Dana, New York *Tribune*, March 4th.

the other hand, Giddings and other Free-soilers thought that he would sustain their doctrines.[1] Horace Mann did not believe that Webster would compromise the great question.[2] All this conjecture was idle. More than six weeks before he made the declaration in public, he had given Clay to understand that he would support substantially the Kentucky senator's scheme of compromise.[3] Before concurring in all the details, he desired to give the subject careful consideration; and between the time of his interview with Clay on January 21st and the delivery of his speech he consulted with men of diverse views.[4] He heard every side advocated; he saw the subject in all its bearings. As the result of his mature and carefully considered judgment, he determined to follow his own first impressions, and devote himself to the advocacy of Clay's plan, "no matter what might befall himself at the North."[5]

The speech produced a wonderful sensation; none other in our annals had an immediate effect so mighty and striking. The reply to Hayne and the reply to Calhoun have more permanent value, and their influence has been lasting; the 7th of March speech dealt with slavery, and when the slavery question ceased to be an issue the discourse of Webster lost all but the historical interest. A careful reading of the speech now fails to disclose the whole reason of its harsh reception at the North. It is probable that the matured historical view will be that Webster's position as to the application of the Wilmot proviso to New Mexico was statesmanship of the highest order. In 1846, 1847, and 1848, the formal prohibition of slavery in the territory to be acquired, or which was acquired from Mexico, seemed a vital and practical question. The latitude of the territory

---

[1] History of the Rebellion, p. 323. Giddings's statement that Webster had made promises to anti-slavery men is probably a mistake. See Curtis, vol. ii. p. 402.

[2] March 4th, Life, p. 293.   [3] Curtis, vol. ii. p. 397.

[4] Lodge, p. 322.   [5] Curtis, vol. ii. p. 397.

in dispute gave reason to suppose that its products would be those of the cotton States, and that it would naturally gravitate towards slave institutions. While many believed that the Mexican law sufficed to preserve freedom in California and New Mexico, it nevertheless was good policy to make extraordinary appropriations for the war only on condition of an express understanding that the territory acquired should be free. But in 1850 the question had changed. California had decided for herself; and the more important half of the controversy was cut off by the action of the people interested. There remained New Mexico.[1] The very fact that California had forbidden slavery was an excellent reason for believing that New Mexico would do likewise. It had now become known that while the latitude of New Mexico assigned her to the domain of slavery, the altitude of the country gave her a different climate from that of the slave States, and subjected her to different economical conditions. It was understood that neither cotton, tobacco, rice, nor sugar could be raised, and no one in 1850 maintained that slave labor was profitable save in the cultivation of those products. The correspondence between Webster and the delegate to Congress from New Mexico shows that no one conversant with the facts had the slightest notion that slavery had any chance of being established in that territory.[2] The people themselves proved that no Wilmot pro-

---

[1] New Mexico then comprised the westerly portions of New Mexico as at present bounded, and Colorado, Nevada, and Utah, most of Arizona, and the southwesterly part of Wyoming. Narrative and Critical History of America, Justin Winsor, vol. vii. p. 552.

[2] This correspondence was published in many of the newspapers of the day, and may be found in Webster's Works, vol. vi. p. 548. Hugh N. Smith, the delegate from New Mexico, under date of April 9th, wrote: "New Mexico is an exceedingly mountainous country, Santa Fé itself being twice as high as the highest point of the Alleghanies, and nearly all the land capable of cultivation is of equal height, though some of the valleys have less altitude above the sea. The country is cold. Its general agricultural products are wheat and corn, and such vegetables as

viso was needed, for in convention assembled in May they
formed a State government, and declared for the absolute
prohibition of slavery.   It seems that Webster had studied
this territorial question more deeply, knew the facts better,
and saw clearer than his detractors.[1]   It certainly is no lack
of consistency in a public man to change his action in conformity with the change in circumstances.   The end desired
was to have California and New Mexico free ; and if that
could be gained by the action of these communities, it was
surely as well as to have it determined by a formal act of
Congress.   To insist upon a rigid principle when it is no
longer applicable or necessary is not good politics ; yet great
blame has been attached to Webster because he did not now
insist on the Wilmot proviso.   Anti-slavery writers have

---

grow in the Northern States of this Union.   It is entirely unsuited for
slave labor.   Labor is exceedingly abundant and cheap.   It may be hired
for three or four dollars a month, in quantity quite sufficient for carrying
on all the agriculture of the territory.   There is no cultivation except
by irrigation, and there is not a sufficiency of water to irrigate all the
land.

"As to the existence at present of slavery in New Mexico, it is the general understanding that it has been altogether abolished by the laws of
Mexico ; but we have no established tribunals which have pronounced as
yet what the law of the land in this respect is.   It is universally considered, however, that the territory is altogether a free territory.   I know
of no persons in the country who are treated as slaves, except such as
may be servants to gentlemen visiting or passing through the country.
I may add that the strongest feeling against slavery universally prevails
throughout the whole territory, and I suppose it quite impossible to convey it there, and maintain it by any means whatever."

[1] Senator Hale, who opposed the compromise, and at this time criticised severely Webster's course, said in the Senate, July 9th, 1856 : " Wise
or unwise," the compromise measures of 1850 "had succeeded in an
eminent degree in restoring peace to the country."   And when Congress assembled, Dec., 1853, "it was literally true, I believe, at the time,
. . . as Mr. Webster said, that there was not a single foot of territory on
the continent where this great question was not settled by what I think
Mr. Webster termed an irrepealable law."—*Congressional Globe*, vol. xxxiii.
p. 846.

pointed to the legislative establishment of slavery in New Mexico in 1859 as proof that Webster made in 1850 a fatal error of judgment. But the practice never actually existed in that territory, and the act of 1859 was the work of a coterie, passed for political effect.[1]

The historian whose sympathies are with the anti-slavery cause of 1850—and it seems clear that he can most truly write the story—can by no means commend the whole of the 7th-of-March speech. The orator dwelt upon the conditions of the annexation of Texas at too great a length, for the bad bargain and the manner in which it was made were not a pleasant recollection to the North. It was not necessary to lay great stress upon the fact that more slave States could be created out of Texas, for, while it is obvious that the intention was to remind the South how well they had fared in the Union, the orator's mode of treating the subject was of a nature to irritate the North; and all the more, because his argument could not legally be impugned. Webster's reference to the abolition societies and their work brought a storm of indignation upon his head from people who were not used to suppress their voice or mince their meaning. Webster was wrong in his estimate of the abolitionists. Yet similar judgments were common ; and for ten years more we find the same pleas against the agitating of slavery. The complete answer to this deprecation was given by Lowell for once and all : " To be told that we ought not to agitate the question of slavery, when it is that which is forever agitating us, is like telling a man with the fever and ague on him to stop shaking, and he will be cured." [2]

But what grieved the old supporters of Webster the most was his severe censure of the North for their action in regard to fugitive slaves. The bill of Mason, which, with some amendments, he proposed to support, was a stringent

---

[1] See Chap. X.

[2] Political Essays, p. 31. This essay was published in the *Atlantic Monthly* for Oct., 1860.

measure; and while Webster's own idea was that the fugitive ought to have a jury trial in case he denied owing service to the claimant,[1] there is no doubt that he would have voted for the Mason bill pure and simple, or, had he been in the Senate at the time, for the actual Fugitive Slave law passed in September, rather than that the compromise should fail. It was thus that the country regarded, and rightly, his position. Webster's remarks on this subject are those of an advocate bound to the letter of the law, fettered by technicality and overborne by precedent. He does not take a broad, statesmanlike view, drawn indeed from the written law, but adapted to changing sentiments and keeping pace with the progress of the century; he who had taught us to seize the essential and eternal principles underlying the record is not true to the standard which he himself erected. Webster could see "an ordinance of Nature," and the "will of God" written on the mountains and plateaus of New Mexico, but he failed to see an ordinance of Nature and the will of God implanted in the hearts of men that led them to refuse their assistance in reducing to bondage their fellows, whose only crime had been desire for liberty and escape from slavery. These feelings in the minds of men of Massachusetts were, in Webster's opinion, "local prejudices" founded on "unreal ghostly abstractions."[2] He could detect the "taunt and reproach" to the South in the Wilmot proviso, but could not discover that a rigorous fugitive slave act was equally a taunt and reproach to the North.

---

[1] See Fugitive Slave bill introduced by Webster, June 3d, 1850, Works, vol. v. p. 373. See his letter of Nov. 11th, 1850, where he states that if he had been in the Senate when the present Fugitive Slave law passed, he "should have moved, as a substitute for it, the bill proposed by myself." Private Correspondence, vol. ii. p. 402.

[2] Remarks in Boston, April 29th, Curtis, vol. ii. p. 438. These expressions are cited from the celebrated Revere House speech, which may be found in full in Life of B. R. Curtis, vol. i. p. 117. The argument as to the duty of Massachusetts is strong.

Other points in this discourse occasioned much comment at the time, but the principal ones, and all that are necessary to a comprehension of what will follow, have been touched upon.   It now remains to relate how the country received this speech.

The Massachusetts Legislature was in session discussing the national question, but dropped the subject in its general aspect to consider their great senator's relation to it.   One member said that Webster was " a recreant son of Massachusetts who misrepresented her in the Senate." Henry Wilson " declared that Webster in his speech had simply, but hardly, stated the Northern and national side of the question, while he had earnestly advocated the Southern and sectional side ; that his speech was Southern altogether in its tone, argument, aim and end." [1]   The anti-slavery Whigs and Free-soil members were anxious to instruct Webster formally to support the Wilmot proviso and vote against Mason's Fugitive Slave bill ; and a resolution with that purport was introduced by Wilson, but they had not the strength to carry it through the legislature.   The speech was received in a like manner by the majority of the Northern representatives in Congress.   No one of the New England Whig members agreed with him. [2]   Horace Mann especially was bitter.   He writes: " Webster is a fallen star! Lucifer descending from heaven !"   " There is a very strong feeling here [at Washington] that Mr. Webster has played false to the North."   " He has not a favorable response from any Northern man of any influence." [3]   Giddings represented the anti-slavery sentiment of Ohio when he says, " By this speech a blow was struck at freedom and the constitutional rights of the free States which no Southern arm could have given." [4]

---

[1] Rise and Fall of the Slave Power, vol. ii. p. 254.
[2] Curtis, vol. ii. pp. 428, 447 ; Boston *Atlas*, April 6th.
[3] Letters of March 8th, 10th, 14th, Life, pp. 293, 294.
[4] History of the Rebellion, p. 324.

A public meeting in Faneuil Hall condemned the action
of Webster. Theodore Parker, who was one of the principal speakers, said : " I know no deed in American history
done by a son of New England to which I can compare
this but the act of Benedict Arnold. . . . The only reasonable way in which we can estimate this speech is as a bid
for the presidency."[1] In the main, the Northern Whig
press condemned the salient points of the speech. The New
York *Tribune* was especially outspoken, and doubted whether
Webster would carry with him a Northern Whig vote.[2] A
large proportion of the Whig newspapers of New England[3]
felt obliged to dissent from the opinion of him whose arguments they had heretofore received with avidity and
spread with zeal. It was regarded as an indication of great
weight when the Boston *Atlas*, whose editor was a warm
personal friend of Webster, combated unreservedly the important positions of the 7th-of-March speech ; and although
this respectful criticism was expressed in emphatic terms,
the editor spoke more in sorrow than in anger.[4] Those
of the Whig journals who, after the flush of surprise, came
to their leader's support could only advocate his principles
in a lukewarm manner ; and it was evident that devotion
to Webster, and not to the cause he had made his own, was
the spring of their action.[5] Nearly all the religious papers
of the North vented their disapproval.[6] Whittier, in a song
of plaintive vehemence called " Ichabod," mourned for the
" fallen" statesman whose faith was lost, and whose honor
was dead.

Curtis and Theodore Parker, who agree in nothing else,
are of the same mind about public sentiment. " This

---

[1] Speech of March 25th.

[2] March 9th and 11th.

[3] Nine-tenths of them, according to the Boston *Atlas*.

[4] See the editorial of April 6th.

[5] Notably the Boston *Advertiser*, the Boston *Traveller*, and the **Spring-**
field *Republican*. See for the latter, Life of Bowles, vol. i. p. 78.

[6] See a list of them in the *Liberator* of April 12th.

speech," writes Curtis, "was received by probably a great majority of Mr. Webster's constituents, if not by a majority of the whole North, with disfavor and disapprobation." [1] " I think," said Parker, " not a hundred prominent men in all New England acceded to the speech." [2]

This was the instant outburst of opinion; but friends for Webster and his cause came with more deliberate reflections. Some prominent Democratic journals approved from the first his position, [3] and there were many Whigs in New England, and especially in Boston, who were sure to follow Webster whithersoever he led. The majority, indeed, would have preferred that he had spoken differently, but their personal devotion induced them to espouse his side. [4] His moral and intellectual influence in the free States was greater than that of any man living, for the people had confidence that his gigantic intellect would discover the right, and that his intellectual honesty would impel him to follow it. The country has listened to but two men on whose words they have hung with greater reverence than on those of Webster. The intellectual force and moral greatness of Washington and of Lincoln were augmented by their high office and the gravity of the existing crises. When the first excitement had subsided, the friends of Webster bestirred themselves, and soon testimonials poured in, approving the position which he had taken. The most significant of them was the one from eight hundred solid men of Boston, who thanked him for " recalling us to our duties under the Constitution," and for his " broad, national, and patriotic views." [5] The tone of many of the Whig papers changed,

---

[1] Vol. ii. p. 410.   [2] Sermon, Oct. 31st, 1852.

[3] Notably the New York *Herald* and the New York *Journal of Commerce.*

[4] For example, George Ashmun, M. C. from the Springfield, Mass., district. Life of Samuel Bowles, vol. i. p. 41.

[5] Among the signers were George Ticknor, George T. Curtis, Benjamin R. Curtis, Rufus Choate, Moses Stuart, W. H. Prescott, and Jared Sparks. The communication was dated March 25th.

some to positive support, others to more qualified censure. The whole political literature of the time is full of the discussion of this speech and its relation to the compromise. It is frequently said that a speech in Congress does not alter opinions; that the minds of men are determined by set political bias or sectional considerations. This was certainly not the case in 1850. Webster's influence was of the greatest weight in the passage of the compromise measures, and he is as closely associated with them as is their author. Clay's adroit parliamentary management was necessary to carry them through the various and tedious steps of legislation. But it was Webster who raised up for them a powerful and much-needed support from Northern public sentiment.

At the South the speech was cordially received; the larger portion of the press commended it with undisguised admiration.[1] Calhoun complimented Webster for many of his declarations. Senator Foote, of Mississippi, was warm in his praise; while Jefferson Davis afterwards said that it contained so little for the South that he "never could see why it was republished in the Southern States."[2]

It now remains for us to consider the justice of the altered verdict on the character of Webster, which dates from the 7th of March. I have already spoken of him at length; but his vigorous personality fills such a vast space of his time that in dwelling upon his attitude towards the question which distracted the country, and the attitude of the country towards him, we are studying in the best manner the history of the period. Tradition has even been unkinder to him than history. It is generally believed that in his later years he was daily flustered with brandy, and that he trod the path of the gross libertine. The truth on this delicate

---

[1] See many extracts from Southern papers in the *Liberator* of April 5th, May 3d and 10th; also Webster's reference thereto in the Senate, March 25th, Curtis, vol. ii. p. 420.

[2] Jan. 26th, 1860, *Congressional Globe*, p. 599.

subject has already been stated.[1] But it is the delight of
story-tellers to make Webster the hero of exaggerated or
wholly apocryphal anecdotes that tickle the ears of listeners
by a tale of his rank excess. When it affects great men, the
"taint of vice whose strong corruptions inhabit our frail
blood" becomes an especially toothsome morsel of gossip
for those who gladly believe that intellectual greatness is
prone to the indulgence of the passions.

It was a common opinion that Webster's intense desire
for the presidency caused him to sacrifice his principles, but
those who are most vehement in their charge refute themselves. Giddings says that Webster thought "his only pathway to the presidential chair lay through the regions of
slavery;" but on the next page the anti-slavery apostle
writes that the reaction from the speech "prostrated in
political death the giant who seemed to have directed his
deadly aim at the heart of liberty."[2] Horace Mann said the
speech was a "bid for the presidency."[3] This, however, was
an after-thought; for on the 8th of March he records the
opinion that Webster "will lose two friends at the North
where he will gain one at the South."[4] Theodore Parker
said that Webster "was a bankrupt politician in desperate
political circumstances, gaming for the presidency;" yet, according to the same authority, the speech did not commend
itself to "a hundred prominent men in all New England."[5]
If one believes that Webster surrendered principle for the
sake of winning the favor of the South, it must be on the
ground that this man of large public experience did not understand the sentiment of the North; or that, with unex-
ampled fatuity, he hoped his position on the sectional question would gain him the support of the South and yet not

---

[1] See p. 143.
[2] History of the Rebellion, pp. 323, 324.
[3] This was written April 6th, Life, p. 299.
[4] Ibid., p. 293.
[5] Discourse, April 12th, 1852, and Sermon, Oct. 31st, 1852.

lose him that of the free States. The charge lies in a mis-
conception of his character. While his desire for the presidency was ardent, he demanded the nomination from his
party as a right rather than begged it as a favor. In truth,
if we carefully estimate the public utterances of Webster we
shall see that the charge of flagrant inconsistency is unjust.
Of all the criticisms of his action from anti-slavery men, that
of Emerson was the least uncharitable and the most truthful. The philosopher could appreciate the conservatism of
the statesman, and could understand that the point of view
of the one might be widely different from that of the other.[1]
If we contrast simply his former sentiments on slavery with
the treatment of it in the 7th-of-March speech, the imputation of inconsistency may, indeed, seem reasonable.[2] But
that is only to look on one side of the question; for if we reflect on Webster's veneration for the Constitution and his

---

[1] "Mr. Webster, perhaps, is only following the laws of his blood and
constitution. . . . He is a man who lives by his memory; a man of the
past, not a man of faith and hope. All the drops of his blood have eyes
that look downward, and his finely developed understanding only works
truly and with all its force when it stands for animal good; that is, for
property. He looks at the Union as an estate, a large farm, and is excellent in the completeness of his defence of it so far. What he finds already written he will defend. Lucky that so much had got well written
when he came, for he has no faith in the power of self-government. . . .
In Massachusetts, in 1776, he would, beyond all question, have been a refugee. He praises Adams and Jefferson, but it is a past Adams and Jefferson. A present Adams or Jefferson he would denounce."—Memoir of
Emerson, Cabot, p. 581.

[2] Webster himself denied that there was any inconsistency. See his
statement in his 7th-of-March speech, and his remarks in the Senate,
March 25th, in reply to Hale. The following he wrote to inhabitants of
Maine in May: "Gentlemen,—One of the exciting questions of the present
moment respects the necessity of excluding slavery by law from the territories lately acquired from Mexico. If I believed in any such necessity,
I should, of course, support such a law. I could not do otherwise consistently with opinions very many times expressed, and which opinions I
have no inclination to change, and shall not change." Curtis, vol. ii. p.
430.

sincere love for the Union, as shown through his whole career, it is easy to see that the main-spring of his action was
the same in 1850 as it was twenty years before, when he
made the reply to Hayne.   His dislike of slavery was strong,
but his love for the Union was stronger, and the more powerful motive outweighed the other; for he believed that the
crusade against slavery had arrived at a point where its further prosecution was hurtful to the Union.   As has been
said of Burke, " he changed his front, but he never changed
his ground." [1]   The mention of Burke cannot fail to suggest
the likeness between the British statesman and the American
in their last important position in public life.   Burke, too,
turned his back upon his old friends and supporters.   He
who for so many years was the strength of the Whigs now
became the idol of the Tories.   So complete was the change
that one historian,[2] more brilliant than solid in his judgments, cannot account for it in any other way than that the
reason of the statesman was tottering.   Other more careful
writers,[3] who better comprehended Burke, see plainly that
he simply followed the laws of his blood and constitution.
So it was with Webster.   He was as conservative as Burke.
Both dreaded fanatics.   The Union and the Constitution
were to the American what the ancient and revered institutions of ages and nations were to the Englishman.   Both
were the means of breaking up their party—the American
Whig party beyond hope of revival; the English Whigs
were deprived of power for a generation.   Party passion
has so affected opinions about Burke that it has remained
for the present generation of Englishmen to measure fairly
the worth of their greatest statesman.   Never has his reputation shone so brightly as to-day, and not until now has his
conservatism been appreciated at its full value.   It is quite
certain that we shall not be less generous in the estimate of

---

[1] Life of Burke, Morley, p. 245.
[2] Buckle.
[3] Bancroft, Lecky, and Morley.   See Morley, pp. 1 and 3.

our great conservative. Until the closing years of our century, a dispassionate judgment could not be made of Webster; but we see now that, in the war of the secession, his
principles were mightier than those of Garrison.[1] It was
not "No Union with slave-holders," but it was "Liberty and
Union" that won. Lincoln called the joint names his watchword,[2] and it was not the liberty or abolitionist, but the Union
party that conducted the war.

Burke likewise suffered calumny in his private life. He
received large gifts of money from a rich and noble lord,
even as Webster had contributions from the merchants of
State Street, and Burke was also accused of getting money
in discreditable ways.[3]

In thinking of the intellectual greatness of Webster, we
are reminded of an American whose grasp was wide, who
stamped his print upon his time, and yet not until our generation has historic justice been done to his memory. When
Webster eulogized Alexander Hamilton with that graphic
and familiar comparison that has now become an estimate
of his work which no one disputes, it was considered a brave
and noble act to speak so warmly of a man whom few cared
to honor.[4]

[1] Webster's "great argument was behind every bayonet, and was carried home with every cannon-shot in the war which saved the Union."—
George F. Hoar, at Plymouth, Aug. 1st, 1889. "The great rebellion of 1861
went down hardly more before the cannons of Grant and Farragut than the
thunder of Webster's reply to Hayne."—Gov. J. D. Long, Jan. 15th, 1882.

[2] History of Nicolay and Hay, *Century Magazine*, vol. xxxviii. p. 413.

[3] It was said that at the time Burke changed his political opinions he
was "overwhelmed with pecuniary embarrassments from which there
seemed no outlet in opposition."—History of England, Lecky, vol. v. p.
460. But Lecky has no doubt of the sincerity of Burke's convictions.

[4] "He smote the rock of the national resources, and abundant streams
of revenue gushed forth. He touched the dead corpse of the public credit,
and it sprang upon its feet."—Webster's Works, vol. i. p. 200. "I admire
your gallantry (and good conduct, too) in vindicating and eulogizing the
fame and character of Hamilton. Few men at this day are magnanimous
to dare it."—Letter of Joseph Gales to Webster, March 27th, 1831, Curtis,
vol. i. p. 399.

I.—11

On the 11th of March, Seward spoke. Although this was his first term in the Senate, and indeed in Congress, for he had never been a member of the House, he was by no means an unknown man. Achieving local reputation by service in the legislature, he had twice held the office of governor. The executive of New York had always been a prominent office, owing to the importance of the State and the power vested in it by the Constitution; but it was unusually so in the case of Governor Seward, for he had to do with affairs that gave him fame beyond the confines of his own State. Indeed, so inseparably was his name connected with this office that after years of renowned service in the Senate his title still remained Governor Seward. He was a good lawyer, and had a large practice in the United States courts. Fond of study, having an especial liking for history and philosophy, he loved the classics, and he read many of the English poets with delight; but he detested mathematics. An active Whig, always supporting the candidate of his party, he leaned decidedly to anti-slavery views. He was a friend of John Quincy Adams, whom he regarded with respect and veneration, and who had a marked influence on his turn of thought. Adams, who brooded constantly during the last years of his life over the slavery question, said to Seward the year before he died, "I shall be here but a little while. I look to you to do a great deal." He had been elected senator by a large majority of the legislature, and it was well understood at home and abroad that he was a strenuous opponent of the extension of slavery. His speech at Cleveland in 1848 had produced a profound sensation. • "Slavery can be limited to its present bounds," he had said; "it can be ameliorated; it *can* and *must* be abolished, and you and I can and must do it."[1]

Beginning with an unanswerable argument in favor of the admission of California, he mentions the demand that

---

[1] See Life by F. W. Seward, vols. i. and ii., and Memoir prefixed to vol. i. of Works.

there shall be a compromise of the questions which have
arisen out of slavery before California shall be allowed to
become a State; and emphatically declares: "I am opposed
to any such compromise, in any and all the forms in which
it has been proposed;" for what do we of the North "receive in this compromise? Freedom in California." But as
"an independent, a paramount question," California "ought
to come in, and must come in, at all events. . . . Under the
circumstances of her conquest, her compact, her abandon-
ment, her justifiable and necessary establishment of a Constitution, and the inevitable dismemberment of the empire
consequent upon her rejection, I should have voted for her
admission even if she had come as a slave State."

In regard to the fugitive slave question, "I say to the
slave States, you are entitled to no more stringent laws;
and that such laws would be useless. The cause of the inef-
ficiency of the present statute is not at all the leniency of its
provisions;" it is the public sentiment at the North, which
will not support the enforcement of the Fugitive Slave
act. "Has any government ever succeeded in changing the
moral convictions of its subjects by force? But these convictions imply no disloyalty. We reverence the Constitution, although we perceive this defect, just as we acknowledge the splendor and the power of the sun, although its
surface is tarnished with here and there an opaque spot.
Your Constitution and laws convert hospitality to the refugee from the most degrading oppression on earth into a
crime; but all mankind except you esteem that hospitality
a virtue. . . . If you will have this law executed, you must
alleviate, not increase, its rigors."

When Seward came to the territorial question, his words
created a sensation. "We hold," he said, "no arbitrary authority over anything, whether acquired lawfully or seized
by usurpation. The Constitution regulates our stewardship;
the Constitution devotes the domain (*i. e.* the territories not
formed into States) to union, to justice, to defence, to welfare, and to liberty. *But there is a higher law than the Con-*

stitution,[1] which regulates our authority over the domain, and devotes it to the same noble purposes. The territory is a part, no inconsiderable part, of the common heritage of mankind, bestowed upon them by the Creator of the universe. We are his stewards, and must so discharge our trust as to secure in the highest attainable degree their happiness." This remark about "*a higher law*," while far inferior in rhetorical force to Webster's "I would not take pains uselessly to reaffirm an ordinance of Nature, nor to re-enact the will of God," was destined to have transcendent moral influence. A speech which can be condensed into an aphorism is sure to shape convictions. These, then, are the two maxims of this debate; the application of them shows the essential points of the controversy.

Seward then proceeds at some length to rebut Webster's argument based on the proposition that climate and soil would prevent the introduction of slavery into New Mexico. He refers "to the great and all-absorbing argument that the Union is in danger of being dissolved, and that it can only be saved by compromise." He had received "with no inconsiderable distrust" the warnings that had been uttered with impassioned solemnity in his hearing every day for nearly three months, "because they are uttered under the influence of a controlling interest to be secured, a paramount object to be gained; and that is an equilibrium of power in the republic. . . . The question of dissolving the Union is a complex question: it embraces the fearful issue whether the Union shall stand, and slavery, under the steady, peaceful action of moral, social, and political causes, be removed by gradual voluntary effort, and with compensation; or whether the Union shall be dissolved and civil war ensue, bringing on violent but complete and immediate emancipation. We are now arrived at that stage of our national progress when that crisis can be foreseen, when we must foresee it. . . . I feel assured that slavery must give

---

[1] The emphasis is mine.

way; . . . that emancipation is inevitable, and is near; that
it may be hastened or hindered; and that whether it shall
be peaceful or violent depends upon the question whether
it be hastened or hindered; that all measures which fortify
slavery, or extend it, tend to the consummation of violence;
all that check its extension and abate its strength tend to
its peaceful extirpation. But I will adopt none but lawful,
constitutional, and peaceful means to secure even that end;
and none such can I or will I forego. . . . There is no reasonable limit to which I am not willing to go in applying
the national treasures to effect the peaceful, voluntary removal of slavery itself. . . . But you reply that, nevertheless, you must have guarantees; and the first one is for the
surrender of fugitives from labor. That guarantee you cannot have . . . because you cannot roll back the tide of social
progress. You must be content with what you have." Nevertheless, "there will be no disunion and no secession." Senator Seward closed with an appeal for the maintenance of
the Union; he pictured the invocation of countless generations that would be the future inhabitants of this region,
demanding sure and complete freedom over the territory
for which they were now legislating.[1]

In a portion of the discourse there are many glittering
generalities, and pedantic references to Bacon, Montesquieu,
and Burke, which add little to the power of the reasoning.
Nor are the transitions naturally made. In classic style,
it is far inferior to Webster's oration; in terse and severe
precision of language he does not equal Calhoun, and he
fails to stick to the question in hand as closely as Clay.
The first part of the speech, the argument in favor of the
admission of California, is divided into categorical propositions, which again are subdivided into points after the
manner of an old-fashioned sermon. This is not a pleasing
form for an oration calculated to gain the attention of the

---

[1] This speech of Senator Seward may be found in vol. i. of his Works,
p. 51.

hearers. A prominent journalist, whose sympathies were
with the side that Seward advocated, thought the speech
"very dull, heavy, and prosy," and he did not stay it out,[1]
for more than three hours were occupied in its delivery. It
was too long by a third. But the last two-thirds make it a
great speech, and it is from that portion that nearly all the
foregoing citations are made. Seward was listened to with
close and earnest attention by Webster, Clay, Calhoun, Benton, Cass, Hale, and Corwin,[2] not from personal sympathy
with him in his maiden effort, but because he represented
faithfully the sentiment of the Empire State, and was, moreover, regarded as the mouthpiece of the President. The
latter supposition was a mistake. Nor did Seward propose
at any time to speak for General Taylor in the Senate ; on
the contrary, he had refused a place on any important committee, lest their intimate personal relations might create
the suspicion that he acted authoritatively for the President.[3] Indeed, the Washington organ of the President assailed Seward for the sentiments expressed, and it was accordingly given out that he had lost all influence with the
administration. Webster sneered at the speech.[4] Clay wrote
that the speech had eradicated the respect of almost all men
for Seward.[5] But one voice came from the South, and that
was the voice of censure ; in this the Northern Democratic

---

[1] Brewer, of the Boston *Atlas*.

[2] Washington correspondence New York *Tribune*, March 11th.

[3] Memoir prefixed to vol. i. of Works, p. lxxxiv. Seward had, however,
consulted the Secretary of the Interior. On the day that he spoke, before
going to the Capitol, he wrote his wife : "I showed my notes confiden-
tially to Mr. Ewing, and he is satisfied."—Life of Seward, vol. ii. p. 125.

[4] "I perceive that my friend Weed laments that it did not happen to
me to make such a great and glorious speech as Governor Seward's. I
thank him sincerely for his condolence, but *Omnia non possumus omnes*."
Webster to Blatchford, July, 1850, Memoir of Thurlow Weed, p. 183.
But Weed did not entirely approve of the speech. See letters of Seward
to him, Life of Seward, vol. ii. p. 129.

[5] Private Correspondence, p. 604.

press for the most part coincided.   The New York *Tribune*, however, said that the speech represented the feeling of the great State of New York; and this was true of the majority of the Whigs, for later in the year, in State convention assembled, they commended by formal resolution the course of their senator.[1]

Seward's reasoning on the fugitive slave question was incapable of refutation; later events plainly demonstrated the force of his position.   His unerring foresight as to what would happen to slavery in case the Union were dissolved is an unfolding of the idea planted in his mind by his political exemplar, John Quincy Adams.[2]   But his confident assertion that "there will be no disunion and no secession" is a revelation of that serene optimism that was a characteristic of Seward throughout his whole career.   The burning assertion that "there is a higher law than the Constitution" would in ordinary times have simply been the averment of a noble abstraction as old as Roman law, and, although it was applied to the territorial question by the senator, the religious and philanthropic people of the country soon seized upon it as justifying resistance to the Fugitive Slave law. The remark undoubtedly received a far wider application than its author purposed.   Of all the anti-slavery partisans in Congress, Seward was perhaps the last man one would have suspected of soaring to such a moral height and laying down a principle that should warrant opposition to the law.   At any rate, the expression would have seemed more natural in the mouth of Chase or Hale, in that of Giddings or Horace Mann.   For Seward did not disdain the arts of the machine politician.   He believed that a shrewd distribution of the patronage was a great assistance even to a party of moral ideas.   His influence with the administration was great enough to control the dealing-out of the offices of the North, and he made an efficient member of the

---

[1] New York *Tribune*, March 12th and Oct. 3d.
[2] See especially Life of Seward, F. W. Seward, vol. i. p. 672.

New York Whig regency whose sphere was practical politics. That the higher-law doctrine should be carried to its
legitimate result was far from his desire; but we shall see
how this maxim became a distinction of the radicals, who
accordingly looked to Seward as their leader.

These four speeches are but a fraction of the congressional
utterances on the question superseding all others; but they
present the case in its different aspects forcibly and plainly.
The four bulky volumes of the *Congressional Globe* containing the records of the session are for the most part a report
of speeches on the subject of slavery, and an account of the
various parliamentary procedures which took place before
arriving at the settlement. We have heard from four men
—a Southern Whig and a Northern Whig in favor of the
compromise, a Southern Democrat and an anti-slavery Whig
opposed to it. The Southerners, however, who afterwards
were proud to own themselves Calhoun's disciples, had no
idea of resting their case on his demand for a constitutional
amendment that should maintain an equilibrium. Jefferson Davis, who aspired to succeed Calhoun as a leader, gave
an exposition of what they actually desired. Out of respect
for Calhoun, he admitted that the amendment might eventually become necessary; but, in common with nearly every
one of his fellow-extremists, he knew that it was a chimer-
ical idea and an impossible demand. It was a good enough
argument to keep in the background; it had a possibility
of future value, for it might serve as one of the pre-
texts for secession. But now it must make place for a tan-
gible claim, and one that the average Southern mind could
comprehend. Davis was quite ready to state what would
satisfy the South. What he preferred, before all, was non-
intervention—" that is, an equal right to go into all territories—all property being alike protected;" but, in default of
this, "I will agree to the drawing of the line of 36° 30′
through the territories acquired from Mexico, with the condition that in the same degree as slavery is prohibited north
of that line, it shall be permitted to enter south of the line;

and that the States which may be admitted into the Union shall come in under such constitutions as they think proper to form."¹ This was his ultimatum. The speeches of Clay, Calhoun, Webster, Seward, and the demand of Davis, being a corollary to the complaint of Calhoun, show the three sides of the controversy. The other speeches are restatements or amplifications of the cogent arguments used by these leaders of the debate.

The discussion went on, not unattended with excitement. Between Benton and Senator Foote a noticeable altercation took place; for some time there had been a bitter personal feeling between the two men.² The Southerners looked on Benton as a renegade, for, although a slave-holder from a slave-holding State, he was bitterly opposed to their object, and the senator from Mississippi was tacitly selected to taunt Benton whenever opportunity offered.³ In the latter part of March he had a spirited controversy with Foote as to what measure should have legislative preference. The senator from Mississippi moved that the territorial bills should be made a special order. Benton objected to this, demanding, with considerable asperity, that the admission of California should first have consideration. This nettled Foote, who was of an excitable temperament, and he replied in words of bitter sarcasm. "The senator," he said, "need not think of frightening anybody by a blustering and dogmatic demeanor. We have rights here, as well as the senator from Missouri, and we mean to maintain them at all hazards and to the last extremity. . . . The honorable senator now says, 'I am the friend of California. . . . I announce—I, sir—I announce—that I will from this day henceforward insist—I, the Cæsar, the Napoleon of the Senate—I announce that I have now come into the war with sword

---

¹ Remarks of Jefferson Davis in the Senate, March 13th and 14th.

² Casket of Reminiscences, H. S. Foote, p. 331.

³ I am indebted to James W. Bradbury, then a senator from Maine, for the statement in the last clause.

and buckler.'" Foote continued in an exasperating manner, ridiculed the notion of Benton posing as "the special friend of California," and insinuated that his zeal for the State was not from "high public reasons," but from "certain personal and domestic considerations."[1] Benton retorted that he believed personalities were forbidden by the laws of the Senate. "And now, sir," he said, "I will tell you what I know. I know that the attacks made upon my motives to-day, and heretofore in this chamber, are false and cowardly." The rejoinder of Foote was not less cutting than his former remarks. It greatly irritated Benton, who exclaimed, "I pronounce it cowardly to give insults where they cannot be chastised. Can I take a cudgel to him here?" Calls to order by the vice-president and several senators, with mollifying remarks by others, terminated the incident for the day.[2] On the morrow, Benton, in a personal explanation, declared his determination, if the Senate did not protect him from insult, thereafter to redress the wrong himself, cost what it might. For some time afterwards the rancor between the two gentlemen did not have a public manifestation. But on the 17th of April, when Foote was pressing his motion for the reference of Clay's resolutions and other cognate matter to a select committee of thirteen, the pent-up enmity broke forth. Benton made the charge that the whole excitement under which the country had labored was due to the address of the Southern members of Congress,[3] and that "there has been a cry of wolf when there was no wolf; that the country has been alarmed without reason and against reason." Foote, in reply, defended the signers of the Southern address, said their action was "worthy of the highest laudation," and that they would be held in "veneration when their calumniators, no matter who they may be, will be objects of general loathing and contempt." When the word

---

[1] Fremont, one of the senators-elect from California, was the son-in-law of Benton.
[2] This was March 26th.   [3] See p. 104.

"calumniators" was uttered, Benton rose from his seat, pushed his chair violently from him, and, without remark or gesture, but with great wrath in his face, quickly strode towards the seat of Foote, which was about twenty feet distant from his own. Benton had no weapon of any kind in his hands or about his person. Foote, seeing at once the movement of Benton, left his place on the floor and ran towards the secretary's table, all the while looking over his shoulder; at the same time he drew a five-chambered revolver, fully loaded, and cocked it; then took a position in front of the secretary's table. Meanwhile Senator Dodge followed Benton, overtook him and grasped him by the arm, when he said, "Don't stop me, Dodge!" to which the reply came, "Don't compromise yourself or the Senate." He was then on the point of going back to his seat when he happened to see the pistol in Foote's hands, at which he became greatly excited. He struggled with the senators who were holding him, with the apparent intention of approaching Foote, and, dramatically throwing open his coat, exclaimed, "I am not armed; I have no pistols; I disdain to carry arms. Let him fire. Stand out of the way and let the assassin fire." In the meantime, Foote was disarmed and Benton was led back to his seat. Senators considered the scene an outrage to the dignity of the Senate, and a committee was appointed to investigate the affair and take proper action. Three months and a half later they reported, reciting fully the facts, but forbore to recommend any action to the Senate. They made one statement of historical interest; namely, that they had "searched the precedents, and find that no similar scene has ever been witnessed in the Senate of the United States." [1]

On the 18th of April the resolutions of Clay and others of similar purport were referred to a select committee of thirteen. Clay was chosen its chairman, and it was further made up by the election of senators Webster, Phelps, Cooper, Whigs, and Cass, Dickinson, Bright, Democrats, from the

---

[1] Report of Committee, July 30th.

free States; King, Mason, Downs, Democrats, and Mangum, Bell, and Berrien, Whigs, from the slave States. Nothing demonstrated more clearly that the question was not a partisan one than the constitution of this committee. There were thirty-four Democrats and twenty-four Whigs in the Senate, yet the Whigs were given a majority of this committee. The division was not on party, but on sectional lines. It had been tacitly understood that there should be six members from the free and six from the slave States, and it was eminently proper that the thirteenth man should be the Nestor of the Senate, as Clay was called. The senators chosen were able, experienced, and moderate men; among them there was only one advocate of the Wilmot proviso, Phelps, of Vermont, and but one Southern extremist, Mason, of Virginia. The committee reported on the 8th of May; their recommendations and views were thus recapitulated:

1. The admission of any new State or States formed out of Texas to be postponed until they shall hereafter present themselves to be received into the Union, when it will be the duty of Congress fairly and faithfully to execute the compact with Texas by admitting such new State or States.

2. The admission forthwith of California into the Union, with the boundaries she had proposed.

3. The establishment of territorial governments, without the Wilmot proviso, for New Mexico and Utah; embracing all the territory recently acquired by the United States from Mexico not contained in the boundaries of California.

4. The combination of these two last-mentioned measures in the same bill.

5. The establishment of the western and northern boundary of Texas, and the exclusion from her jurisdiction of all New Mexico, with the grant to Texas of a pecuniary equivalent; and the section for that purpose to be incorporated in the bill admitting California and establishing territorial governments for Utah and New Mexico.

6. More effectual enactment of law to secure the prompt

delivery of persons bound to service or labor in one State, under the laws thereof, who escape into another State.

7. In the District of Columbia the slave-trade, but not slavery, was to be prohibited under a heavy penalty.

No minority report was made; but Phelps, Cooper, Mason, Downs, and Berrien dissented from some of the views of the majority, and made statements to that effect in open Senate. The committee, however, were unanimously agreed on the first proposition, relating to the formation of more States from Texas. It will be seen that the practical bearing of these recommendations was the same as that of Clay's resolutions introduced in January;[1] bills to carry them out had been prepared, and were offered in connection with the report. The discussion on these measures in various shapes continued for nearly five months, and nearly every senator spoke. Among the supporters of the compromise scheme in the Senate were Clay, Webster, Cass, Douglas, and Foote. It was opposed by Seward, Chase, Hale, John Davis, of Massachusetts, and Dayton—all of them anti-slavery Whigs or Free-soilers; by Benton, an independent Democrat; and by Jefferson Davis and a following of Southern extremists.[2] Every one was astonished at the fire and vigor of Clay. He was the especial champion of the plan, and right nobly did he advocate it in spite of his age and infirmity. Greeley, a looker-on at Washington, was amazed at his energy, and wrote the *Tribune:* "He is . . . an overmatch in the engineering of a bill by sharp corners and devious passages for any man in the Senate. Webster is more massive and ponderous in a set debate, but does not compare in winning support to a measure."[3]

Meanwhile, the Nashville convention met. From the first

---

[1] See p. 122.

[2] "All the Union men, North and South, Whigs and Democrats, for the period of six months were assembled in caucus every day, with Clay in the chair, Cass upon his right hand, Webster upon his left hand, and the Whigs and Democrats arranged on either side."—Douglas, speech at Cincinnati, Sept. 9th, 1859.   [3] Letter of June 9th.

the Whigs in the South were either opposed to it, or were silent on the subject. The supporters of the project were mainly Democrats; but in many of the States, after the introduction of the compromise resolutions, they joined in the opposition. It was patent, however, from Webster's allusion to it in his 7th-of-March speech, that the proposed convention attracted attention at Washington as a disunion move. He intimated that if any persons should meet at Nashville "for the purpose of concerting measures for the overthrow of this Union over the bones of Andrew Jackson," the old hero "would turn in his coffin." By the latter part of March the feeling in favor of the convention had largely subsided, as shown by the fact that, out of sixty newspapers published in ten slave-holding States, from Maryland to Louisiana, there were not more than fifteen that gave it a decided support.[1] In fact, there was little enthusiasm for it outside of South Carolina and Mississippi. The convention met on the 3d of June; nine States were represented. There were six delegates from Virginia, seventeen from South Carolina, twelve from Georgia, twenty-one from Alabama, eleven from Mississippi, one from Texas, two from Arkansas, six from Florida, and a large number from Tennessee;[2] but the credentials of the delegates from most of the States were not of a character to give great weight to the proceedings of the convention. The important proposition in its address was the demand for a division of the territory acquired from Mexico by the parallel of 36° 30', with a right to carry slaves below that line. This was called "an extreme concession on the part of the South;" and if the convention represented the Southern people, it was virtually their ultimatum. But this assemblage was not a wave, but only a ripple, of Southern sentiment. It deserves a mention here more from the hopes and fears it had excited than from its active or enduring effects.

---

[1] Wilmington, N. C., *Chronicle.* Cited in Boston *Advertiser*, March 23d.
[2] *National Intelligencer*, June 8th.

The influence of the administration was exerted against the plan of the committee of thirteen. The second, third, and fifth recommendations [1] were combined in one measure, which the President himself in derision had called the omnibus bill,[2] and he warmly encouraged Hannibal Hamlin, Senator from Maine, to oppose it.[3] A few days after the report of the committee, Clay, in a speech, held out the olive branch to the administration. It was not accepted; on the contrary, " war, open war, undisguised war, was made by the administration and its partisans against the plan of the committee." [4] This the senator thought was unfair. What he deemed he had a right to expect was well stated in his witty retort to John Bell, a Whig senator from Tennessee, who defended the President. Bell said : " The President announced that he still adhered to the plan he had proposed ; and the old question is presented whether Mahomet will go to the mountain, or the mountain come to Mahomet. I do not undertake to say which is Mahomet or which the mountain." The reply from Clay came quickly : " I beg pardon, but I only wanted the mountain to let me alone." He said, moreover, that with the concurrence, or even the forbearance, of the administration the measure would have passed both Houses without difficulty.

These remarks of Clay were made on the 3d of July, and it was the last time that he had occasion to criticise the course of the President. Personal and sectional passion were stilled by the entrance of grim death into the White House. General Taylor on Thursday morning, the Fourth of July, was apparently in robust health. He attended the exercises in commemoration of the day at the Washington Monument, and listened to the oration of Senator Foote. The heat was of unusual intensity ; he was for a long time

---

[1] See p. 172.

[2] Statement of Clay in the Senate, July 3d.

[3] Life of Clay, Schurz, vol. ii. p. 351 ; Life of Thurlow Weed, vol. ii. p. 178.   [4] Remarks of Clay, July 3d.

exposed to the sun, and to quench his raging thirst drank a large quantity of iced water. Returning to the house, he ate freely of cherries and wild fruits, and took copious draughts of iced milk. An hour after dinner he was seized with cramps, which took the form of violent cholera morbus. The usual remedies were applied, but the illness increased, until by midnight serious results were threatened. The patient continued in this condition until Saturday, the 6th, when it was deemed best to call in counsel ; two other physicians were sent for, and Dr. Wood, his son-in-law, was summoned from Baltimore. By Monday the skill of his doctors had checked the visible stages of cholera morbus, but typhoid fever set in, and there were signs of mental distress. He said to his medical attendant : " I should not be surprised if this were to terminate in my death. I did not expect to encounter what has beset me since my elevation to the presidency. God knows that I have endeavored to fulfil what I conceived to be my honest duty. But I have been mistaken. My motives have been misconstrued, and my feelings most grossly outraged." He was undoubtedly brooding over an interview between himself and Stephens and Toombs, which occurred on the second day of his illness.[1] It was reported that they had called upon him as representatives of a cabal of ultra Southern Whigs to protest against his course on the slavery question, and it was said that they warned him, unless his policy were changed, they would vote a resolution of censure on his conduct in the Galphin business.[2] This day, Monday, the 8th, the physicians and family became much alarmed ; by evening hope was abandoned. That night and the next morning all was gloom at the executive mansion ; bulletins were issued every hour, which crowds anxiously awaited with tearful sympathy for the illustrious hero in his last fight. At ten o'clock Tuesday morning a rumor was started that the President had rallied ; at one in the after-

---

[1] See Life of John A. Quitman, Claiborne, vol. ii. p. 32.
[2] What the Galphin business was will be later on explained.

noon, that he was dead; but the official bulletin of 3.30 P.M. stated that the crisis had been passed, and he was beyond immediate danger. The city ran wild with joy. Bells were rung and bonfires were built to show the relieved anxiety of the people. Crowds of officials and many of the diplomatic body repaired to the White House to offer their congratulations. But the exultation was short-lived. By seven o'clock it was known that the physicians had refused to give more medicine, saying their patient was in the hands of God; and the bulletin announced that the President was dying. In response to his earnest inquiry, his doctor and friend told him he had not many hours to live. The general knew it too well, but he met death like a hero. He prayed with his spiritual adviser; he bade farewell to his wife and children, who were overcome with grief; and he uttered his last words with emphatic distinctness: "I have always done my duty: I am ready to die. My only regret is for the friends I leave behind me."

There was deep and sincere sorrow all through the Northern States at the death of the President. One correspondent on his journey from Boston to Washington saw everywhere signs of mourning; he had never known anything like the depth of feeling which pervaded the masses. "It seemed, indeed," he wrote, "as if our journey lay through the dark valley and shadow of death." [1] "I never saw grief," Seward wrote, "public grief, so universal and so profound." [2] The wide-felt sorrow was a testimony to the sterling honesty and patriotism of General Taylor. It extended to the border States, where he had a powerful hold on the Whigs, while but little regret for his death was shown in the cotton States outside of his own Louisiana. The grief of the Freesoilers and anti-slavery Whigs was especially great, for they had given their adherence to the President's plan, and they felt that now its strongest prop was gone: they soon had

---

[1] Correspondent of Boston *Atlas*, July 14th.
[2] Seward to his wife, Life of Seward, vol. ii. p. 144.

reason to feel that the succession of Fillmore boded ill to their scheme.[1]

Millard Fillmore was a self-educated, self-made man, and a safe though not brilliant lawyer. He early entered into politics, became a sturdy Whig, and served several terms in the House of Representatives, where he was marked for his industry, his anti-slavery views, and his support of John Quincy Adams in the fight for the right of petition. When he took the oath of office as Vice-President, the difference between him and Seward was apparently not one of principle, but one centring on the disposition of the offices. There was a lack of harmony between the two divisions of the party, beginning soon after the inauguration of General Taylor, but Seward acquired the ascendant, and his influence with the administration, as we have seen, became powerful.[2] Fillmore was distinguished for his suavity of manners. He had presided over the Senate during the heated debates on the compromise measures with impartiality and dignity. His idea of the decorum proper for the presiding officer of the Senate was so high that he had confided to only one person his own view of the question which agitated Congress. The debate had stirred the conservative feelings of his nature, and he had told the President privately that in case there should be a tie in the Senate, and it should devolve upon him to give the casting vote, his decision would be in favor of the scheme devised by Clay. While there was uncertainty about the policy of the new President,[3] Webster felt confident that it would promote the scheme of the committee of thirteen. He writes: " I believe Mr. Fillmore favors the compromise, and there is no doubt that recent

---

[1] This account of the illness and death of President Taylor is made up from detailed reports at the time to the Philadelphia *Bulletin* and New York *Independent ;* from references to the illness in Congress; from allusions to his death by President Fillmore, and in the eulogies delivered in the Senate and the House,

[2] See p. 102.   [3] Life of Horace Mann, p. 307.

events have increased the probability of the passage of that measure."[1] Clay confides to his daughter his opinion that the death of General Taylor " will favor the passage of the compromise bill,"[2] while Seward lamented that " Providence has at last led the man of hesitation and double opinions to the crisis where decision and singleness are indispensable."[3]

The announcement of the cabinet set at rest all doubts. President Fillmore, on receiving the resignation of the old cabinet, had at once determined to offer the office of Secretary of State to Clay or Webster; Clay, however, called upon him and recommended Webster. Thereupon he tendered the office to Webster, who after some deliberation, but with a great deal of reluctance, accepted it and advised the President regarding the other selections.[4] Thomas Corwin, of Ohio, received the Treasury portfolio; Charles M. Conrad, of Louisiana, became Secretary of War; William A. Graham, of North Carolina, had the Navy Department; A. H. H. Stuart, of Virginia, was Secretary of the Interior; Nathan K. Hall, of New York, Postmaster-General, and John J. Crittenden, of Kentucky, was Attorney-General.

Four of the members came from the slave-holding States, but they were men of moderate views. It was a cabinet favorable to the compromise; and Webster, who dominated the new administration, used its whole influence and power in favor of the scheme for which he had contended in the Senate. The President, moreover, knew well the use of official patronage, and before long the cry went out that when-

---

[1] Letter of July 11th, Webster's Private Correspondence, vol. ii. p. 376.

[2] Letter, July 13th, Private Correspondence, p. 611.

[3] Letter of Seward to his wife, July 12th, Life of Seward, vol. ii. p. 145.

[4] See letter of Fillmore to G. T. Curtis, Life of Webster, vol. ii. p. 465; also Webster's letter to Haven, ibid.; and his letters to Harvey and Blatchford, July 21st, Webster's Private Correspondence, vol. ii. p. 378.

ever practicable Seward men were removed and their places
filled with conservative Whigs.

In the meantime, a few men at Santa Fé, with an eye to
their own advantage, had taken steps towards the formation
of a State government for New Mexico. This move was suggested by the acting military governor of the territory, being in accordance with advice from General Taylor's Secretary of War. The governor called a convention, which assembled May 15th, and in ten days framed a constitution for
the State of New Mexico. This constitution prohibited slavery; it was adopted by the people in June, the vote being
8371 for and 39 against ratification. A governor, legislature and a congressman were chosen, and in July the Legislature assembled and elected senators. Before the question
of the admission of New Mexico as a State could be formally
brought before Congress, a territorial government had been
established, and the matter of conferring statehood on her
was not considered. The project could not have received
warm support, for the population was of far different character from that of California. While there were one hundred thousand souls in the territory, two-fifths were Indians,
three or four thousand were proud to call themselves Castil-
ians; fifteen hundred were emigrants from the United States,
and the remainder were Mexicans—that is, of the Spanish-In-
dian mixed race.[1] To the sprinkling of Americans was due
the political organization. "Their superior intelligence and
energy," said John Bell in the Senate, "will exercise a controlling influence over the more passive and tractable Mexicans and Indians." They had, indeed, formed a carpet-bag-
ger government on a magnificent scale; and, as Clay said
when it was foreshadowed that New Mexico might apply
for admission as a State, "It would be ridiculous, it would
be farcical [to admit her]; it would bring into contempt the
grave matter of forming commonwealths as sovereign mem-

---

[1] The population of the territory, exclusive of Indians, according to the
census of 1850, was: white, 61,525; free colored, 22; slaves, none.

bers of this glorious Union." On the death of President Taylor the project fell to the ground and made no figure in the adjustment of the controversy.[1]

After General Taylor's funeral and the customary eulogies, the discussion in the Senate continued on the so-called omnibus bill until the 31st of July, when the bill was ordered to be engrossed for a third reading; but it had been so cut down by the amendments that nothing remained of the original measure but the part which provided a territorial government for Utah without the interdiction of slavery; in that shape, it was passed. From the debate and the vote on the various amendments, however, it seemed highly probable that every recommendation of the committee of thirteen could be made law, provided each article, standing as an independent measure, were considered separately. Senator Douglas, chairman of the committee on territories, immediately introduced a bill for the admission of California. After this had been discussed for a few days, a bill was brought in which devised the settlement of the Texas boundary, and proposed to pay Texas ten million dollars for the relinquishment of her claims on New Mexico. The debate on these two measures went on side by side, a part of each sitting being devoted to California and a part to the Texas boundary. A vote on the latter question was first reached; it was taken August 9th, and the bill passed by 30 to 20. There were twelve votes against the Texas boundary measure from the slave and eight from the free States; in the main they were those of extremists from the South and anti-slavery Whigs and Free-soilers from the North. Benton, whom it is difficult to classify, joined Seward and Jefferson Davis, Chase and Atchison, Hale and Mason, in opposing the measure. The division on the California bill was had August 13th; there were 34 yeas and 18 nays. The yeas were fifteen Northern Democrats, eleven North-

---

[1] Arizona and New Mexico, H. H. Bancroft, pp. 342, 446 *et seq.*; Speech of Clay, May 31st, and of John Bell, July 5th, in the Senate.

ern Whigs, four Southern Whigs, and Chase, Hale, Benton, and Houston of Texas. The nays were all from the slave States, and all Democrats but three. The next day ten Southern senators, among whom were Jefferson Davis, Atchison, and Mason, presented a solemn protest against the action of the Senate in admitting California.[1] On the 15th of August the measure establishing a territorial government, without the Wilmot proviso, for New Mexico was passed. The vote was a light one, 27 to 10; the nays were all from the North. On August 23d the Fugitive Slave law was ordered to be engrossed for a third reading, which was equivalent to its passage, by a vote of 27 to 12. The nays were eight Northern Whigs, among them Winthrop (the successor of Webster), three Northern Democrats, and Chase; there were fifteen Northern senators who did not vote. The last of the series of the compromise measures, the abolition of the slave-trade in the District of Columbia, passed September 16th by 33 to 19; the nays were thirteen Southern Democrats and six Southern Whigs.

The different acts embraced in the compromise were disposed of more summarily in the House. The Texas Boundary bill, to which was added the New Mexico Territorial bill, was passed September 6th by 108 to 97. The division was on practically the same lines as in the Senate on the Texan act; as, for example, every member from South Carolina and Mississippi, all Democrats, voted against it; and on the same side were Giddings, Horace Mann, Julian, and Thaddeus Stevens. The California Admission bill went through the next day by 150 to 56. All the nays were from the slave States, and among them were two prominent Whigs, Clingman and Toombs, who had, however, but seven party associates. Two days later the House agreed to the Senate Utah bill. On September 12th, the Fugitive Slave law was

---

[1] This was signed by the two Senators from Virginia, South Carolina, and Florida, and by one each from Tennessee, Louisiana, Mississippi, and Missouri—nine Democrats and one Whig.

carried through the House, under the operation of the previous question, by 109 to 76; thirty-one Northern members
voted for it, among them three Whigs.   Thirty-three representatives from the North were either absent or paired or
dodged the vote.   There were enough of the latter to give
force to the dry remark of Thaddeus Stevens: "I suggest
that the Speaker should send a page to notify the members
on our side of the House that the Fugitive Slave bill has been
disposed of, and that they may now come back into the
hall."   The House some days afterwards concurred in the
Senate bill for the abolition of the slave-trade in the District of Columbia, and the series of measures received the
approval of the President.

The compromise was now complete.   It accorded substantially with the scheme outlined by Clay in January.[1]   I
have made the analysis of the vote on the different articles
with prolix detail, because it shows clearly how the compromise was carried in parts when it was impossible to enact
it as a whole.   Indeed, there were only four senators who
voted for every one of the measures which made up the
plan.[2]   Clay's name is recorded only on the bill for the abolition of the slave-trade in the District of Columbia; for,
worn out with his indefatigable exertions, he had sought the
air of the sea to regain his strength, and was at Newport
pending the determination of the other matters.   Of course,
had he been in the Senate, he would have supported every
one of the acts.   Douglas favored them all, but was un-
avoidably absent when the Fugitive Slave law was considered.
Had he been in Washington at the time, he would have given
his voice for the act.[3]   Dickinson, of New York, was a friend
to each one of the series of measures, and his name is not recorded for the New Mexico bill and the Fugitive Slave law,

---

[1] See p. 122.

[2] Houston, of Texas; Dodge, of Iowa; Sturgeon, of Pennsylvania, Democrats; and Wales, of Delaware, Whig.

[3] Life of Douglas, Sheahan, p. 160.

as he had paired with his colleague Seward, whose state
of health had made an absence from Washington necessary.

The influence of the administration was powerfully felt in
bringing about the result. "Here," writes Horace Mann, "are
twenty, perhaps thirty, men from the North in this House,
who, before General Taylor's death, would have sworn, like
St. Paul, not to eat nor drink until they had voted the proviso, who now, in the face of the world, turn about, defy the
instructions of their States, take back their own declarations,
a thousand times uttered, and vote against it."[1] Webster
was as active in his support of the compromise as when in
the Senate, and his private letters at this time testify how
much his heart was bound up in the success of the scheme
he had advocated at so great a cost. When the affair was
practically concluded, he writes: "I confess I feel relieved.
Since the 7th of March, there has not been an hour in which
I have not felt a 'crushing' weight of anxiety and responsibility. . . . It is over. My part is acted, and I am satisfied."[2]

The success of the compromise measures was due to their
almost unvarying support by the Northern Democrats and
Southern Whigs, although in the House many Northern
Whigs, owing to the influence of Webster, gave strong aid
to all the articles except the Fugitive Slave law. In the
Senate, while the conservative Northern Whigs supported
the Texas Boundary bill, they did not vote for the territorial
acts and the Fugitive Slave bill. The whole strength of the
North was exerted for the admission of California and the
abolition of the slave-trade in the District of Columbia; that
of the South in favor of the more effectual act for the rendition of runaway slaves. The Southern ultras, with the exception of Jefferson Davis, voted for the territorial bills.

The vote on the compromise measures portended a disso-

---

[1] Letter of Sept. 6th, Life of Horace Mann, p. 322.
[2] Private Correspondence, vol. ii. p. 385, Letter to Harvey, Sept. 10th.

lution of the existing political parties. One might then have conjectured that each would equally suffer; but the actual tendency was towards breaking up the Whig and cementing the Democratic party.

The reader who peruses the foregoing pages will understand sufficiently the scope of each of the acts of the compromise except the Fugitive Slave law. That deserves a fuller notice, for its effect on the North was greater than any of the others, and it was, moreover, one of the most objectionable laws ever passed by the Congress of the United States. Under the provisions of the act, *ex-parte* evidence determined the identity of the negro who was claimed. Even the affidavit of the owner was not necessary; that of his agent or attorney would suffice. The testimony of the alleged fugitive was expressly denied. These cases were ordinarily to be determined by commissioners appointed by the United States circuit courts, and these courts were enjoined to increase the number of commissioners from time to time, "with a view to afford reasonable facilities to reclaim fugitives from labor." It was the duty of a commissioner (or of a court or judge) "to hear and determine the case of a claimant in a summary manner." When the negro was adjudged to the claimant, the latter had authority "to use such reasonable force and restraint as may be necessary" to remove the fugitive to the State from which he escaped. No process could be issued "by any court, judge, or magistrate, or other person whomsoever" for the "molestation" of the slave-owner, his agent, or attorney, after the ownership of the negro was determined in the manner recited in the act. The United States marshals and their deputies were obliged to make unusual exertions to execute the law under penalty of a heavy fine. In case the slave escaped, they were liable to a civil suit for his value. In the event of an attempt being made to prevent the arrest or to rescue the alleged fugitive, the commissioners, or persons appointed by them, were empowered "to summon and call to their aid the bystanders or posse comitatus of the proper county; . . . and all good citizens are hereby commanded to aid and assist in the prompt and efficient execution of this law, whenever their services may be required, as aforesaid, for that purpose." If any person shall "willingly hinder or prevent" the claimant from arresting the fugitive, or "shall rescue or attempt to rescue, . . . or shall harbor or conceal" the fugitive, such person is "subject to a fine not exceeding one thousand dollars or imprisonment not exceeding six months; . . . and shall, moreover, forfeit and pay by way of civil damages to the party injured by such illegal conduct the sum of one thousand dollars for each fugitive so lost." In case the commissioner determined that the service of the negro was due the claimant, his fee was ten dollars, and one-half of that amount if the alleged fugitive was discharged.

The mere statement of the provisions of this law is its condemnation. It was a maxim among Roman lawyers that if a question arose about the civil status of an individual, he was presumed to be free until proved to be a slave.[1] The burden of proof lay on the master, the benefit of the doubt was on the side of the weaker party. Under this act of ours, the negro had no chance: the meshes of the law were artfully contrived to aid the master and entrap the slave. It seems amazing that recent legislation in Christian America on this vital point went backward from pagan Rome, and it is almost impossible to portray the spirit of the time in a manner that shall enable us to make allowance for the men who passed this act. The Northern men who supported the law or dodged the vote went counter to public sentiment at the North, which was decidedly against such a measure. Nor was it indispensable to prevent disunion. The cotton States might rally for an overt act of secession in case the Wilmot proviso were passed, or if slavery were abolished in the district; but they would not on the fugitive slave question. Indeed, when the law passed the Senate it

---

[1] Lecky's History of Morals, vol. i. p. 313; Webster's Works, vol. v. p. 309.

was generally supposed that it would undergo amendment in the House in a manner to soften its requirements.[1]

The cotton States were not the great sufferers from the loss of negroes. There were more fugitives from the four border States of Maryland, Virginia, Kentucky, and Missouri than from all the rest of the slave States,[2] and most of the congressmen from the border States would have been satisfied with a less stringent measure than the actual one. It was apparent to every one who knew anything of the sentiments of the North that this law could not be executed to any extent. Seward had truly said that if the South wished their runaway negroes returned they must alleviate, not increase, the rigors of the law of 1793;[3] and to give the alleged fugitive a jury trial, as Webster proposed, was the only possible way to effect the desired purpose.

If we look below the surface we shall find a strong impelling motive of the Southern clamor for this harsh enactment other than the natural desire to recover lost property. Early in the session it took air that a part of the game of the disunionists was to press a stringent fugitive slave law, for which no Northern man could vote; and when it was defeated, the North would be charged with refusing to carry out a stipulation of the Constitution.[4] Douglas stated in the Senate that while there was some ground for complaint on the subject of surrender of fugitives from service, it had been greatly exaggerated. The excitement and virulence were not along the line bordering on the free and slave States, but between Vermont and South Carolina, New Hampshire and Alabama, Connecticut and Louisiana.[5] Clay gave vent to his astonishment that Arkansas, Louisiana, Georgia,

---

[1] Remarks of Douglas in the Senate, Dec., 1851, Life, by Sheahan, p. 161.

[2] The number of slaves escaped for the year ending June 1st, 1850, from Maryland, Kentucky, Virginia, and Missouri, was 540; from all other States, 470. Compiled for New York *Tribune* from census returns. *Tribune,* Aug. 28th, 1851.   [3] See p. 163.

[4] New York *Tribune,* Feb. 2d.   [5] Speech, March 13th.

and South Carolina, States which very rarely lost a slave, demanded a stricter law than Kentucky, which lost many.[1] After the act was passed Senator Butler, of South Carolina, said: "I would just as soon have the law of 1793 as the present law, for any purpose, so far as regards the reclamation of fugitive slaves;" and another Southern ultra never thought it would be productive of much good to his section.[2] Six months after the passage of the law, Seward expresses the matured opinion "that political ends — merely political ends—and not real evils, resulting from the escape of slaves, constituted the prevailing motives to the enactment."[3] The admission of California was a bitter pill for the Southern ultras, but they were forced to take it. The Fugitive Slave law was a taunt and reproach to that part of the North where the anti-slavery sentiment ruled supremely, and was deemed a partial compensation.

President Fillmore's notoriety of later years came for the most part from his writing "Approved Sept. 18th, 1850," under the Fugitive Slave law. This infamous act has blighted the reputation of every one who had any connection with it, and he has suffered with the rest; yet it appears to me unjustly. It would have been a rash move on the part of the President to unsettle by his veto a question which had so long distracted the country, and which Congress had apparently composed, unless he could do so on constitutional grounds. Before signing the law, he requested the opinion of his Attorney-General on its constitutionality: this Crittenden affirmed in positive terms.[4] Webster, his Secretary of State, and the ablest lawyer in the country, likewise believed the law constitutional.[5] It is, therefore,

---

[1] Remarks in Senate, May 13th and 21st.

[2] In Senate, Feb. 22d, 1851. "We have no faith in this Fugitive Slave bill."—*De Bow's Review*, Nov., 1850.

[3] Letter to a Massachusetts convention opposed to the Fugitive Slave law, April 5th, 1851, Works, vol. iii. p. 446.

[4] For this opinion, see Life of Crittenden, Coleman, vol. i. p. 377.

[5] Private Correspondence, vol. ii. p. 402.

difficult to see how the President could do otherwise than give his approval to the compromise which had the seal of Congress.

A few considerations on the compromise as a whole may be proper before proceeding to relate how the country received the action of its representatives. It has sometimes been set forth as an abject surrender to the South,[1] but this is an unwarranted judgment. If we might eliminate the insulting provisions of the Fugitive Slave act, it would be safe to say that it was an eminently fair settlement for the North.[2] The essential and permanent advantage gained in the whole series of measures was the admission of California as a free State. The territorial question has been already considered.[3] Giddings made an impassioned appeal against the Texas Boundary bill. He said: "Sir, the payment of this ten million of dollars constituted the most objectionable feature of the 'omnibus bill.' It is designed to raise Texas scrip from fifteen cents upon the dollar to par value; to make every dollar of Texas scrip worth six and a half; to make many splendid fortunes in a short time; to rob the people, the laboring men of the nation, of this vast sum, and place it in the hands of stock-jobbers and gamblers in Texas scrip."[4] Yet it is undeniable that Texas had a claim on the United States for a portion of her debt,[5] and this bill caused little dissatisfaction at the North. The only plan besides the compromise which had Northern friends was that of Presi-

---

[1] Jefferson Davis, in a speech made at Jackson, Miss., July 6th, 1859, spoke of 1850 as "that dark period for Southern rights," and said, "Though defeated on that occasion, Southern rights gained much by the discussion."—New York *Tribune*, Aug. 31st, 1859.

[2] "I think, *regarding the thing as a compromise*, Mr. Clay has done very well."—Letter of Horace Mann, Feb. 14th, Life, p. 289.

[3] See p. 149 *et seq.*

[4] Speech in the House, Aug. 12th.

[5] H. H. Bancroft, in New Mexico and Arizona, p. 457, states that about one-half of the $10,000,000 was bonus, the intimation being that the other half was a just payment. See also New York *Tribune*, June 18th.

dent Taylor, and this left the Texas boundary question un-settled. In case Texas should endeavor to assert her claim by force of arms, General Taylor determined to resist with Federal troops any invasion into New Mexico, and he doubt-ed not that he would be successful. His military confidence was, indeed, well founded; but danger existed that in case blood were shed, the South would take sides with Texas. "The cause of Texas in such a conflict will be the cause of the entire South," wrote Alexander H. Stephens,[1] and he expressed the almost unanimous feeling of the cotton States.

Overt secession, immediate disunion, were not the dangers that Clay and Webster most feared. Both of them pro-claimed where they would be found in any such event. Clay said in the Senate: "I should deplore, as much as any man living or dead, that arms should be raised against the authority of the Union either by individuals or by States. But ... if any one State, or the portion of the people of any State, choose to place themselves in military array against the government of the Union, I am for trying the strength of the government. I am for ascertaining whether we have got a government or not. . . . Nor, sir, am I to be alarmed or dissuaded from any such course by intimations of the spilling of blood."[2] The cabinet circular, written by Web-ster in October, which he wanted sent to every official of the United States, shows clearly that he was ready to resist with the whole power of the government any overt act on the part of the South;[3] and the following June he said to a Virginian audience: "But one thing, gentlemen, be as-sured of, the first step taken in the programme of seces-

---

[1] To the editor of the *National Intelligencer*, July 4th.

[2] Remarks in the Senate, Aug. 1st.

[3] This paper was objected to by the cabinet, for political reasons, and was not used. It was not printed till 1882. Lodge, p. 331; Webster Cen-tennial volume, Oct. 12th, 1882. I am indebted for this latter reference to Mr. Lodge.

sion, which shall be an actual infringement of the Constitution or the laws, will be promptly met." [1]

But the key to the course of Webster and Clay is not found in a desire to preserve merely an external Union. They strove for a union of hearts as well as a union of law. They hoped to see exist between the two sections, as Webster said, "the sense of fraternal affection, patriotic love, and mutual regard;" [2] or, as Clay put it, "dissolution of the Union . . . may not in form take place; but next to that is a dissolution of those fraternal and kindred ties that bind us together as one free, Christian, and commercial people. In my opinion, the body politic cannot be preserved unless this agitation, this distraction, this exasperation, which is going on between the two sections of the country, shall cease." [3]   That their work came to naught was not their fault. Clay did not think the present crisis more serious than that of 1820. [4] The Missouri Compromise had, in his view, prevented disturbance thirty years, and from his point of view the hope was reasonable that the present settlement might endure as long.

When Congress met, it was admitted on all hands that legislative action was necessary. Clay and Webster were the foremost men in Congress; the responsibility of carrying a scheme devolved upon them. The plan which they should adopt must be one that could win a majority of both Houses, even if they had to sacrifice some personal predilections. It was apparent at the outset that while the Wilmot proviso might obtain a majority of the House, it could not carry the Senate, and it was therefore excluded. And while an undoubted majority of both Houses favored the admission of California, it seemed impossible to bring that question fairly before the House. Fifty members could block legislation, and more than that number were ready to op-

---

[1] Speech at Capon Springs, June, 1851.   [2] 7th-of-March speech.
[3] Speech in Senate, May 21st.   [4] Ibid.

pose by any means an attempt to force through the California bill without a settlement of the other matters in dispute; and the leaders trumped up plausible reasons for those who needed them. Unless I greatly deceive myself, these two considerations, with what has been previously urged, are sufficient to justify the compromise devised by Clay and supported by Webster.[1] No one can read carefully the debates in which these two men took part, at the same time illuminating their public utterances by the light of their private letters, without arriving at the conclusion that the mainspring of their action was unselfish devotion to what they believed the good of their country. But their course brought censure on them both, for, in the opinion of their respective sections, Clay yielded too much to the North, and Webster too much to the South. The senator from Kentucky was abused by the South, the senator from Massachusetts condemned by the North. Clay, being a consummate party leader, finally rallied to his support most of the Southern Whigs; Webster, lacking that art, and having to deal with a greater independence of sentiment, never won the thinkers and persuaders of the Northern Whig party to his side.

In awarding this praise to the two great Unionists, does it follow that the muse of history must condemn the anti-slavery Whigs and Free-soilers who opposed the compromise? By no means. It is true that had these men co-operated with the compromisers, the scheme as finally enacted might have been more favorable to the North, and it is certain that the Fugitive Slave law could have been modified or defeated. The parting of the ways was at the Wilmot proviso. The same information which Webster and Clay had in regard to the territories was open to Seward, Chase, and their coadjutors. They must have known that

---

[1] Clay is not responsible for the actual Fugitive Slave law. The bill reported from the committee of thirteen was a milder measure. As I have before stated, he was not in the Senate when the law was passed.

the probabilities were against the introduction of slavery into New Mexico and Utah.[1] But they felt that a stand must be made on the principle of permitting no more slavery in the national domain, and, while the Southern ultras were dreaming and talking of the conquest of Mexico and Cuba, they determined it should be known that there was a band of men totally opposed to the conquest of more territory, unless it were expressly understood that it should be dedicated to freedom. Hale urged, also, that if the Wilmot proviso were conceded, it would only satisfy the South for a little while, when they would make new demands.[2] It was, moreover, obvious to an astute politician like Seward, and probably to others, that a dissolution of political parties was imminent; that, to oppose the extension of slavery, the different anti-slavery elements must be fused into an organized whole; it might be called Whig or some other name, but it would be based on the principle of the Wilmot proviso. All through Seward's speeches and letters one may discover his confident belief, not only in the ultimate triumph of this principle, but in the success of the party organization that should make it a platform. The impartial years, therefore, have vindicated as right the course of Seward, Chase, Hale in the Senate, and that of Giddings, Mann, and Thaddeus Stevens in the House. Yet even the opposers of the compromise must, in after-life, have admitted to themselves that it was exceedingly fortunate that Clay's scheme was adopted. Looked on merely as a truce between the two sections, what a victory for the North it turned out to be! Not only was the North relatively more powerful when the trial came, but the Northwest, which in 1850 was as closely connected commercially with the South by the Mississippi River as it was with the East by the lakes, had become joined to New York and New England by iron bands that brought closer mercantile

---

[1] For example, see letter of Horace Mann, Life, p. 294.
[2] Remarks of Hale, Senate, May 28th.

I.—13

ties and more intimate social and political intercourse. The Northwest was in sentiment as well as in population a far stronger tower in 1860 than it would have been ten years earlier.[1] The Northwestern States in 1850 were Indiana, Illinois, Michigan, Wisconsin, and Iowa; their ten senators, and all their representatives in Congress but four, were Democrats. Considering that the slavery question in 1850 was not a party one, this is not a fact of the greatest moment, but from the subsequent political leaning of these States it is one of interest.

The response of the North to the action of Congress was on the whole favorable. The question had been a disquieting one for two years, and the settlement caused a marked feeling of relief. In the United States an accomplished fact, a decision of the majority, has wonderful power; and many who objected to the compromise before its enactment became its firm friends after it was engrossed in the statute-book. Business interests and men had, in the main, favored the proposed adjustment, and were well satisfied with the conclusion of the matter, for trade loves political repose. The iron manufacturers of Pennsylvania, the cotton and woollen manufacturers of New England, had an additional reason of satisfaction. They were especially glad to see the slavery question disposed of, for now they thought Congress could turn its attention to raising the duties fixed by the tariff of 1846. They had no hope of accomplishing anything at this session, for it had already continued longer than any previous sitting; but they thought the field was clear for action when Congress should next assemble.

The people testified in the usual way their sanction of the work of their representatives. Boston seemed especially enthusiastic. A national salute of one hundred guns was fired on the Common "as a testimonial of joy on the part of the citizens of Boston, of both political parties, at

---

[1] This idea was suggested to me by James W. Bradbury, a senator from Maine in 1850, and an influential supporter of the compromise.

the adoption of the late measures of Congress."[1] Ten
thousand names signed the call for a Union meeting at
New York City.[2] It was large and enthusiastic; it cordially approved the compromise, declared the Fugitive Slave
law constitutional, promised to support the execution of it,
and deprecated the further agitation of slavery. At Philadelphia there was a meeting of six or seven thousand;[3]
the resolutions were similar to those of New York, but, in
addition, they demanded the repeal of the Pennsylvania
statute which conflicted with the execution of the Fugitive
Slave law. A Union meeting at Concord, N. H.,[4] which
was addressed by Franklin Pierce, approved the compromise, opposed the higher-law doctrine, and gave a mild
approbation to the measure for the recovery of runaway
negroes. An enthusiastic assemblage at Dayton, O.,[5] urged
thereto by the eloquence of Clement L. Vallandigham,
declared that the settlement was the "best attainable,"
and that "the Union, the Constitution, and the laws must
and shall be maintained." A Union meeting in Cincinnati[6]
adopted similar resolutions, and condemned further agitation of the slave question. Finally, Faneuil Hall resounded
with the eloquence of Rufus Choate and Benjamin R. Curtis,[7] the great lawyers of Boston. Their hearers resolved
that the adjustment "ought to be carried out in good faith,"
and that "every form of resistance to the execution of a
law, except legal process, is subversive and tends to anarchy."

---

[1] Boston *Advertiser*, Sept. 21st.

[2] Oct. 30th. New York *Tribune;* but this journal thinks that, "considering the threats held out of publishing the names of all traders
who refused to sign as men to be avoided by Southern purchasers
in our market, it is rather surprising that they were not able to sweep
clean the mercantile streets." Perkins, Warren & Co. published a card
in the *National Intelligencer* of Dec. 17th denying that they were abolition
merchants, a report which had got into circulation in the South.

[3] Nov. 21st, New York *Tribune.*   [4] Nov. 20th, Boston *Advertiser.*

[5] Oct. 26th, *National Intelligencer.*   [6] Nov. 14th, ibid.

[7] Nov. 26th, Boston *Advertiser.*

When it was known that the compromise would certainly be adopted, the *National Intelligencer* remarked that it could fill a double sheet of forty-eight columns with extracts full of joy and gratulation from the Southern and Western papers alone at the success of the measure.[1] The States of Maryland, Virginia, Kentucky, and Missouri were thoroughly satisfied. The Georgia convention was held in December. It was a representative body; over 71,000, or three-quarters of the voters of the State, had taken part in the election of delegates.[2] While it did not wholly approve of the compromise, it would abide by it as a "permanent adjustment of the sectional controversy." The fifth resolution stated, "That it is the deliberate opinion of this convention that upon the faithful execution of the Fugitive Slave bill by the proper authorities depends the preservation of our much-loved Union."[3] New Orleans held an enthusiastic Union meeting. In fact, the people of the South, outside of South Carolina and Mississippi, were generally satisfied with the result, and even in Mississippi a strong Union feeling existed. An adjourned meeting of the Nashville Convention was held in November; the attendance was small, and the proceedings attracted little attention. The convention complained of the failure to extend the Missouri Compromise line to the Pacific, of the admission of California, of the organization of the territories without protection to property of the South, of the dismemberment of Texas, and of the abolition of the slave-trade in the District of Columbia; it asserted the right of secession,[4] but these declarations had little responsive echo beyond South Carolina and Mississippi.

A large number of active and influential people at the North, however, totally condemned the Fugitive Slave law. An immense Free-soil meeting at Lowell, Mass., a gathering of all parties in Syracuse, N. Y., an indignation meeting at

---

[1] Sept. 17th.
[2] Boston *Atlas*, Dec. 17th.
[3] *National Intelligencer*, Dec. 14th.
[4] *National Intelligencer*, Nov. 26th.

Springfield, Mass., denounced the enactment.[1] On October
14th several thousand people filled Faneuil Hall with a like
purpose; they were presided over by Charles Francis Adams;
a sympathetic letter from the veteran Josiah Quincy was
read, and the burning eloquence of Wendell Phillips and
Theodore Parker animated the people. They resolved that
the law was against the golden rule and God's own command; that it was contradictory of the Declaration of Independence and inconsistent with the Constitution.[2] In the
latter part of the same month the common council of Chicago declared that the act for the recovery of fugitive slaves
violated the Constitution of the United States and the laws
of God; that senators and representatives from the free
States who voted for the bill, or " basely sneaked away from
their seats and thereby evaded the question, . . . are fit only
to be ranked with the traitors Benedict Arnold and Judas
Iscariot." One of the resolutions requested citizens, officers,
and police of the city to abstain from all interference in the
capture of any fugitive. But while one meeting of citizens
sustained the resolutions of the city council, a larger one,
succeeding the first, though mainly composed of the same
people, was over-persuaded by the vigorous oratory of Senator Douglas, and resolved that all laws of Congress ought
to be faithfully executed. Douglas afterwards boasted in
the Senate that this speech of his was the first public one
" ever made in a free State in defence of the Fugitive law,
and the Chicago meeting was the first public assemblage in
any free State that determined to support and sustain it."[3]
Charles Sumner addressed a Faneuil Hall meeting early in
November. He did not believe that the Fugitive Slave law
would be executed in Massachusetts, but he continued: " I
counsel no violence. There is another power, stronger than

---

[1] These meetings took place in October. Rise and Fall of the Slave
Power, vol. ii. pp. 305 and 306 ; Boston *Advertiser*, Oct. 2d.

[2] Boston *Atlas*, Oct. 15th.

[3] Life of Douglas, Sheahan, p. 162 *et seq.*

any individual arm, which I invoke; I mean that irresistible public opinion inspired by love of God and man, which, without violence or noise, gently as the operations of nature, makes and unmakes laws. Let this public opinion be felt in its might, and the Fugitive Slave bill will become everywhere among us a dead letter." [1]

A very potent influence on political sentiment now began to be exerted on the anti-slavery side. Preachers in their pulpits, in meetings, in conference, in synod, pronounced against the Fugitive Slave act as being in conflict with the law of God. [2] The great majority of the Protestant clergy of the North unquestionably sympathized with this sentiment. The working of this act was in one respect especially iniquitous. Applied to fugitive slaves, no matter when they had escaped, it was an *ex post facto* law: it thus brought under its provisions negroes who had been living in peace and quiet for many years at the North. There was no statute of limitations for the escaped bondman. All over the North, immediately on the passage of the act, these negroes took alarm, and thousands fled to Canada, abandoning their homes and forsaking situations which gave them a livelihood. [3] There was so much excitement among the negro population of Boston that the Faneuil Hall meeting before referred to pledged their colored citizens their help, advised them to stay, and to have no fear of being taken back to bondage.

---

[1] Rise and Fall of the Slave Power, vol. ii. p. 308.
[2] Ibid., p. 310.
[3] Life of William Lloyd Garrison, vol. iii. p. 302.

CHAPTER III

For the sake of riveting the attention of the reader on the compromise measures, certain events have been passed over which, before leaving the year 1850, should receive mention.

The most important diplomatic achievement of the Taylor administration was the negotiation of the Clayton-Bulwer treaty. A ship-canal from the Atlantic to the Pacific was dreamed of as early as 1826, and is referred to by Clay in one of his diplomatic instructions. Should such a canal be constructed, "the benefits of it," he wrote, "ought not to be exclusively appropriated to any one nation, but should be extended to all parts of the globe." Nine years later the Senate and President Jackson assented to the same principle; and President Polk carried the idea into execution in the treaty with New Granada, by which the United States agreed to guarantee the neutrality of the Isthmus of Panama so that a canal or railroad might be constructed between the two seas, and the Panama route be "open to all nations on the same terms." [1] There were three passes from ocean to ocean—the Panama, the Nicaragua, and the Tehuantepec; and it was deemed practicable to build a railroad or canal by any one of them.

When Clayton entered upon the duties of the State Department, he found the Nicaragua route demanding immediate attention. Two companies of capitalists—one British, one American, the latter headed by Commodore Vanderbilt—

---

[1] Message of President Polk in transmitting the treaty, *Congressional Globe*, vol. xxvii. p. 253.

were each endeavoring to get a grant from the government
of Nicaragua for the purpose of constructing a ship-canal,
the American company seeking the aid of their own government. The commercial question was complicated by a difference between Nicaragua and the British government.
Long before our Revolution, England had a settlement at
Balize, in the Bay of Honduras, and assumed a protectorate
over the Mosquito Indians who occupied a strip of the coast
along the Caribbean Sea. It was claimed by England that
the port of San Juan fell within the limits of this protectorate, but this was denied by Nicaragua. In January,
1848, two British ships of war entered the San Juan River,
stormed the fort, and gained possession of the town.

At this time, owing to the efforts which were made by the
rival American and English companies, a jealous feeling existed on the part of both of "these great maritime powers,"
each being "desirous of obtaining some exclusive advantage
to itself in reference to the opening of this route of inter-
oceanic communication."[1] It was absolutely necessary that
there should be an understanding between the United States
and Great Britain, and a treaty was concluded April 19th between Clayton and Henry Lytton Bulwer, the British Minister.

The purpose of the convention was stated to be "for fa-
cilitating and protecting the construction of a ship-canal between the Atlantic and Pacific oceans" by the Nicaragua
route. Both governments pledged themselves never to obtain exclusive control over said canal; never to erect fortifi-
cations commanding the same; and not to colonize, or assume or exercise any dominion over, Nicaragua, Costa Rica,
the Mosquito coast or any part of Central America. They
agree to protect the company that shall undertake the work,
and they will exert the influence which they possess with
the Central American governments to facilitate its construction. The United States and Great Britain will guarantee

---

[1] The words of Edward Everett, Senate, March 21st, 1853.

the neutrality and security of the canal when completed, so long as no unfair discriminations are made or unreasonable tolls exacted; and they invite all friendly States to enter into similar stipulations with them, as the great design of this convention was the construction and maintenance of a ship-communication between the two oceans "for the benefit of mankind on equal terms to all." By the eighth article of the treaty, the governments of the United States and Great Britain expressed the desire not only " to accomplish a particular object, but to establish a general principle, and they agree to extend their protection by treaty stipulations" to a canal or railway that may be constructed by the way of Tehuantepec or Panama.

Before the ratifications of the treaty were exchanged, Bulwer notified Clayton that he was instructed to insist on an explanatory declaration that the stipulations as to the neutral territory did not apply to Balize, or, as it was more frequently called, British Honduras. Before replying, the Secretary of State asked William R. King, who was chairman of the Committee on Foreign Relations, what was the understanding of the Senate when the treaty was confirmed. King wrote that " the Senate perfectly understood that the treaty did not include British Honduras." [1] Clayton then answered Bulwer to that effect.

The treaty was ratified in the Senate by a vote of 42 to 10.   In the affirmative may be found the names of Webster, Clay, Seward, and Cass, each of whom, at some portion of his life, occupied the State department, and three of whom are renowned for their diplomatic achievements. Seward and Edward Everett, another Secretary of State and accomplished diplomat, afterwards defended the treaty in the Senate. [2]

The treaty was favorable to unrestricted commercial intercourse, and was in line with our traditional policy. Yet it has given rise to many disputed questions, for the United

---

[1] Seward's Works, vol. i. p. 385.   [2] Jan. 10th and March 21st, 1853.

States and England drew a different meaning from several
of the articles. Less than three years after its conclusion
its provisions were severely criticised in the Senate; and
under the Pierce and Buchanan administrations it became a
subject of controversy with England. Although, after this,
the question slept for a long time, it was revived by the discussion which grew out of the undertaking of the French
company to construct a canal across the Isthmus of Panama,
and the policy of our government in making such a treaty
was then much questioned.[1]

The Galphin affair has been referred to,[2] and it is now
time to give an account of it. The Galphin claim dated back
to a time before the Revolutionary War, and was originally
on the colony and State of Georgia. George W. Crawford,
the Secretary of War under President Taylor, became in 1835
attorney for the claimants, with a contingent fee of one-half
of the claim, and he urged it before the Georgia legislature
without success. It afterwards appears as a claim on the
United States. On what ground it was turned over to the
general government is irrelevant to my narrative; but in
the hot August days towards the end of the Congressional
session of 1848 it was carried through the House during an

---

[1] Treaties and Conventions, Haswell, p. 440; International Law Digest,
Wharton, § 150 f. See the debate in the Senate, Jan. and March, 1853,
especially the speeches of Seward, Clayton, and Everett, defending the
treaty; the speech of Douglas, criticising it; and the remarks of Cass,
censuring Clayton severely for his "unprecedented error" in coming to
an understanding with Bulwer, which changed the construction and
"vital point" of the treaty without the knowledge of the Senate. *Congressional Globe*, vols. xxvi. and xxvii.; Seward's Works, vol. i. p. 376. See
also article "British Honduras," Encyclopædia Britannica. For the am-
biguity in the construction of the treaty, see Curtis's Life of Webster, vol.
ii., and Life of Buchanan, by same author; see Buchanan's message, Dec.
3d, 1860. Appendix to *Congressional Globe*, p. 4; also article "Treaties,"
in Lalor's Cyclopædia of Political Science, by J. Bancroft Davis; and
diplomatic correspondence between Secretary Blaine and Lord Granville
in 1881, and between Secretary Frelinghuysen and Granville in 1882 and
1883.   [2] See p. 176.

exhausting night sitting, unnoticed and without a word of discussion. This order, which became a law, directed the Secretary of the Treasury " to examine and adjust the claim of the late George Galphin, . . . and to pay the amount which may be found due." In the closing days of the Polk administration, Crawford received $43,518.97, this being the principal of the claim; but no interest was allowed, although the demand for it had been made. After Crawford became Secretary of War, his client requested him to prosecute the claim for interest. Crawford's name now disappears from the record as attorney, but the affair was pressed with such vigor that the demand for back interest was submitted by the Secretary of the Treasury to the comptroller, a man of large business experience and sound judgment, by whom it was disallowed. The question was then put to the Attorney-General whether the law of 1848 did not require the payment of interest. The answer was yes; whereupon, although Congress was in session, the Secretary of the Treasury paid the claimant interest from May 2d, 1775, amounting to $191,352.89, of which the attorney of record received $3000, and George W. Crawford one half the remainder, or $94,176.44.

When this fact became known there was severe comment on it by the press, in which the New York *Tribune*, a Whig and administration journal, joined.[1] This prompted Crawford to demand an investigation from the House, and a committee was appointed, who reported that the payment of interest was not "in conformity with law and precedent." From the evidence it appeared that Crawford had made a partial statement of the matter to the President, who saw noth-

---

[1] "Thoughtlessness has brought the administration into a strait from which they cannot escape with honor and safety without the resignation of at least the Secretary of War and the Attorney-General, if not also of the Secretary of the Treasury; $192,000 of *interest* allowed contrary to settled custom, and nearly half of it going into the hands of the Secretary of War, makes a startling case!"—Seward to Weed, April 1st, 1850, Life of Seward, vol. ii. p. 130.

ing inconsistent between his cabinet position and his share
in the claim. Crawford testified that he had never told the
Secretary of the Treasury or the Attorney-General of his
connection with the business, but that he had urged them to
make a prompt disposition of the case. Meredith and Johnson[1] denied that they had any knowledge of Crawford's
interest, which demonstrates that their examination of the
papers on file was cursory, since these plainly showed that
he was acting in the affair. Even from such a brief relation,
it will be seen that this was an administration scandal of no
mean proportions. It would have attracted much greater
attention had the slavery question not so absorbed Congress,
but, nevertheless, the relation of the cabinet ministers to the
affair was a subject of severe animadversion in the House.
On the day of General Taylor's death this body was considering a resolution which disapproved of and dissented
from the opinion of the Attorney-General and the action of
the Secretary of the Treasury, reflected severely on the relation of the Secretary of War to the matter as being an
improper and dangerous precedent, and implied a censure
of the President for the opinion he had given Crawford;
but during the discussion the House received the news that
the condition of the President was so critical that he could
not survive an hour, and it therefore adjourned. After his
death and the appointment of a new cabinet, the subject
ceased to attract attention. The affair, however, was the
greatest trouble General Taylor had during his short term
of office. It was charged in the House that Crawford had
plundered the public treasury, and that the President and
other members of the cabinet had "connived at and sanctioned the enormous allowance." General Taylor, in money
affairs, was strictly honest;[2] in fact, he was very sensitive
on that point, and it is not to be wondered at that his death-
bed was disturbed by reflections on the indiscretion or dis-

---

[1] The Secretary of the Treasury and the Attorney-General.

[2] Scott's Autobiography, vol. ii. p. 390.

honesty of his chosen advisers.[1] General Taylor did not understand the matter fully: he either supposed that the claim for interest would come before Congress, or he was too confiding to suspect that Crawford suppressed a part of the story to obtain his approval. But before his death he comprehended the situation, and was on the point of making those changes in his cabinet which the affair imperatively demanded.[2]

The diplomatic history of this year would not be complete without a notice of the Hülsemann letter, the most striking of any of Webster's state papers while he was connected with the Fillmore administration. During the progress of the Hungarian revolution, under the leading of Louis Kossuth, President Taylor sent a special agent to Europe to watch and report upon the progress of events, with a possible view to the recognition of Hungary. This, coming to the knowledge of the Austrian government, caused offence, and there ensued between the two countries a correspondence which was still pending when Webster became Secretary of State. In September, Hülsemann, the Austrian *chargé-d'affaires* sent a haughty and dictatorial letter. The reception of such a missive proved a lucky chance for an American Secretary of State gifted with rare command of language; it paved the way for a declaration of sentiments that have ever a zealous response from the American heart. Webster's reasoning was a complete refutation of the position Hülsemann had taken. He earnestly defended our right to view with great interest "the extraordinary events" which have occurred not only in Austria, but "in many other parts of Europe since February, 1848." But the Secretary goes further, "and freely admits that in proportion as these extraordinary events appeared to have their origin

---

[1] See p. 176.

[2] Autobiography of Thurlow Weed, p. 589. I have made up this account from the three reports of the House committee, and the debate on them in the House.

in those great ideas of responsible and popular governments
on which the American constitutions themselves are wholly
founded, they could not but command the warm sympathy
of the people of this country. . . . The power of this republic, at the present moment, is spread over a region, one of
the richest and most fertile on the globe, and of an extent
in comparison with which the possessions of the House of
Hapsburg are but as a patch on the earth's surface." Then
follow well-chosen words depicting our present and increasing population, our navigation and commerce, our protection to life, liberty, property, and personal rights. "Nevertheless, the United States have abstained, at all times, from
acts of interference with the political changes of Europe.
They cannot, however, fail to cherish always a lively interest in the fortunes of nations struggling for institutions like
their own." The style, while not of the "spread-eagle"
character, approaches it as closely as dignity and good taste
would allow. Webster himself thought the letter "boastful
and rough," but one of his excuses was that he wished to
"touch the national pride and make a man feel sheepish
and look silly who should speak of disunion." [1] The letter
was received with great enthusiasm in the Senate, the sentiments being cordially endorsed by both parties; and although hardly more than a stump speech under diplomatic
guise, it received commendation among liberal circles in
England. [2]

The President, in his message to Congress on their re-
assembling in December, praised highly the compromise. It
was, however, true that the beneficent purpose of this series
of measures had not yet been wholly realized. "It would be
strange," he said, "if they had been received with immediate approbation by people and States prejudiced and heated
by the exciting controversies of their representatives. I believe those measures to have been required by the circumstances and condition of the country. . . . They were adopted

---

[1] Curtis, vol. ii. p. 537.   [2] *Westminster Review*, Jan., 1853.

in the spirit of conciliation and for the purpose of conciliation.   I believe that a great majority of our fellow-citizens sympathize in that spirit and purpose, and in the main
approve, and are prepared, in all respects, to sustain, these
enactments."

In January, 1851, a pledge was signed by several members of Congress which declared that they would not support for any office whatever any man " who is not known
to be opposed to the disturbance of the settlement, and to
the renewal, in any form, of agitation upon the subject of
slavery."   This had ten signatures from the free States
and thirty-four from the slave States; among the latter were
the names of Clay, Howell Cobb, the speaker of the House,
Alexander H. Stephens, and Robert Toombs.   The President in his message made a fair and intelligent statement
of the public sentiment on the compromise prevailing at
the North in the early months of the new year.   The
Northern Democrats, with the exception of a diminishing
number of Free-soilers, unreservedly accepted the adjustment, and so did the Webster and Fillmore Whigs.   The
Seward Whigs took the position that these measures were
the law of the land ; that whatever in them was irrepealable no one would be mad enough " to attempt to repeal ;"[1]
and that the Fugitive Slave law demanded obedience, but
that it ought to be abrogated.   The abolitionists, who may
be defined as those who determined to agitate the question
not only until the extension of slavery should be restricted,
but until it was abolished in the States, did not accept the
compromise, and sympathized with resistance to the Fugitive
Slave law.   The Concord philosopher, who was esteemed a
moderate abolitionist, plainly expressed the sentiment of
these people : " The act of Congress of September 18th,
1850, is a law which every one of you will break on the
earliest occasion—a law which no man can obey, or abet the
obeying, without loss of self-respect and forfeiture of the

---

[1] Letter of Seward, Works, vol. iii. p. 448.

name of a gentleman." [1]   Nothing better illustrates the difference between the position of the anti-slavery statesman and the agitator than certain corrections made by Sumner in an article on slavery written by Theodore Parker for the use of a Massachusetts legislative committee. The additions of Sumner are the words in brackets. " We regard the Fugitive Slave law as morally [not legally, but morally] invalid and void; and [though binding on the conduct] no more binding on the conscience of any man than a law would be which should command the people to enslave all the tall men or all the short men, and deliver them up on claims to be held in bondage forever." [2]

The Fugitive Slave law did not work as smoothly as its supporters wished; and while Clay maintained that it had been executed in Indiana, Ohio, Pennsylvania, in New York City, and, in fact, everywhere except in Boston, other senators from the South declared that its operation left much to be desired. Not only had two runaway negroes been spirited away from Boston to England, but Mason, of Virginia, told of what happened to a neighbor who had pursued two slaves to Harrisburg, Pa., where he had had them arrested. The owner finally recovered his property. But it was only after a tedious delay of two months, during which time he and his

---

[1] Life of Emerson, Cabot, p. 578, Emerson's address at Concord, May 3d, 1851. " Cette loi [the Fugitive Slave law] est en ce moment la pierre d'achoppement contre laquelle le *compromis* est toujours près de se briser."—Promenade en Amérique, Ampère, tome i. p. 408.

[2] The book referred to, containing this essay, was Parker's own, and is in the Boston Public Library. In Parker's own pencil handwriting on the margin I find: " these in [ ] added by Sumner." The article was written March, 1851. I take this opportunity of saying that in the preparation of this work I have used freely the Boston Public Library, the Athenæum, the College Library of Harvard University, the Astor Library of New York, the Congressional Library of Washington, the Case and Public Libraries and the library of the Historical Society of Cleveland. I desire to recognize the intelligent aid of Mr. Brett, the librarian of the Public Library of Cleveland, and to acknowledge my indebtedness to Mr. Frederic Bancroft, the librarian of the Department of State.

companions were put in prison and subjected to a trial for riot. The expenses of the Virginian in this affair were fourteen hundred and fifty dollars, and when he carried his slaves home he sold the two for fifteen hundred dollars.[1] Only after litigation of ten days or a fortnight had a fugitive been reclaimed in New York City; the slave was carried home and sold, but the proceeds of the sale barely met the expenses, although Mason had heard it stated that a committee of citizens in New York had actually contributed five hundred dollars to the owner.[2] In Ohio, the Senator had heard of one case where the fugitive was easily recovered, but that was a woman who confessed to being a slave, and of course had been sent back. In Detroit, Mich., a runaway negro was reclaimed, but a mob had gathered, and only after the military were called out had the undertaking been successful. Although, according to trustworthy estimates, there were fifteen thousand fugitives in the free States, another Southern senator complained that only four or five had been recaptured under the law of September, 1850.

This interesting discussion in the Senate was prompted by a noteworthy affair which had just taken place in Boston. On the 15th of February a negro by the name of Shadrach, employed in the Cornhill coffee-house, was arrested on the charge of having escaped the previous May. On being brought before the commissioner, George Ticknor Curtis, he, finding the fugitive unprepared with counsel, adjourned the proceedings to the next day. Under the law of Massachusetts her jails could not be used for the imprisonment of fugitive slaves, and as Shadrach had been remanded

---

[1] Clay mentioned to Mason that the comptroller had just passed an account in which twelve hundred or thirteen hundred dollars were allowed to the marshal for carrying back the fugitive slaves in that case.

[2] Senator Dickinson, of New York, assured Mason that the expenses of the claimant in this case were entirely paid by the citizens of New York City.

I.—14

to the custody of the deputy marshal, he was detained in
the United States court-room in the court-house, situated
in the heart of the city.   A mob of colored men broke into
the room, took off the alleged fugitive, who soon got to
Canada, beyond the clutches of the United States law, and,
owing to the time-honored decision of Lord Mansfield, became a freeman.   When Theodore Parker heard of the
arrest he went immediately down to Court Square, intending to help in the rescue, but the act had been accomplished
before he arrived.   He writes in his journal: "This Shadrach
is delivered out of his burning, fiery furnace without the
smell of fire on his garments. . . . I think it is the most
noble deed done in Boston since the destruction of the tea
in 1773."   This rescue created a great deal of excitement,
and nowhere more than among the law-givers at Washington.   The President immediately issued a proclamation
which appealed in the usual terms to all good citizens, commanding all civil and military officers to assist in putting
down any combinations whose purpose was to resist the law,
and to aid in the arrest of those who had set the law at defiance.   No practical result came from the energetic action
of the administration.   Five of the rescuers were indicted
and tried, but, as the jury could not agree, they were not convicted.   The incident demonstrated that in Massachusetts the
Fugitive Slave law would only be enforced with difficulty.
Undoubtedly the vast majority of the citizens of Boston had
a passive, if not an active, sympathy with the officers of the
government; but every one well understood that back of
this negro mob which rescued Shadrach was a vigilance
committee composed of men of influence and good position.
This committee had an efficient organization, and aimed to
prevent the arrest of fugitives, or, when they were seized, to
give them legal aid and interpose every lawful obstacle to
their rendition.[1]

---

[1] This account I have made up from the debate in the Senate on the
subject in Feb.,1851; from the Life of Webster, by Curtis; Rise and Fall of

Yet law in Boston was clothed with majesty, and the majority of the citizens felt that even an unjust law were better executed than resisted. The common council, with praiseworthy motives, directed that the mayor and city marshal should use the police force most energetically in support of the law and maintenance of the public peace. On the 3d of April the city police, on a warrant issued by commissioner Curtis, arrested Thomas Sims, a slave who had escaped from a Georgia owner, and confined him in the court-house. Fearing an attempt at rescue, a strong guard was set and the court-house surrounded with heavy chains. The fugitive had good volunteer counsel, but the case was plain. He was adjudged to the claimant, and the Shadrach affair had so excited apprehension that he was taken from his place of imprisonment at five o'clock in the morning, escorted by three hundred police disposed in hollow square around him. The militia were under arms in Faneuil Hall, but they were not needed, as the police met not the slightest resistance. The negro was safely put on board a vessel which took him to Savannah.[1]

Since the Revolutionary War not a slave had been sent back from Boston by legal process,[2] and this rendition caused intense feeling. On the day of the arrest a meeting was held on the Common, where Wendell Phillips spoke; in the evening Theodore Parker addressed a gathering at Tremont Temple. Five days later, a convention met at the latter place, presided over by Horace Mann, who alluded in scathing words to the fact that Faneuil Hall had been denied

---

the Slave Power, Wilson; and Life and Correspondence of Theodore Parker, Weiss. Parker and Phillips were members of this vigilance committee. For other members, and an account of it, see Life of Parker, Frothingham, p. 401.

[1] Rise and Fall of the Slave Power, vol. ii.; Life of Theodore Parker, vol. ii. The placard given on following page, which was posted at all corners by the vigilance committee, is an illustration of their manner of work. See Life of Parker, Weiss, vol. ii. p. 104.

[2] Life of Parker, vol. ii. p. 107.

them. "But then there is a melancholy propriety in this," he said; "when the court-house is in chains, Faneuil Hall may well be dumb." Among the speakers were Henry Wilson and Thomas W. Higginson, and William Lloyd Garrison addressed another assemblage. The burden of all these meetings was a protest against the Fugitive Slave law and severe denunciation of all who were concerned in the arrest

---

PROCLAMATION!!

TO ALL

THE GOOD PEOPLE OF MASSACHUSETTS!

Be it known that there are now

THREE SLAVE-HUNTERS OR KIDNAPPERS

IN BOSTON

Looking for their prey. One of them is called

"DAVIS."

He is an unusually ill-looking fellow, about five feet eight inches high, wide-shouldered. He has a big mouth, black hair, and a good deal of dirty bushy hair on the lower part of his face. He has a Roman nose; one of his eyes has been knocked out. He looks like a Pirate, and knows how to be a Stealer of Men.

The next is called

EDWARD BARRETT.

He is about five feet six inches high, thin and lank, is apparently about thirty years old. His nose turns up a little. He has a long mouth, long thin ears, and dark eyes. His hair is dark, and he has a bunch of fur on his chin. He had on a blue frock-coat, with a velvet collar, mixed pants, and a figured vest. He wears his shirt collar turned down, and has a black string—not of hemp—about his neck.

The third ruffian is named

ROBERT M. BACON, *alias* JOHN D. BACON.

He is about fifty years old, five feet and a half high. He has a red, intemperate-looking face, and a retreating forehead. His hair is dark, and a little gray. He wears a black coat, mixed pants, and a purplish vest. He looks sleepy, and yet malicious.

Given at Boston, this 4th day of April, in the year of our Lord, 1851, and of the Independence of the United States the fifty-fourth.

God save the Commonwealth of Massachusetts!

and surrender of Sims. On the day that the fugitive was delivered over to his claimant funeral bells were tolled.

But Faneuil Hall was not closed only against the abolitionists. In this same month of April, the board of aldermen refused the use of it to many Whig and Democratic citizens of Boston who wished to unite in a public reception to Webster, then at Marshfield. The excuse made was that since the hall had been denied to Wendell Phillips and his associates, it could not consistently be opened for a meeting on the other side which purposed approval of the compromise measures; but every one understood the action to be a reflection on Webster's course for the past year. This awoke a storm of indignation that was not lessened by the dignified and manly way in which the Secretary of State met the occasion. Afterwards the city council offered him the use of Faneuil Hall, but this he declined in a courteous manner, adding that he should not " enter Faneuil Hall till its gates shall be thrown open, wide open, ' not with impetuous recoil, grating harsh thunder,' but with ' harmonious sound on golden hinges moving,' to let in freely and to overflowing . . . all men of all parties who are true to the Union as well as to liberty."

Webster's path for the last year had indeed been among the thorns of the world. In February a brutal attack was made in the House upon his private character by Allen, a Free-soil member from the Worcester, Mass., district. While the slander was at bottom prompted by partisan motives, yet the bit of truth in it stung Webster to the very depth of his honest soul. The point under discussion was the appropriation of the money for the last instalment of the indemnity due Mexico under the treaty of 1848, amounting to more than $3,000,000, due in May, 1852. The Secretary of State had contracted with a syndicate of bankers of Boston, New York, and Washington for the payment and transfer of this, as well as the previous instalment, to Mexico. These bankers paid three and one half per cent. premium for the privilege. It was shown during the discus-

sion that four per cent. premium might have been obtained
from the Rothschilds, so that the government had not done
as well by about $30,000 as it might have done. This gave
Allen an opportunity to object decidedly to the Secretary of
State having anything to do with the pecuniary concerns of
the government, because he held his place " less as a servant
and stipendiary of the government than a servant and stipendiary of bankers and brokers." Allen said there was
undoubted authority for the statement that when the President offered Webster the position of Secretary of State he
wrote to Boston to know what would be done for him in a
financial way. An arrangement had then been made with
the bankers and brokers of Boston and New York by which
$25,000 should be raised for him in each city as a compensa-
tion for taking the position in the cabinet ; that the amount
was collected in New York, but that it fell somewhat short
in Boston, for " gentlemen in Boston had bled so freely on
former occasions of a similar character that it was difficult
to raise the full amount." In fact, Allen continued, our Secretary of State was the pensioner of Wall Street and State
Street, and this lucrative contract with these bankers gave
them a chance to recoup themselves at the government's
cost. This charge was baseless, and it was felt on all sides
of the House to be a shameful one. Although neither Webster himself nor his friends interposed any obstacle to a full
inquiry into the matter, the House, by the overwhelming
vote of 119 to 35, refused to consider a resolution providing
for the appointment of a committee of investigation, and
passed the appropriation, which, however, for want of time,
failed in the Senate. At the next session all amendments
putting any limitations on the administration as to the manner of payment were rejected, and the appropriation pure
and simple passed both Houses. This completely vindicated
Webster. The bit of truth in the scandal was the fact that,
some weeks after he had taken the position of Secretary of
State, a gift of money for the extraordinary expenses of his
table was presented him by some men from Boston ; but

most of those who joined in the subscription were gentlemen retired from affairs, only two of them being bankers, and Webster did not know the name or position of any one of the subscribers. Allen's charge, however, was so positive and direct that it lived in brass, while the denial was written in water.[1] Any one who understood Webster knew that he was incapable of making a sordid bargain with his moneyed friends for accepting a cabinet position. In fact, lack of thrift and no knack at bargaining brought him into this and other trouble. This charge has here been baldly stated, for one who takes up the cudgels for Webster need not suppress any fact. Unquestionably many people will consider it a surprising *naïveté* of judgment to assert that Webster was honest at heart. But if we can only view his failing with the same charity which we every day employ in judging our acquaintances and our friends, we shall have a complete key to his conduct in affairs. Do we not all know men—and men in the noblest professions—who, morally sound, yet lack thrift, and who are continually in trouble on this account? But we make excuses for them; knowing them through and through, we do not say that their hearts are rotten. If we judge Webster with like charity, we shall arrive at a similar conclusion.

In the history of the decade between 1850 and 1860 the overpowering question is slavery, and to that must our attention chiefly be directed. Yet it is a gratification for the historian to record that though the public mind was so fully engrossed with this one idea, legislators still found time to enact measures that were in the line of true progress. There has been so much descant on the commercial, social, and intellectual benefits of cheap postage that in civilized

---

[1] For the charge of Allen, see *Congressional Globe*, vol. xxiii. pp. 686, 696, vol. xxiv. p. 371 *et seq.* For the defence, see Ashmun's remarks, vol. xxiii. pp. 687, 697; Davis's remarks, vol. xxiv. p. 373; Franklin Haven's letter to Boston *Transcript* of May 17th, 1851, ibid., p. 375; Curtis, voL ii. p. 492 *et seq.* The salary of the Secretary of State was then $6000.

countries it has become a governmental axiom that the increase in the revenue of the post-office department and the decline of rates of postage is a true mark of growth in civilization. The Congress which adjourned March 3d, 1851, took a step in this direction. The rates of postage at the organization of the post-office department were, for a single letter (that is, a single piece of paper), from eight to twenty-five cents, according to the distance, with a minimum distance of forty miles and a maximum of five hundred. These charges had been twice reduced, and on the opening of this session of Congress the postage for a letter not exceeding one-half ounce in weight was five cents under three hundred miles; over three hundred miles, ten cents; and to the Pacific territories, via Panama, forty cents. The revenues of the Postmaster-General's department exceeding the expenditures, he therefore recommended a reduction in the inland letter postage to three cents. The President concurred in this recommendation, and the subject was soon taken up by Congress. That body appreciated that the rapid extension of steam transportation for the past two years, with the abundant promise of further progress in that direction, was certain to result in a great reduction in the cost of the service. It was stated during the discussion that, while ten cents was the postage on a letter from Detroit to Buffalo, a barrel of flour was carried between the two cities on the same conveyance for the same money.[1] The bill which passed Congress made the rate for a prepaid letter, not weighing over half an ounce, three cents for under three thousand miles ; six cents for over that distance.

The most exciting event of the summer was the expedition to Cuba under the lead of Lopez. This adventurer had engaged in two unsuccessful attempts to give freedom to his adopted country, and with dauntless spirit was ready to head another enterprise. He fell in with a clique of

---

[1] That is, by steamboat. There was then no railroad between Buffalo and Detroit.

speculators at New Orleans, who cherished wild dreams of magnificence and wealth which the expected easy conquest of Cuba would realize. These men were willing to risk their money, though not their lives, and in Lopez they found a ready instrument. He, in fact, was only too glad to meet persons who would back with money his visionary schemes. Cuban bonds were issued, signed by General Narciso Lopez, " chief of the patriotic junta for the promotion of the political interests of Cuba, and the contemplated head of the provisional government, and commander-in-chief of the revolutionary movement about to be now undertaken through my agency and permissive authority for the liberation of Cuba." Everybody knew that the payment of the bonds was based on the success of the revolution, but those who invested large amounts of money in them at from three to twenty cents on the dollar thought the speculation one of great promise. Lopez and the schemers deluded themselves; it was easy for them to dupe others. The ways and means being provided, a man of ability and influence was desired as leader of the expedition. Lopez offered the command to Jefferson Davis, then a United States senator, who, deeming it inconsistent with his duty, declined it, at the same time recommending Robert E. Lee. Lee was then invited to take the leadership of the expedition, but, believing that his position in the United States army should prevent him from giving heed to such a proposal, he refused it.[1] General Lopez was therefore left in sole command; but it was not difficult to get more followers than he could use, for the undertaking was called an easy one, and unusual inducements were held out to those who would enlist. It was said that not only were the creoles anxious to rebel against Spain, but they had decided upon that step, and a well-planned revolution was already in progress. The Spanish army had been tampered with and would frater-

---

[1] Memoir of Jefferson Davis, by his Wife, vol. i. p. 412; Life of Robert E. Lee, Long, p. 72.

nize with the invaders ; all the officers of the Spanish navy in the West Indies were favorable to the patriotic cause. The landing of General Lopez and his followers would be the signal for a general uprising ; an easy victory was assured ; it would only remain for the Congress to dictate terms. Those who were so fortunate as to share in this expedition as officers would receive confiscated sugar-plantations, well furnished with slaves ; even the common soldiers were each to get the sum of five thousand dollars. Sympathy for the acquisition of Cuba was very strong at the South, and the promoters played upon this feeling. It was thought by the least sanguine of them that if a fairly successful demonstration were made, public sentiment would be so aroused that the United States would lend their assistance, or at any rate would not interfere with additional expeditions ; for the object of the patriots was to establish a republic, or annex Cuba to our country on favorable terms. The Secretary of State, however, appreciated fully what honest neutrality meant ; and, as he had stated in the Senate the year previous,[1] Spain had well-grounded reasons to count on our friendship, for we had at different times given her assurances that if she would abstain from the voluntary surrender of Cuba to a European power, " she might be assured of the good offices and the good-will of the United States . . . to maintain her in possession of the island." Nor did the President shrink from his duty. The invaders first purposed to start from Savannah, but this was prevented by the energetic action of the government. That the shipload of adventurers finally got away from New Orleans was not due to negligence at Washington, but to the dereliction in duty of the collector of the port from whence they set sail. On the early morning of August 3d, the steamer *Pampero* left New Orleans, with Lopez and nearly five hundred men ; they were mostly ill-informed youths, and the majority of them were American citizens. When the

---

[1] May 21st, 1850.

steamer arrived off the coast of Cuba, she was badly piloted
and ran aground, so that the invaders were forced to land
at a place not of their choosing.   They went ashore on the
night between the 11th and 12th of August, at a spot
about sixty miles from Havana.   The force was divided,
the main body proceeding into the interior under Lopez,
while two hundred men, commanded by Colonel Crittenden,
remained to guard the stores until transportation could be
obtained.   On the 13th, when marching to join Lopez,
Crittenden was attacked by a superior force.   The officers
displayed bravery, but the men were dispirited from the
first hours on shore.   Instead of finding the whole island
in revolution and fourteen towns in the hands of patriots,
as they had been led to believe, they saw no evidence whatever of an uprising; instead of being received as friends,
they found themselves in a hostile country.   To fight dis-
ciplined troops with the odds against them was peril enough,
yet, to add to the misery of the invaders, they had no artillery and no rifles; their arms were condemned muskets.
Such a contest could only be of short duration.   Colonel
Crittenden and his men soon retreated to the place of dis-
embarkation; about fifty of them took boat and were making for the United States, when they were captured by a
Spanish ship of war which was cruising on the coast.   They
were carried to Havana, tried and sentenced by a military
court, and were publicly shot.   The men under Lopez were
attacked at the same time as was Crittenden's detachment;
many of them were killed or wounded, and they were forced
to retreat; they went into the interior and sought refuge
in the mountains, but they were pursued by the troops and,
after two skirmishes, were dispersed on the 24th of August.   Those who had not been killed, or who had not
died of hunger or fatigue, were made prisoners.   Some
days afterwards Lopez was taken and garroted in the public square opposite the prison in Havana.   Some of his followers were pardoned, and the rest, one hundred and sixty-
two in number, most of them American citizens, were sent

to Spain, where it was understood they would be put to work in the mines.[1]

In the meantime a crowd of adventurers had come to New Orleans and were anxiously awaiting news from Lopez; if the intelligence were favorable, another expedition would be fitted out, and this they intended to join. The Cuban question was the sole topic of discussion on the streets, in the cafés and bar-rooms, of this excitable Southern city, then at the zenith of its importance. Spurious despatches giving accounts of victories by Lopez appeared in the New Orleans *Delta*, whose editor was the chief promoter of the enterprise, and whose faith and money were alike engaged. There was enough opposition to the prevailing opinion to increase the earnestness with which the side of the filibusters was advocated. The newspaper *La Union* espoused with vigor the Spanish cause, and vehemently denounced the Americans. The excitement had risen to fever heat when the news arrived, on August 21st, of the shooting of Colonel Crittenden and fifty of his companions. It was at the same time learned that many of the unhappy victims had written letters to their friends, leaving them in the care of the Captain-General, who had forwarded them by the secretary of the Spanish consul at New Orleans. The letters arrived on the same steamer that brought the woful intelligence; and it was reported that they were detained and had not been given up when asked for. This stirred up a mob to

---

[1] My authorities, in addition to what have been cited, for this account are two letters of Colonel Crittenden—one to Dr. Lucien Hensley, the other to his uncle, the Attorney-General—both of them written just before he was shot; a letter from Philip Van Vechten, a lieutenant under Lopez, who was pardoned; the personal narrative of C. N. Howell, who accompanied the expedition; Commander C. T. Platt's official despatch to the Navy Department from Havana, dated Sept. 1st; Memorias sobre el Estado Político, Gobierno y Administracion de la Isla de Cuba, por el Teniente-General Don José de la Concha, Madrid, 1853; Annual Message of President Fillmore, Dec. 2d, 1851; Cincinnati *Commercial*, cited by *National Intelligencer* of Oct. 4th; Life of Webster, Curtis.

gut the office of *La Union* and sack the cigar-store called
La Corina, whose proprietor had been insulting in his talk
about Americans. The rioters broke into the office of the
Spanish consul; the portraits of the Queen of Spain and of
the Captain-General of Cuba were defaced, and the Spanish
flag was torn to pieces. Other buildings were attacked and
more property was destroyed. At different times the rioters were addressed by the mayor, sheriff, and district attorney; finally, having wreaked their vengeance on the
chief offenders, the violence of the mob came to an end;
no one was killed and only one man was injured.

This occurrence gave rise to a nice diplomatic question.
The Spanish minister at Washington demanded redress for
the insult to the flag and pecuniary indemnity for the personal losses. After a certain amount of correspondence, in
which the provocation was duly pointed out as showing
that the outrage " was committed in the heat of blood, and
not in pursuance of any premeditated plan or purpose of
injury or insult," the Secretary of State frankly acknowledged the wrong, expressed regret in the most handsome
terms, and said that when a Spanish consul was again sent
to New Orleans, instructions would be given to salute the
flag of his ship " as a demonstration of respect, such as may
signify to him and his government the sense entertained by
the government of the United States of the gross injustice
done to his predecessor by a lawless mob, as well as the
indignity and insult offered by it to a foreign State with
which the United States are, and wish ever to remain, on
terms of the most respectful and pacific intercourse." The
satisfactory manner in which Webster concluded the matter
deserves much higher praise than the vigorous outburst of
nationality in the Hülsemann letter. In our country, where
every citizen holds pronounced opinions on the most delicate questions of diplomacy, the Secretary of State who
desires political advancement is tempted to court an opportunity such as Hülsemann gave Webster, and to shun an
occasion like the matter in hand. That he treated the Span-

iard as justly as he did the Austrian added to the laurels
he had already won in the State department. Enthusiastic
meetings of sympathy with Cuban independence and the
cause of the filibusters had been held in Nashville, Cincinnati,
Baltimore, Philadelphia, Pittsburgh, and New York City;
the cotton States did not need to express their feeling, for
every one knew that they were decidedly for Cuba. When
the historian reflects that our State department has sometimes been influenced against its better judgment by strong
popular sentiment, he writes a grateful page in recording
that the astute and experienced Lord Palmerston unreservedly praised the note addressed by Webster to the Spanish
Minister. He called it "highly creditable to the good faith
and sense of justice of the United States government," and
said that the Secretary "more rightly consulted the true
dignity of the country by so handsome a communication
than if the acknowledgment of wrong and the expression
of regret had been made in more niggardly terms." When
Congress met, an appropriation was made, on the recommendation of the President, to indemnify the Spanish consul and other Spanish subjects at New Orleans for their personal loss.[1]

In the autumn of this year there were two important
illustrations of the working of the Fugitive Slave law.
Gorsuch, a resident of Maryland, with his son, several
friends, and a United States officer, all well armed and
bearing the warrant of the commissioner at Philadelphia,
went to Christiana, Lancaster County, Pa., in search of two
fugitives who had escaped three years previously. Arriving at a house about two miles from the village where they
supposed the negroes were secreted, they demanded their

---

[1] Report of account of the riot by the District Attorney and Mayor of
New Orleans to the State Department, Senate documents, 1st Sess., 32d
Cong., vol. i.; debate on the subject in Congress, *Congressional Globe*, vol.
xxiv.; New Orleans *Bee*, cited by the New York *Tribune*, Sept. 1st; Life
of Webster, Curtis, vol. ii.

property, and broke into the lower part of the house.   The colored inmates kept possession of the upper story, the fugitives saying they would rather die than go back to slavery, and their associates decisively refusing to give them up. Meanwhile, a horn was blown as a signal to the negroes in the neighborhood, with the result of bringing together from fifty to one hundred men armed with guns, axes, corn-cutters, and clubs.   The slave-hunters having left the house, an angry parley ensued, which was at length interrupted by the arrival of Castner Hanaway and another gentleman, both Quakers living in the neighborhood.   The deputy marshal summoned them to aid him in making the arrest of the fugitives, which they indignantly refused to do; but they endeavored to calm the wrath of the negroes, and at the same time warned Gorsuch and his companions that it would be madness to persist, saying, " The sooner you leave the better, if you would prevent bloodshed."   Gorsuch emphatically refused to quit his ground; words of irritation led to firing, and a general fight resulted.   The slave-owner and his son fell — the one dead and the other wounded, while none of the negroes received more than slight wounds.

This affair caused great excitement throughout the whole country.   The anti-slavery people did not defend the violence of the negro mob; but the moral which they drew from the affair was: " But for slavery such things would not be; but for the Fugitive Slave law, they would not be in the free States." [1]   The United States marshal, district attorney, and commissioner from Philadelphia, with forty-five United States marines from the navy-yard, repaired immediately, by the orders of the President, to the scene of the trouble.   A posse of about forty of the city marshal's police, with the assistance of a large body of special constables, scoured the country, and made arrests of those who were supposed to have been engaged in the fight; the fugitive slaves, however, had escaped.   Castner Hanaway and his

---

[1] New York *Tribune.*

associate, hearing that warrants were issued for them, voluntarily surrendered themselves. The prisoners were taken to Philadelphia and indicted for treason. Castner Hanaway was first tried; prominent among his counsel was Thaddeus Stevens, and Justice Grier, of the United States Supreme Court, presided. His charge was so clearly in favor of the prisoner that the jury speedily agreed upon a verdict of not guilty. One of the negroes was tried, but not convicted; the rest were not brought to trial.[1]

The other case is that of the "Jerry rescue," which took place at Syracuse, N. Y. On the first day of October, Jerry McHenry, an athletic mulatto and industrious mechanic, who had been living in that city for several years, was claimed as a fugitive slave by a man from Missouri. Jerry had made one ineffectual attempt to escape, and the courage which he displayed, together with the one-sided character of the proceedings incident to a claim made under the Fugitive Slave law, aroused active sympathy for the negro from the citizens and sojourners of Syracuse. The city was full of people, for on that day were held a meeting of the county agricultural society and the Liberty party's annual convention. Jerry was imprisoned overnight in the police-office to await the conclusion of the examination on the morrow. He had, unknown to himself, many ardent friends, among whom were the Rev. Samuel J. May and Gerrit Smith. May,[2] who had charge of the Unitarian Society of Syracuse, was a rare combination of perfect courage and gentleness of spirit. Gerrit Smith, a great-hearted man, and a deep

---

[1] The Underground Railroad, William Still, particularly the account cited from the *Pennsylvania Freeman*, a local newspaper, edited by a Quaker, p. 349. The New York *Independent*, Sept. 18th and 25th; notably a letter from Rev. Mr. Gorsuch, a son of the man who was killed, which purports to be a reliable narrative of the bloody affray; also Rise and Fall of the Slave Power, vol. ii. p. 327. The fight took place Sept. 11th.

[2] See p. 65.

thinker on moral and religious subjects, had early espoused the cause of the slave. Shrewd in his investments, he had accumulated large wealth, which he devoted to the good of his kind; and later, as a noted worker in the Liberty party, he was elected to Congress as its candidate from one of the northern districts of New York.

Under the lead of these two gentlemen, twenty or thirty resolute men determined to rescue the negro. Early in the evening they made an attack upon the police-office, and beat down the prison door with a battering-ram; they encountered little resistance, and easily overpowered the police, without, however, inflicting any personal injury. They then led Jerry out, put him in a buggy drawn by a swift pair of horses, and took him to a place of refuge in the city, where he remained concealed for several days, being finally sent safely through to Canada. The anti-slavery people exulted greatly over this affair, and their elation was increased by the failure to convict any of the eighteen rescuers who were indicted. Several were tried, but the United States district attorney did not venture to bring to trial the leaders in the affair, although they defied him to do so; Samuel J. May, Gerrit Smith, and another gentleman, uniting in a published acknowledgment to the effect that they had done all they could in the rescue of Jerry; that they were ready for trial, and would give the court no trouble as to the fact, but would rest their defence upon the unconstitutionality and extreme wickedness of the Fugitive Slave law.[1]

Since the passage of this law one year had now elapsed. The fact was patent that in most Northern communities it could not be enforced without more trouble and expense than were worth the taking. This law violated the fundamental principle of democratic government,—that laws are futile unless upheld by public sentiment. It was a curious commentary on a statute that gentlemen of the very high-

---

[1] Recollections of Anti-slavery Conflict, Samuel J. May, p. 373 *et seq.;* Life of Gerrit Smith, Frothingham, p. 117.

I.—15

est character, like Samuel J. May and Gerrit Smith, should lead a mob of earnest, unarmed men to resist the execution of it. Most of the anti-slavery men would not advise resistance to the law ; the law-abiding sentiment of the North was strong, and did not sympathize with forcible opposition to those invested with public authority; but to fair-minded men it was clear that the attempt to carry into effect the Fugitive Slave act in many parts of the North would simply be kicking against the pricks.

During the year the South had gained in union feeling. The compromise measures, as we have seen, were generally satisfactory outside of South Carolina and Mississippi. In May a convention of Southern Rights associations of South Carolina, held at Charleston, resolved in favor of secession, with or without the co-operation of other Southern States.[1] This feeling was then apparently strong throughout the State, since of thirty newspapers, only two were opposed to secession.[2] The election in October showed that the Southern Rights convention and the newspapers had not represented the sentiment of the people, or else that between May and October a great change had taken place in public opinion. The issue was made in the election of delegates to a State convention. One set of delegates opposed action by South Carolina alone ; the other set were unconditionally in favor of secession. Two-thirds of the delegates chosen belonged to the former party, and in the country at large this was regarded as a Unionist victory ; and well it might be, for to vote co-operation with the other Southern States meant to abide by the Union.[3]

In Mississippi a very exciting and significant canvass took place between Jefferson Davis and Senator Foote. One had been a strong opponent, and the other an ardent supporter, of the compromise measures in the Senate, and they now

---

[1] *National Intelligencer*, May 13th.

[2] Von Holst, vol. iv. p. 34.

[3] *Tribune Almanac*, 1852, p. 43 ; New York *Independent*, Oct. 23d, 1851.

went before the people of their State for vindication. Davis was the candidate for governor of the States-rights party, which believed in the right of secession and favored a Southern convention for action, while Foote was the candidate of the Unionists. The question was thoroughly discussed on the stump by both men, and the contest was exceedingly close, Foote having but 1009 majority over his competitor.[1] The majority would have been larger had it not been for the personal popularity of Davis, who was stronger than his party. The State convention which had been elected previous to the gubernatorial contest declared that the people of Mississippi would abide by the compromise measures, and that the right of secession was utterly unsanctioned by the Federal Constitution.[2]

The Thirty-second Congress met on December 1st. There was little change in the relative strength of the political parties in the Senate; the Democrats had made a slight gain. Charles Sumner, of Massachusetts, and Benjamin F. Wade, of Ohio, took their seats in the Senate; they resembled each other in nothing but personal courage and hatred of slavery. Sumner was a graduate of Harvard, a representative of the culture of Boston, and the intimate friend of nearly every one of that brilliant set of scholars, poets, and *literati* to whose performances during the twenty years before the civil war we may point with a just feeling of pride. Himself a ripe scholar, he loved the classics; he was a profound student of history, delving into the past so earnestly that his desire to visit the old countries grew into a passion. He went abroad furnished with letters from the wise and influential of America to the men of distinction across the sea; he returned with a mind broadened by contact with the thinkers, writers, and politicians of Europe. He had charming manners and rare social accomplishments; he and Chase

---

[1] *Tribune Almanac*, 1852, p. 44; Rise and Fall of the Confederate Government, vol. i. p. 20. The election took place in November.

[2] *Congressional Globe*, vol. xxiv. p. 35.

were considered the handsomest men in the Senate. A favorite child of fortune, kind friends ever stood ready to give their help; opportunities were made for him. Sumner was not a great lawyer; the bent of his mind was towards politics rather than law. Possessed of strong moral feelings, politics especially attracted him on account of the moral element that now entered into public questions. From an early day he had hated slavery; the *Liberator* was the first paper he had ever subscribed for, having read it since 1835, yet he was opposed to Garrison's doctrines on the Constitution and the Union. A Whig until 1848, he then became a Free-soiler, and by a well-managed coalition of the Free-soilers and Democrats he was this year elected senator.[1]

Benjamin F. Wade, also a son of New England, was in character of the rugged heroic type. Born of poor parents, he worked on the western Massachusetts farm in the summer, and had only the common schooling of two or three months in the winter. His religious education was wholly under the guidance of his pious mother; he read the Bible with diligence, and knew the Westminster Catechism by heart. When twenty-one, he went to Ohio and took up his home on the Western Reserve. The problem then with him was how to get a living in this new rough country. He worked as a drover and as a common laborer; but finally deciding to adopt law as a profession, he studied in a lawyer's office, was admitted to the bar, and was fortunate in forming a partnership with Joshua R. Giddings, a leading lawyer in northeastern Ohio. Only by a strong effort of the will was Wade able to overcome his constitutional diffidence in public speaking, which at the outset threatened to defeat his intention of becoming an advocate; but he grew to be a vigorous speaker.

---

[1] For a detailed account of this coalition, see relation of Henry Wilson, who was one of the prime movers, Rise and Fall of the Slave Power, chap. xxvii. This estimate of Sumner I have mainly derived from Edw. L. Pierce's Memoir and Letters of Charles Sumner.

His second legal associate, Rufus P. Ranney, became the best lawyer and soundest judge of Ohio, taking rank with the most carefully trained legal minds of the country.   The bar of the Western Reserve was an able body of men; they had but few law-books, and those they mastered; their literature was the Bible and Shakespeare, and their forensic contests were apt displays of logic, invective, and wit.   In that community influence went for nothing; if a man rose to the top it was through ability and industry.   In those days the best lawyers went to the legislature and sat on the bench.   There they took great interest in the enactment of necessary measures, and were careful that the phraseology should be simple and exact, considering the deliberate yet positive expounding of the law a grave and solemn duty. It was an honor to be a member of the legislature, and an honor to be a judge.

Wade had been a State circuit judge, had served in the legislature, and was this year elected to the Senate as a Whig of well-known anti-slavery principles.   He was thoroughly honest; his manners were rough, and his style of address was abrupt.[1]

There were now five men in the Senate who, though differing in party antecedents, were ready to work together in opposing the extension of slavery: Seward, of New York; Chase and Wade, of Ohio; Sumner, of Massachusetts; and Hale, of New Hampshire.   Their ages were respectively fifty, forty-three, fifty-one, forty, and forty-five.   The absence of Benton from this Senate was conspicuous; after thirty years of eminent service he had failed to secure a re-election because he would not abate his principles one jot at the dictation of the pro-slavery Democrats of Missouri.[2]

The members of the House of Representatives who assembled December 1st had all been elected since the passage

[1] I have drawn this characterization of Wade largely from his biography, by A. G. Riddle.
[2] Life of Benton, Roosevelt, p. 341.

of the compromise measures, and their political classification in contrast with that of the last Congress affords a good
idea of public sentiment at the time.   There were in this
House one hundred and forty Democrats, eighty-eight
Whigs, and five Free-soilers.[1]   There was almost no change
in the delegation from the slave States; the Democrats had
lost two seats, which the Whigs had gained.   But at the
North, the Whigs had lost twenty-four, while the Democrats
had gained twenty-six members.[2]   Two causes had contributed to effect this result.   In some districts the Democrats
won because they were more earnest than the Whigs in the
advocacy of the compromise; in other districts Whigs lost
their seats because they had supported the compromise or had
failed to vote against the Fugitive Slave law.   Of twenty-
eight Northern Democrats who had voted for that act, fifteen were candidates for re-election, of whom twelve were
returned.   Only three Northern Whigs had voted for the
bill; one of them was a member of the present House.

On the first day of the session a debate took place in the
House as to which party was the more faithful to the compromise.   The Democratic caucus had laid on the table a
resolution endorsing those measures, while the Whig caucus,
in a formal declaration, had approved them.   Neither action had any significance; it was simply clever political
fencing.   To this complexion had it, however, come: every
article of the compromise was regarded as a finality at the
North except the Fugitive Slave law, while the touchstone
of fidelity to the settlement of 1850 was opposition to the
repeal of the Fugitive Slave act and willingness to support
the strict execution of it.

The President, in his annual message, reflected fairly
the tendency of public opinion.   "The agitation," said he,

---

[1] This is the classification of the New York *Tribune;* that of the *Congressional Globe* is 142 Democrats, 91 Whigs.   For the classification of
the Thirty-first Congress, see p. 116 *et seq.*

[2] The Democrats had gained the two members from California.

"which for a time threatened to disturb the fraternal relations which make us one people, is fast subsiding;" and " I congratulate you and the country upon the general acquiescence in these measures of peace which has been exhibited in all parts of the republic."

The concern about the general acceptance of the compromise and the execution of the Fugitive Slave law was now overshadowed by the interest taken in the visit of Kossuth. The Hungarian revolution had failed ; this was owing largely to the fact that Russia came to the assistance of Austria. Kossuth fled to Turkey, and had been there some time under detention, when the President was directed by Congress to offer one of the ships of our Mediterranean squadron to convey him and his associates to the United States. Austria pressed Turkey very vigorously not to release the refugees without her consent ; but, through the exertions of the American minister and of the English and Sardinian representatives at the Porte, the government of Turkey was induced to consent to their departure, and they left in the summer of this year on the frigate *Mississippi*. Kossuth turned aside to visit England, in order to arouse enthusiasm for his cause and get help for down-trodden Hungary. He then came to America, arriving at New York quarantine on Friday, December 5th, at one o'clock in the morning. A salute of twenty-one guns, an address of welcome by the health officer, a hearty greeting on shore from people who had gathered at this unseasonable hour, showed that the country would receive the refugee as a conquering hero. When day came, the citizens of Staten Island turned out to congratulate Kossuth that he had set foot in the land of liberty. The morning was given up to callers ; among those who paid their respects were Foresti, an Italian exile, and an Indian chief, who referred to himself as being also " one of the unfortunate." At noon there was a general procession, and a formal address of welcome, to which Kossuth made an appropriate reply. This was but the prologue ; the play was on the morrow. On this Saturday, nature vied with the people. The deep-blue sky, the clear, brilliant atmosphere, the crisp yet mild air of the December day, seemed to set off fitly the enthusiasm of the multitude. Kossuth and his party left Staten Island at eleven o'clock on the steamer *Vanderbilt*, which had come for him in the charge of the reception committee of the New York Common Council. As the boat steamed by, Governor's Island fired a salute of thirty-one guns, New Jersey one hundred and twenty, and then guns were fired on every side. As the *Vanderbilt* passed the navy-yard, the war-ships *North Carolina* and *Ohio* saluted, and all the ferry-boats whistled. On nearly all the vessels—steamers and smaller craft—in the bay, Hungarian and United States flags floated together. New York had never seen a finer sight. One hundred thousand people were waiting on the Battery; Castle Garden was full to overflowing. When Kossuth could be seen, a tumultuous roar broke forth; when he landed, it seemed, said one reporter, as if the shout would raise the vast roof of the reception hall; the cheer continued uninterruptedly for fifteen minutes. The mayor, who was primed with a speech, in vain besought silence. At last, from sheer exhaustion of the crowd, the uproar ceased; the address of welcome was made; but when Kossuth rose to reply, the enthusiasm again burst out. Only those near him could hear a word, yet he went through the form of speaking, and written copies of this carefully prepared declaration of his self-imposed errand were furnished the reporters. The speech over, Kossuth, mounted on Black Warrior, a war-horse which had been in many battles of the Florida and Mexican wars, reviewed the troops that had turned out to escort him. Then the procession began to move. Besides the military display there was a large number of civic bodies, and it took an hour to pass a given point. When Kossuth's carriage entered Broadway, an inspiring sight met his eyes. All the shops and houses were decorated, many of them with mottoes of sympathy for Hungary and welcome for her governor, as everybody called him. The street was jammed

with people ; every window was alive with human beings.
There was, says the reporter, "a continuous roar of cheers
like waves on the shore." Every one agreed that, since the
landing of Lafayette, no such enthusiasm had been seen in
New York; and it is certain that no foreigner except that
gallant Frenchman ever received a similar ovation. The
greatest of Roman generals might have been proud of such
a triumph.

This splendid testimonial was not so much to the man as
to the principle of which he was the incarnation. The different manifestations of the revolutionary spirit which began
in Europe in 1848 had been followed with deep interest in
America. The readers of newspapers were fully informed
of the progress of the events. Though European news came
slower then than now, it was more trustworthy. The American correspondents abroad were almost always men of education and culture; many of them had attainments which
gave them access to the best society of the countries to
which they were sent. They knew what was taking place;
they knew how to discriminate the true from the false, and
they had time before mail-day to sift the rumors from the
facts and to give an orderly arrangement to their narrative.
Our countrymen, therefore, of this time had correct knowledge of contemporary events in Europe. These revolutionary movements seemed to them due to American example ;
the contemplation of the free, united, and happy country
created a yearning, they thought, for the like, and this
yearning stirred up the people on the European continent
to rebel against their tyrants. Never had there been a
more unquestioned faith in our institutions, a greater desire
to propagate the principles underlying them, or a more sublime confidence in their virtue. This feeling found an official expression in the Hülsemann letter,[1] and a popular expression in the triumph to Kossuth. The blows struck for
Hungarian liberty had indeed been in vain; but the hero of

---

[1] See p. 205.

the revolution was here to tell us that the mighty movement had been not crushed, but only delayed. In his speech he frankly avowed his object. " I come here," he said, " to invoke the aid of the great American republic to protect my people, peaceably, if they may, by the moral influence of their declarations, but forcibly if they must, by the physical power of their arm—to prevent any foreign interference in the struggle about to be renewed for the liberties of my country." He explained why it was that he had such hopes of the United States. " Your generous act of my liberation is taken by the world for the revelation of the fact that the United States are resolved not to allow the despots of the world to trample on oppressed humanity." It was soon well understood that he expected the United States and England would combine to prevent the interference of Russia in Austro-Hungarian affairs, and that he wanted to raise in this country one million dollars on Hungarian bonds, payable when the independence of the country should be achieved. It is quite certain that if, in these December days, a popular vote of New York City could have decided the foreign policy of the nation, it would have been in favor of intermeddling in European affairs, for the metropolitan people had seemingly lost their heads. On the evening of Kossuth's arrival, there was a torchlight procession in his honor; some of the banners had legends proposing intervention by the United States in behalf of oppressed liberty in Europe; others denoted regret for neglect in the past, and bore the inscription, " May our future atone for the past !"

On the Monday morning following his arrival the New York *Tribune* maintained that while non-intervention in European affairs was the correct principle, there might be circumstances when our own interests, as well as our duty in the family of States, would command us to step beyond the straight line of this policy. Most of the New York press were favorable to Kossuth, and the editor of the journal which was the most active in exposing the folly of the craze was denounced as " a mercenary and time-serving political parasite," and "the exorbitant and unblushing eulogist of the bloody house of Hapsburg." The friends of Kossuth delighted to compare him with Lafayette; his enemies said he rather called to mind another Frenchman, Gênet, who, at first received with great enthusiasm, finally became a stench in the nostrils of the public. One extravagant journalist, wrought up to a high pitch of feeling by one of Kossuth's speeches, declared that the Washington of the eighteenth century was interpreted by the Washington of the nineteenth. Steady people in other parts of the country thought New York had run mad; they were amazed at the wild infatuation, and called it the folly of the day.

Kossuth showed wonderful tact in steering clear of anything that should excite partisan or sectional feeling. A delegation of the American and Foreign Anti-slavery Society called upon him and made an address. He replied: "I know you are just and generous, and will not endeavor to entangle me with questions of a party character while I am with you. I must attend to one straight course and not be found to connect myself with any principle but the one great principle of my country's liberation." A party of several thousand men who called themselves the European Democracy, composed of foreigners from Italy, Germany, Poland, Austria, and France, marched to his hotel and delivered an address revealing that they were socialists. Kossuth replied discreetly; he was not a socialist, and, indeed, that question was not the one at issue in Hungary. He received successively deputations from colored men, the presbytery of Brooklyn, the faculty and alumni of Columbia College, Cuban exiles, the students of Yale College, and the Whig Central Committee, to all of whom he made appropriate remarks. The city of New York gave him a banquet at the Irving House; four hundred guests sat down at table, and among them was George Bancroft. At the Astor House there was an editorial banquet in his honor, presided over by the poet-editor William Cullen Bryant, which every one considered it a high privilege to attend. The reading of a let-

ter from Webster, coldly declining to attend on account of
public duties, was received with hisses and groans. Toasts
were responded to by Bancroft, Henry J. Raymond, Parke
Godwin, Henry Ward Beecher, and Charles A. Dana. Two
days after this banquet, the New York Democratic Central
Committee presented Kossuth the resolutions which they had
adopted. They declared that the time for American neutrality had ceased, and promised that "at the tap of the drum one
hundred thousand armed men will rally around the American
standard to be unfurled on the field when the issue between
freedom and despotism is to be decided." A large meeting
in Plymouth Church raised twelve thousand dollars for the
Hungarian cause, and a dramatic benefit was given at Niblo's
Garden for the fund. An imposing reception by the bar of
New York, and an afternoon entertainment by the ladies at
the Metropolitan Opera House were a fitting close of the
honors which had been showered on the Hungarian hero
in this hospitable city.

It was, indeed, a curious spectacle to see the descendants
of sober-blooded Englishmen and phlegmatic Dutchmen
roused to such a pitch of enthusiasm over a man who was
not the benefactor of their own country, and whose only
title to fame was that he had fought bravely and acted
wisely in an unsuccessful revolution.

It is evident that we were even then an excitable people.[1]

---

[1] J. J. Ampère, Promenade en Amérique, speaks of the reception of
Kossuth at New York: "Je vois que dans cette ivresse de New York
entrait pour beaucoup ce besoin d'excitation, de manifestations bruyantes,
qui est le seul amusement vif de la multitude dans un pays où l'on ne
s'amuse guère. Ce vacarme est sans conséquence et sans danger; tout
cela se borne, comme me le disait un homme d'esprit, à lâcher la vapeur
('let out the steam'), ce qui, comme on sait, ne cause point les explosions
de la machine, mais les prévient."—Tome ii. p. 53. "The American is
shrewd and keen; his passion seldom obscures his reason; he keeps his
head in moments when a Frenchman, or an Italian, or even a German,
would lose it. Yet he is also of an excitable temper, with emotions capable of being quickly and strongly stirred. . . . Moreover, the Americans

Yet if we had gained vivacity in this electric air of ours, what was occurring at Washington demonstrated that we had not lost the habit of deliberating wisely before taking a resolve. On the first day of the session a resolution was introduced into the Senate providing a welcome from Congress to Kossuth on his arrival, and tendering, in the name of the whole American people, the hospitalities of the metropolis of the Union. But objection was made to taking action of any official character, and this gave rise to considerable discussion. Before a vote was reached Kossuth arrived at New York. The project of greeting him when he first set foot on our shores was then suspended by a proposition to welcome him at the capital of the country. Even this simple resolution provoked a four days' debate, for by this time the Senate had the report of his first speech. The notion that the fixed foreign policy of this government, exacting non-interference in European affairs, could, under any circumstances, be altered was entertained by only a few senators. Yet there was no lack of enthusiasm. "There has been but one Washington and there is but one Kossuth," Foote declared in eager tones. "The great Hungarian leader will live in the brightest pages of history," said Cass. The occasion prompted Sumner to make his maiden speech. Kossuth deserves our welcome, he exclaimed, "as the early, constant, and incorruptible champion of the liberal cause in Hungary." He is "a living Wallace— a living Tell— I had almost said a living Washington." Seward spoke of him as "the representative of the uprising liberties of Europe." Yet several senators were opposed to offering Kossuth the hospitalities of Congress, unless it should be expressly declared in the resolution that we did not intend to depart from the settled policy of our government. The discussion generated so much heat that one senator did not hesitate to say "that there have been more unpleasant and

---

like excitement. They like it for its own sake, and go wherever they can find it."—American Commonwealth, Bryce, vol. ii. p. 191.

hard things said of Kossuth in this Senate than have been said of him in all Europe, except by the bribed and hireling prints of some of the despots of the Old World." It was, however, resolved to give him a cordial welcome to the capital. There was anxiety in the State department in regard to his reception. " It requires great caution," wrote Webster, "so to conduct things here when Mr. Kossuth shall arrive as to keep clear both of Scylla and Charybdis;" [1] and " his presence here will be quite embarrassing. . . . I hope I may steer clear of trouble on both sides." [2] Kossuth, after an enthusiastic reception at Philadelphia and Baltimore, arrived at Washington on the 30th of December; he was met at the station by Seward and Shields, of the Senate committee. A large crowd awaited his arrival and greeted him with demonstrations of respect. At noon the Secretary of State called upon him. Webster wrote that Kossuth was a gentleman " in appearance and demeanor; . . . he is handsome enough in person, evidently intellectual and dignified, amiable and graceful in his manners. I shall treat him with all personal and individual respect; but if he should speak to me of the policy of 'intervention,' I shall 'have ears more deaf than adders.' " [3] The next day Kossuth was presented to the President, and later in the week he dined at the White House.[4]

---

[1] Letter to Haven, Dec. 23d, Private Correspondence, vol. ii. p. 497.

[2] Letter to Paige, Dec. 25th, ibid., p. 499.

[3] Letter to Blatchford, Dec. 30th, ibid., p. 501.

[4] Ampère assisted at this dinner, and writes: " Là, j'ai été témoin d'une nouvelle scène de ce drame de la venue de Kossuth en Amérique, dont j'avais vu à New York, il y a quelques semaines, l'exposition si brillante et en apparence si pleine de promesses; . . . ni avant, ni pendant, ni après le dîner, il n'a été fait, à ma connaissance, aucune allusion à la cause de la Hongrie. Je n'ai vu que de la politesse pour l'homme, mais nulle expression à haute voix de sympathie pour sa cause. . . . Kossuth, qui a le tort d'aimer les costumes de fantaisie, portait une lévite de velours noir, et m'a semblé beaucoup moins imposant dans cette tenue que quand il haranguiat, appuyé sur son grand sabre, dans la salle de Castle Garden, à New York."—Promenade en Amérique, tome ii. p. 98.

Four days of the new year had gone by before the much-canvassed reception of the Senate took place. The ceremony was the same as that which twenty-seven years before governed the welcome to Lafayette. At one o'clock on the 5th of January the doors were opened, and Governor Kossuth, escorted by the committee—Shields, Seward, and Cass—entered and advanced within the bar, all the senators at the same time rising. The suite of the honored guest, in military uniforms, stood below the bar. Shields said: "Mr. President, we have the honor to introduce Louis Kossuth to the Senate of the United States." The presiding officer addressed him: "Louis Kossuth, I welcome you to the Senate of the United States. The committee will conduct you to the seat which I have caused to be prepared for you." He was then conducted to a chair in front of the President's desk; the Senate, in order to give the senators an opportunity of paying their respects to their guest, adjourned, and they were individually presented. General Houston attracted special notice. The presence of the hero of San Jacinto in the chief council of the nation could not fail to suggest to the Hungarian how much happier than his own lot had been that of the Texas liberator. Senator Houston said, in his rough, hearty way, "Sir, you are welcome to the Senate of the United States;" to which Kossuth replied, "I can only wish I had been as successful as you, sir." Houston with ready sympathy rejoined, "God grant that you may yet be so!"

Two days after this reception, a banquet was given to Kossuth by members of Congress of both parties, at which Webster made a noteworthy speech. His allusion to England was exceedingly felicitous, being possibly a delicate reference to remarks that had been made in the Senate, which seemed to assume that all the political virtue of the world was centred in the United States. "On the western coast of Europe," he said, "political light exists. There is a sun in the political firmament, and that sun sheds his light on those who are able to enjoy it." In the course of his speech he made a strong argument for the independence of Hungary, based on her distinctive nationality and the home-rule principle.

The House had passed without debate the joint resolution to welcome Kossuth; but when a motion was made for the appointment of a committee to introduce him to the House, the different feelings in regard to the Hungarian hero were strikingly manifest. By the many instrumentalities which the rules of the House put in their power, members tried to prevent the consideration of the resolution, and it was not until the day of Kossuth's arrival at Washington that the subject was fairly brought before this body. Then for many days the representatives strove and wrangled over the question; amendments were offered, counter-motions were made, until finally, when the 5th of January had come, and it was stated that the Hungarian purposed leaving on the ninth, the majority rose in their might, suspended the rules and adopted the resolution. The form of reception was the same as in the Senate, and it took place without incident.

Soon after Kossuth left for the West, and visited several cities, where there was great curiosity to see the lion of the day; crowds turned out to greet him and showed some enthusiasm, but it was patent before he left Washington that his mission had failed. Indeed, from the moment that he avowed his expectations, it was apparent everywhere, except in New York City, that his hope for a pronunciamento in favor of intervention, should Russia take a hand hereafter in the affairs of Hungary, was utterly vain; and a very short time after his departure sufficed to bring the citizens of the metropolis around to the opinion of the rest of the country. By the middle of January a correspondent wrote that the excitement had wholly died down, and the name of Kossuth was rarely heard in New York. One vote taken in the House of Representatives had decided significance. An amendment to the resolution of welcome had been offered, providing that the committee on the reception of Kossuth should be instructed to inform him that the

United States would not look with indifference on the intervention of Russia against Hungary in any struggle for liberty she might hereafter have with the despotic power of Austria. The mover of this amendment, seeing that it met with no favor, desired to withdraw it, but this was not permitted. A division was therefore taken, but the proposition received only seven votes.

Nor was Kossuth much more successful in his quest for sinews of war. At Pittsburgh he complained bitterly that while one hundred and sixty thousand dollars had been raised, only thirty thousand dollars remained for the purchase of muskets; the rest had been wasted in costly banquets and foolish parades. He appealed no longer for intervention, but for money, and urged that the salt-mines of Hungary would be ample security for the loan. Although he remained in the country until July, it is certain that the net amount of the contributions to his cause was less than one hundred thousand dollars.

The reason of the interest taken in Kossuth's visit is now plain enough to be seen, but at the time it was stated that the excitement had been worked up by politicians with an eye to the German vote in the approaching presidential election. This view was not correct. The movement was spontaneous, and the politicians took hold of it so as to keep in the popular current. In the honor done to this representative of European revolution there was the exultation of the young republic which rejoiced in the strength of a lusty giant. Two years previously the arrival of Kossuth would have stirred up but little enthusiasm, for then the unhappy sectional controversy which had threatened disaster engrossed the attention of the people; now, however, it was felt that the country was united and harmonious. With sweet forgetfulness the memory of past danger faded away, and a serene optimism would not anticipate evil. From the debate it was apparent that members of Congress generally thought we were quite a match for Austria and Russia combined, although at the present moment there

I.—16

was no desire to put forth our strength. But there was
grim truth in the rebuke by Clemens, of Alabama, when he
reminded certain senators who were willing to fight, if necessary, for liberty in Europe that "but recently a bitter sectional conflict was raging in our midst, which threatened at
one time to shatter our Confederacy into atoms; that the
embers of that strife were still unquenched, and that it was
the part of wisdom to secure internal peace before we engaged in external war."

Horace Mann and others of his persuasion were mainly
wrong when they attributed to the influence of the slave
power the opposition to Kossuth which came from the
South.[1] No one was a more enthusiastic champion of the
Hungarian than Senator Foote, a devoted supporter of
Southern institutions. It was he who exclaimed: "At such
a moment, does it behoove the American people to join the
side of despotism, or to stand by the cause of freedom? We
must do one or the other. We cannot avoid the solemn
alternative presented. . . . Those who are not for freedom
are for slavery."[2] Hale tried to drag the slavery question
into the debate, but his political friends frowned upon his
endeavor; for Seward and Cass, Sumner and Shields, went
hand in hand in the affair. In the House, a member from
North Carolina charged that the abolitionists had taken the
lead in the matter, and, while this accusation added somewhat to the heat of the debate, there is no doubt that most
of those who objected to conferring the proposed honor on
Kossuth did so because he had assailed the non-intervention
doctrine of Washington.

The heroic play which began in New York changed into
a farce when Congress came to audit the hotel bill of the
Hungarian governor and his suite. The bill, amounting to
nearly four thousand six hundred dollars, was considered
by the Senate enormous in its magnitude. The senators

---

[1] Life of Horace Mann, p. 356.
[2] Remarks in Senate, Dec. 3d, 1851.

did not pry into the items; but the House had no such reserve, and before passing it they examined narrowly the itemized statement; whence it appeared that the apartments had been large and luxurious, and that champagne, madeira, and sherry had flowed freely. Kossuth was defended from all participation in debauchery, it being asserted that he was abstemious in all his habits except smoking, and that, while he sometimes drank claret at dinner, he was moderate in the pleasures of the table.[1]

Early in the session a resolution was introduced into the Senate by Foote which declared that the compromise measures were a definite adjustment of the distracting questions growing out of slavery. This occasioned a rambling discussion, but the proposition was never brought to a vote. On the 5th day of April a division in the House was attained on a resolution similar in purport. One hundred and three members voted that the compromise should be regarded as a permanent settlement, and seventy-four voted against such a declaration. The nays were made up of twenty-six Northern Democrats,[2] twenty-eight Northern Whigs, nineteen Southern Democrats, and one Southern Whig, viz., Clingman. It was noticeable that, while every representative present from South Carolina voted against the resolution, every representative from Mississippi but one voted for it; the delegation from both States were all Democrats. Twenty Southern and only seven Northern Whigs voted in the affirmative. Many of the latter were absent.

It is now my intention to narrate the proceedings of the national conventions of the Democratic and Whig parties,

---

[1] My authorities for this relation are the New York *Tribune* and the *National Intelligencer*. Both of these newspapers give copious extracts from contemporary journals; the debates in the Senate and House, vol. xxiv., *Congressional Globe;* Life of Webster, Curtis, vol. ii.; Webster's Private Correspondence, vol. ii. See also Promenade en Amérique, Ampère, tome i. p. 370. The curious may find the itemized bill in *Congressional Globe*, vol. xxiv. p. 1692.

[2] In these are included Rantoul and Durkee, Free-soilers.

two bodies which assembled with a fresher mandate from the people than had the representatives in Congress. The Democratic convention was held on June 1st at Baltimore, and the prominent candidates were Cass, Douglas, Buchanan, and Marcy. Cass was now nearly seventy years old, but temperate habits and a regular life had preserved his native vigor. A son of New England, his education had been mainly acquired in the academy of Exeter, N. H., his native place. In early life he came West, and as governor of Michigan territory from 1813 to 1831 his administration of affairs was marked with intelligence and energy.[1] His experience during this term of office with the British stationed in Canada, who constantly incited the Indians to wage war on the settlers of the Northwest, caused him to imbibe a hatred of England which never left him, and whose influence is traceable throughout his public career. He held the war portfolio under Jackson, later was Minister to France, and had now for several years represented Michigan in the Senate. His anglophobia and his readiness to assert vigorous principles of American nationality made him popular in the Northwest. He tried a solution of the slavery question in the Nicholson letter, written a few months before he was selected as the candidate of the Democratic party in 1848. In this letter he invented the doctrine which afterwards became widely known as the doctrine of popular sovereignty. He maintained that Congress should let the people of the territories regulate their internal concerns in their own way; and that in regard to slavery the territories should be put upon the same basis as the States.

Douglas was only thirty-nine years old, being remarkably young to aspire to the highest office in the State. Clay had reached the age of forty-seven when he became a candidate for the presidency, and Webster was forty-eight when he

---

[1] See a paper read by Prof. A. C. McLaughlin before the American Historical Association, Dec., 1888, "The Influence of Governor Cass on the Development of the Northwest;" see also his Life of Cass.

began to dream that it might be his lot to reach the desired goal. Douglas was a son of New England, and, like many New England boys, worked on a farm in the summer and attended school in the winter. By the time he was twenty, he had wrought for two years at a trade, had completed the classical course at an academy, and had begun the study of law. He then went to Illinois, and before he had attained his majority was admitted to the bar; he became a member of the legislature at twenty - three, a Supreme judge at twenty-eight, a representative in Congress at thirty, and a senator at thirty-three.

Douglas's first political speech gained him the title of the "Little Giant;" the name was intended to imply the union of small physical with great intellectual stature. Yet he was not a student of books, although a close observer of men. He lacked refinement of manner; was careless of his personal appearance, and had none of the art and grace that go to make up the cultivated orator. John Quincy Adams was shocked at his appearance in the House when, as the celebrated diary records, in making a speech he raved, roared, and lashed himself into a heat with convulsed face and frantic gesticulation. "In the midst of his roaring, to save himself from choking, he stripped off and cast away his cravat, unbuttoned his waistcoat, and had the air and aspect of a half-naked pugilist."[1] But Douglas took on quickly the character of his surroundings, and in Washington society he soon learned the ease of a gentleman and acquired the bearing of a man of the world. He was a great friend to the material development of the West, and especially of his own State, having broad views of the future growth of his section of country.[2] He vied with Cass in his dislike of

---

[1] Memoirs of J. Q. Adams, vol. xi. p. 510.

[2] "M. Douglas est un des hommes dans le congrès dont le discours et l'aspect m'ont le plus frappé. Petit, noir, trapu, sa parole est pleine de nerf, son action simple et forte. . . . Il me parait un des hommes de ce pays qui ont le plus d'avenir; il pourra arriver au pouvoir quand l'Ouest,

England. He believed in the manifest destiny of the United States. He thought that conditions might arise under which it would become our bounden duty to acquire Cuba, Mexico, and Central America. He was called the representative of young America, and his supporters antagonized Cass as the candidate of old-fogyism. His adherents were aggressive, and for months had made a vigorous canvass on his behalf. A Whig journal ventured to remind Douglas that vaulting ambition overleaps itself, but added, "Perhaps the little judge never read Shakespeare, and does not think of this."[1]

James Buchanan was born in Pennsylvania in 1791. He had a fair school and college education, studied law, soon acquired a taste for politics, was sent to the legislature, served as representative in Congress ten years, and was elected three times senator. In the Senate he distinguished himself as an ardent supporter of President Jackson. He was Secretary of State under Polk, but since the close of that administration had remained in private life. He was a gentleman of refinement and of courtly manners.[2]

Marcy was a shrewd New York politician, the author of the phrase "To the victors belong the spoils."[3] He had been judge, United States senator, and three times governor. He held the war portfolio under Polk, but the conduct of this office had not added to his reputation, for it had galled the administration to have the signal victories of the Mexican war won by Whig generals, and it was currently believed that the War Minister had shared in the

---

qui n'y a pas encore été représenté, voudra à son tour avoir son président. L'esprit de M. Douglas me semble, comme sa parole, vigoureux, ardent, ce qui en fait un représentant très-fidèle des populations énergiques qui grandissent entre la forêt et la prairie."—Promenade en Amérique, J. J. Ampère, tome ii. p. 56.

[1] Pike, in New York *Tribune*, cited by Von Holst, vol. iv. p. 165. In this characterization of Douglas I have used the Lives of Douglas by Sheahan and by H. M. Flint.   [2] See Life of Buchanan, Curtis.

[3] For the speech in which Marcy used this expression, see The Lives of the Governors of New York, p. 564.

endeavor to thwart some of the plans of Scott and Taylor. Always an honored citizen of New York, it has seemed fitting that the highest mountain-peak in the State by bearing his name should serve as a monument to his memory.

The hall in which the convention met at Baltimore was one of the largest in the country; it could accommodate five thousand people. There was then nothing like the outside pressure on the delegates which is seen now at every one of these national conventions when the nomination is contested; but the city thronged with people, and it was apparent that the friends of Douglas had mustered in full force. On the evening of the first day an immense meeting took place in Monument Square, where an enthusiastic crowd listened to eloquent speakers. The first two days of the convention were occupied in organization and in confirmation of the two-thirds rule. It was decided to make the nomination before the adoption of the platform. This action did not by any means portend differences in agreeing upon a declaration of principles, but rather showed the desire of delegates to settle the important affair first. Owing to the confident feeling that this year's nomination was equivalent to an election, the contest became exceedingly animated.

A year previous Clay had serious doubts of the success of his own party, and, regarding it as nearly certain that a Democrat would be elected in 1852, he hoped that the nomination would fall to Cass, whom he considered quite as able and much more honest and sincere than Buchanan.[1]

On the first ballot Cass had 116, Buchanan 93, Marcy 27, Douglas 20, and all the other candidates 25 votes. The number necessary to a choice was 188. Cass had 75 from the free, and 41 from the slave, States; Buchanan, 32 from the free, and 61 from the slave, States; while Douglas had only two votes from the South. The interest centred in these three candidates. Their names and the announcement of their votes never failed to bring prolonged ap-

---

[1] Private Correspondence, p. 619.

plause. The voting began on the third day of the convention, and seventeen ballots were that day taken. Douglas
gained considerably at the expense of Cass, but it looked
improbable that any of the three favorites could secure the
nomination, which seemed likely to go to a dark horse.
The merits of several others were canvassed, and among
them Franklin Pierce. On the fourth day Douglas steadily increased until the twenty-ninth ballot, when the votes
were: for Cass, 27; for Buchanan, 93; for Douglas, 91; and
no other candidate had more than 26. On the morning of
the fifth day, on the call of the States for the thirty-fourth
ballot, the Virginia delegation retired for consultation, and
coming back cast the fifteen votes of their State for Daniel
S. Dickinson, of New York. This was received with favor.

Dickinson was a delegate; he immediately took the floor
and said: "I came here not with instructions, but with expectations stronger than instructions, that I would vote for
and endeavor to procure the nomination of that distinguished citizen and statesman, General Lewis Cass." After saying he highly appreciated the compliment paid him by "the
land of Presidents, the Ancient Dominion," he declared, emphatically: "I could not consent to a nomination here without incurring the imputation of unfaithfully executing the
trust committed to me by my constituents—without turning
my back on an old and valued friend. Nothing that could
be offered me—not even the highest position in the government, the office of President of the United States—could
compensate me for such a desertion of my trust." [1]

On the next ballot, Virginia cast her fifteen votes for
Franklin Pierce, and then Cass reached his greatest strength,
receiving 131. As the weary round of balloting continued,
Pierce gained slowly, until, on the forty-eighth trial, he received 55, while Cass had 73, Buchanan 28, Douglas 33, and
Marcy 90. On the forty-ninth ballot there was a stam-
pede to Pierce, and he received 282 votes to 6 for all oth-

[1] Letters and Speeches, Dickinson, vol. i. p. 370.

ers. The convention nominated William R. King, of Alabama, for Vice - President, and then adopted a platform. Its vital declarations were : " The Democratic party of the Union . . . will abide by, and adhere to, a faithful execution of the acts known as the compromise measures settled by the last Congress—the act for reclaiming fugitives from service or labor included ; which act, being designed to carry out an express provision of the Constitution, cannot with fidelity thereto be repealed, nor so changed as to destroy or impair its efficiency. The Democratic party will resist all attempts at renewing in Congress, or out of it, the agitation of the slavery question, under whatever shape or color the attempt may be made."

The platform was adopted with but few dissenting voices. When the resolution endorsing the compromise measures was read, applause resounded from all sides ; many delegates demanded its repetition ; it was read over again, and a wild outburst of enthusiasm followed. There was no question that while the delegates had differed widely in regard to men, they were at one in desiring this resolution, a vital and popular article of Democratic faith.[1]

Franklin Pierce, of New Hampshire, was now in his forty-eighth year. He had in his boyhood drunk in patriotic principles from his father, an old Revolutionary soldier, at whose hearthstone the fellow-veterans were always welcome, and whose greatest joy was mutually to revive the sentiments which had animated them in 1776. Pierce was graduated from Bowdoin College, Maine, and afterwards became a lawyer. The prominent position which his father occupied in the Democratic party in the State was a help to the son's political advancement. He served in the legislature four years, when twenty-nine he went to Congress as representative, and became United States senator at thirty-three, being the youngest man in the Senate. He resigned

---

[1] New York *Tribune;* Presidential Elections, Stanwood ; Life of Pierce, Hawthorne ; Life of Pierce, Bartlett.

before the expiration of his term, and, coming home, devoted himself with diligence to the practice of his profession. He was a good lawyer and a persuasive advocate
before a jury. He declined the position of Attorney-General offered him by Polk, the appointment of United States
senator, and the nomination for governor by his own political party. He enlisted as a private soon after the outbreak of the Mexican war, but, before he went to Mexico,
was commissioned as brigadier-general, and served under
Scott with bravery and credit. He was a strong supporter
of the compromise measures. An eloquent political speaker,
graceful and attractive in manner, his integrity was above
suspicion, and he was also deeply religious. He had not the
knack of making money, and the fact received favorable
mention that while long in public life, and later enjoying
a good income from his profession, he had not accumulated
ten thousand dollars.

Such was the man who had been chosen by the reunited
Democratic party to lead it on to assured victory. It could
only be said that he was a respectable lawyer, politician,
and general, for he had tried all three callings, and in none
of them had he reached distinction. There can be no better commentary on the fact that he was not a man of mark
than the campaign biography written by his life-long friend,
Nathaniel Hawthorne. The gifted author, who had woven
entrancing tales out of airy nothings, failed, when he had his
bosom friend and a future President for a subject, to make
an interesting narrative. The most graceful pen in America, inspired by the truest friendship, labored painfully in
the vain endeavor to show that his hero had a title to greatness ; and the author, conscious that his book was not valuable, never consented to have the " Life of Pierce" included
in a collected edition of his works.[1]

Yet the book, in truthfulness and sincerity, was a model for
a campaign life. Hawthorne would not set down one word

---

[1] See the New York *Critic*, Sept. 28th and Nov. 23d, 1889.

that he did not believe absolutely true. Pierce evidently wished to appear before the public in his real character, for otherwise, knowing this quality of honesty in his friend, he would not have requested Hawthorne to write the biography, but would have been content with the fulsome panegyric that had already appeared. The author in his preface apologizes for coming before the public in a new occupation; but " when a friend, dear to him almost from boyish days, stands up before his country, misrepresented by indiscriminate abuse on the one hand, and by aimless praise on the other," it is quite proper " that he should be sketched by one who has had opportunities of knowing him well, and who is certainly inclined to tell the truth." The idea one gets of Pierce from the little book of one hundred and forty pages is that he was a gentleman of truth and honor, and warmly loved his family, his State, and his country. Having the inward feelings of a gentleman, he lacked not the external accomplishments; his fine physical appearance was graced by charming manners.[1] It is quite certain that Pierce did not desire the nomination; even if his sincerity in his letter of January 12th be doubted, the statement of Hawthorne is conclusive. It is possible he shrank from public life on account of an unfortunate weakness, or that he did not wish to expose the feeble health of his wife to the social demands entailed by the position.[2]

The nomination of Pierce was a complete surprise to the country. With the mass of the Democratic party, astonishment was mixed with indignation that the leaders who had borne the brunt of partisan conflict should be passed over for one whose history must be attentively studied, in order to know what he had done to merit the great honor. Yet the nomination was not the spontaneous affair which it

---

[1] See Life of Pierce, Hawthorne; Hawthorne and his Wife, Julian Hawthorne, vol. i.; Life of Pierce, Bartlett; Memoir of J. Q. Adams, vol. ix. p. 103; Memoir of Jefferson Davis, by his Wife, vol. i. p. 541.

[2] See Memories of Many Men, M. B. Field, p. 158.

seemed, for the candidature of Pierce had been carefully
nursed and his interests were in competent hands. The
idea of putting him forward originated early in the year
among the New England Democrats, who deemed it quite
likely that Cass, Douglas, and Buchanan would fail to secure the coveted prize. The favorite son of New Hampshire was eligible, as the State had been steadfastly Democratic, and Pierce was undoubtedly the most available man
in New England. Several conferences were held to decide
upon a plan of action, and it was determined that New
Hampshire should not present his name nor vote for him
until some other State had started the movement.[1] Pierce
was privy to much of this negotiation, and it is said that
the delicate matter of his excessive conviviality was talked
over with him, and that he promised to walk circumspectly
should he become President. At all events, a letter written
by him a few days before the convention shows a change
of feeling from his expression of January in regard to the
nomination;[2] and if his personal objections still remained,
they were overruled in the interest of the New Hampshire
and New England Democracy. Pierce promptly accepted
the nomination, " upon the platform adopted by the convention, not because this is expected of me as a candidate,
but because the principles it embraces command the approbation of my judgment, and with them I believe I can safely
say there has been no word nor act of my life in conflict."[3]

The Whig convention met at Baltimore June 16th, in
the same building that the Democrats had used, and it was
noticed that greater taste had presided over the decoration
of the hall than two weeks before. Among the delegates

---

[1] Account of Edmund Burke, one of the editors of the Washington
Union, of the events that led to the nomination of Pierce, cited by the
New York *Tribune* of Nov. 28th, 1853, from the *National Era.* The Boston *Atlas* said, June 7th, 1852, that, while Pierce's nomination would surprise the country, it was not wholly a surprise to many in the secrets of
the Democratic party; also conversation with J. W. Bradbury.
[2] Life of Pierce, Bartlett, p. 247.   [3] Ibid., p. 258.

were many able and earnest men.   Choate and Ashmun, of
Massachusetts, Dayton, of New Jersey, and Clayton, of
Delaware, were well known; and among those who afterwards gained distinction were Fessenden, of Maine, Dawes,
of Massachusetts, Evarts, of New York, Sherman, of Ohio,
and Baker, of Illinois.

The candidates for the presidential nomination were Webster, Fillmore, and General Scott; but the delegates differed
in regard to the platform as well as in their preferences for
men, and whether the Fugitive Slave law should be declared a finality was almost as important a question as who
should be the nominee.   There were more strangers in the
city than at the time of the Democratic convention, and
the outside pressure in favor of Webster was strong; but
it was apparent to cool observers that the chances of success were for Scott.   Fillmore had a large number of delegates pledged to him, for his friends had used unsparingly
in his favor the patronage of the government, yet had effected little at the North; his supporters were almost entirely from the South, where he was, moreover, popular on
account of his vigorous execution of the Fugitive Slave act.
Clay, likewise, had declared for Fillmore.[1]   Constant demonstrations in favor of each of the three candidates were
made in the form of processions headed by noisy bands,
and evening meetings addressed by eulogistic orators.   The
leaders of the party and managers of the respective candidates were constantly in conference, seeking to win outside
support for their man.

The platform which was submitted on Friday, the third
day of the convention, had the approval of the delegates
from the South, of Webster's friends, and of Webster himself.[2]   The important resolution declared that the compromise acts, "the act known as the Fugitive Slave law included, are received and acquiesced in by the Whig party of

---

[1] Private Correspondence, p. 628.
[2] See War between the States, A. H. Stephens, vol. ii. p. 237.

the United States as a settlement in principle and substance
of the dangerous and exciting questions which they embrace. . . . We insist upon their strict enforcement . . . and
we deprecate all further agitation of the question thus settled." Rufus Choate rose to advocate this resolution. His
appearance was striking; tall, thin, of a rich olive complexion, his face was rather that of an Oriental than an American. Raven locks hanging over a broad forehead, and pierc-
ing dark eyes, complete the picture. He had represented
Massachusetts in the Senate, but his greatest triumphs had
been won in the forum. His speech this day was the first
example of that brilliant convention-oratory which animates
and excites the hearers, and its beauty and power may still
be felt when the issue that inspired this impassioned oration
is dead. He said: "Why should we not engage ourselves
to the finality of the entire series of measures of compromise ? . . . The American people know, by every kind and degree of evidence by which such a truth ever can be known,
that these measures, in the crisis of their time, saved this
nation. I thank God for the civil courage which, at the
hazard of all things dearest in life, dared to pass and defend
them, and 'has taken no step backward.' I rejoice that the
healthy morality of the country, with an instructed conscience, void of offence towards God and man, has accepted
them. Extremists denounce all compromises ever. Alas!
do they remember such is the condition of humanity that
the noblest politics are but a compromise, an approximation
—a type—a shadow of good things—the buying of great
blessings at great prices? Do they forget that the Union
is a compromise, the Constitution—social life—that the harmony of the universe is but the music of compromise, by
which the antagonisms of the infinite Nature are composed
and reconciled? Let him who doubts—if such there be—
whether it were wise to pass these measures, look back
and recall with what instantaneous and mighty charm they
calmed the madness and anxiety of the hour! How every
countenance, everywhere, brightened and elevated itself!

How, in a moment, the interrupted and parted currents of fraternal feeling reunited! Sir, the people came together again as when, in the old Roman history, the tribes descended from the mount of Secession — the great compromise of that Constitution achieved—and flowed together behind the eagle into one mighty host of reconciled races for the conquest of the world. Well, if it were necessary to adopt these measures, is it not necessary to continue them? ... Why not, then, declare the doctrine of their permanence? In the language of Daniel Webster, 'Why delay the declaration? Sink or swim, live or die, survive or perish, I am for it.'"[1]

Few Americans have surpassed Choate in burning eloquence. He was a scholar, a student of words, and a master of language. The exuberance of his vocabulary was poured out through an organ of marvellous richness; dramatic gestures gave a point to his words, and he swayed that great audience as a reed is shaken with the wind. The enthusiastic and excited demonstrations of delight as Choate sat down displeased Botts, of Virginia, who was for Scott, and he took the orator to task for the attempt to excite enthusiasm for a particular candidate, when the ostensible object was to advocate the platform. This gave Choate the opportunity to name his candidate in a most felicitous way: "Ah, sir," he said, "what a reputation that must be, what a patriotism that must be, what a long and brilliant series of public services that must be, when you cannot mention a measure of utility like this but every eye spontaneously turns to, and every voice spontaneously utters, that great name of Daniel Webster!"[2] If a vivid and appropriate speech could have changed the tide of that convention, Choate would have been rewarded by the success of the man whom he venerated and loved. A delegate from Ohio objected to the crucial resolution, and he spoke for an influential body of delegates, but the platform as a

---

[1] Memoir of Rufus Choate, Brown, p. 270.   [2] Ibid., p. 277.

whole was adopted by a vote of 227 to 66. The nays were all from the North, and all were supporters of Scott.

The convention was now ready to ballot. Fillmore and Webster were of course in full sympathy with the platform, and it now became an important question—was Scott satisfied with the Fugitive Slave law ? He was the candidate of the Seward Whigs, and many strong anti-slavery men were enthusiastic in his favor; yet to be nominated he must have Southern votes, and carry Southern States to be elected. Goaded to it by an insinuation of Choate, Botts, before the vote on the platform was taken, produced a letter from Scott which could be interpreted to mean that he was a strong friend of the compromise measures.

On the first ballot Fillmore had 133, Scott 131, and Webster 29 votes. Webster had votes from all the New England States except Maine, and five votes outside of New England ; but from the South, none.[1] Fillmore received all the votes from the South except one given to Scott by John Minor Botts, of Virginia. Scott had all the votes from the North except those given to Webster and sixteen to Fillmore.[2] For fifty ballots there was no material change ; thirty-two votes were the highest number Webster reached. On the fiftieth ballot, Southern votes began to go to Scott, and on the fifty-third he had enough of them to secure the nomination, the ballot standing : Scott, 159; Fillmore, 112; Webster, 21.[3] In the Whig convention a majority nominated.

It is apparent that the conservative Whigs might have controlled the nomination, for the strength of Fillmore and Webster united on either one was sufficient. Fillmore was the second choice of Webster's friends, and, in the opinion

---

[1] New Hampshire four, Vermont three, Massachusetts eleven, Rhode Island two, Connecticut three, New York two, Wisconsin three, California one.

[2] Twenty Years of Congress, Blaine, vol. i. p. 101.

[3] On the last ballot Virginia gave Scott eight, Tennessee and Missouri each three votes.

of most of the Fillmore delegates, Webster was preferable to Scott. Considering the cordial relations existing between the President and Secretary of State, the fact that they were both in Washington, and that a Sunday intervened between the days of balloting, it may seem surprising that their friends did not get together and decide to concentrate their votes. The President had written a letter withdrawing his name from the consideration of the convention. This had been confided in secrecy to the delegate from Buffalo, N. Y., with instructions to present it whenever he should deem proper, but it was never laid before the convention.[1] But, in truth, it was impossible to deliver over the whole Fillmore strength to Webster. A determined effort was made to nominate the Massachusetts statesman, and his chances were greater than the number of his votes would seem to indicate. He had strong supporters at the South, among whom were Robert Toombs and Alexander H. Stephens.[2] Nearly all the Southern delegates, however, were instructed to vote for Fillmore, and this they felt bound to do, until it should be apparent that he could not be nominated. This point was seemingly reached on Saturday. The Southern friends of Webster made a careful canvass and found that of the one hundred and twenty-eight votes for Fillmore, which was his average number, twenty-two of them would probably go to Scott when the break came, but that one hundred and six could be relied upon for Webster. This number they promised if Webster would come to the line of Maryland forty strong, which would make one hundred and forty-six; he was always sure, in addition, of one vote from California, and one hundred and forty-seven was the number necessary for a choice. The Northern managers worked industriously to bring this about. They endeavored to win over enough from the New York delegation, but that was controlled by

---

[1] The Republic, Ireland, vol. xiii. p. 314.

[2] See The War between the States, A. H. Stephens, vol. i. p. 336; vol. ii. p. 239.

I.—17

Seward and would not quit Scott. They plied the Maine
delegates, who coldly refused their aid to the greatest son
of New England, for the defeat of Webster was a consummation as devoutly wished for as the success of Scott.
Powerful and almost tearful appeals were made to Dawes
and Lee to give their votes for Webster, if only for one ballot, in order that the Massachusetts delegation might be
unanimous; but they absolutely declined to do so, and voted
for Scott to the end. It was then impossible to secure the
requisite number of Northern votes, and the Southern delegates, unless they could be assured that their accession would
nominate Webster, would not leave Fillmore.[1]

Either before the convention met or immediately on its
assembling, a tacit bargain had been made between the
Northern managers for Scott and some Southern delegates.
It is evident from the debates in Congress that Scott had
influential supporters at the South, many of whom did not
scruple to declare their preference,[2] and while the congressional politicians might have been willing to take him without platform or personal pledges, they knew it was idle to
think of carrying a Southern State for him unless the convention should declare the Fugitive Slave law a finality. It
was therefore arranged that in case the Scott men should

---

[1] See an article entitled "Doings of the Convention" in the Boston
Courier, June 25th, of which the editor said this article was "furnished
by a gentleman whose character and standing in this community are a
guarantee for its fidelity and fairness." This article was attributed to
Choate and to a Mr. Swan, but it was probably written by William Hayden, a delegate, and a former editor of the Boston *Atlas*. The Springfield *Republican* of June 28th copied the article entire, and said: "We are
assured by another Massachusetts delegate that, so far as it goes, its
statements are strictly true." See also Life of Choate, Brown, p. 279, and
Reminiscences, Peter Harvey, p. 239. "It was stated by the chairman of the
Mississippi delegation that nine-tenths of the Southern delegates were
willing to leave Fillmore and go for Webster, although they were deterred
from doing so for fear that when their phalanx was broken, enough delegates would go to Scott to nominate him."—Boston *Daily Advertiser*.

[2] See *Congressional Globe*, vol. xxiv. p. 1077 *et seq.*, also p. 1159.

support the declaration of principles agreeable to the South, the Southern delegates, on the breaking-up of the Fillmore vote, would go to Scott in numbers sufficient to nominate him.   The vote at that time against the platform was by no means a representation of the entire Northern opposition, for many delegates sacrificed their cherished opinions in order to make sure the nomination of their candidate. The New York *Tribune* spoke for a large number of faithful Whigs when it said that while there was no probability that the Fugitive Slave law would be altered by Congress during the present generation, to declare it a finality was irritating and useless.   Agitation will not be stopped by resolution, the editor argued, but if the hunting of fugitive slaves at the North should cease, it might be checked.[1]

Scott was a Virginian by birth, a gentleman of honorable character and conservative principles, but his claim to the nomination was solely on account of his brilliant campaign in the Mexican war.   As one of his enthusiastic advocates said in the Senate, he was "greater than Cortez in his triumphant, glorious, and almost miraculous march from Vera Cruz to the old city of the Aztecs."[2]   It would be unfair to judge the man from his autobiography, for it was written in a garrulous old age, and is the most egotistical of memoirs.[3]   At this time he was inflated with vanity and puffed up with his own importance.   It should be the prayer of his friends that he may be estimated by his actions rather than by his words, for to his adversary it was a delight that he had written a book.   Many of the Whig politicians had a superstition that only a general could lead them to victory, for they had never been successful except under Harrison and Taylor.   If it were military glory which

---

[1] The *Tribune*, June 22d.   In addition to the authorities already cited I have used in this account of the Whig convention the New York *Tribune;* History of Presidential Elections, Stanwood; Memories of Rufus Choate, Neilson; Life of Webster, Curtis, vol. ii.

[2] Mangum, of North Carolina, April 15th.

[3] The autobiography of Lieutenant-General Scott was written in 1863.

won the populace, why was not Scott, a greater general than either, an eminently strong candidate?

Fillmore took his defeat with equanimity, but to Webster the action of the convention was the eclipse of the bright hopes with which he had long deluded himself. The account given by his Boswell[1] of the great man's interview with Choate immediately after the convention is inexpressibly sad. The deep grief exhibited on that handsome face, the studied avoidance of the subject of which his mind was too full for utterance, at the silent meal of which the three partook, and then the hour's private conversation, made the scene linger long afterwards in the memory of Choate as the most mournful experience of his life.[2] The words of the Preacher, " Vanity of vanities, all is vanity," must have come to the great statesman with a force felt only by deep and strong natures. Had he served the law or literature[3] with half the zeal with which he served the public, he would not in his age have been left naked to his enemies. What a comment it is on the disappointments that hedge about political life that the author of the reply to Hayne and of the Bunker Hill and Plymouth orations should sigh in vain for the position to which so many mediocre men have been called! It is easy to censure ambition like Webster's, yet we know that unless, in a democracy, the best statesmen desire the highest office in the State, political dry rot has set in—a fact which it is our fashion to ignore when we moralize on the desire for the presidency that lays such strong hold of our public men. Many writers who believe that Webster sold himself to the South gloat over the fact that

---

[1] Peter Harvey, Lodge so calls him, p. 95.   [2] Harvey, p. 195.

[3] "I make no progress towards accomplishing an object which has engaged my contemplations for many years, A History of the Constitution of the United States and President Washington's Administration. This project has long had existence as an idea; and as an idea I fear it is likely to die."—Webster to Edward Everett, Nov. 28th, 1848, Private Correspondence, vol. ii. p. 289.

he did not receive a single Southern vote in the convention, and, with reckless disregard of his physical condition, aver that the disappointment at not receiving the nomination actually killed him.[1]

The usual noisy rejoicings over the result of the convention disturbed the founder of the Whig party, Clay, as he lay upon his death-bed in the National Hotel at Washington. He had come to the capital at the opening of Congress, but had only been able to go once to the Senate. His disease was consumption, and death had now stared him in the face many months. He had a sincere Christian faith, and, retaining his mental faculties to the last, awaited with composure the inevitable summons which came on the 29th day of June. As he had been loved, so was he mourned by the people of the nation. The funeral progress was made through many cities on the way to Lexington. New York testified its grief by a most imposing demonstration. The city was draped in mourning, and appropriate inscriptions were everywhere displayed; the favorite one, "the man who would rather be right than President," seemed to sum up best the life of Clay. Minute-guns were fired from the forts in the bay, and bells tolled, as the long procession accompanied the funeral-car through the streets, marching to the dirge and the mournful measure of the muffled drums. Never had the city seen such a general manifestation of popular grief. Political differences were forgotten. A great countryman was dead, and he was mourned not as a Whig, but as an American.[2] Everywhere those who had loved and admired him, those who had been swayed by his voice and influenced by his words, paid a last respectful tribute to his remains. The lament of the nation was loud and sincere, and Kentucky mourned for him as a mother sorrows for a son.[3]

---

[1] "It was the fashion in certain quarters to declare that it killed him; but this was manifestly absurd."—Life of Webster, Lodge, p. 340; see what follows.   [2] New York *Herald*, July 21st.

[3] For an account of the obsequies, see Last Years of Henry Clay, Colton, p. 438 *et ante*.

Scott's letter of acceptance was published a few days after the adjournment of the convention. "I accept," he wrote, "the nomination with the resolutions annexed."[1] The action of the convention was coldly received by the Whigs. Those who liked the platform did not like the candidate, and those who were warm for the candidate objected decidedly to the platform.[2] Many thought: the voice is Jacob's voice, but the hands are the hands of Esau. Seward was the political juggler, or Mephistopheles, as some called him, and the result was regarded as his triumph. The notion prevailed that Scott, if he became President, would be controlled by Seward, and this was certain to hurt the candidate at the South. Seward therefore, five days after the nomination, took the unusual course of writing a public letter, in which he said he would not ask or accept "any public station or preferment whatever at the hands of the President of the United States, whether that President were Winfield Scott or any other man."[3]

Some of the prominent Whig newspapers of Georgia declined to sustain Scott, because his election would mean Free-soilism and Sewardism.[4] An address was issued on the 3d of July by Alexander H. Stephens, Robert Toombs, and five other Whig representatives, in which they flatly refused to support Scott because he was "the favorite candidate of the Free-soil wing of the Whig party," and he had not clearly said that he regarded the compromise measures as a finality.[5] The business men of New York city disliked the nom-

---

[1] The letter was published in the *National Intelligencer* of June 29th. It is dated June 24th. He received his official notification the 22d.

[2] The phrase "We accept the candidate, but spit upon the platform," became very common among Northern Whigs.

[3] Seward's Works, vol. iii. p. 416. The letter is dated June 26th.

[4] The Augusta *Chronicle* and the Savannah *Republican*. The Savannah *News* disliked the nomination exceedingly.

[5] Von Holst, vol. iv. p. 208; McCluskey's Political Text-book, p. 682. Three of the signers were from Georgia, two from Alabama, one each from Mississippi and Virginia.

ination, as they were afraid of Seward's influence. There was no enthusiasm in Boston and Massachusetts; the State was Whig to the core, but the active people and most of the newspapers were disaffected because Webster had not been nominated. In other places, also, there was discontent at the turn affairs had taken.[1]

A Union convention of Georgia and a Native American convention, held at Trenton, N. J., nominated Webster for President; later, a Webster electoral ticket was put into the field in Massachusetts; but he neither accepted nor declined any of these nominations. The happiest day of this, the last year of Webster's life, was the 9th of July, when he received an enthusiastic reception and heart-felt greeting from the citizens of Boston. It was the fashion then to compare all demonstrations with the one made in honor of Lafayette in 1824,[2] and those who took part in both declared Webster's reception much more imposing than that given to the gallant Frenchman.[3] The estrangement between Massachusetts and her favorite son, which had existed since the speech of the 7th of March, had passed away. Webster's address was in exquisite taste. He did not touch the political questions of the day, but he paid an eloquent tribute to Boston and to Massachusetts, for he was as proud of Massachusetts as was she of her great statesman.[4]

---

[1] "The dissatisfaction in the early part of the summer took a somewhat active form in the States of New Jersey, Pennsylvania, Georgia, Tennessee, North Carolina, and Massachusetts."—Life of Webster, Curtis, vol. ii. p. 650.

[2] Those who are interested in these matters will find an entertaining account of this in Josiah Quincy's Figures of the Past.

[3] Curtis, vol. ii. p. 628.

[4] In Theodore Parker's Scrap-Book, in the Boston Public Library, is an account of this reception to Webster, taken from the Boston *Atlas* of July 10th. Among the men who rode in the carriages was George T. Curtis. Parker underscores his name, and writes in lead pencil: "N. B. That Nemesis is never asleep. Webster must be attended with the Kidnapper. The Sims brigade ought also to have been on parade. The court-house should have been festooned with chains."

While the candidacy of Scott repelled the most conservative Whigs, the platform made it impossible for the Freesoilers to come to his support. They held a convention in August and nominated Hale for President and Julian for Vice-President. They epigrammatized their principles in the words " Free soil, free speech, free labor, and free men." The drift of anti-slavery opinion, as well as its varying shades, is illustrated by the fact that Henry Wilson, Charles F. Adams, of Massachusetts, and Giddings supported Hale, while Wade, Seward, and Greeley advocated the election of Scott. All of these men were of Whig antecedents.

The Democrats soon recovered from the surprise of Pierce's nomination, and began to feel a genuine enthusiasm for their candidate, and for their declaration of principles. They were joyful to have the party reunited; they were certain that the platform represented the prevailing sentiment; and when they had read up about Pierce, they were satisfied that he was not a vulnerable candidate. The men who were prominent before the Baltimore convention did not delay the announcement that they would give Pierce their cordial support. The New York *Evening Post*, which upheld powerfully the Free-soil movement of 1848, and whose editor had strong anti-slavery views, now advocated Pierce, and was followed by other journals which got their cue from the metropolitan organ.[1] The argument of the *Post*, that the Democratic candidate and platform were really more favorable to liberty than the Whig, was somewhat strained; the editor failed to look the situation squarely in the face.[2] He was, however, acting in perfect harmony with the prominent New York Democrats who had, four years previously, bolted the regular nomination. Van Buren himself had announced that he should vote for Pierce.[3] Yet it was perfectly evident that anti-slavery men

---

[1] Life of William Cullen Bryant, Godwin, vol. ii. pp. 43, 62.

[2] See especially an article cited in *National Intelligencer* of July 15th.

[3] Letter of July 1st, Life of Pierce, Bartlett, p. 295.

had more to hope from the success of the Whigs than of the Democrats.[1] Chase, although still a Democrat, would not support Pierce, but gave his adherence to the Free-soil nominations, and tried hard, though in vain, to bring to their support his former New York associates.[2]

Although the session of Congress lasted until August 31st, 1852, its proceedings are devoid of interest, as is apt to be the case in the year devoted to the making of a new President. "A politician," writes Horace Mann from Washington, "does not sneeze without reference to the next Presidency. All things are carried to that tribunal for decision." "Congress does little else but intrigue for the respective candidates." "Our debates lately are mostly on the presidential question." "Our political caldron is beginning to seethe vehemently."[3]

But there was one senator who felt that he owed allegiance to neither political party, and who, with an entire disregard of the effect his words might have on the fortune of either candidate, was determined to have his say. In May, Sumner presented a memorial from the representatives of the Society of Friends in New England, asking the repeal of the Fugitive Slave law. In introducing it he made a few remarks, laying down this aphorism : "Freedom, and not slavery, is national; while slavery, and not freedom, is sectional." This sententious truth proclaimed by the independent senator was destined to be of greater worth, even as a party shibboleth, than the verbose declarations of the Democratic and Whig conventions. In July, Sumner wanted leave to introduce a resolution instructing the judiciary committee to consider the expediency of reporting a bill for the immediate repeal of the Fugitive Slave act ; but permission was refused, only ten senators voting for it. The short de-

---

[1] This is well stated by Horace Mann, Letter of June 24th, Life, p. 370.

[2] Life of Chase, Schuckers, p. 130.

[3] Letters of Feb. 3d, March 27th, April 24th, May 8th, Life, pp. 358, 362, 363.

bate on the subject is interesting from the fact of one of the senators from Mississippi[1] stating that a convention of his State had solemnly declared that the repeal of this law would be regarded as sufficient ground for the dissolution of the Union. This, he said, was no idle threat. While it was true that his people did not think this act of any essential benefit, as slaves from Mississippi seldom escaped, and when they did the cost and trouble of recapturing them amounted to more than their value, yet the repeal " would be an act of bad faith," and show that the North would not live up to any bargain. One of the senators from Georgia[2] followed in a similar strain. His State stood pledged to dissolve the ties which bound her to the Union the moment the Fugitive Slave law was repealed, and this interdependence he pointed impressively by quoting the prophetic saying of the pilgrims:

> "While stands the Coliseum, Rome shall stand;
> When falls the Coliseum, Rome shall fall."

Although Sumner failed to get a hearing this day, he was resolved to speak before the session came to an end. Five days before the final adjournment an amendment to one of the appropriation bills was under consideration, which provided for the payment of extraordinary expenses incurred in executing the laws of the United States. It was plain that the intent was to have the general government bear the cost of capturing runaway negroes. Sumner moved that the Fugitive Slave act be excepted from the operation of this amendment, and that the act itself be repealed. This gave him the opportunity to speak on the question, which, in his view, far transcended the importance of President-making.

"I could not," he said, "allow this session to reach its close, without making or seizing an opportunity to declare myself openly against the usurpation, injustice, and cruelty of the late enactment by Congress for the recovery of fugi-

---

[1] Brooke.   [2] Charlton.

tive slaves." He made an elaborate argument in favor of his thesis that slavery was sectional, not national. He showed that this was true from a legal point of view; it was historically confirmed; the statesmen who made the nation bore witness to its truth; the church and the colleges supported the statesmen; the literature of the land condemned slavery; and it was abhorred by the "outspoken, unequivocal heart of the country" at the time the Constitution was adopted.

He examined the history of the fugitive slave clause of the Constitution, and pointed out that it was not one of the compromises; he averred that the Fugitive Slave act of 1793 "was not originally suggested by any difficulty or anxiety touching fugitives from labor." He argued that the act of 1850 was unconstitutional, dissecting it with severity, and exposing its merciless provisions in terse statements. Congress had no power to pass such a law, he maintained; but if it had, it was bound by a provision of the Constitution to give the fugitive a jury trial. "Even if this act could claim any validity or apology under the Constitution, which it cannot, *it lacks that essential support in the public conscience of the States where it is to be enforced, which is the life of all law, and without which any law must become a dead letter.*"

As pertinent to the subject, he introduced an original historical document in the shape of a letter from Washington, which had never before seen the light. One of Washington's slaves had fled to New Hampshire. In a letter to the collector at Portsmouth, after describing the fugitive and expressing the desire of her mistress, Mrs. Washington, for her return, he says: "I do not mean, however, by this request that violent measures should be used, *as would excite a mob or riot—which might be the case if she has adherents—or even uneasy sensations in the minds of well-disposed citizens.* Rather than either of these should happen, I would forego her services altogether; and the example also, which is of infinite more importance."

The orator impressively added: "Sir, the existing slave act cannot be enforced without violating the precept of Washington. Not merely uneasy sensations among well-disposed persons, but rage, tumult, commotion, mob, riot, violence, death, gush from its fatal, overflowing fountains. Not a case occurs without endangering the public peace."

He closed with an application of the higher-law doctrine to the subject. "The slave act violates the Constitution and shocks the public conscience. With modesty, and yet with firmness, let me add, sir, it offends against the divine law. No such enactment can be entitled to support. As the throne of God is above every earthly throne, so are his laws and statutes above all the laws and statutes of man."[1]

This was Sumner's first elaborate oration in the Senate. He spoke for four hours in an elegant and finished manner.[2] It was the speech of a lawyer, a scholar, an historian, and a moralist, for he had the equipment of them all. To intellectual strength and moral feeling was joined the physical courage that dared anything. Here was a new and dangerous foe of slavery. Clemens, of Alabama, with a levity certainly not shown by his Southern associates, thought the speech unworthy of notice; "the ravings of a maniac," he said, "may sometimes be dangerous, but the barking of a puppy never did any harm." Hale complimented the orator; he had placed himself "side by side with the first orators of antiquity, and as far ahead of any living American orator as freedom is ahead of slavery." Chase declared that the speech "will be received as an emphatic protest against the slavish doctrine of finality in legislation which two of the political conventions recently held have joined in forcing upon the country;" this speech "will mark an era in American history." Horace Mann wrote home: "The 26th of August, 1852, redeemed the 7th of March, 1850."[3]

For Sumner's amendment there were only four votes, viz.:

---

[1] These quotations are from vol. xxv. *Congressional Globe.*
[2] Life of Horace Mann, p. 381.   [3] Ibid., p. 381.

Chase, Hale, Sumner, and Wade. It was noted as significant that Seward was not present during this debate, but there was nothing inconsistent in his not caring at this time to make a record upon a question of no practical value, for it was clearly impossible to repeal the Fugitive Slave law, and in a political campaign, where report spoke of him as the exponent of the Whig candidate, it would have been impolitic for him to enter upon this question. He knew well enough that the anti-slavery cause had more to hope from Scott than from Pierce, and, in his view, it was a duty of anti-slavery men to work and vote for the success of the Whig party. William Cullen Bryant, a keen observer and, though supporting Pierce, a strong opponent of slavery, thought this effort of Sumner useless. Bryant undoubtedly expressed the best political wisdom of the time when he wrote: "I see not the least chance of a repeal or change of the Fugitive Slave law. Its fate is to fall into disuse. All political organizations to procure its repeal are attempts at an impracticability. We must make it odious, and prevent it from being enforced." [1]

No presidential campaign is so hopeless that the weaker candidate and his friends do not at some time during its progress sincerely entertain anticipations of success. [2] In a few weeks after the nomination of Scott, the bitter disappointment of Webster's and Fillmore's friends had, in some degree, subsided, and the faithful party-men began to rally to the support of the regular nominee. The Scott managers tried to work up enthusiasm for their candidate in the manner that had been so successful in 1840. Scott was a greater general than Harrison. It seemed possible that Lundy's Lane and Mexico might arouse as great enthusiasm as had been inspired by the watchword of Tippecanoe. As a beginning, a mass-meeting was held on the anniversary of the

---

[1] Life of Bryant, Godwin, vol. ii. p. 63.

[2] Rufus Choate, as late as Sept. 26th, "thought Scott's chances of an election were very good." See Reminiscences by Parker, p. 259.

battle as near as possible to the classic spot of Lundy's Lane. The gathering hosts could not assemble on the battle-field where Scott had so gallantly and successfully fought, for that was in Canada; they therefore came together at Niagara Falls. Delegations arrived from many States. Two hundred and twenty officers and soldiers of the war of 1812 were present, and some of them had also taken part in the battle which they were now glad to celebrate. The meeting lasted two days; the number present varied decidedly, according as the count was Democratic or Whig, but no doubt remains that it was an imposing assemblage. Thos. Ewing, of Ohio, acted as president of the day, and among the speakers were Henry Winter Davis, Greeley, and William Schouler. The New York *Tribune* judged that it surpassed the most enthusiastic of the Harrison meetings of 1840.[1]

Nevertheless, this was a quiet campaign. There was no principle at stake. The New York *Tribune*, which could not accept the Whig platform, and yet in deference to its position as a party organ kept its anti-slavery views in the background, dragged into the canvass the tariff question. Elaborate articles constantly appeared in its columns, advocating the principle of protection, and endeavoring to prove that the economic interests of the people would be better cared for by the Whigs than by the Democrats. The *Tribune* quoted the approval of Pierce by the London *Times*, "as a valuable practical ally to the commercial policy" of England,[2] and added, let Americans "choose between the British and American candidate." In another issue, with an eye to an important part of the foreign vote, the editor asks:

---

[1] July 29th. The meeting was July 27th and 28th.

[2] *Tribune*, July 21st. "We greatly prefer General Pierce to either General Cass, Mr. Douglas, or Mr. Buchanan; . . . to descend to minor particulars in his political creed, he is at once a man of New England and yet a decided champion of free trade."—London *Times*, June 24th, cited in New York *Herald*, July 9th.

" Will Irishmen support British policy ?" [1]   The New York
Evening Post took up the gauntlet, arguing gravely that the
cause of freedom of trade was a vital one, and that it demanded the election of Pierce.   Yet everybody knew that
Greeley and Bryant were stifling their honest convictions;
that instead of combating one another's economic notions,
they ought to have joined in denunciation of the Fugitive
Slave law and of the platform that declared it a finality.
The discussion of the tariff attracted no interest, and had
no appreciable effect upon the result. [2]

The campaign soon became characterized by apathy.
After the Lundy's Lane celebration, the Whig mass-meet-
ings were small and lacked enthusiasm, while those of the
Democrats were not much, if any, better. [3]   Evening meetings were held, and idle crowds were attracted by torchlight
processions and amused by transparencies which paraded
the virtues of one or set forth the failings of the other candidate. But the heart of the people was not in it.   The
cynical chronicler of the times wrote : " It is all a contest
between the politicians for the spoils." [4]

As there could be no sober discussion of principles, the
campaign degenerated into one where personal detraction
of the candidates became the feature. Pierce was called a
drunkard ; he was said to be a coward ; the story ran that
on the field of Churubusco fear overcame him and he fainted.
It did not matter that the charge of cowardice was effectually disproved by the official report of General Scott ; [5] the
partisan journals would not retract the slander, and a favorite doggerel ditty had for its burden the contrast between
the bravery of Scott and the cowardice of Pierce. [6]   At the

---

[1] Sept. 9th.   [2] See New York *Herald*, Aug. 21st.
[3] Ibid., Sept. 19th.   [4] Ibid., Aug. 21st.
[5] See New York *Herald*, July 22d ; Autobiography of General Scott,
p. 494 ; Life of Pierce, Hawthorne, p. 102.

[6]   " Two generals are in the field,
            Frank Pierce and Winfield Scott,

South, strangely enough, Pierce was charged with being an abolitionist, though garbled extracts from an imperfect report of a speech were all that could give color to this imputation. He was also accused of being opposed to religious liberty. There had been until recently a provision in the New Hampshire constitution that certain State offices should be held only by Protestants. It was said that Pierce did not desire the removal of this religious test, while, in truth, he had made continued efforts for that very object.[1] His utterances in general had not been of the kind to attract large attention, but it was evident from his public letter of May 27th that he was inclined to side with the South rather than with the North on the sectional question;[2] and it is a perfect indication of public sentiment at the North that this most serious objection to Pierce was little used.

The charge against Scott which had the greatest influence on the result has been already alluded to: he was the Seward candidate and tinctured with Free-soilism. Accused of Nativism, the basis for the charge was a letter more than ten years old to the American party men of Philadelphia. "I now hesitate," the general had written, "between ex-

---

Some think that Frank's a fighting man,
    And some think he is not.
'Tis said that when in Mexico,
    While leading on his force,
He took a sudden fainting fit,
    And tumbled off his horse.

"But gallant Scott has made his mark
    On many a bloody plain,
And patriot hearts beat high to greet
    The Chief of Lundy's Lane.
And Chippewa is classic ground,
    Our British neighbors know,
And if you'd hear of later deeds,
    Go ask in Mexico."

—From Theodore Parker's Scrap-book, Boston Public Library.
[1] Life of Pierce, Hawthorne, p. 123.   [2] Life of Pierce, Bartlett, p. 246.

tending the period of residence before naturalization and a total repeal of all acts of Congress on the subject : my mind inclines to the latter." [1]   The large Irish and German immigration of the past few years had given the foreign vote an importance never before attached to it, and this is the first presidential campaign in which we light upon those now familiar efforts to cajole the German and Irish citizens.   It is apparent that Scott's opinion was a dangerous expression for a presidential candidate.

Scott's vanity and egotism became a familiar subject of ridicule, and the nickname of " Fuss and Feathers," given him in the army, was circulated gleefully by the Democrats. An example of the inclination of Americans to look on the humorous side of things was shown in this campaign.   At the beginning of the Mexican war, when Scott, the general of the army, was, as he relates, in the habit of spending fifteen to eighteen hours a day in his office, he happened one day to be absent at the moment when the Secretary of War called.   In explanation, Scott wrote that regular meals being out of the question, he had only stepped out to take " a hasty plate of soup."   On another occasion, when it was proposed to send him to the Rio Grande, he, appreciating the Democratic jealousy of Whig generals, represented to the administration that unless he could have their steady support for his plans, it would be useless to go, " for soldiers had a far greater dread of a fire upon the rear than of the most formidable enemy in front." [2]   It is not easy to perceive why "a hasty plate of soup" and "a fire upon the rear" should have seemed so ridiculous ; but these words of the stately general had, nevertheless, their place among the materials of the canvass, and were the cause of great merriment to the Democrats.

It is pleasant to record some of the amenities of this cam-

[1] Boston *Post*, June 30th ; New York *Herald*, July 15th.   The date of the letter was Nov. 10th, 1841.

[2] Autobiography of Lieutenant-General Scott, p. 385.

paign. A scurrilous letter from Concord, charging Pierce
with gross intemperance, having appeared in the New York
Tribune, the editor the next day apologized for its insertion,
and said that had he known its character, it would not have
been printed; he added that while General Pierce was not
"a temperance man in our sense of the term, we know nothing with regard to his habits that should subject him to public reprehension." [1] Martin Van Buren wrote: "The Whig
nominee, in that chivalrous spirit which belongs to his character, has commenced his first political campaign with a
frank admission of the private worth and claims to public
confidence of his opponent—a concession which I am very
sure General Pierce will be at all times ready to recipro-
cate." [2] Hawthorne, in his campaign life of Pierce, spoke
of Scott as "an illustrious soldier, indeed, a patriot, and one
indelibly stamped into the history of the past." [3] The New
York *Herald*, which supported Pierce, said: "For the private reputation of General Scott, as well as for his military
character, we have always had the highest regard and deepest veneration. He is a hero—the pink of chivalry in his
profession; and as a gentleman in social life, he is without
stain or blemish." [4]

The elation of the Whigs at the success of their big
Lundy's Lane meeting was of short duration, for the August
State elections were favorable to the Democrats. The Free-
soil convention followed hard upon and its nominations
augured ill for the Whigs. While this party called itself
the Free-soil Democracy, it was patent that it would this
year draw away more Whigs than Democrats in the doubtful States of New York and Ohio. The September elections afforded the Whigs no comfort. They cast about how
the tide of public sentiment might be turned, and it was determined that General Scott should make a tour of the country and show himself to the people, in the hope that his mag-

---

[1] New York *Tribune*, June 11th.   [2] Life of Pierce, Bartlett, p. 294.
[3] Life of Pierce, Hawthorne, p. 137.   [4] Sept. 26th.

nificent martial presence might kindle enthusiasm. Although Harrison had made several speeches in 1840, it was considered beneath the dignity of a presidential candidate to take the stump; but a pretext was found for this proposed journey. An act of Congress had made the general of the army one of a board to examine Blue Lick Springs, Ky. with a view to locate there the Western military asylum for sick and disabled soldiers; and, as Scott took with him two associates, this was the avowed object of his leaving the headquarters at Washington.[1] His first important stop was at Pittsburgh, where he made an off-hand speech, expressing his love for Pennsylvania on account of the patriotism and many great virtues of the people.

In 1852, the only rail route from Pittsburgh to Cincinnati, which were necessary points of the journey, was *via* Cleveland, and this fitted well the object of the political managers, for it gave their candidate the opportunity to traverse the State of Ohio, which the Free-soil nominations had put in the doubtful column. Scott was received at Cleveland in a drenching rain by crowds of people. " I was pained," he said in his harangue, "that while I was comfortably sheltered in a covered carriage, you should have been exposed to rain and mud." A voice in the crowd, bidding him welcome, with pronounced Hibernian accent, suggested the propriety of explaining that he had changed his notions about Nativism, upon which Scott warmly exclaimed : " I hear that rich brogue—I love to hear it ; it makes me remember noble deeds of Irishmen, many of whom I have led to battle and to victory."

The country between Cleveland and Columbus was thickly settled, and crowds turned out at every station to greet the candidate and general. He repeated at Shelby what he had many times said : " I have not come to solicit your votes. I go on a mission of public charity." At Columbus he made

---

[1] See the indignant article in the New York *Tribune* of Sept. 27th, denying that Scott had taken the stump.

a spirited and manly speech to a deputation of Germans, denying that he had hanged fifteen of their countrymen in Mexico.

In all of his many addresses, Scott steered clear of political questions; he thanked the people for their hearty greetings; he praised their cities and their States. Ohio was "the Empire State of the West;" Kentucky was "famous for the valor of her troops and for the beauty of her daughters;" Indiana was "one of the great Northwestern States— one of the States most devoted to the Union—one of its main props and supports." At Madison, Ind., he again had compliments for our adopted as well as our native-born citizens. "I have," he said, "heard several times since I landed on your shores the rich brogue of the Irish and the foreign accent of the German. They are welcome to my ear, for they remind me of many a well-fought and hard-won field on which I have been nobly supported by the sons of Germany and of Ireland." Remaining over Sunday in this city, he showed his liberality by attending mass at the Catholic church in the morning, and the service of the Episcopal church in the evening.

Scott left Ohio on his return trip just before the October State election. Pennsylvania and Indiana voted on the same day for State officers. All three went Democratic, and this indicated beyond doubt that Pierce would carry them in November, which would make his election certain. The Whig cause was not helped by the stumping tour of their candidate. Scott was far from happy in his off-hand addresses; all but one were commonplace and some afforded fit subjects for ridicule. The New York *Herald* published them as a Democratic campaign document under the title of "The Modern Epic. Fifty-two Speeches by Major-General Winfield Scott, embracing a Narrative of a Trip to the Blue Licks and back to Washington in Search of a Site for a Military Hospital. The Iliad of the Nineteenth Century."[1]

---

[1] In this relation of the tour of General Scott, I have carefully compared

Instead of travelling around to be stared at by gaping crowds, Pierce spent the period of his candidacy in dignified retreat at his Concord home, varied only by a short visit to the Isles of Shoals, where he enjoyed the companionship and unrestrained talk of his intimate friend Hawthorne.[1] He had occasion to write a few letters and make a few short speeches. His most important effort was when the news of Webster's death came: he paid a feeling tribute to the personal friend, the son of New Hampshire, and the American citizen.

That Pierce was elected in November surprised few; that his victory should be so overwhelming astounded Democrats as well as Whigs. Scott carried only four States—Vermont, Massachusetts, Kentucky, and Tennessee. Pierce had 254 electoral votes and Scott 42. It was the largest majority since the era of good feeling when every elector but one cast his vote for Monroe; and the majority in the popular vote of Pierce over Scott was more than 200,000—a larger majority than had been received since record was made of the popular vote. The Free-soil following showed a marked falling-off as compared with 1848.[2]

The reason of Democratic success was because that party unreservedly endorsed the compromise, and in its approval neither platform nor candidate halted. Other causes contributed to increase the majorities of Pierce, but the greater fidelity of the Democratic party to the settlement of 1850 was in itself sufficient for his election. The country was tired of slavery agitation. The people were convinced that the status of every foot of territory in the United States, as regards slavery, was fixed; that it had ceased to be a polit-

---

the accounts and reports of speeches in the New York *Tribune* and New York *Herald*.

[1] See Hawthorne and his Wife, vol. i. p. 466; Hawthorne's American Note-books, vol. ii.

[2] History of Presidential Elections, Stanwood. Free-soil vote, 1848, 291,263; 1852, 155,825.

ical question. It is true that a part of this settlement was
a slave-catching bill, obnoxious to the North; but as it was a
part of the bargain, it must be enforced in good faith. The
benefit in politics, thought the majority, seldom comes unmixed. With the great good of forever settling the slavery
question, it is surely only a small ill that the constitutional
provision for the rendition of fugitive slaves shall be carried
out. Thus thought, after the election, nearly everybody who
voted for Pierce; and the majority of voters for Scott did
not differ widely from this opinion.

The business interests of the country were on the side of
the Democrats. The *Tribune* complained that the mercantile Whigs of New York City either kept away from the
polls or voted for Pierce, because they would not endorse
the Seward candidate.[1] Trade was good, the country was
very prosperous, and this state of affairs would likely continue under settled political conditions, of which there appeared to the commercial interests greater promise under
Democratic than Whig rule.

The Democratic party seemed to have a noble mission
confided to it. It had control of the Senate and the House,
and the country had now given into its charge the executive department. It had gained the confidence of the people because it professed to be the party essentially opposed
to the agitation of slavery; because it was the party of pac-
ification; and because it insisted upon observing sacredly the
compromises of the Constitution, and all other compromises.

For a proper understanding of our history, the events of
the decade between 1850 and 1860 must be considered in their
bearing on the success of the Republican party in the latter
year. One of the most important causes that led to this result was the publication of "Uncle Tom's Cabin." Of the
literary forces that aided in bringing about the immense
revolution in public sentiment between 1852 and 1860, we

---

[1] New York *Tribune*, Nov. 8th.

may affirm with confidence that by far the most weighty
was the influence spread abroad by this book.

This story, when published as a serial in the *National
Era*, an anti-slavery newspaper at Washington, attracted
little attention, but after it was given to the world in book
form in March, 1852, it proved the most successful novel
ever written. The author felt deeply that the Fugitive
Slave law was unjust, and that there was cruelty in its execution; this inspired her to pour out her soul in a protest
against slavery. She thought that if she could only make
the world see slavery as she saw it,[1] her object would be accomplished; she would then have induced people to think
right on the subject.

The book was composed under the most disheartening
circumstances. Worn out with the care of many young
children; overstrained by the domestic trials of a large
household; worried because her husband's small income did
not meet their frugal needs; eking out the poor professor's
salary by her literary work in a house too small to afford a
study for the author—under such conditions there came the
inspiration of her life. "Uncle Tom's Cabin" was an outburst of passion against the wrong done to a race, and it
was written with an intensity of feeling that left no room
for care in the artistic construction of the story. The style
is commonplace, the language is often trite and inelegant,
sometimes degenerating into slang, and the humor is
strained. Yet Macaulay, a severe critic and lover of literary form, was so impressed by the powerful book that he
considered it on the whole "the most valuable addition that
America has made to English literature;"[2] and Lowell felt
"that the secret of Mrs. Stowe's power lay in that same
genius by which the great successes in creative literature
have always been achieved."[3]

---

[1] Mrs. Stowe lived in Cincinnati from 1832 to 1850.
[2] Macaulay's Life and Letters, vol. ii. p. 271.
[3] Life of H. B. Stowe, by C. E. Stowe, p. 328.

The author had been satisfied to gain four hundred dollars a year by her pen, but she had now written a book of which there were sold three thousand copies on the first day of publication, and in this country over three hundred thousand within a year. England received the story with like favor—the sale went on in the mother country and her colonies until it reached the number of one and a half million copies.[1] The book was soon translated into twenty different languages.[2] The author was now the most famous woman in America; she had gained a competence and secured undying glory.

The effect produced by the book was immense. Whittier offered up "thanks for the Fugitive Slave law; for it gave occasion for 'Uncle Tom's Cabin.'" Longfellow thought it was one of the greatest triumphs in literary history, but its moral effect was a higher triumph still. Lowell described the impression which the book made as a "whirl of excitement."[3] Choate is reported to have said: "That book will make two millions of abolitionists."[4] Garrison wrote the author: "All the defenders of slavery have let me alone and are abusing you."[5] Sumner said in the Senate: "A woman, inspired by Christian genius, enters the lists, like another Joan of Arc, and with marvellous powers sweeps the chords of the popular heart. Now melting to tears, and now inspiring to rage, her work everywhere touches the conscience, and makes the slave-hunter more hateful."[6]

---

[1] Life of H. B. Stowe, pp. 160 and 190. It is not known what has been the total sale in the United States since its publication. See Life-Work of the Author of Uncle Tom's Cabin, McCray, p. 120. "An immense edition of Uncle Tom, prepared for Sunday-schools, has been published in England."—Lieber to Hillard, April, 1853, Life and Letters of Lieber, p. 261.   [2] Life of H. B. Stowe, p. 195.   [3] Ibid., p. 327.

[4] New York *Independent*, Aug. 26th, 1852.

[5] Life of H. B. Stowe, p. 161.

[6] Speech on the Fugitive Slave law, Aug. 26th, 1852, *Congressional Globe*, vol. xxv. p. 1112. Emerson said, in 1858: "We have seen an American woman write a novel, of which a million copies were sold, in

The story appealed particularly to the emotional nature of women. Tales are told of their sitting up all night absorbed in the work, touched to the heart at the recital of the death of little Eva, and weeping bitter tears at the cruel murder of Uncle Tom. One woman wrote that she could no more leave the story than she could have left a dying child. A cool-headed London printer took the book home at night to read, with the view of deciding whether it would be a paying publication. He was so affected, first by laughter and then by tears, that he ended with a distrust of his literary judgment, thinking that his emotion came from physical weakness; so he tried the story on his wife, a strong-minded woman, and got her approval before he deemed it wise to print the book.[1]

The novel was published as a serial in three daily newspapers of Paris; and one journal, noted for its excellent literary criticism, said that the intense interest awakened by "Uncle Tom" surpassed that which had been excited by the publication of "The Three Guardsmen" of Alexander Dumas, or Eugène Sue's "Mysteries of Paris."[2] In Italy the

---

all languages, and which had one merit, of speaking to the universal heart, and was read with equal interest to three audiences—namely, in the parlor, in the kitchen, and in the nursery of every house."—Lecture on Success.

[1] Life of H. B. Stowe, pp. 161 and 191.

[2] *Le Temps.* Life-Work of the Author of Uncle Tom's Cabin, McCray, p. 110.

" Our most prominent and extraordinary representative abroad is really Uncle Tom. . . . Creameries, dry-goods and eating shops are named after his humble abode. . . . Four or five children's books are published in cheap form by societies of religious instruction, extracted from or built upon Mrs. Stowe's masterpiece, and bearing its title as their best recommendation. You have not forgotten George Sand's generous homage of admiration paid to Mrs. Stowe and her book; now we have Heinrich Heine, the greatest living wit of Europe, taking lessons in reading the Scriptures from the American slave, introducing him with honor and by name among the first creators and creatures of European literature."— Paris correspondence New York *Tribune*, Sept. 28th, 1854. "Everybody

book was received with such fervor that the pope felt obliged to prohibit its circulation in his dominions.[1]

Never but once before had a novel produced such an excitement. One cannot fail to be struck with the likeness between the impression occasioned by Rousseau's story and that made by " Uncle Tom." Kant became so engrossed in the perusal of the " Nouvelle Héloïse" that he failed, for the only time in his life, to take his accustomed afternoon walk ;[2] and Lord Palmerston, who had not read a novel for thirty years, read " Uncle Tom's Cabin " three times, and, instead of making a flippant criticism, which one might have expected from a statesman who shocked grave men by his levity, he admired the book, " not only for the story but for the statesmanship of it."[3]

The " Nouvelle Héloïse " spoke for the liberty and dignity of the peasant, implying that he as well as the king was a man; while " Uncle Tom " pleaded for the liberty of the slave. The one had its part in the social revolution of 1789, and the other had an influence on the political revolution of 1860.

The dramatic strength of the story was not lost upon the theatrical managers. It soon appeared on the stage in Boston, and the first time that Mrs. Stowe, then a woman of forty-one, ever went to the theatre was when she saw a dramatization of her own immortal work. She was sensibly moved at the exquisite interpretation of Topsy by Mrs. Howard, and by the acting of little Cordelia Howard, who struck the audience with wonder, and drew tears from the most callous by a lifelike impersonation of little Eva.[4] In New York the play proved the theatrical success of the sea-

---

in Germany has read Uncle Tom's Cabin."—Letter of Motley, Dec. 23d, 1852, Motley's Letters, vol. i. p. 148.

[1] American Almanac, 1854, p. 348 ; New York *Herald*, May 31st, 1853.

[2] Life of Rousseau, John Morley, vol. ii. p. 33.

[3] Life-Work of the Author of Uncle Tom's Cabin, McCray, p. 109.

[4] Ibid., p. 121.

son. The effect it produced on the frequenters of the Chatham Street and Bowery theatres—at both of which places
"Uncle Tom's Cabin" remained long on the boards—was a
most curious study. The men and boys who sought their
amusement at those theatres belonged to the mobs that
hooted and insulted abolitionists, and broke up anti-slavery
conventions. But when they saw "abolition dramatized,"
as the play was cleverly called, they went wild at the escape of Eliza across the river; they were heartily in sympathy with the forcible resistance to the Fugitive Slave law
made by George Harris and his friends; they applauded
vociferously the allusions to human rights; they were dis-
gusted with the professional tone of the auctioneer and the
business-like action of the negro-buyers in the slave-market
scene; and they wept sincerely at the death of Uncle Tom.[1]
Men and boys who never read a book were impressed and
swayed by this dramatic performance. In the day when
the fashion of even the metropolitan theatres was a nightly change of programme, the run of "Uncle Tom's Cabin"
was counted by more than a hundred performances;[2] and
when little Cordelia Howard had a benefit on her three
hundred and twenty-fifth consecutive impersonation of Eva,
it was spoken of as being without a parallel in the history
of the stage.[3] In every city north of Mason and Dixon's
line where there was a theatre, the managers found it profitable, and even necessary, to comply with the popular demand for a representation of this powerful play.

It was, perhaps, not surprising that "Uncle Tom's Cabin"
should be given at two theatres in London, for the philanthropic mind of England was exercised on the subject of
slavery in America; but it was remarkable that the gay
Parisians should have filled two theatres nightly to laugh

---

[1] New York *Tribune*, Aug. 8th and Sept. 19th, 1853.
[2] Life-Work of the Author of Uncle Tom's Cabin, McCray, p. 132.
[3] New York *Tribune*, May 13th, 1854.

at Topsy and weep at the hard fate of Uncle Tom.' Certainly the inhabitants of this brilliant city knew less and cared less for the oppressed black than did their neighbors across the Channel, and the interest which they took in this portrayal of life among the lowly is an earnest tribute to the dramatic character of the work.[2]

Some writers have depreciated the political effect of "Uncle Tom's Cabin" because the results were not immediate. "It deepens the horror of servitude," wrote George Ticknor, "but it does not affect a single vote."[3] In reviewing the election of 1852 one could not then have written otherwise.[4] It is probably true that the seed sown by works of fiction germinates slowly. The "Nouvelle Héloïse" and "Émile" were published nearly a generation before the French Revolution began. Because many people of France applauded the democratic sentiment implied by the words in the "Nouvelle Héloïse"—"I would rather be the wife of a charcoal-burner than the mistress of a king"—they did not hurl Pompadour from her seat of power; and although "Uncle Tom's Cabin" was directed against the Fugitive Slave law, it did not effect its repeal.

The great influence of Mrs. Stowe's book, however, was shown in bringing home to the hearts of the people the conviction that slavery is an injustice; and, indeed, the impression it made upon bearded men was not so powerful as its appeal to women and boys. The mother's opinion was a potent educator in politics between 1852 and 1860, and boys in their teens in the one year were voters in the

---

[1] Life of H. B. Stowe, p. 192; Bibliographical Account of Uncle Tom's Cabin, prefaced to edition of 1887, p. xlvi.

[2] The hold it still has (in 1890) on the American stage is similar evidence. It is one of those plays that each generation must see. The book is still widely read, as every bookseller and librarian knows. In 1888 and 1889 it headed the list in fiction in greatest demand at the New York free circulating library. *The Critic*, vol. xii. p. 156; *The Nation*, vol. l. p. 222.

[3] Dec. 20th, 1852. Life of George Ticknor, vol. i. p. 286.

[4] See p. 278.

other. It is often remarked that previous to the war the
Republican party attracted the great majority of schoolboys, and that the first voters were an important factor in
its final success. The bright boys of France, who in their
youth read the "Nouvelle Héloïse" and "Émile" became
revolutionists in 1789, and the youth of America whose first
ideas on slavery were formed by reading "Uncle Tom's
Cabin" were ready to vote with the party whose existence
was based on opposition to an extension of the great evil.

It is quite true that the moral and literary causes which
aided in bringing about the abolition of slavery needed political events to give them force and to shape their action.
Had it not been for the fatuity of the one party and the
wisdom of the other in forcing an issue that was broad
enough to include many shades of opinion, "Uncle Tom's
Cabin" and other anti-slavery literature might have made
many abolitionists, but would not have made enough Republicans to elect Lincoln in 1860. The Republican party,
however, could not have succeeded without the backing of
a multitude of men and women who were Republicans because they believed slavery to be a cruel wrong, opposed to
the law of God and to the best interests of humanity.

The election of 1852 gave the death-blow to the Whig
party; it never entered another presidential contest.[1] Webster, as well as Clay, died before his party received this
crushing defeat, which, indeed, he had predicted.[2] His physical frame worn out, he went early in September home to
Marshfield to die. The story of his last days, as told with
loving detail by his friend and biographer, is of intense interest to the hero-worshipper, and has likewise pointed the
moral of many a Christian sermon. The conversations of
great minds that, unimpaired, deliver themselves at the approach of death to introspection are, like the most famous

---

[1] That is, with an independent nomination. See Chap. VIII.
[2] New York *Herald*, Nov. 3d; Harvey's Reminiscences, p. 199.

of all, the discourse of Socrates in the Phædo, a boon to humankind. The mind of Webster was perfectly clear, and when all earthly striving was over, his true nature shone out in the expression of thoughts that filled his soul. Speaking of the love of nature growing stronger with time, he said: "The man who has not abandoned himself to sensuality feels, as years advance and old age comes on, a greater love of mother Earth, a greater willingness and even desire to return to her bosom and mingle again with this universal frame of things from which he sprang." [1]   Two weeks before he died, he wrote what he wished inscribed on his monument: "Philosophical argument, especially that drawn from the vastness of the universe in comparison with the apparent insignificance of this globe, has sometimes shaken my reason for the faith that is within me; but my heart has assured and reassured me that the Gospel of Jesus Christ must be a divine reality." The day before his death, he said with perfect calmness to his physician: "Doctor, you have carried me through the night, I think you will get me through to-day; I shall die to-night." The doctor honestly replied: "You are right, sir." [2]

His family, friends, and servants, having assembled in his room, he spoke to them "in a strong, full voice, and with his usual modulation and emphasis: 'No man who is not a brute can say that he is not afraid of death. No man can come back from *that* bourn; no man can comprehend the will or works of God. That there is a God, all must acknowledge. I see him in all these wondrous works, himself how wondrous!'" [3]

Eloquent in life, Webster was sublime in death. He took leave of his household one by one, addressing to each fitting words of consolation. He wanted to know the gradual steps towards dissolution, and calmly discussed them with his physician. At one time, awaking from a partial stupor which preceded death, he heard repeated the words of the psalm

---

[1] Curtis, vol. ii. p. 668.   [2] Ibid., p. 696.   [3] Ibid., p. 697.

which has smoothed the death-pillow of many a Christian:
" Yea, though I walk through the valley of the shadow of
death, I will fear no evil, for thou art with me; thy rod
and thy staff, they comfort me." The dying statesman exclaimed: " ' Yes, thy rod—thy staff—but the fact, the fact I
want,' . . . for he was not certain whether the words that had
been repeated to him were intended as an intimation that he
was already in the dark valley."[1] Waking up again past
midnight, and conscious that he was living, he uttered the
well-known words, " I still live." Later he said something
about poetry, and his son repeated one of the verses of Gray's
Elegy. He heard it and smiled. In the early morning Webster's soul went out with the tide.[2]

It was a beautiful Sunday morning of an Indian summer's
day when the sad tidings reached Boston, which came home
to nearly all of her citizens as a personal sorrow. In all the
cities of the land mourning emblems were displayed and
minute-guns were fired. New York City and Washington
grieved for him as for a friend. During the week there
were the usual manifestations of mourning by the government at Washington; the various departments were closed,
and the public buildings were draped with emblems of woe.
Festal scenes and celebrations were postponed, and on the
day of his funeral business was suspended in nearly all the
cities during the hours when he was borne to his last resting-
place. " From east to west," said Edward Everett, " and
from north to south, a voice of lamentation has already gone
forth, such as has not echoed through the land since the
death of him who was first in war, first in peace, and first in
the hearts of his countrymen."[3]

By Webster's own request, he had a modest country funeral. The services were conducted in his Marshfield home.

---

[1] Curtis, vol. ii. p. 700.
[2] Ibid., p. 701. Webster died Oct. 24th; he was in his seventy-first year.
[3] Speech at Faneuil Hall, Oct. 27th, Works, vol. iii. p. 158. See also
diary of R. H. Dana, Life, by C. F. Adams, vol. i. p. 222.

The coffin was borne to the tomb by six of the neighboring farmers, and the multitude followed slowly and reverently. To the Marshfield farmers and Green Harbor fishermen Webster was a companion and a friend; by them he was mourned sincerely as one of their own fellowship. It could not be said of him that a prophet is not without honor save in his own country. One man in a plain and rustic garb paid the most eloquent of all tributes to the mighty dead: "Daniel Webster, the world without you will seem lonesome."[1] A Massachusetts orator of our day has truly said: "Massachusetts smote and broke the heart of Webster, her idol, and then broke her own above his grave."[2]

On Sunday, the 31st of October, one week after his death, nearly all the preachers of the North delivered sermons on the life and death of Daniel Webster.[3] In the main, they were highly eulogistic. If, indeed, a preacher permitted himself to speak of the failings of the great man, it was in such a manner as one might in all gentleness speak of the frailty of a dear departed friend. To this there was one notable exception—the sermon of Theodore Parker, delivered in the Boston Melodeon. The preacher appeared to want the good which Webster did interred with his bones and the evil to live after him. Even had the discourse been true, it was, considering the occasion, indecent. But in it there was much of error. The current gossip of Boston and the pungent tales of Washington correspondents were crystallized into a serious utterance and given the stamp of a scholar.

---

[1] Curtis, vol. ii. p. 704. "As for thinking of America without Webster, it seems like thinking of her without Niagara, or the Mississippi, or any other of the magnificent natural features which had belonged to her since I grew up, and seemed likely to endure forever."—Letter of J. L. Motley, from Dresden, Dec. 23d, 1852, Motley's Correspondence, vol. i. p. 149.

[2] J. D. Long, Webster Centennial, vol. i. p. 165.

[3] There were more than one hundred and fifty sermons on the death of Webster printed in pamphlet form. Memorandum of Theo. Parker on bound collection of them in Boston Public Library.

He, who felt competent to separate the fable from the truth in the Old and New Testaments, showed great credulity in estimating the history of his own day. Apparently Parker had misgivings about his facts, for a few months later we find him writing Sumner and Giddings in the endeavor to get evidence concerning Webster's recreancy to the anti-slavery cause and acceptance of money gifts.[1] A teacher of young men, for it was to them that this discourse was addressed, should have made sure of his facts before he gave vent to such vituperative and vindictive words.[2]

Yet we may not utterly condemn Parker. He was sincere, and meant to be truthful; but he had that mental constitution which could only see his side of any question, and he thought himself a second Luther, commissioned to rebuke sin in high places.[3] He was, however, a scholar; he knew many languages; his books were his friends and companions.[4] While not so profound a student of philosophy and theology as his German contemporaries, he illuminated transcendentalism by a practical knowledge of man; and had he not enlisted in the anti-slavery cause he would undoubtedly have left behind him a theological work of merit, for he was the exponent of radical Unitarianism. "Suppose," he writes in his diary, "I could have given all the attention to theology that I have been forced to pay to politics and slavery, how much I might have done! I was meant for a philosopher, and the times call for a *stump orator*."[5]

_____

[1] See letters from Giddings and Sumner of Jan., 1853, to Parker, furnished by F. B. Sanborn to the Springfield *Republican*, copied into the Boston *Transcript*, Jan. 25th, 1882. I am indebted to Mr. Lodge for this reference. See also Parker's preface to this sermon, written March 7th, 1853.

[2] The important statements in this sermon are carefully examined, and many of them refuted, by George T. Curtis in his monologue on Last Days of Daniel Webster, written in 1877. Frothingham says the sermon was prepared with care. Life of Parker, pp. 339, 420.

[3] Recollections and Impressions, O. B. Frothingham, p. 54.

[4] His library of 13,000 volumes was left the Boston Public Library.

[5] Life and Correspondence of Theo. Parker, Weiss, vol. ii. p. 115.

I.—19

Parker was, said Emerson, "a man of study fit for a man of the world."[1] Though sympathizing for many years with the abolitionists, it was not until after the passage of the Fugitive Slave law that he devoted himself heartily to their work. He was the pastor, the especial friend and counsel, of runaway negroes. His efforts in their behalf were untiring. At the time of the Shadrach rescue he wrote in his diary : " These are sad times to live in, but I should be sorry not to have lived in them. It will seem a little strange one or two hundred years hence that a plain humble scholar of Boston was continually interrupted in his studies, and could not write his book, for stopping to look after fugitive slaves —his own parishioners!"[2] Parker was bitter and harsh towards his opponents, for years of religious contention fitted him for the part of the political iconoclastic reformer. Deeming Webster responsible for the Fugitive Slave law, he could not do otherwise than magnify the vices and belittle the virtues of this great statesman.

Parker spoke every Sunday to two or three thousand people in the Melodeon or the Music Hall, and exercised great influence. He lacked many graces of oratory ; it was the pregnant matter of his discourse that held his large audience captive. His sermon on Webster moulded many opinions. Of all indictments it is the most severe. It would, indeed, be deplorable if it presented the true character of the man who had received so much honor from his countrymen, and it is gratifying that fewer men now believe the charges than when the sermon was delivered ; that instead of acknowledging " its analytical justice, its fidelity,"[3] it is regarded as the raving of an honest fanatic.

Parker and Wendell Phillips may be said to be the exponents of abolitionism in the decade of 1850–60. They do

---

[1] Life of Parker, Frothingham, p. 549.

[2] Feb. 21st, 1851, Life and Correspondence of Theo. Parker, Weiss, vol. ii. p. 105.

[3] Expressions of the *New Hampshire Independent* (Dem.), 1852.

not fill the period as Garrison did that of 1830–40; for the
reformer who begins the agitation has the hardest work and
receives the greatest honor. It had now become respectable
to be an abolitionist; his political power was not to be despised. The abolitionists shed no tears over the defeat of
Scott; they had no more regard for the Whig than for the
Democratic party.[1] Most of them were dismayed at the
falling-off of the Free-soil vote; but Garrison, who did not
believe in political action, had even for this no regret.[2]

The President graced his administration by the appointment of Edward Everett, of Massachusetts, as Secretary of
State to succeed Webster. Everett graduated from Harvard
at the age of seventeen, taking the first college honors of
his class; two years later he became a Unitarian preacher,
and then gave promise of that eloquence for which in after-
years he was so famed. When twenty-one, he was appointed
professor of Greek literature at Harvard College, and to fit
himself for the place he went abroad and studied four years,
two of which were passed at the University of Göttingen.
Victor Cousin, the philosopher and the translator of Plato,
who met Everett in Germany, said he was one of the best
of Greek scholars. In 1820, when twenty-six, he preached
a sermon in the hall of the House of Representatives at
Washington on the text, "Brethren, the time is short," de-
lighting the orators, the jurists, and the men of state who
went to hear him. Justice Story wrote: "The sermon was
truly splendid, and was heard with breathless silence." Rufus
King, much affected, said that he "had never heard a discourse so full of unction, eloquence, and good taste."[3] John
Quincy Adams, who was nothing if not critical, confided to
his diary that "it was without comparison the most splendid

---

[1] See Life of Garrison, vol. iii. p. 370; also letter of Theo. Parker to
Sumner, Dec. 20th, 1852. "In the Senate of the United States there is
but one party; it is the party of slavery. It has two divisions—the *côté
droit* and the *côté gauche,* the Democrat and the Whig."—Life and Correspondence, Weiss, vol. ii. p. 216.   [2] Life of Garrison, vol. iii. p. 371.

[3] Life and Letters of Joseph Story, vol. i. p. 382.

composition as a sermon that I ever heard delivered." [1] In
this same year Everett became editor of the *North American Review;* he was then and afterwards a frequent contributor, and shared with many other gifted minds the honor
of making this quarterly a monument of American scholar-
ship and fair-minded criticism. He was elected representative and served ten years in Congress. He made a diligent
and conscientious member, for he knew thoroughly what it
was his business to know ; his name is connected with many
important measures, but his service was rather useful than
brilliant. Afterwards the people chose him governor of his
commonwealth for three terms, and for a fourth he was only
defeated by one vote. He did not grieve, however, at quitting active politics, for he had again the yearning of a
scholar for Europe. Webster, writing to him in Italy, spoke
of the enjoyment " that Italy tenders to the taste of the cultivated," and especially " to you, so full and fresh with history and the classics." [2] This same year Webster became
Secretary of State, and was able to secure for his friend the
appointment of minister to England.

No American ever divined or appreciated Europe better
than Everett, yet he was as intensely national in feeling and
expression as were those Western politicians who paraded
their contempt of Europe on the stump and in Congress.
His friend Hillard even criticised his orations for their
vaunting strain in regard to our country and institutions.
Knowing thoroughly many tongues, this true patriot still
could say : " The sound of my native language beyond the
sea is a music to my ear beyond the richest strains of Tus-
can softness or Castilian majesty."

Everett returned to the United States in 1845, and one
year later was chosen president of Harvard College. He
retained the position three years, until obliged to resign it on
account of ill-health.

---

[1] Memoir of John Quincy Adams, vol. iv. p. 52.
[2] Private Correspondence, vol. ii. p. 101.

In this hurrying country and this hurrying age of ours, what a delight there is in the review of the life of such a ripe scholar, accomplished diplomat, and finished orator! As we view the constant strife for wealth and political power and reflect that Everett might well have aspired to either, how impressive is his choice of the better part— that of laboring his whole life for accurate learning and aiming at the highest eloquence! In a time when so much superficial work is done, how worthy of admiration are the consummate art and the painstaking care, in the study and on the platform, of Everett, whose very stuff of conscience would not let him do aught but perfect work! His orations, wrote Hillard, are "nearly faultless as literary productions. He is as careful to select the right word as a workman in mosaic is to pick out the exact shade of color which he requires."

The unalloyed friendship that existed between Webster and Everett is a beautiful trait, ennobling them both. Jealousy did not exist on the part of the one, nor envy on the part of the other. "When I entered public life," Everett said, "it was with his encouragement."[1] Webster wrote Everett: "I feel that you are among the foremost of those who, in the course of the last thirty years, have helped me along, by favor, by good advice, and by large contributions to my stock of knowledge." Everett, by the choice of his friend, edited Webster's works, and wrote the chaste and temperate biographical memoir prefixed to the first volume. Three months before his death, Webster penned to Everett these words of deep feeling: " We now and then see, stretching across the heavens, a long streak of clear, blue, cerulean sky, without cloud or mist or haze. And such appears to me our acquaintance, from the time when I heard you for a week recite your lessons in the little school-house in Short Street to the date hereof."[2]

---

[1] Speech on the death of Daniel Webster, Oct. 27th, 1852.
[2] Letter of July 21st, 1852. In addition to authorities already cited, I

While Everett's greatest triumphs were gained on the platform before the cultivated people who naturally assembled to hear him, and with whom he felt in perfect accord, yet when called to more active duty he acquitted himself with credit. Entering upon his brief service in the State department, he was immediately obliged to take up the Cuban question and give an answer to official notes from England and France. These two nations had proposed a tripartite convention with the United States, by virtue of which the three powers should guarantee the possession of Cuba to Spain and jointly and severally disclaim, now and forever, all intention to obtain possession of that island. In his reply Everett's endeavor was, " to assert a line of principle and of policy which would be generally approved by the country ; which would show that it was possible to reconcile the progressive spirit and tendency of the country and of the age with the preservation of the public faith, with the sanctity of the public honor, and with the dictates of an enlightened and liberal conservatism." [1]

Never had the success of a Secretary of State been more complete; and yet the Cuban question was an extremely delicate one to handle. The South had for years been anxious to acquire Cuba, and this desire was now increased by the disappointment at the outcome of the Mexican conquests, for slavery, on both economical and political grounds, needed expansion. On the other hand, the majority of the Northern people were opposed to the acquisition of more slave

---

have, in this characterization of Everett, drawn from Everett's Works, vol. i. and iii. ; article by George S. Hillard, *North American Review*, Jan., 1837 ; article by C. C. Felton, *North American Review*, Oct., 1850 ; article on Edward Everett, in Appletons' Cyclopædia of Biography, by S. A. Allibone; article in Encyclopædia Britannica, by Rev. E. E. Hale; Forney's Anecdotes of Public Men, vol. ii. " À ceux qui douteraient qu'on pût rencontrer aux États-Unis le type parfait du scholar et du gentleman, je citerais M. Ed. Everett, qui vit à Cambridge." — Promenade en Amérique, Ampère, tome i. p. 45.

[1] Statement by Everett, speech in the Senate, March 21st, 1853.

territory, although a portion of the Democratic party, of
which Cass and Douglas were the exponents, had heartily
embraced the doctrine of manifest destiny, which meant
that this government, when it honorably could, should acquire territory by conquest and purchase, ignoring the fact
whether it was slave or free soil.

The Secretary respectfully declined the proposition of
England and France. One strong objection to the proposed
agreement was, "Among the oldest traditions of the federal
government is an aversion to political alliances with European powers." This was a policy counselled by Washington
and by Jefferson. There is, moreover, a great difference between the interest, in regard to Cuba, of France and England
on the one side and the United States on the other. "Cuba
lies at our doors. It commands the approach to the Gulf of
Mexico, which washes the shores of five of our States. It
bars the entrance to that great river which drains half the
North American continent."

To understand our position, England and France must
suppose an island like Cuba, a Spanish possession, guarding
the entrance of the Thames or the Seine, and consider what,
in that case, their answer would be should we propose to
them a similar tripartite convention.

"Territorially and commercially, Cuba would, in our
hands, be an extremely valuable possession. Under certain
contingencies, it might be almost essential to our safety.
Still, for domestic reasons the President thinks that the incorporation of the island into the Union at the present time,
although effected with the consent of Spain, would be a
hazardous measure; and he would consider its acquisition
by force, except in a just war with Spain (should an event
so greatly to be deprecated take place), as a disgrace to the
civilization of the age."

Before closing, the Secretary went into a history of our
territorial acquisitions, defending them all, although he limp-
ed when attempting to justify the annexation of Texas. He
then vindicated the doctrine of manifest destiny as applied

to the past, calling it "the undoubted operation of the law of our political existence," as being a name less harsh than the other to European ears; and then, in a burst of national enthusiasm, he said: "Every addition to the territory of the American Union has given homes to European destitution, and gardens to European want." [1]

The commendation of this letter was general, and from both parties. [2] Cass said in the Senate: "It is marked by a lofty, patriotic, American feeling. I have seldom seen a document more conclusive in its argument, or more beautiful in its style or illustrations;" [3] and Douglas testified that it was "applauded by the almost unanimous voice of the American people." [4]

When Fillmore, in his last message, said that he had discharged the arduous duties of his high trust "with a single eye to the public good," he was believed by everybody except by some of the Seward Whigs and the abolitionists. The slavery question and the sectional differences weighed heavily on his mind, and he felt that it was a duty of his high office to attempt their solution. He proposed in his last message to Congress a scheme of negro colonization, and advocated its adoption; he believed that there was the path in which might be solved the difficulties which were raised by slavery and the antagonism of race. This part of his message was suppressed by the advice of his cabinet; but even had this not been done, there is no reason to suppose that the plan would have been adopted by Congress.

---

[1] Everett to the Comte de Sartiges, Dec. 1st, 1852, Senate Documents, 2d Sess., 32d Cong., Doc. 13.

[2] "Mr. Everett's letter has been received by Congress and the country as a very able exposition of the American sentiment in regard to Cuba." —*Harper's Magazine*, Feb., 1853. See also New York *Herald*, Jan. 7th, 1853.

[3] Jan. 15th, 1853. The letter was written Dec. 1st, 1852, but was not given to Congress and the public till Jan. 5th, 1853.

[4] Senate, March 16th, 1853.

Yet in after-life it was a satisfaction to Fillmore that he had thought out a plan which might have produced satisfactory results.[1]

Fillmore was a man of imposing physical presence; he looked like a ruler, and graced the White House.[2] He was strictly temperate, industrious, orderly, and his integrity was above suspicion.

Besides the charge against Webster, already mentioned,[3] there were two attempts to implicate members of the cabinet in unworthy transactions. One was the affair of the Lobos Islands, in which the Secretary of State was concerned. Webster had, indeed, acted with precipitancy in this matter, but there is no evidence of corrupt motive or action.[4]

The other charge was against the Secretary of the Treas-

---

[1] See Address of James Grant Wilson on Fillmore before the Buffalo Historical Society, Jan. 7th, 1878. I am indebted to Mr. Barnum, corresponding secretary of that society, for the portion of the address which referred to the colonization plan. General Wilson informs me that the suppressed portion of the message never appeared in print, but that ex-President Fillmore once permitted him to peruse the proof-slip, which at the time was submitted to the cabinet. "Previous to his retirement from office, some friends of President Fillmore contributed one thousand dollars to make him a life member of the Colonization Society. In his letter of acknowledgment, he took occasion to express his decided approval of the objects of the society, and to say that it appeared to him to have pointed out the only rational mode of ameliorating the condition of the colored race in this country."—*Harper's Magazine*, April, 1853.

[2] "M. Fillmore avait un cachet de simplicité digne et bienveillante, qui me semble faire de lui le type de ce que doit être un président Américain."—J. J. Ampère, Promenade en Amérique, tome ii. p. 100.

[3] See p. 213.

[4] See Curtis, vol. ii. The President's Message, Dec. 6th, 1852; Boston *Courier* and New York *Tribune*, Aug. 13th and 20th; New York *Tribune*, Nov. 8th. *Per contra*, see editorials in New York *Evening Post*, Nov. 9th and 12th; for the correspondence, see Senate Document 109, 32d Cong., 1st Sess. The letter of Webster to Captain Jewett, authorizing him to take guano from the Lobos Islands, has written on the last sheet of the letter "App^d. June 5th. M. F." See MSS. State department archives.

ury.   While a senator, Corwin had become attorney for Dr.
Gardiner, who had a claim against Mexico.   It was one of
those claims that, by the treaty of 1848, were to be adjudi-
cated and paid by the United States.   Less than a year after
being employed as attorney, Corwin, in conjunction with his
brother, bought an interest in the claim for which they actually gave $22,000.   On the accession of Fillmore he was
offered the Secretaryship of the Treasury, but he would not
accept it until he had disposed of his interest in this and
other claims.   He therefore made in good faith an unconditional transfer of his share.   The matter would probably
have never been noticed had not the Gardiner claim turned
out to be "a naked fraud upon the treasury of the United
States,"[1] and had not Corwin realized for his share in the
transaction a handsome profit.   A personal and political
enemy charged that the transfer of this interest was a blind,
and the inference followed that Corwin had used his influence as Secretary of the Treasury with the board of commissioners, which had the adjustment of these claims, to have
passed a fraudulent claim in which he was directly interested.   The matter attracted considerable attention in Congress and in the country.   Committees of investigation were
appointed both by the Senate and the House.   The House
committee, a majority of whom were Democrats, reported
that there was no evidence to show that Corwin knew that
the claim was fraudulent; they virtually said that his transfer was unconditional and made in good faith.   The subject
gave rise to an animated debate in the House, in which the
defenders of the Secretary of the Treasury had altogether
the better of the argument.[2]   The reputation which Corwin

---

[1] Report of the House Committee of Investigation.

[2] See especially speeches of Andrew Johnson and Olds of Ohio attacking Corwin, and those of Barrere of Ohio, Chapman of Connecticut, and A. H. Stephens in his defence, vol. xxvii. *Congressional Globe*,
Jan., 1853; for the report of the House committee and a large amount
of testimony, see Reports of Committees, 2d Sess. 32d Cong., Rep.
No. 1.

had always borne as an honest man was an efficient factor towards causing the explanation of his friends to be accepted as true, and in making up public sentiment in his favor.[1] Indeed, in his own home he was not less esteemed for his moral purity than he was celebrated for his wit and eloquence.

It would have been an ungrateful task to write down Corwin as having prostituted his high office to the purpose of private gain, for he is one of the characteristic men of the ante-bellum period. A son of Western soil, his speeches have a flavor of the wild surroundings of his youth. He was a born orator, exactly fitted for the rollicking campaign of 1840, when he made the reputation of being the best stump-orator of Ohio, and that before audiences who were wont to listen attentively to public speakers and weigh carefully their merits.

People went to hear Corwin to be entertained as well as instructed. His fine head, sparkling hazel eyes, cheery, pleasing manners, together with the facial expression of a wonderful actor, set off his abundant humor, his knack at telling stories, and his skill at repartee.

The survivors of the generation who listened to Corwin were never weary of telling of his marvellous eloquence, apt replies, and fitting anecdotes;[2] though it is true that his wit

---

[1] For a view of the case, criticising Corwin, see editorials in the New York *Evening Post*, March 4th and 6th, 1854.

[2] Corwin's complexion was very dark. He was on several occasions supposed to be of African descent, and he was fond of relating these ludicrous mistakes. One of his keen retorts was made when addressing a Whig mass-meeting at Marietta, O. He had then great anxiety not to offend the abolitionists, who were beginning to cast a large vote. A sharp-witted opponent, to draw him out, asked: "Shouldn't niggers be permitted to sit at the table with white folks, on steamboats and at hotels?" "Fellow-citizens," exclaimed Corwin, his swarthy features beaming with suppressed fun, "I ask you whether it is proper to ask such a question of a gentleman of my color?" The crowd cheered, and the questioner was silenced. Ben: Perley Poore's Reminiscences, vol. i. p. 209.

sometimes degenerated into coarseness. He was the best-
known man in Ohio; everybody called him Tom. A formal resolution of a Whig State convention proclaimed him
"a man of the people, and a champion of their rights," and
declared, amid the enthusiastic acclaim of the multitude, "we
esteem him, and we love him."

But Corwin was more than a witty stump-speaker. He
was a good lawyer, who thought deeply on the principles
of government and political questions. His friends had
hopes that he might even reach the presidency; but he
destroyed his political prospects by an indiscreet though
brave speech in the Senate in February, 1847, on the Mexican war.[1]

It was a scathing arraignment of the policy of conquest,
a severe invective against the "destiny doctrine," and a
fierce retort to the statement of Cass, "We want room."
"If I were a Mexican," said Corwin, "I would tell you,
'Have you not room in your own country to bury your dead
men? If you come into mine, we will greet you with bloody
hands and welcome you to hospitable graves.'"[2] It is inconsistent, but it is the inconsistency of a vigorous nationality, to
condemn this utterance of Corwin as an unpatriotic expression to utter during a war in which his country was engaged, while we praise the parallel saying of Chatham during our Revolution, and print it in every schoolboy's book
of oratory.[3]

Corwin's position on the compromise of 1850 was the
same as that of Clay and Webster, and he suffered, as did

---

[1] Corwin "is a truly kind, benevolent, and gifted man. He seems to
forego all hope of the presidency, just now at least."—Seward to his wife,
from Washington, Jan. 23d, 1848, Life of Seward, F. W. Seward, vol. ii.
p. 62.

[2] See Corwin's Speeches; also memoir prefixed to them; Public Men
and Events, Sargent; Reminiscences, Ben: Perley Poore.

[3] "If I were an American, as I am an Englishman, while a foreign troop
was landed in my country I never would lay down my arms—never—
never—never!"

the Massachusetts statesman, from the alienation of friends
who thought that his opposition to slavery had weakened.
"I did agree that Mr. Fillmore should approve" the Fugitive Slave law, he said in 1859, "though I did not like it; I
thought it was constitutional, and that Congress were the
best judges of its policy."[1]

The President, influenced by the attempt to bring home
the charge of corruption to his administration, suggested in
his last message new legislation to protect the government
against mischief and corruption, although he bore testimony
to the efficiency and integrity with which the several executive departments were conducted.

In the debate in Congress on the Gardiner claim, few
found fault with Corwin for being, while a senator, the attorney of the claimant, since there were many precedents
to justify such a position; but it was nevertheless felt that
it ought to be made improper for a senator, a representative, or any officer of the United States to act as attorney
for a claim against the country, or to be interested in any
way in the prosecution of it. This feeling found expression in a law passed at this session of Congress;[2] the offence was made a misdemeanor, punishable with fine and
imprisonment.

When Fillmore withdrew from the presidential office, the
general sentiment proclaimed that he had filled the place
with ability and honor.[3] The country abounded with prosperity; the administration was identified with the compromise, and the compromise had now become very popular.
If Northern people did not approve the Fugitive Slave law,
they at least looked upon it with toleration. It is quite
true, however, that after-opinion has been unkind to Fill-

---

[1] House of Representatives, Dec. 8th, 1859.

[2] Approved Feb. 26th, 1853.

[3] Public Men and Events, Sargent, vol. ii. p. 394. "There was at that
time but one voice heard from one end of the country to the other—that
of 'Well done, good and faithful servant.'"

more.   The judgment on him was made up at a time when
the Fugitive Slave law had become detestable, and he was
remembered only for his signature and vigorous execution
of it.   After Johnson had been President, it was asserted,
with the taste for generalization that obtains in politics,
that all of our Vice-Presidents who succeeded to the presidential office turned out badly.   This was maintained until
the wise administration of President Arthur became confessedly an exception to the rule; yet the plaudits for Arthur were not more general than were those for Fillmore at
the close of his administration.   Fillmore retained as strong
a hold on his party as did the other; both were candidates
for renomination, and showed great strength in their party
conventions.

In a just estimate, therefore, of our Vice-Presidents who
have become Presidents, we should class Fillmore with Arthur, and not with Tyler and Johnson.

CHAPTER IV

I⊤ will be well, at this point of my narrative, to examine the institution of negro slavery as it existed in the South. So forcibly has the word slavery come in the closing years of our century to signify a practice utterly abhorrent, that we find it difficult to realize how recently it was defended and even extolled. It is my wish to describe the institution as it may have appeared before the war to a fair-minded man. In such an inquiry it is quite easy for one of Northern birth and breeding to extenuate nothing; more care must be taken to set down naught in malice. Nevertheless, this chapter can only be a commentary on the sententious expression of Clay: "Slavery is a curse to the master and a wrong to the slave."

It was the cultivation of the semi-tropical products, cotton, sugar, and rice, that strengthened the hold of slavery on the South. No one was able to contend, with any success, that grain and tobacco could be as well cultivated by slave as by free labor. After a very careful investigation into the agricultural system of Virginia, Olmsted, who worked a farm in New York, arrived at the conclusion that one hand in New York did as much labor as two slave hands in Virginia.[1] Yet taking as a basis the price paid for slaves when

---

[1] Cotton Kingdom, Frederick Law Olmsted, vol. i. p. 134. This was a low estimate. A New Jersey farmer, who had the superintendence of very large agricultural operations in Virginia, conducted with slave labor, thought four Virginia slaves did not accomplish as much as one ordinary free farm laborer in New Jersey. This statement was confirmed by several who had a similar experience. I shall have frequent occasion to

they were hired out—a common custom in Eastern Virginia
—he was well satisfied that the wages for common laborers
were twenty-five per cent. higher in Virginia than in New
York.[1] What was true of Virginia was substantially true
of the other border slave States. It should have been clear
that, in the portion of the South where the climate was un-
suitable for cotton-raising, slavery was an economical failure;
and before the war, as at present, this conclusion necessarily
followed the inquiries of an impartial observer. If there
had been any justification for slavery it must have been
found in the cotton, rice, or sugar regions.

---

refer to Olmsted's books, The Seaboard Slave States, Texas Journey,
A Journey in the Back Country, and The Cotton Kingdom, the last based
on the three others. This gentleman made several journeys through
the slave States between 1850 and 1857, travelling over a large part of
country on horseback, which gave him unusual facilities for seeing the
life of the people. His aim was to see things as they were and describe
them truthfully. He has admirably succeeded, and his books are in-
valuable to one making a study of this subject.

In reviewing A Journey in the Back Country, James R. Lowell wrote
in the *Atlantic Monthly* for Nov., 1860: "No more important contributions to contemporary American history have been made than in this
volume and the two that preceded it. We know of no book that offers
a parallel to them except Arthur Young's Travels in France. To discuss
the question of slavery without passion or even sentiment seemed an
impossibility; yet Mr. Olmsted has shown that it can be done, and, having no theory to bolster, has contrived to tell us what he saw, and not
what he went to see—the rarest achievement among travellers." This
was a happy comparison of the reviewer, for there was a great resemblance between Young and Olmsted in tastes, manner of observing, and
impartiality of judgment. But the most important resemblance Lowell
could not know in 1860. Both wrote on the eve of a great convulsion.
One was the greatest historical event of the eighteenth century, and the
other will probably be adjudged the greatest of the nineteenth century.

George Wm. Curtis, in the *Atlantic Monthly* for Aug., 1863, makes the
statement that first of all the literature on the subject of slavery are, "in
spirit and comprehension, the masterly, careful, copious, and patient works
of Mr. Olmsted." The epithet of "that wise and honest traveller," which
John Morley applied to Young, may likewise be said of Olmsted.

[1] Cotton Kingdom, vol. i. p. 118.

What was there in mitigation of the wrong done the slave? It used to be said that the slaves were better fed, better clothed, and better lodged than laborers in the cities and manufacturing districts at the North. Yet no statement more completely false was ever made. A report to the Secretary of the Treasury from forty-six sugar-planters of Louisiana stated that the cost of feeding and clothing an able-bodied slave was thirty dollars per year. Olmsted estimates that the clothing would amount to ten dollars, which would leave twenty dollars for the food, or five and one half cents per day.[1] "Does the food of a first-rate laborer," he asks, "anywhere in the free world cost less?" This was a fair example of the cost of supporting the negroes on the large sugar and cotton plantations of the Southwest. Corn-meal was the invariable article of food furnished the slaves; bacon and molasses were regularly provided on some plantations, while on others they were only occasional luxuries. Fanny Kemble, the accomplished actress, who spent a winter on her husband's rice and cotton plantations in Georgia, says that animal food was only given to men who were engaged in the hardest kind of work, such as ditching, and to them it was given only occasionally and in moderate quantities. Her description of the little negroes begging her piteously for meat is as pathetic as the incident of the hungry demand of Oliver Twist.[2] This rude fare was generally given the slave in sufficient quantity; the instances are rare in which one finds the negroes did not have enough to eat. Frederick Douglass, however, tells us that, when a child, although belonging to a wealthy and large landed proprietor of Maryland, he was often pinched with hunger, and used to dispute

---

[1] Cotton Kingdom, vol. ii. p. 238.

[2] Journal of a Residence on a Georgian Plantation in 1838–39, Frances Anne Kemble, p. 134; see also p. 65. This was not published until 1863. In the *Atlantic Monthly* for August, 1863, George Wm. Curtis says: "This book is a permanent and most valuable chapter in our history; for it is the first ample, lucid, faithful, detailed account from the actual head-quarters of a slave plantation in this country."

I.—20

with the dogs the crumbs which fell from the kitchen table.[1] In comparison with slaves who had plenty, the prison convicts of the North had a greater variety of food, and it was not so coarse.[2] " Ninety-nine in a hundred of our free laborers," wrote Olmsted, " from choice and not from necessity, live, in respect to food, at least four times as well as the average of the hardest-worked slaves on the Louisiana sugar plantations."[3] The negroes on the large cotton plantations of the Southwest fared no better. A Louisiana cotton-planter furnished De Bow an itemized estimate of the cost of raising cotton, in which the expense of feeding one hundred slaves, furnishing the hospital, overseer's table, etc., was put down at $750 for the year. This was $7.50 for each one, or, in other words, the cost of food for the slave was less than $2\frac{1}{12}$ cents per day.[4] The overseers everywhere endeavored to bring the keeping of the slaves down to the lowest possible figure. This was a large item in the cost of cotton production; and on the large plantations, where in some cases as many as five hundred slaves were worked, economy in feeding these human cattle was studied with almost scientific precision. The supply of food to the slaves was made a subject of legislation. Louisiana required that meat should be furnished, but this law became a dead letter. North Carolina fixed the daily .allowance of corn; in the other States the law was not specific, but directed in general terms that the provisions should be sufficient for the health of the slave.

It was in the line of plantation parsimony that the clothes furnished the field hands should be of the cheapest material and as scant as was consistent with a slight regard for de-

---

[1] Life of Frederick Douglass, by himself, p. 22; see also pp. 45, 61, 108.

[2] Cotton Kingdom, vol. ii. p. 241.

[3] Ibid., p. 239; Despotism in America, Hildreth, pp. 58, 60; Slave States of America, Buckingham, vol. i. pp. 87, 134.

[4] De Bow's Resources of the South and West, vol. i. p. 150.

cency and health.   All observers agree that the slaves who labored on the cotton and sugar plantations presented a ragged, unkempt, and dirty appearance.[1]

Comfortable houses were in many places built for the negroes;[2] but, owing to their indolent and filthy habits, which were aggravated by their condition of servitude, neatness and the appearance of comfort soon disappeared from their quarters.   The testimony is almost universal that the negro cabins were foul and wretched.[3]

In the cotton, sugar, and rice districts the negroes were hard worked.   The legal limit of a day's work in South Carolina was fifteen hours; on cotton plantations, during the picking season, the slaves labored sixteen hours, while on sugar plantations at grinding time eighteen hours' work was exacted.[4]   Many of the large owners of land and of negroes in the Southwest were absentees, whose authority was delegated to their overseers.   Indeed, in all cases where the agricultural operations were on a large scale, the overseer was the power.   Patrick Henry described the overseers as "the most abject, degraded, unprincipled race."[5]   Years had not improved them, and on the lonely plantations of the Southwest they were hardly amenable to public opinion or subject to the law's control.   They were generally igno-

---

[1] The Louisiana cotton-planter before referred to said the cost of clothing one hundred slaves, shoeing them, furnishing bedding, sacks for gathering cotton, etc., was $750 per annum.

[2] Cotton Kingdom, vol. i. p. 320.

[3] I quote observations of Frances Kemble on several Georgia plantations.   "I found there [at St. Annie's] the wretchedest huts, and most miserably squalid, filthy, and forlorn creatures I had yet seen here," p. 187.   "The negro huts on several of the plantations that we passed through were the most miserable human habitations I ever beheld," p. 242.   "Miserable negro huts" which "were not fit to shelter cattle," p. 248.   See also Slave States of America, Buckingham, vol. i. p. 134.

[4] Cotton Kingdom, vol. i. p. 328; vol. ii. p. 180.

[5] Life of Patrick Henry, Wirt, cited in Stroud's Slave Laws, p. 74; see also Mrs. Davis's remarks on overseers, Memoir of Jefferson Davis, vol. i. p. 477.

rant, frequently intemperate, always despotic and brutal. Their value was rated according to the bigness of the cotton crop they made, and, with that end in view, they spared not the slave.   The slaves always worked under the lash.   " It is true," said Chancellor Harper, in his defence of slavery, "that the slave is driven to labor by stripes." [1]   With each gang went a stout negro driver whose qualification for the position depended upon his unusual cruelty; he followed the working slaves, urging them in their task by a loud voice and the cracking of his long whip.   That the negroes were overtasked to the extent of being often permanently injured, was evident from the complaints made by the Southern agricultural journals against the bad policy of thus wasting human property.   An Alabama tradesman told Olmsted that if the overseers make "plenty of cotton, the owners never ask how many niggers they kill;" [2] and he gave the further information that a determined and perfectly relentless overseer could get almost any wages he demanded, for when it became known that such a man had made so many bales to the hand, everybody would try to get him. [3]

In the rich cotton-planting districts the negro was universally regarded as property.   When the newspapers mentioned the sudden death of one of them, it was the loss of money that was bewailed, and not of the light which no Promethean heat can relume.   Olmsted found that "negro life and negro vigor were generally much less carefully economized than I had always before imagined them to be." [4]   Louisiana sugar-planters did not hesitate to avow openly that, on the whole, they found it the best economy to work off their stock of negroes about once in seven years, and then buy an entire set of new hands. [5]   An over-

[1] Pro-slavery Argument, p. 34.
[2] The same man, however, expressed the opinion that "niggers is generally pretty well treated, considerin'."   Cotton Kingdom, vol. ii. p. 184.
[3] Ibid., p. 186.   [4] Ibid., p. 191.
[5] Frances Kemble's Journal, p. 28; Society in America, H. Martineau,

seer once said to Olmsted : "Why, sir, I wouldn't mind killing a nigger more than I would a dog."[1] The restraint of
the law did not operate powerfully to prevent the killing of
these unfortunates. While the wilful, malicious, and premeditated murder of a slave was a capital offence in all the
slave-holding States, it was provided in most of them that
any person killing a slave in the act of resistance to his
lawful owner was guilty of no offence, nor was there
ground for an indictment in the case where a slave died
while receiving moderate correction.[2] But what protected
the overseers on plantations remote from settlements and
neighbors was the universal rule of slave law, that the testimony of a colored person could not be received against a
white.[3] This gave complete immunity to the despotic overseer. On but few plantations were there more than two
white men, and they were always interested parties, being
owner, manager, or overseer. As a matter of fact, only refractory slaves, or negroes attempting to run away, were
killed, and these murders were not frequent. Except in
rare instances the slaves had no incentive to work, save the
fear of a whipping.[4] "If you don't work faster," or "if you
don't work better, I will have you flogged," were words
often heard.[5] No one can wonder that it was a painful
sight to see negroes at work. The besotted and generally
repulsive expression of the field hands ; their brute-like
countenances, on which were painted stupidity, indolence,
duplicity, and sensuality ; their listlessness ; their dogged
action ; the stupid, plodding, machine-like manner in which
they labored, made a sorrowful picture of man's inhumanity

---

vol. i. p. 308; Weld's Slavery as It Is, cited in Key to Uncle Tom's Cabin,
p. 41.

[1] Cotton Kingdom, vol. ii. p. 203. See account of the murder of a slave
in Life of Frederick Douglass, p. 57.

[2] Stroud's Slave Laws, pp. 56 and 61.   [3] Ibid., p. 41.

[4] Life of Frederick Douglass, by himself, p. 117.

[5] Cotton Kingdom, vol. ii. p. 203.

to man.[1]   General Sherman, who was for a time stationed
at New Orleans and later lived more than a year in Louisiana, states that the field slaves were treated like animals.[2]
Fanny Kemble noticed that those who had some intelligence, who were beyond the brutish level, wore a pathetic
expression — a mixture of sadness and fear.[3]   Frederick
Douglass, himself a slave and the only negro in his neighborhood who could read, relates the effect of unceasing and
habitual toil on one in whom there was a gleam of knowledge: " My natural elasticity was crushed; my intellect
languished ; the disposition to read departed ; the cheerful
spark that lingered about my eye died out ; the dark night
of slavery closed in upon me, and behold a man transformed
to a brute."[4]   An observer who visited an average rice
plantation near Savannah was impressed with the fate of
the field hands : " Their lot was one of continued toil from
morning to night, uncheered even by the hope of any
change or prospect of improvement in condition."[5]   Harriet
Martineau wrote : " A walk through a lunatic asylum is far
less painful than a visit to the slave quarter of an estate."[6]
This state of affairs is perfectly comprehensible; it was an
accessory of the system.   It was Olmsted's judgment that a
certain degree of cruelty was necessary to make slave labor
generally profitable.[7]

The institution bore harder on the women than on the
men.   Slave-breeding formed an important part of plantation economy, being encouraged as was the breeding of animals.   " Their lives are, for the most part, those of mere
animals ;" wrote Fanny Kemble, " their increase is literally
mere animal breeding, to which every encouragement is

---

[1] See Cotton Kingdom, vol. i. pp. 142, 245 ; vol. ii. p. 202.
[2] *North American Review*, Oct., 1888.
[3] Frances Kemble's Journal, p. 98.
[4] Life of Frederick Douglass, p. 119.
[5] Slave States of America, Buckingham, vol. i. p. 133.
[6] Society in America, vol. i. p. 224.
[7] Cotton Kingdom, vol. i. p. 354.

given, for it adds to the master's live-stock and the value of his estate." [1] The women worked in the fields as did the men. When it became known that they were pregnant, their task was lightened, yet, if necessary, they were whipped when with child, and, in some cases, were put to work again as early as three weeks after their confinement, although generally the time of rest allowed was one month. Fanny Kemble's woman heart bled at the tales of suffering she heard, of the rapid child-bearing, the gross disregard of nature's laws of maternity, and the consequent wide prevalence of diseases peculiar to the sex; her daily record of what she saw and heard is as pitiful as it is true. [2]

The money return for this degradation of humankind came mainly from the growth of cotton. Of the 3,177,000 slaves in 1850, De Bow estimated that 1,800,000 of them were engaged in the cotton-culture. [3] The value of this crop amounted to much more than that of the combined production of sugar and rice. [4] Cotton was then, as now, not only the most important article of commerce of the South, but was by far the greatest export from the whole country. [5] It formed the basis of the material prosperity of the South,

---

[1] Frances Kemble's Journal, p. 122. "A woman thinks . . . that the more frequently she adds to the number of her master's live-stock by bringing new slaves into the world, the more claims she will have upon his consideration and good-will. This was perfectly evident to me from the meritorious air with which the women always made haste to inform me of the number of children they had borne, and the frequent occasions on which the older slaves would direct my attention to their children, exclaiming, 'Look, missis! little niggers for you and massa; plenty little niggers for you and little missis!' "—Frances Kemble's Journal, p. 60.

[2] See Frances Kemble's Journal, pp. 60, 200, 251.

[3] De Bow's Resources of the South and West, vol. iii. p. 419; Cotton Kingdom, vol. i. p. 17.

[4] Value of crops in 1850: cotton, $105,600,000; sugar, $12,396,150; rice, $3,000,000. De Bow's Resources, vol. iii. p. 40.

[5] The total domestic exports for the year ending June 30th, 1850, were $136,946,912, of which cotton furnished $71,984,616, and bread-stuffs and provisions, $26,051,373. De Bow's Resources, vol. iii. pp. 388, 391, 392.

and there was economic foundation for the statement, so arrogantly made, that " Cotton is king."

The profits of cotton-growing in a new country were very large. Harriet Martineau, who visited Alabama in 1835, was told that the profits were thirty-five per cent. One planter whom she knew had two years previously invested $15,000 in land, which he could then sell for $65,000; but he expected at this time to make fifty or sixty thousand dollars out of his growing crop.[1] Land was so plenty that no one took any pains to prevent its exhaustion, and when a good yield of cotton could no longer be had, the land was abandoned, and more virgin soil was purchased. When Olmsted visited the South, Mississippi and Louisiana were the States which offered the largest returns. He visited one Mississippi plantation where five hundred negroes were worked, the profit in a single year being $100,000.[2] The rich country tributary to Natchez, as well as that along the Yazoo River, was all owned by large proprietors, none of whom were worth less than $100,000, and the property of some was popularly estimated by millions. The ignorant newly-rich seemed to be as large an element of society in Mississippi as they were in New York.[3] A Southern lawyer truly describes a phase of the cotton industry. Wealth was rapidly acquired by planters who began with limited means, and whose success was due to their industry, economy, and self-denial. They devoted most of their profits to the increase of their capital, with the result that in a few years, as if by magic, large estates were accumulated. "The fortunate proprietors then build fine houses, and surround themselves with comforts and luxuries to which they were strangers in their earlier years of care and toil."[4]

An unwise and wasteful conduct of the business, however,

---

[1] Society in America, vol. i. p. 228.
[2] Cotton Kingdom, vol. ii. p. 83.   [3] Ibid., pp. 158, 159.
[4] Letter to *Harper's Weekly*, Feb., 1859, quoted in Cotton Kingdom, vol. ii. p. 158.

accompanied this prosperity. The profits were laid out in
more land and negroes ; the prospect of enlarged gains and
greater social consideration were alike an incentive to increase
these holdings.   Frequently the coming crop was mortgaged
for money at high rates of interest, and the plantation supplies were furnished by factors at extravagant prices. No system could be more ruinous ; yet the demand for the world's
great staple continued to be so active, and the profit of raising cotton so enormous, that the cotton regions of the Southwest were, in the decade before the war, very prosperous.
This prosperity was the boast of the Southerner, and the
notion widely prevailed that in material well-being the South
went ahead of the North.'   The acme of this idea was attained when Senator Hammond taunted the North with the
results of the financial panic of 1857.   " When the abuse of
credit," said he, "had destroyed credit and annihilated confidence ; when thousands of the strongest commercial houses
in the world were coming down, and hundreds of millions of
dollars of supposed property evaporating in thin air ; when
you came to a dead-lock, and revolutions were threatened,
what brought you up ?   Fortunately for you, it was the
commencement of the cotton season, and we have poured
upon you one million six hundred thousand bales of cotton
just at the crisis to save you from destruction." ²   Every one
knows that those were bragging words ; nevertheless, the
prosperity of the cotton States was real.   Nowhere else existed such a union of soil and climate adapted to the growth

---

¹ See various articles in De Bow's Resources ; *De Bow's Review ;* Southern Wealth and Northern Profits, by T. P. Kettell, New York, 1861 ; also
speech of Hammond, of South Carolina, in the United States Senate,
March 4th, 1858.   But in 1890 the leading senator of South Carolina
saw the matter in a different light. " I assert, what I believe is not denied, that the institution of slavery retarded and hindered the material
development of those States where it existed ; certainly so as compared
with their sister free States."—Butler, in the Senate, Jan. 16th, 1890.

² In the Senate, March 4th, 1858, Speeches and Letters of J. H. Hammond, p. 317.

of the staple, which was always in brisk and increasing demand. The Southerners maintained that their wealth was due to their peculiar institution; that without slavery there could not be a liberal cotton supply.[1] This assertion has been effectually disproved by the results since emancipation, while even in the decade before the war it could with good and sufficient reason be questioned. It was apparent to the economist that the rich gifts of nature, the concentration of capital and the combination of laborers accounted for the fruitful returns of cotton-planting. It was patent that with free white labor better results could be obtained.[2] It is quite true, however, that the practical question did not lie between slave labor and free white labor, but between the negro bondman and the negro freeman. Northern and English observers, for the most part, staggered when confronted with the horns of the dilemma; yet they certainly amassed sufficient facts to venture the assertion that if the slaves were freed, cotton-planting would be as remunerative to the master as before, and that the physical condition of the laborer would be improved. The demand for cotton and negroes went hand in hand; a high price of the staple made a high value for the human cattle. A traveller going through the South would hear hardly more than two subjects discussed in public places—the price of cotton and the price of slaves.[3]

This kind of property was very high in the decade before

---

[1] "The first and most obvious effect [of abolition of slavery] would be to put an end to the cultivation of our great Southern staple."—Chancellor Harper, Pro-slavery Argument, 1852, p. 86. "The average annual yield [of cotton] during the twenty years previous to 1861 was 1,335,000,000 pounds; during the twenty-three years from 1865 to 1886 it was 2,207,-000,000 pounds, an increase of 65.3 per cent."—The United States, Whitney, p. 383. The crop of 1850 was 2,233,718 bales, value $105,600,000. The crop of 1880 was 5,757,397 bales, value $275,000,000.

[2] This subject is thoroughly discussed in A Journey in the Back Country, Olmsted, p. 296, and in his Texas Journey, p. xiii. See also Cotton Kingdom, vol. ii. p. 202.   [3] See Cotton Kingdom, vol. i. p. 51.

the war, a good field hand being worth from one thousand to fifteen hundred dollars. Since the adoption of the Constitution the price of slaves had increased manifold, and after 1835 the advance was especially marked.[1] The need of slaves in the cotton region kept slavery alive in the border States; for the Southwest was a ready purchaser of negroes, and Maryland, Virginia, and Kentucky, which States could employ slave labor to little advantage, always had a surplus for sale. The salubrious climate of these States produced a hardy laborer who was in great request in the cotton and sugar districts. The negroes of Virginia and Kentucky considered it a cruel doom to be sold to go South, as it was well understood that harder work and poorer fare would be their lot. The annual waste of life on the sugar plantations of Louisiana was two and one-half per cent. over and above the natural increase.[2] On the cotton estates the increase, if any, was slight. On one of the best-managed estates in Mississippi, Olmsted learned that the net increase amounted to four per cent.; on Virginia farms, however, it was frequently twenty per cent. Nevertheless, between 1830 and 1850 the slave population of Maryland decreased and that of Virginia remained stationary, while Louisiana more than doubled, Alabama nearly trebled, and Mississippi almost quintupled their number of slaves. These facts disclose the internal slave-trade and the most wretched aspect of the institution—that of breeding slaves for market.

Even so methodical and frugal a planter as Washington found that if negroes were kept on the same land, and they and all their increase supported upon it, "their owner would gradually become more and more embarrassed or impover-

---

[1] The Slave-trade, Carey, p. 112; Southern Wealth and Northern Profits, Kettell, pp. 130 and 135; Thirty Years' View, Benton, vol. ii. p. 782; A Journey in the Back Country, Olmsted, pp. 326 and 374.

[2] Report of the Agricultural Society of Baton Rouge, La.; letter of Johnson, M. C. from Louisiana, to the Secretary of the Treasury, cited on p. 174, Notes on Uncle Tom's Cabin, Stearns (1853). The author was an Episcopal clergyman of Maryland, and the book a defence of slavery.

ished." Yet the financial remedy was not adopted by Washington; he made a rule neither to buy nor sell slaves.[1] Jefferson, although in easy circumstances when he retired from the presidency, could not make both ends meet on his Monticello estate, and died largely in debt.[2] Madison sold some of his best land to feed the increasing number of his negroes, but he confessed to Harriet Martineau that the week before she visited him he had been obliged to sell a dozen of his slaves.[3] We may be certain it was with great reluctance that the gentlemen of Virginia came to the point of breeding negroes to make money; but it was the easiest way to maintain their ancient state, so they eventually overcame their scruples. Even before Madison died, the professor of history and metaphysics in the college at which Jefferson was educated wrote in a formal paper: " The slaves in Virginia multiply more rapidly than in most of the Southern States; the Virginians can raise cheaper than they can buy; in fact, it is one of their greatest sources of profit;" and the writer seemed to exult over the fact that they were now "exporting slaves" very rapidly.[4] He wrote his defence of slavery in 1832, and then thought that Virginia was annually sending six thousand negroes to the Southern market.[5] For the ten years preceding 1860 the average annual importation of slaves into seven Southern States from the slave-breeding States was not far from twenty-five thousand.[6] In Virginia the number of women exceeded that of men, and

---

[1] Bancroft, vol. vi. p. 179. See also letter of Washington, printed in the *Athenæum*, July 11th, and cited by the New York *Nation*, July 30th, 1891.

[2] Life of Jefferson, Morse, p. 335.

[3] Retrospect of Western Travel, vol. i. p. 192.

[4] Prof. Dew, Pro-slavery Argument, pp. 362, 370. He afterwards became President of William and Mary College.

[5] Ibid., p. 378.

[6] Cotton Kingdom, vol. i. p. 58, note. See Slavery and Secession, Thos. Ellison, p. 223. The slave-exporting States were Maryland, Virginia, Kentucky, North Carolina, Tennessee, and Missouri; see also Pike's First Blows of the Civil War, pp. 386, 392.

were regarded in much the same way as are brood-mares.[1]
A Virginia gentleman, in conversation with Olmsted, con-
gratulated himself "because his women were uncommonly
good breeders; he did not suppose there was a lot of women
anywhere that bred faster than his; he never heard of babies
coming so fast as they did on his plantation; . . . and every
one of them, in his estimation, was worth two hundred dollars,
as negroes were selling now, the moment it drew breath."[2]
Frederick Douglass had a master, professedly a Christian,
opening and closing the day with family prayer, who boasted that he bought a woman slave simply "as a breeder."[3]
When James Freeman Clarke visited Baltimore, a friend
who had been to a party one night said there was pointed
out to him a lady richly and fashionably dressed, and apparently one moving in the best society, who derived her
income from the sale of the children of a half-dozen negro
women she owned, although their husbands belonged to
other masters.[4] Sometimes a negro woman would be advertised for sale as being "very prolific in her generating
qualities."[5]

The law in none of the States recognized slave marriages;[6]
in all of them the Roman principle, that the child followed
the condition of its mother, was the recognized rule. Except in Louisiana, there was no law to prevent the violent
separation of husbands from wives, or children from their
parents.[7] The church conformed its practice to the law.
The question was put to the Savannah River Baptist Association, whether in the case that slaves were separated, they

---

[1] Cotton Kingdom, vol. i. p. 57.   See debate in Virginia legislature,
1831–32.

[2] Cotton Kingdom, vol. i. p. 59.   [3] Life of Douglass, p. 118.

[4] Anti-slavery Days, James Freeman Clarke, p. 32.

[5] Goodell's American Slave Code, p. 84.

[6] There was a faint recognition by statute in Maryland, and by judicial
decision in Louisiana; but neither was of practical value.   They did not
prevent the separation by sale of husband from wife.   Notes on Uncle
Tom's Cabin, Stearns, p. 38.   [7] Stroud's Slave Laws, p. 82.

should be allowed to marry again.   The answer was in the affirmative, because the separation was civilly equivalent to death, and the ministers believed "that in the sight of God it would be so viewed."   It would not be right, therefore, to forbid second marriages.   It was proper that the slaves should act in obedience to their masters and raise up for them progeny.[1]   The negro women lacked in chastity ; it is true this was a natural inclination of the African race, but that this tendency should be fostered was an inevitable result of slavery.   "Licentiousness and almost indiscriminate sexual connection among the young," said Olmsted, "are very general."[2]

Slaves were chattels.[3]   They could be transferred by a simple bill of sale as horses or cattle ; they could even be sold or given away by their masters without a writing.[4] The cruelty of separating families, involved by the business of selling slaves who were raised expressly for market, or by the division of negroes among the heirs of a decedent, or their forced sale occasioned by the bankruptcy of an owner, appealed very forcibly to the North.   It especially awakened the sympathy of Northern women, who counted for much in educating and influencing voters in a way that finally brought about the abolition of slavery.   These separations were not infrequent, although they were not the general rule.   There was a disposition, on the score of self-interest, to avoid the tearing asunder of family ties, for the reason that if slaves pined on account of parting from those to whom they had become attached, they labored less obediently and were more troublesome.   Humane masters would, whenever possible, avoid selling the husband apart from the

---

[1] Goodell's American Slave Code, p. 109; Memorials of a Southern Planter, Smedes, p. 77.

[2] Seaboard Slave States, Olmsted, p. 132.

[3] In Louisiana and Kentucky they were in some cases considered real estate, but they did not partake enough of the quality of real property to prevent their being sold off from an estate. See Goodell, pp. 24, 25, 71, 75.

[4] *De Bow's Review*, vol. viii. p. 69.

wife, or young children away from the mother. The best
public sentiment of the South frowned upon an unnecessary
separation of families. It was not unusual to find men
making a money sacrifice to prevent a rending of family attachments, or generous people contributing a sum to avert
such an evil.[1] The prominence given in their arguments by
the abolitionists to this feature of the system undoubtedly
influenced the South to abate this cruelty. The apologists
of slavery never defended the separation of families; it was
admitted to be a necessary evil, and pains were taken to give
Northern and foreign visitors the impression that such cases
were of rare occurrence.

It is very probable that a good deal of the Northern sympathy on this subject was misplaced. Heart-rending scenes
at slave auctions certainly took place, and the many incidents recounted in the abolition literature are perhaps all of
them trustworthy relations,[2] yet they as surely represent

---

[1] Lyell, Second Visit to the United States, vol. i. p. 209; Notes on Uncle
Tom's Cabin, p. 40; Pro-slavery Argument, p. 132. For the subject discussed thoroughly, from the abolitionist standpoint, see Key to Uncle
Tom's Cabin, p. 133. The Key to Uncle Tom's Cabin is mainly a collection of *pièces justificatives.* For confirmation of statements in the text,
see p. 137. Memorials of a Southern Planter, Smedes, p. 48. The result
of Edmund Yates's observations was that separations were frequent. "At
Richmond and New Orleans I was present at slave auctions, and did not
see one instance of a married pair being sold together; but, without exception, so far as I was able to learn from the negroes sold by the auctioneers, every grown-up man left a wife, and every grown-up woman a
husband."—Letter to the Women of England, cited in Greeley's American
Conflict, p. 70.

[2] See the account of the editor of the *Pennsylvania Freeman*, Dec. 25th,
1846, of a sale at Petersburg, Va., cited in Key to Uncle Tom's Cabin,
p. 137. When the negroes found out that they were to be sold "the
effect was indescribably agonizing." A mother cried "in frantic grief"
when her boy was sold. "During the sale, the quarters resounded with
cries and lamentations that made my heart ache."

Edmund Yates writes: "I saw Mr. Pulliam [of Richmond] sell to different buyers two daughters away from their mother, who was also to be
sold. This unfortunate woman was a quadroon; and I shall not soon

only a phase and not the universal rule. The detailed, minute, and celebrated account of a slave auction at Richmond by William Chambers, the publisher, of Edinburgh, is undoubtedly a fair example of what many times occurred. At one establishment there were ten negroes offered for sale. The intending purchasers examined the slaves by feeling the arms of all and the ankles of the women; they looked into their mouths and examined carefully their hands and fingers. One of the lots was a full-blooded negro woman with three children. "Her children were all girls, one of them a baby at the breast, three months old, and the others two and three years of age. . . . There was not a tear or an emotion visible in the whole party. Everything seemed to be considered a matter of course; and the change of owners was possibly looked forward to with as much indifference as ordinary hired servants anticipate a removal from one employer to another." Chambers took an offered opportunity to converse with the woman, who told him she had been parted from her husband two days, and that her heart was almost broken at the thought of the lasting separation. The writer continues: "I have said that there was an entire absence of emotion in the party of men, women, and children thus seated, preparatory to being sold. This does not correspond with the ordinary accounts of slave sales, which are represented as tearful and harrowing. My belief is that none of the parties felt deeply on the subject, or at least that any distress they experienced was but momentary—

---

forget the large tears that started to her eyes as she saw her two children sold away from her."

"Who was the greatest orator you ever heard?" asked Josiah Quincy of John Randolph. "The greatest orator I ever heard," replied Randolph, "was a woman. She was a slave. She was a mother, and her rostrum was the auction-block."—Figures of the Past, p. 212.

See account of Lewis Hayden, Key to Uncle Tom's Cabin, p. 155; Anti-slavery Manual (1837), p. 109; Slave States of America, Buckingham, vol. i. p. 183; also Retrospect of Western Travel, Martineau, vol. i. p. 235.

soon passed away and was forgotten. One of my reasons for this opinion rests on a trifling incident which occurred. While waiting for the commencement of the sale, one of the gentlemen present amused himself with a pointer-dog which, at command, stood on its hind-legs and took pieces of bread from his pocket. These tricks greatly entertained the row of negroes, old and young; and the poor woman whose heart three minutes before was almost broken now laughed as heartily as any one." [1] Chambers spent a forenoon in visiting different establishments where slaves were sold at auc-

---

[1] Things in America, W. Chambers, pp. 279, 280. The whole account is worth reading. A similar account of a slave auction, which took place at Savannah, may be found in the New York *Tribune* of April 28th, 1860, translated from *Das Ausland;* see also Promenade en Amérique, J. J. Ampère, tome ii. p. 113. See also account of the " great auction sale of slaves at Savannah, March 2d and 3d, 1859," by a correspondent of the New York *Tribune*, published in the New York *Tribune*, and in pamphlet in 1863.

When Seward visited Virginia, in 1846, there were on the steamboat on which he travelled seventy-five slaves who were on the way to New Orleans to be sold. As they arrived at a port of entry where the ship lay at anchor which was to take them south, Seward watched them with intense interest as they filed from the steamboat to the ship, which had already one hundred and twenty-five fellow negroes doomed to the same destiny. He writes: " As I stood looking at this strange scene a gentleman stepped up to my side and said, ' You see the curse that our forefathers bequeathed to us.'

" I replied, ' Yes,' and turned away, to conceal manifestations of sympathy I might not express.

" ' Oh,' said my friend, ' they don't mind it; they are cheerful; they enjoy the transportation and travel as much as you do.'

" ' I am glad they do,' said I, ' poor wretches !'

" The lengthened file at last had all reached the deck of the slaver, and we cut loose. The captain of our boat, seeing me intensely interested, turned to me and said : ' Oh ! sir, do not be concerned about them; they are the happiest people in the world.' I looked, and there they were— slaves, ill protected from the cold, fed capriciously on the commonest food —going from all that was dear to all that was terrible, and still they wept not. I thanked God that he had made them insensible. And these were ' the happiest people in the world !' "—Life of Seward, vol. i. p. 778.

I.—21

tion. His blood boiled with indignation to see a human being, though with a black skin, sold "just like a horse at Tattersall's;" yet he closed his narrative with: "It would not have been difficult to speak strongly on a subject which appeals so greatly to the feelings; but I have preferred telling the simple truth."

Jefferson, who hated slavery and who studied negroes with the eye of the planter and philosopher, thus compared them with the whites: "They are more ardent after their female; but love seems with them to be more an eager desire than a tender, delicate mixture of sentiment and sensation. Their griefs are transient. Those numberless afflictions which render it doubtful whether heaven has given life to us in mercy or in wrath, are less felt and sooner forgotten with them."[1] A careful study of the slaves of the generation before the civil war must lead to the same conclusion.[2] The earnest and educated women of the North unconsciously invested the negroes with their own fine feelings, and estimated the African's grief at separation from her family by what would be their own at a like fate. The selling of a wife away from her husband, or a mother away from her children, appeared to their emotional natures simply horrible. It seemed a cruel act, for which there could be no excuse or mitigation. It was a vulnerable part of the system; the abolitionists, attacking it with impetuosity, gained the sympathy of the larger portion of thinking Northern women. This earnestness was not simulated, for the injustice likewise appealed strongly to the emotional temperaments of the abolitionists. Garrison identified himself so closely with the negroes, whose cause he had made

---

[1] Notes on Virginia, Jefferson's Works, vol. viii. p. 382.

[2] See account of a slave auction at Richmond in Travels of Arforedson, Anti-slavery Manual, p. 114 ; also Key to Uncle Tom's Cabin, p. 152; Olmsted's Seaboard Slave States, p. 556 ; Promenade en Amérique, J. J. Ampère, vol. ii. p. 115. "The negro [in Africa] knows not love, affection, or jealousy."—Cited by Herbert Spencer, Sociology, vol. i. p. 663. "The negro race do not understand kissing."—Ibid., vol. ii. p. 17.

his own, that in addressing a body of them he said that he was ashamed of his own color.[1]

It could not be denied that an extensive traffic in slaves existed all through the South. "Cash for Negroes," "Negroes for Sale," and "Negroes Wanted," were as common advertisements in the Southern papers as notices of proposed sales of horses and mules. Indeed, the two kinds of property were frequently advertised and sold together. An administrator offers "horses, mules, cattle, hogs, sheep, and several likely young negroes;" a sheriff announces the sale of "ten head of cattle, twenty-five head of hogs, and seven negroes;" an auctioneer bespeaks attendance at the court-house in Columbia, S. C., for an opportunity such as seldom occurs, for he will offer one hundred valuable negroes, among whom are "twenty-five prime young men, forty of the most likely young women, and as fine a set of children as can be shown." A dealer at Memphis offers the highest cash price for slaves, and one at Baltimore wants to buy five thousand negroes and announces that families are "never separated." A firm at Natchez, Miss., advertises "fresh arrivals weekly of slaves," and promises to keep constantly "a large and well-selected stock." A competitor in the same city offers "ninety negroes just arrived from Richmond, consisting of field hands, house-servants, carriage-drivers, several fine cooks, and some excellent mules, and one very fine riding-horse;" and he advises his patrons that he has "made arrangements in Richmond to have regular shipments every month, and intends to keep a good stock on hand of every description of servants." An auctioneer in New Orleans announces for sale three splendid paintings, "The Circassian Slave," "The Lion Fight," and "The Crucifixion;" also, "Delia, aged seventeen, a first-rate cook; Susan, aged sixteen, a mulatress, a good house-girl; Ben, aged fourteen, and Peyton, aged sixteen, smart house-boys;" and adds, "The above slaves are fully guaranteed and sold for no fault." A

---

[1] Life of Garrison, vol. i. p. 158.

storekeeper of New Orleans, who was likewise a colonel, at
the request and for the amusement of his many acquaintances got up a raffle, and the prizes were a dark-bay horse,
warranted sound, with a trotting buggy and harness, and
"the stout mulatto girl Sarah, aged about twenty - nine
years, general house-servant, valued at nine hundred dollars
and guaranteed."[1]   There might be seen now and then in
the New Orleans papers an advertisement of a lot of pious
negroes.[2]   A curious notice appeared in the *Religious Herald*, a Baptist journal published in Richmond : " Who wants
thirty-five thousand dollars in property?   I am desirous to
spend the balance of my life as a missionary, if the Lord
permit, and therefore offer for sale my farm—the vineyard
adjacent to Williamsburg . . . and also about forty servants, mostly young and likely, and rapidly increasing in
numbers and value."[3]   By actual count made from the advertisements in sixty-four newspapers published in eight
slave States during the last two weeks of November, 1852,
there were offered for sale four thousand one hundred negroes.[4]   The good society of the South looked upon slave
dealers and auctioneers with contempt.   Their occupation
was regarded as base, and they were treated by gentlemen
as the publicans were by the Pharisees.   The opening scene
of " Uncle Tom's Cabin " was criticised as inaccurate, for it
showed a Kentucky gentleman entertaining at table a vul-
gar slave-dealer.[5]   The utter scorn with which such men

---

[1] New Orleans *True Delta*, Jan. 11th, 1853, cited in Key to Uncle Tom's
Cabin, p. 182 ; New Orleans *Picayune*, Jan., 1844 ; Second Visit to America, Lyell, vol. ii. p. 126 ; Key to Uncle Tom's Cabin, p. 134 *et seq.*, where
copies of large numbers of similar advertisements may be found.   See
description and illustration of an auction in the rotunda of the St. Louis
Hotel, New Orleans, of estates, pictures, and slaves.   Slave States of
America, Buckingham, vol. i. p. 334.
[2] Retrospect of Western Travel, Martineau, vol. i. p. 250.
[3] New York *Independent*, March 21st, 1850.
[4] Key to Uncle Tom's Cabin, p. 142.
[5] Notes on Uncle Tom's Cabin, Stearns, p. 145.

were regarded was a condemnation of slavery in the house of its friends.[1]

A feature of the institution that aroused much indignation at the North was its cruelty, as evidenced by the rigor with which the lash was used. We have seen that flogging necessarily accompanied this system of labor.[2] The master and the overseer held the theory that the negroes were but children and should be chastised on the principle of the ancient schoolmaster who carried out the injunctions of Solomon. This was also in the main the practice, but wanton cruelty did not rule.[3] At times, however, a fit of drunkenness, an access of ill-temper, or a burst of passion would incite the man who had unrestrained power to use it like a brute.[4] Abolition literature is full of such instances, well attested.

Slaves were sometimes whipped to death.[5] The murderers were occasionally tried, and once in a while convicted,

---

[1] "You [*i. e.* the Southern people] have among you a sneaking individual of the class of native tyrants known as the slave-dealer. He watches your necessities, and crawls up to buy your slave at a speculating price. If you cannot help it, you sell to him; but if you can help it, you drive him from your door. You despise him utterly. You do not recognize him as a friend, or even as an honest man. Your children must not play with his; they may rollick freely with the little negroes, but not with the slave-dealer's children. If you are obliged to deal with him, you try to get through the job without so much as touching him. It is common with you to join hands with the men you meet; but with the slave-dealer you avoid the ceremony—instinctively shrinking from the snaky contact. . . . Now, why is this? You do not so treat the man who deals in corn, cattle, or tobacco."—Lincoln at Peoria, Oct. 16th, 1854. Life by Howells, p. 276.

[2] See pp. 308 and 309.

[3] Cotton Kingdom, vol. i. p. 354; Kemble, p. 229. "The slave-owners, as a body, are not cruel, and many of them treat their slaves with paternal and patriarchal kindness."—Life and Liberty in America, Chas. Mackay, vol. i. p. 314.

[4] Olmsted's Seaboard Slave States, p. 485; Kemble, p. 175; Life of Fred. Douglass, pp. 38, 111. See also the graphic account of the whipping of a woman which Olmsted witnessed, Cotton Kingdom, vol. ii. p. 205.

[5] See Key to Uncle Tom's Cabin, pp. 60–80, 92 *et seq.*

but they were never hanged; more frequently, however, as the violent act was usually witnessed only by negroes, no proof could be obtained,[1] and the perpetrator was not even arrested. When negroes themselves committed a capital crime, there were instances of burning them to death at the stake.[2]

One finds, however, notice of plantations on which the slaves were never whipped. Ampère, who had no sympathy with slavery, visited a German who owned a plantation near Charleston, and who, having no cruelty or tyranny in his nature, appeared to be literally oppressed by his blacks. He was so humane that he would not whip his slaves. The slaves showed him little gratitude, and labored sluggishly and with great carelessness. When he went into a cabin where the negresses were at work cleaning cotton, he confined himself to showing them how badly their task was done and explaining to them the considerable damage which their negligence caused him. His observations were received with grumbling and sullenness. Ampère saw in this case an excellent argument against slavery. Had the gentleman hired his laborers he would have dismissed them if they did not work to his liking; but under the Southern system his choice lay simply between whipping them or becoming a victim to their idleness.[3] Masters like this were

---

[1] See p. 309.

[2] See Cotton Kingdom, vol. ii. pp. 348, 354. "That slaves have ever been burned alive has been indignantly denied. The late Judge Jay told me that he had evidence in his possession of negro burnings every year in the last twenty." See also New York *Weekly Tribune*, Oct. 3d, 1857; Anti-slavery History of the John Brown Year, p. 205; Debate in the House of Representatives, March 8th, 1860; New York *Tribune*, March 12th, 20th, and Aug. 24th, 1860. The grave historian Richard Hildreth so abhorred slavery that, before writing his serious work, Despotism in America, he gave to the press anonymously a novel, The White Slave, in which he describes with fidelity the burning of a negro at the stake, who was a fugitive and a murderer, see chap. xlv.

[3] Promenade en Amérique, J. J. Ampère, tome i. p. 114.

certainly rare in the cotton region, but as one travelled
northward, slavery appeared under milder features. A
New England girl became a governess upon a Tennessee
plantation where no slave had been whipped for seven
years; she became reconciled to slavery, and did not find in
reality the "revolting horrors" in it for which a Northern
education had prepared her.[1] In Virginia, Olmsted saw no
whipping of slaves except of wild, lazy children as they
were being broken in to work; and he heard of but little
harshness or cruelty.[2]

In our time, when the desire for education is common to
all, and the need of it universally acknowledged, it is interesting to inquire how this matter was dealt with by the slave-
holders. North Carolina, South Carolina, Georgia, Alabama,
and Louisiana forbade, under penalties, the teaching of slaves
to read or write. In Virginia the owners, but no one else,
might instruct their negroes, and in North Carolina the slaves
might be taught arithmetic. Some of these enactments
were on the statute-books before 1831, but everywhere after
that date the laws were made more stringent and were more
effectually enforced.[3] This year was memorable for the Nat
Turner insurrection and for the beginning of a systematic
abolition agitation by Garrison in the *Liberator*. The usual
apology at the South for these laws was their alleged necessity to prevent the negroes from reading the abolition documents sent to the slave States, which were incitements to
insurrection. The course which legislation took after 1831
has led many Northern writers to infer that the anti-slavery
agitation was the cause of slaves being treated more inhu-
manly than before. In so far as the withholding of privileges of education and association was a cruelty they are
right; but they are wrong when they have assumed that

---

[1] The Sunny South, Ingraham, pp. 59, 143.
[2] Cotton Kingdom, vol. i. pp. 94 and 131.
[3] Stroud's Slave Laws, p. 138 *et seq.*; Goodell's American Slave Code,
p. 20.

more positive brutality prevailed. A careful examination of the slavery literature will hardly fail to lead to the conclusion that the flood of light which the abolitionists threw upon the practice influenced the slave-owners to mitigate its most cruel features.[1] The thesis that slavery is a positive good began to be maintained after 1831, but no amount of arrogant assertion could prevent the advocates of slavery from being put on the defensive. Their earnest endeavors to convince Northern and foreign visitors of the benefits of the system show their appreciation of the fact that it was under the ban of the civilized world; and this very necessity of justifying their peculiar institution made them desirous of suppressing, as far as possible, what they themselves admitted to be its evils.

The ideas about the education of negroes were not everywhere alike, and there were other defences of their being kept in ignorance than the one which I have mentioned. A Georgia rice and cotton planter said that "the very slightest amount of education, merely teaching them to read, impairs their value as slaves, for it instantly destroys their contentedness; and since you do not contemplate changing their condition, it is surely doing them an ill service to destroy their acquiescence in it."[2] The Georgia gentleman was only partly right. A mass of advertisements of slaves for sale shows that knowledge made them more valuable, although it

---

[1] See, for example, Baltimore *American*, quoted in Slavery and Color, W. Chambers, p. 173. Seward made a visit to Culpepper Court-house and wrote his wife, Dec. 14th, 1857: "It is quite manifest that the long debate about slavery has made a deep impression on the minds and hearts of the more refined and generous portion of the families in Virginia. The word 'slaves' is seldom used. They are 'servants,' 'hands.' They are treated with kindness, and they appear clean, tidy, and comfortable. I happened to fall in upon a husking frolic on Mr. Pendleton's plantation, and it was indeed a merry and noisy scene. My visit was very pleasant. Mrs. Pendleton is a lady you would respect and love. She is sad with cares and responsibilities which she has too much conscientiousness to cast off."—Life of Seward, vol. ii. p. 331.

[2] Kemble, p. 9.

is also true that it made them more dangerous.[1]   The problem of the master was to impart sufficient knowledge to make the slave useful without making him restless.[2]

Chancellor Harper, in defending the law of South Carolina, reasoned that the slaves had to work during the day with their hands, and in their intervals of leisure few cared to read for amusement or instruction. "Of the many slaves," he writes, "whom I have known capable of reading, I have never known one to read anything but the Bible, and this task they impose on themselves as matter of duty ;" but this is an inefficient method of religious instruction, for "their comprehension is defective, and the employment is to them an unusual and laborious one." [3]   Another South Carolina judge, of equal prominence, took an entirely different view. He advocated the repeal of the law which forbade the instruction of the slaves. "When we reflect as Christians," he writes, "how can we justify it that a slave is not to be permitted to read the Bible?   It is in vain to say there is danger in it.   The best slaves in the State are those who can and do read the Scriptures.   Again, who is it that teach your slaves to read?   It generally is done by the children of the owners.   Who would tolerate an indictment against his son or daughter for teaching a favorite slave to read? Such laws look to me as rather cowardly." [4]   In spite of the law, then, house-servants were frequently taught to read.[5] Field hands, on the contrary, remained in gross ignorance, even where there were no prohibitory statutes.   In Maryland the teaching of slaves was not forbidden by law,[6] yet an apologist of slavery admits that as a general thing they were not taught to read in that State.[7]   Frederick Douglass

---

[1] See Despotism in America, Richard Hildreth, p. 63 ; also Cotton Kingdom, vol. ii. p. 82.

[2] See Cotton Kingdom, vol. i. p. 61.   [3] Pro-slavery Argument, p. 36.

[4] Judge J. B. O'Neall, De Bow's Resources, vol. ii. p. 269.

[5] See, for example, Memorials of a Southern Planter, Smedes, p. 79.

[6] The Negro in Maryland, Brackett, p. 197.

[7] Notes on Uncle Tom's Cabin, Stearns, p. 86.

relates that he had to teach his fellow-slaves on the plantation by stealth, and that when the secret was discovered his school was broken up; he was told, moreover, that if he were striving to be another Nat Turner he would very speedily meet that negro's fate.[1] Douglass himself had been taught to read while a boy by his Baltimore mistress, whose houseservant he was; but he relates that, though eager to learn, and though the teacher was proud of the rapid progress of the pupil, when the master came to hear of this instruction, further progress was peremptorily forbidden, because it was thought learning would spoil the best negro in the world by making him disconsolate and unhappy.[2]

And there were exceptions even to the crass ignorance of field hands. Olmsted visited a Mississippi plantation where all the negroes knew how to read: they had been taught by one of their number, and with the permission of the owner. They were well fed, and did good, honest work. The master was growing rich from the fruits of their labor, and, though illiterate himself, was proud of his instructed and religious slaves.[3]

Closely allied with the subject of education is that of religious nurture. It must be borne in mind that the Southern people were very pious, and held strictly to the orthodox faith. Liberal religious movements made no headway among them. If anything were needed to make the names of Garrison and Parker more opprobrious in the South, it

---

[1] Life of Fred. Douglass, p. 105.

[2] Ibid., p. 70. Sarah Grimke received a severe rebuke for teaching her little negro maid to read. The Sisters Grimke, Birney, p. 12. "Slavery and knowledge cannot live together. To enlighten the slave is to break his chain. . . . He cannot be left to read in an enlightened age without endangering his master; for what can he read which will not give at least some hint of his wrongs? Should his eye chance to fall on the Declaration of Independence, how would the truth glare on him 'that all men are born free and equal?' "—Channing on Slavery, p. 75.

[3] Cotton Kingdom, vol. ii. p. 70.

was that they were reproached with being infidels.[1] The
practice of giving religious instruction to the slaves varied
greatly, according to the temper of the master.   Bishop
Polk, of Louisiana, who owned four hundred slaves, was
very careful about their religious training.   They were
baptized and taught the catechism; at a proper age many
of them were confirmed; marriages were solemnized according to the ritual of the Episcopal Church.   The influence of the bishop among the church people of his diocese
was beneficial.[2]   Other masters, from indolence, paid little
attention to the matter, while still others discouraged religious instruction from a belief of its danger.   Religious exercises among the slaves, however, were rarely forbidden.[3]
It was the opinion of Fanny Kemble that the systematic
preaching to the negroes, common in her neighborhood, was
largely due to the exposure in the abolition literature of
former neglect.   Sometimes the slaves of an estate were
preached to by one of their own number, or by one from
a neighboring plantation.   After the day of Nat Turner, it
was customary at these meetings to have white men present, and in some States this was required by law.   There
were also legal restrictions in regard to negroes assembling
at night for worship.   Free blacks, who were itinerant
preachers, were everywhere frowned upon, and frequently
prevented from pursuing their calling.

There was a strong feeling that the religious instruction
should be given by white preachers.   Many of these moved
in the same sphere of society as the slave-holders, and practically all of them had the feelings of the dominant class.
"Servants, obey in all things your masters," was their favorite text, and the slaves were solemnly enjoined to be satisfied with their lot on earth; though the conditions were

---

[1] In regard to Garrison, see his Life, vol. iii. p. 374.

[2] See note, p. 213, vol. ii. Cotton Kingdom.

[3] Ibid., p. 222; see also Promenade en Amérique, Ampère, tome ii.
p. 144.

often hard, they were assured that if they remained faithful and steadfast, their reward hereafter would be exceeding great.[1] Following the teaching of the fathers of the
church, they took pains to impress upon the slaves that
while they suffered from the fall of Adam, they labored
likewise under the curse of Canaan; that to this were due
their black skin and hard hands; that these were manifestations of God's displeasure, and pointed them out as proper
subjects of slavery.[2]

The slaves were fond of religious exercises. Even the
arid discourses of the white clergymen were a relief from
their monotonous daily toil, while to attend upon the ex-
hortations of one of their own color gave unalloyed delight. Yet there did not seem to be in the minds of the
slaves any necessary connection between religion and morality. An entire lack of chastity among the women, and
an entire lack of honesty among the men, did not prevent
their joining the church and becoming, in the estimation of
their fellow-slaves, exemplary Christians. It is obvious that
if the white preachers inculcated these virtues, such preaching, when accompanied with the averment that slavery was
a necessary relation between the blacks and the whites, must
be without effect; for to the slaves an absolute condition
of the system seemed to be that the labor of the man and
the person of the woman belonged to the master. No moralist would undertake to preach honesty to men who did not

---

[1] A ragged old negro whom Olmsted met in Mississippi showed that
such preaching had taken root by discoursing thus: "Rough fare's good
enough for dis world. . . . Dis world ain't nothin'; dis is hell, dis is hell
to what's a-comin' arter. . . . I reckon de Lord has 'cepted of me, and I
'specs I shall be saved, dough I don't look much like it. . . . De Lord am
my rock, and he shall not perwail over me; I will lie down in green past-
ures and take up my bed in hell, yet will not his mercy circumwent me."
—Cotton Kingdom, vol. ii. p. 90.

[2] Kemble, p. 57; Life of Frederick Douglass, p. 155. A curious yet
characteristic catechism for slaves was published in the *Southern Episco-
palian*, and cited in the New York *Weekly Tribune*, June 10th, 1854.

own their labor, nor chastity to women who did not own their bodies. This was appreciated by Southern reasoners. Chancellor Harper argued that unchastity among female slaves was not a vice or a crime, but only a weakness; and that theft by a negro was not a crime, but only a vice.[1]

It is easy to sum up the intellectual and moral condition of the vast proportion of the slaves; they were in a state of dismal ignorance and moral darkness.[2] If some travellers and novelists have represented slavery in a different light from that in which it is here presented, it is because they have dwelt upon it as seen in the least painful aspect. The household servants were different in all respects from the field hands. They were naturally brighter, and effort was made to train them; they were better fed and clothed, and their close contact with white people, owing to the imitative faculty of the race, was an education in itself. A common picture in literature is the joyful welcome given the master and mistress on their return from a journey by the troops of house-servants, and that such scenes were of frequent occurrence is undoubted. That a breach in the custom was unwelcome is well illustrated by a master who gave his servants a cruel beating because on coming home he was not met by demonstrations of joy and professions of attachment.[3] Olmsted saw some of these welcomes that came from the heart; they were greetings from the house-slaves; the field hands, however, seemed indifferent; " barely touched their tattered hats and grinned." [4] " The slaves in a family," said Henry Clay, "are treated with all the kindness that the children of the family receive;" [5] and it is General Sher-

---

[1] Pro-slavery Argument, pp. 39 and 43. See instance related by Lyell, Second Visit, vol. i. p. 272.

[2] "The field-hand negro is, on an average, a very poor and very bad creature. . . . He seems to be but an imperfect man, incapable of taking care of himself in a civilized manner."—Cotton Kingdom, vol. ii. p. 339.

[3] Slavery as It Is, Thos. D. Weld, p. 129.

[4] A Journey in the Back Country, Olmsted, p. 286.

[5] Speech on Compromise Measures, Feb. 6th, 1850.

man's recollection that "the family servants were treated as well as the average hired servants of to-day."[1] That these remarks were in a measure true of some houses in the South cannot be denied, but there is abundant testimony to show that these statements by no means represent the average condition of household slaves.[2] This is what we should expect, for the relation described by Clay was an inherent impossibility, and the assertion of General Sherman is refuted by the fact that the servant of to-day has a check upon the master in his privilege of quitting the service.

For the sake, however, of putting this aspect of slavery in its fairest light, I am glad to refer to the observations of two English travellers. Buckingham thought that the condition of the " slaves of the household was quite as comfortable as that of servants in the middle ranks of life in England. They are generally well-fed, well-dressed, attentive, orderly, respectful, and easy to be governed, but more by kindness than by severity."[3] Sir Charles Lyell was of the opinion that the house-slaves had many advantages " over the white race in the same rank of life in Europe."[4] A witty English novelist, struck with the fact that, under the system, a good cook or an honest butler could not be tempted away by an offer of higher wages, said that negro slavery in America was a charming domestic institution.

The existence of mulattoes, quadroons, and of slaves fairer still than these, calls attention to the fact of the mixture of the white and negro races. This union was between the white man and the negress.[5] The giving birth to a colored child by a white woman was almost unknown ; the

---

[1] *North American Review*, Oct., 1888.

[2] See A Journey in the Back Country, Olmsted, p. 288.

[3] The Slave States of America, Buckingham, vol. i. p. 131.

[4] Second Visit, Sir Charles Lyell, vol. i. p. 263; see also Homes of the New World, F. Bremer, vol. i. p. 277.

[5] " The tell-tale faces of children, glowing with their master's blood, but doomed for their mother's skin to slavery."—Sumner's speech on the Barbarism of Slavery.

bringing into the world of children fairer than herself by the female slave was a common thing, and was evidence that the ownership of her person by her master was not merely a theoretical right. While the Southerners frequently charged that amalgamation of the two races was the aim of the Northern abolitionists, to an impartial judge it was apparent that where the negro was free, no danger existed of a mixture of blood. The reason for this did not escape the keen observation of De Tocqueville. "Among the Americans of the Southern States," he writes, "nature, sometimes, reasserting her rights, re-establishes for a moment equality between the whites and the blacks. At the North, pride restrains the most imperious of human passions. The Northern man would perhaps consent to make the negress the transient companion of his pleasure if the legislators had declared that she could never aspire to share legitimately his bed; but as she may legally become his wife, he shrinks from her with a kind of horror."[1]

The lack of chaste sentiment among the female slaves is exemplified by their yielding without objection, except in isolated cases, to the passion of their master. Indeed, the idea of the superiority of the white race was so universally admitted that the negress felt only pride at bearing offspring that had an admixture of the blood of the ruling class. Such children, on account of their greater capacity, and because in many cases the master would look after his own progeny, were frequently destined for house-servants; thus their lot might be easier than their mothers' had been. So loose was the tie of marriage among the slaves, that the negro husband felt little or no displeasure when the fancy of the master chanced to light upon his wife. One finds instances, however, scattered through the abolition literature, of the black resenting these intrusions upon his fam-

---

[1] De la Démocratie en Amérique, De Tocqueville, vol. ii. p. 308. It is a certain fact that since the negroes have become free, amalgamation has nearly ceased at the South.

ily by killing the offending white, but such cases are rare. If, indeed, the desire to revenge the injury had been common, the negro's feelings would have been held in check by the certainty of punishment; for when such murders were committed, execution was prompt, generally according to lynch law, and the offender was occasionally burned at the stake.

The practice of gentlemen seeking illicit pleasure among the slaves of their households and estates introduced into the best society of the South a discordant element which one cannot contemplate without feeling profound pity for the suffering of many noble and refined women whose lot was cast in a country where such a system prevailed. A planter's wife is only "the chief slave of a harem," declared, in the bitterness of her heart, the wife of a lordly slave-holder.[1] "We Southern ladies are complimented with the name of wives," said a sister of President Madison, "but we are only the mistresses of seraglios."[2] Harriet Martineau wrote that in the Southwestern States "most heart-rending disclosures were made to me by the ladies, heads of families, of the state of society, and of their own intolerable sufferings in it."[3] Madison avowed to her that there was great licentiousness on the Virginia plantations, "and that it was understood that the female slaves were to become mothers at fifteen."[4] It had become a proverb and a byword that "the noblest blood of Virginia runs in the veins of slaves."[5] Fanny Kemble writes that almost every Southern planter admitted one or several of his female slaves to the close intimacy of his bed, and had a "family more or less numerous of illegitimate colored children."[6] A planter told Olmsted: "There is not a likely-looking black girl in this State that is not the concubine of a white man. There is not an old plantation in which the grand-

[1] Society in America, Martineau, vol. ii. p. 118.
[2] Goodell's American Slave Code, p. 111.
[3] Society in America, vol. i. p. 304.   [4] Ibid., vol. ii. p. 118.
[5] Goodell, p. 84.   [6] Kemble, pp. 15 and 23; see also p. 140.

children of the owner are not whipped in the field by his overseer." [1]

That attractiveness of form and feature which arose from the mixture of bloods increased in a marked degree the selling value of female slaves. A number of cases are cited in the anti-slavery books where comely mulattoes and beautiful quadroons were sold for mistresses; and while unfounded suspicions might sometimes be asserted as positive facts, no one, knowing the system of slavery and understanding human nature, can doubt that many such transactions must have taken place. "I have," writes General Sherman, "attended the auction sales of slaves in the rotunda of the St. Louis Hotel [New Orleans]. . . . I have seen young girls in new calico dresses, inspected by men-buyers as critically as would be a horse by a purchaser—eyes, hair, teeth, limbs and muscles—and have seen spirited bidding for a wench of handsome form and figure by men of respectable standing." [2] A letter of slave-dealers, which was widely circulated in anti-slavery publications, was a bald admission of this feature of the traffic. A free negro woman in New York interested some humane people in the fate of her daughter, a beautiful young quadroon girl who was held for sale by a firm in Alexandria, Va. With a view of raising the money for the purchase of this slave, they asked what was her price. The slave-dealers replied, "We cannot afford to sell the girl Emily for less than eighteen hundred dollars . . . We have two or three offers for Emily from gentlemen from the South. She is said to be the finest-looking woman in this country." [3] Harriet Martineau reports a circumstance that exhibits this feature of slavery in its baldest form. "A Southern lady, of fair reputation

---

[1] Cotton Kingdom, vol. i. p. 308.

[2] *North American Review*, Oct., 1888.

[3] Letter of Bruin and Hill, cited in New York *Independent* from the Cleveland *Democrat*, Jan., 1850. It may be found in Key to Uncle Tom's Cabin, p. 169.

I.—22

for refinement and cultivation, told a story of which a favorite slave, a very pretty mulatto girl, was the heroine. A young man came to stay at her house and fell in love with the girl. ' She came to me,' said the lady, ' for protection, which I gave her.' The young man went away, but after some weeks he returned, saying he was so much in love with the girl that he could not live without her. ' I pitied the young man,' concluded the lady, ' so I sold the girl to him for fifteen hundred dollars.' " [1]

This phase of the morals of slavery may be best studied at New Orleans. The occupation of this city by three distinct nationalities had given it a cosmopolitan air such as was seen in no other city of the country before the war. The graceful qualities of the Latin race were blended with the manly virtues of the Anglo-Saxon stock. The city was a centre of wealth, and the abode of refinement, elegance, and luxury. [2] The Spanish and French mixed their blood freely with the negroes, and the result at New Orleans was the production of beautiful quadroons and octoroons which reached their highest type in the female sex. Such girls were frequently sent to Paris to be educated. They were generally healthy in appearance, and often very handsome; they were remarked for a graceful and elegant carriage, and showed exquisite taste in dress; their manners were refined; in short, they were accomplished young women who would, perhaps, have been fitted for the highest society in the land, had it not been for the taint of African blood. They could not marry with a white man; paying the universal homage to the superiority of the Caucasian race,

---

[1] Society in America, vol. ii. p. 123.

[2] " À la Nouvelle Orleans, nous avons retrouvé avec plaisir l'opéra français et la société française. Un bal chez M. Slidell est ce que j'ai vu jusqu'ici de plus parisien en Amérique. Dans trois salons se pressait un monde fort brillant. Une certaine grâce créole se remarquait chez plusieurs des belles danseuses que j'admirais : le mélange du sang français et du sang anglo-saxon avait produit de très-beaux résultats."—Promenade en Amérique, J. J. Ampère, tome ii. p. 153.

they would not marry a man who had negro blood in his veins. They became, therefore, the mistresses of the wealthy curled darlings of New Orleans. Yet such relations were not entered into blindly; they were the result of systematic arrangement. The young man who fancied the young woman must have the consent of her mother, who was a free person, and who in youth had been placed in like manner. He must have means to provide for the girl and her children, and must agree to settle a certain amount on her when he should leave her and take to himself a lawful wife. All the conditions being satisfactory, the pair lived together in an establishment as husband and wife. The young man led a dual life, frequenting the quadroon society with his mistress, and moving likewise in the best society of New Orleans with his parents and friends. Such connections lasted sometimes for life, but more frequently the marriage of the gentlemen broke them off. The girls that resulted from the union were sometimes sent permanently abroad, where their color did not prevent them from leading reputable lives; but as a general rule they continued in the same rank of life as their mothers, and were destined to a like fate.[1]

That the evil here referred to prevailed throughout the South to any great extent was sometimes denied.[2] The defenders of Southern institutions could point to the observations of two unprejudiced travellers to bear them out in this denial. De Tocqueville testified that mulattoes were far from numerous in the United States;[3] and it is true that the proportion of them was much smaller than in French, Spanish, or Portuguese colonies where slavery had existed or still continued in operation. Sir Charles Lyell was told that mulattoes did not constitute more than two and one-half per

---

[1] For a complete account of this peculiar state of society, see Cotton Kingdom, vol. i. p. 302, and Society in America, vol. ii. p. 116.

[2] See denial of Senator Hammond, Pro-slavery Argument, p. 118.

[3] De la Démocratie en Amérique, vol. ii. p. 331.

cent. of the population, which he was quite ready to believe, and from this he drew a conclusion very favorable to the morals of the Southern States. He writes : " If the statistics of the illegitimate children of the whites born here could be compared with those in Great Britain, it might lead to conclusions by no means favorable to the free country. Here (*i. e.*, in the Southern States) there is no possibility of concealment; the color of the child stamps upon him the mark of bastardy, and transmits it to great-grand-children born in lawful wedlock ; whereas, if in Europe there was some mark or indelible stain betraying all the delinquencies and frailties, not only of parents, but of ancestors for three or four generations back, what unexpected disclosures should we not witness !" [1]

De Tocqueville and Lyell, however, wrote before any count was taken of mulattoes in our decennial census.[2] Such an enumeration was first made in 1850, and a comparison of the figures of 1850 and 1860 shows that the mixture of blood was greater than De Tocqueville and Lyell imagined, while yet it did not reach the proportions that might be supposed from many statements occurring in the abolition literature. It must be understood that, as the mulatto is the product of a union between the white and the black, the term, as used in the census reports, was intended to comprise those having a mixture of white blood from one-half to seven-eighths, but not designed to cover the issue of connections between mulattoes and blacks where there would be a preponderance of African blood. In the slave States, in 1850, ten per cent. of the colored people were mulattoes, and the proportion was twelve per cent. in 1860.[3] The su-

---

[1] Second Visit to the United States, vol. i. p. 271.

[2] De Tocqueville travelled in this country in 1831–33, and Lyell made his second visit in 1845–46.

	1850.	1860.	Proportion. 1850.	Proportion. 1860.
[3] Blacks	3,093,605	3,697,274	89.86	87.70
Mulattoes	348,895	518,360	10.14	12.30
Total colored population,	3,442,500	4,215,634		

perintendent of the census estimated, from certain figures and a fair calculation, that the total births of mulattoes in the whole country from 1850 to 1860 were 273,000. More than six-sevenths of these must have been born in the South. Of every hundred births of colored infants in the United States, seventeen were mulattoes, of whom fifteen saw the light in the slave States; these must have been, for the most part, the issue of white men and female slaves.[1]

Among the Southern apologists for slavery were men of great candor, who admitted the evil which we have considered. Such were Chancellor Harper and W. Gilmore Simms; and they excused it on the ground that, as irregular sexual indulgence had contributed to the misery and degradation of man in all nations, ages, and under all religions, its existence at the South was not due to slavery, but proceeded from man's unbridled passion, whose effects were equally baneful at the North and in Europe.[2] When Seward was

---

[1] The historian must be careful not to make any radical deductions from these census figures. The count of mulattoes was made in 1850, 1860, and 1870. The figures for 1870 show that in the old slave States the number of mulattoes had decreased from 1860. As the war had intervened, this is not satisfactory evidence that the mixing of races had decreased with the emancipation of the slaves; but that fact is so universally acknowledged that no statistics are needed to sustain it. Why the count of the mulattoes was abandoned in 1880 is explained by a letter of Francis A. Walker, President of the Massachusetts Institute of Technology, who was superintendent of the census for 1870 and 1880. He writes, Dec. 20th, 1889: "The reason for the omission of the class mulatto from the census of 1880 was found in the conviction that the returns had always been inaccurate in this particular, and were becoming increasingly so as each successive generation produced a larger admixture of blood. Not one person in ten makes the faintest discrimination between three negroes who are respectively five-eighths, three-fourths, and seven-eighths black. Most persons fail to make the distinction between the whole and the three-fourths of color. Every ten years the admixture becomes more complicated, while there is even less interest than formerly in observing and preserving the distinctions resulting."

[2] See Pro-slavery Argument, pp. 40 and 230. See also, in this connection, Lecky's History of Morals, vol. ii. p. 282.

at Richmond he had an interview with the governor of Virginia, in which the latter spoke of the danger of amalgamation at the North; "and when," as Seward himself reports the conversation, "I told him that commerce of the races was less frequent there than in the South, he forgot the question and extolled that commerce as freeing the white race from habits of licentiousness." [1] The discussion of this defence is the part of the moralist, not of the historian. Our concern is simply with the facts. The most scathing review of this practice may be found in Harriet Martineau's chapter on the " Morals of Slavery," which occurs in " Society in America." Some notion of this part of her book may be had when I mention that all the references but one which have been made to it in the present consideration of the matter were drawn from this chapter. [2] The treatise is admirably written. It is not that of a one-sided agitator who searches only for facts which will square with his theory, but it is the work of a student of social science who has gathered facts with care, and only drawn legitimate deductions. It was this chapter that brought down on the author that indiscriminate abuse in which the critics vied with one another in making ungenerous allusions to her infirmity of deafness, and insulting references to her maidenhood; for it was an offence to put the finger upon the plague-spot.

One of the authoritative apologists of slavery admits that Miss Martineau was correct. The chapter on " Morals of Slavery," writes W. Gilmore Simms, "is painful because it is full of truth. . . . It gives a collection of statements, which are, no doubt, in too many cases founded upon facts, of the illicit and foul conduct of some among us who make their slaves the victims and the instruments alike of the most licentious passions. . . . We do not quarrel with Miss Mar-

---

[1] Life of W. H. Seward, vol. i. p. 777.
[2] The one on p. 336, to vol. i.; this chapter occurs in vol. ii.

tineau for this chapter. The truth—though it is not all truth—is quite enough to sustain her and it." [1]

The child is father of the man. What effect had the institution of slavery on the bringing-up of children? One aspect is best described by Jefferson. "The whole commerce between master and slave," he writes, "is a perpetual exercise of the most boisterous passions, the most unremitting despotism on the one part and degrading submissions on the other. Our children see this and learn to imitate it. . . . The parent storms, the child looks on, catches the lineaments of wrath, puts on the same airs in the circle of smaller slaves, gives a loose to the worst of passions, and thus nursed, educated, and daily exercised in tyranny, cannot but be stamped by it with odious peculiarities." [2] " Everybody in the South," wrote Fred. Douglass, "seemed to want the privilege of whipping somebody else." [3]

The close and habitual association of children with slaves was objectionable on account of the lascivious imagination and gross talk of the negroes. It was a companionship mutually agreeable, but especially dangerous ; for, as chastity was not a restraint upon the blacks, their conversation lacked decency. A Southern merchant told Olmsted that he begged his brother, who was a planter, to send his children North to school, for "he might as well have them educated in a brothel as in the way they were growing up." [4] Fortunately, the custom prevailed for wealthy people at the South to send their daughters and sons away to school and to college, and they generally went to the North. Girls seem to have gone through this corruption scatheless, but boys suffered from the early contact with licentiousness, both physically and morally. [5]

---

[1] Pro-slavery Argument, p. 228.
[2] Notes on Virginia, Works, vol. viii. p. 403.   [3] Life, p. 31.
[4] Cotton Kingdom, vol. ii. p. 230.
[5] See ibid., vol. i. p. 222; vol. ii. p. 229; Martineau's chapter on Morals of Slavery, p. 128.

I have spoken of the effect of slavery on the slaves and slave-holders, but there was another large class in the South that must be considered. The poor whites were free; they had the political privileges of the planters, but their physical condition was almost as bad, and their lack of education almost as marked as that of the negroes. Yet they asserted the aristocracy of color more arrogantly than did the rich; it was their one claim to superiority, and they hugged closely the race distinction. Driven off the fertile lands by the encroachments of the planter, or prevented from occupying the virgin soil by the outbidding of the wealthy, they farmed the worn-out lands and gained a miserable and precarious subsistence. As compared with laborers on the farms or in the workshops of the North, their physical situation was abject poverty, their intellectual state utter ignorance, and their moral condition grovelling baseness.[1] Nor did this proceed entirely from the fact that they were forced to work the barren, unproductive lands. Olmsted drew an instructive comparison between the poor whites of Georgia and the inhabitants of Cape Cod. In all New England the sterility of the soil of the cape was a proverb; yet this careful observer declared that "there is hardly a poor woman's cow on the cape that is not better housed and more comfortably provided for than a majority of the white people of Georgia." He has shrewdly appreciated the peculiar character common to the people of Cape Cod and the "sand-hillers" and "crackers" of Georgia. "In both," he writes, "there is frankness, boldness, and simplicity; but in the one it is associated with intelligence, discretion, and an expansion of the mind, resulting from considerable education; in the other, with ignorance, improvidence, laziness, and the prejudices of narrow minds."[2]

---

[1] For the contrast of illiteracy and common intelligence North and South, see Cotton Kingdom, vol. ii. p. 331.

[2] Olmsted's Seaboard Slave States, p. 538. The difference is thoroughly discussed, and the inducements to a seafaring and fishing life are considered.

The poor whites of the South looked on the prosperity of the slave-holding lord with rank envy and sullenness; his trappings contrasted painfully with their want of comforts, yet he knew so well how to play upon their contempt for the negro, and to make it appear that his and their interests were identical, that when election-day came the whites, who were without money and without slaves, did the bidding of the lord of the plantation. When Southern interests were in danger, it was the poor whites who voted for their preservation. The slave-holders, and the members of that society which clustered round them, took the offices. It was extremely rare that a man who had ever labored with his hands was sent to Congress from the South, or chosen to one of the prominent positions in the State.

The political system of the South was an oligarchy under the republican form. The slave-holders were in a very disproportionate minority in every State.[1] " Two hundred thousand men with pure white skins in South Carolina," said Broderick to the senators, "are now degraded and despised by thirty thousand aristocratic slave-holders."[2] The governor of South Carolina was in favor of doing something to elevate their poor, but feared they were " hopelessly doomed to ignorance, poverty, and crime."[3] In 1850 there were 347,525 slave-holders,[4] who with their families may have numbered two millions.[5] The total white population of the slave States was 6,125,000, so that less than one-third of the white people of the South could possibly have derived any benefit from the institution of slavery. In other words, this imperial domain, covering more square miles than there were in the free States, was given up to two million people;

[1] Seward's Works, vol. i. p. 74.

[2] March 22d, 1858, *Congressional Globe*, vol. xxxvii. p. 193.

[3] Olmsted's Seaboard Slave States, p. 505.

[4] Census Report for 1850.   See Life of Garrison, vol. iii. p. 272.

[5] The superintendent of the census; see Seward's speech, Oct., 1855, Works, vol. iv. p. 237; Henry Wilson's speech, July 2d, 1856, *Congressional Globe*, vol. xxxiii. p. 793.

and more than seven millions, bond and free,[1] labored for them or were subservient to their interests. Yet these figures by no means represent the exclusive character of the slave-holding oligarchy. In the enumeration of slave-holders were included many men from the laboring class who by unusual industry or economy had become possessed of one slave or perhaps more, but who politically and socially belonged only to the class from which they had sprung.[2] Of the large planters owning more than fifty slaves, whose elegance, luxury, and hospitality are recited in tales of travellers, over whose estates and lives has shone the lustre of romance and poetry, there were less than eight thousand.[3] They were the true centre of the oligarchy. Around them clustered the few educated people of the country, also the high societies of the cities, composed of merchants, doctors, lawyers, and politicians; which society was seen to the best advantage in New Orleans, Charleston, and Richmond. Including all these, the total number must have been small; but it was for them that slavery existed. What has been here adduced is sufficient to show that slavery was certainly not for the advantage of the negro. No one seriously maintained that there were any benefits in the system for the poor whites; since it degraded labor, and therefore degraded the white man who had to work with his hands.[4] It is one of the striking facts of our history that these despised people fought bravely and endured much for a cause adverse to

---

[1] The total population of the slave States for 1850 was 9,569,540—composed of whites, free colored, and slaves.

[2] The holders of one slave were 68,820; of more than one and less than five, 105,683—more than half of the whole number, which was 347,525.

[3] De Bow's U. S. Census Report; Olmsted's Cotton Kingdom, vol. i. p. 20.

[4] For a full account of the poor whites, see Olmsted's Seaboard Slave States, pp. 505, 508, 514; Kemble, pp. 76 and 146; Cotton Kingdom, vol. i. p. 22; Key to Uncle Tom's Cabin, p. 185; Helper's Impending Crisis, *passim.*

their own interests, following Lee and Stonewall Jackson with a devotion that called to mind the deeds of a more heroic age.

It was then for a small aristocracy that slavery continued to be, and it is among them that we must look for its advantages. An apologist of the institution, who was himself one of the select few, maintained that by the existence of slavery they had greater leisure for intellectual pursuits and better means of attaining a liberal education. " It is better," he declares, " that a part [of the community] should be fully and highly cultivated, and the rest utterly ignorant." [1]

The South did, indeed, produce good lawyers and able politicians. Their training was excellent. The sons of the wealthy almost always went to college, and there they began to acquire the knack at public speaking which seemed natural to the Southerner. The political life of their State was early opened to them, and by the time the promising young men were sent to Congress they had learned experience and adroitness in public affairs. If they made their mark in the national House or the Senate, they were kept there, and each year added to their usefulness and influence. [2] The aspirants for political honors being almost wholly from the small privileged class, it was not difficult to provide places for those eminently fitted. Moreover, the men who wielded the power were convinced that continu-

---

[1] Chancellor Harper, Pro-slavery Argument, p. 35. " In all social systems there must be a class to do the menial duties, to perform the drudgery of life; that is, a class requiring but a low order of intellect and but little skill. Its requisites are vigor, docility, fidelity. Such a class you must have, or you would not have that other class which leads progress, civilization, and refinement. It constitutes the very mud-sill of society and of political government; and you might as well attempt to build a house in the air as to build either the one or the other except on this mud-sill. Fortunately for the South, she found a race adapted to that purpose to her hand."—Senator Hammond, of South Carolina, Senate, March 4th, 1858, Speeches and Letters, p. 318.

[2] This custom is well described in Lowell's Political Essays, p. 135.

ance in office was the proper reward of those who had shown capacity and honesty. The absurd practice which prevailed at the North, of rotating their representatives in the lower house in order to make room for as many as possible of those who had political claims, never gained foothold in the South. This was, indeed, one reason why the South won advantages over the North, in spite of its inferior numerical strength.[1]

It is not surprising that the Southerners shone in the political sphere. Their intellect tended naturally to public affairs; they had the talent and leisure for politics which a landed aristocracy is apt to have under a representative government; and when the slavery question assumed importance at Washington, their concern for shaping the course of national legislation became a passion, and seemed necessary for the preservation of their order. But it was only in law and politics that the South was eminent. She did not give birth to a poet, nor to a philosopher after Jefferson, and his philosophy she rejected. She could lay claim only to an occasional scientist, but to no great historian; none of her novelists or essayists who wrote before the war has the next generation cared to read.[2] Whoever, thinking of the opportunities for culture in the ancient world given by the existence of slavery, seeks in the Southern community a trace even of that intellectual and artistic development which was the glory of Athens, will look in vain. Had the other causes existed, the sparse settlements of the South, the lack of a compact social body,[3] made utterly im-

---

[1] This superiority is boastfully asserted in De Bow's Resources, vol. iii. p. 63.

[2] A partial exception must be made of W. Gilmore Simms. A new edition of his books was published in 1882, and his revolutionary tales are still read by schoolboys, although to nothing like the extent that Cooper's novels are read. "The South has no literature," said Rufus Choate, Recollections, Parker, p. 265.

[3] In 1852, Mrs. Davis rejoiced in "our mail twice a week." Memoir of Jefferson Davis, vol. i. p. 475.

possible such results as mark Grecian civilization. The physical and economic conditions of the South presented insuperable obstacles to any full development of university education. While efforts were made to promote the establishment of colleges, the higher fields of scientific and literary research were not cultivated with eminent success; for the true scientific spirit could never have free play in a community where one subject of investigation of all-pervading influence must remain a closed book.

When one thinks of the varied forms under which the intellect of New England displayed itself, and remembers the brilliant achievements there in the mind's domain which illumine the generation before the war, he cannot but feel that the superiority of the South in politics, after the great Virginia statesman had left the stage, was held at too great cost, if it was maintained at the sacrifice of a many-sided development such as took place at the North.

The great majority of the slave-holders lacked even ordinary culture. Nothing illustrates this better than the experience of Olmsted while on a horseback journey of three months, from the banks of the Mississippi to the banks of the James. In the rural districts of that country there were no inns. The traveller's stopping-places for the night were the houses of the farmers along his route, many of whom made it a practice to accommodate strangers, and were willing to accept in payment for their trouble the price which would have been demanded by an inn-keeper. A majority of Olmsted's hosts in this journey were slave-holders, and a considerable proportion cotton-planters. He observed that certain symbols of civilization were wanting. "From the banks of the Mississippi to the banks of the James," he writes, "I did not (that I remember) see, except perhaps in one or two towns, a thermometer, nor a book of Shakespeare, nor a piano-forte or sheet of music, nor the light of a Carcel or other good centre-table or reading lamp, nor an engraving or copy of any kind of a work of art of the slightest merit."[1]

The lack of schools was painfully apparent. The deficiency in the rudiments of education among the poor whites and smaller slave-holders was recognized, and attracted attention from the Southern newspapers, and occasionally from those high in office. Much vain declamation resulted, but no practical action. Indeed, the situation was one of difficulty. To plant schools in a sparsely settled country, among a people who have not the desire of learning and who do not appreciate its value, requires energy, and this energy was lacking. Nevertheless, there must have been among the slave-holding lords a secret satisfaction that the poor whites were content to remain in ignorance;[2] for in the decade before the war great objections were made to school-books prepared and published at the North, and yet there were no others. In the beginning of the abolitionist agitation, Duff Green, perceiving that the benefits of slavery

---

[1] Cotton Kingdom, vol. ii. p. 285. This whole chapter, "The Condition and Character of the Privileged Classes of the South," should be read by every one who is interested in the social state of that section before the war. See also Despotism in America, Hildreth, p. 147.

Lieber wrote from Columbia to Hillard, May, 1851: "Every son of a fool here is a great statesman, meditating on the relations of State sovereignty to the United States government; but as to roads, common schools, glass in the windows, food besides salt meat, as to cheerily joining in the general chorus of progress, what is that for Don Ranudo de Colobrados, of South Carolina—out at elbows, to be sure; but then, what of that ?"—Life and Letters, p. 254.

[2] "We imagine that the propriety of shooting a Yankee schoolmaster, when caught tampering with our slaves, has never been questioned by any intelligent Southern man. This we take to be the unwritten law of the South. . . . Let all Yankee schoolmasters who purpose invading the South, endowed with a strong nasal twang, a long Scriptural name, and Webster's lexicographic book of abominations, seek some more congenial land, where their lives will be more secure than in 'the vile and homicidal slave States.' "—Richmond *Examiner*, 1854, cited in a pamphlet entitled A Bake-pan for Doughfaces, published at Burlington, Vt., by C. Goodrich.

ought to be taught to the young, obtained a charter from South Carolina for a Southern Literary Company, whose object was to print school-books adapted to a slave-holding community;[1] but this company had apparently not achieved its purpose, for in *De Bow's Review*, in 1855, there is a complaint that " our text-books are abolition books." The chapter on slavery in Wayland's Moral Science " was heretical and unscriptural." We are using " abolition geographies, readers, and histories," which overrun " with all sorts of slanders, caricatures, and blood-thirsty sentiments." " Appletons' Complete Guide of the World " is "an elegant and comprehensive volume," but contains " hidden lessons of the most fiendish and murderous character that enraged fanaticism could conceive or indite." " This book and many other Northern school-books scattered over the country come within the range of the statutes of this State [Louisiana], which provide for the imprisonment for life or the infliction of the penalty of death upon any person who shall ' publish or distribute' such works ; and were I a citizen of New Orleans," adds the writer, " this work should not escape the attention of the grand jury."[2] A year later, a writer in the same review[3] maintains that " our school-books, especially, should be written, prepared, and published by Southern men ;" and he inveighs against the readers and speakers used in the schools, and gives a list of those which are objectionable. One of them was the " Columbian Orator," and it is interesting to know that this was the first book which the slave, Frederick Douglass, bought. In it were speeches of Chatham, Sheridan, and Fox, and in reading and pondering these speeches the light broke in upon his mind, showing him that he was a victim of oppression, and that, if what they said about the rights of man was true, he ought not to be a slave.[4] The writer in the

---

[1] Life of Garrison, vol. ii. p. 79.   [2] Cotton Kingdom, vol. ii. p. 358.
[3] *De Bow's Review*, vol. xx. p. 69, Jan., 1856.
[4] Life of Douglass, p. 75.

Review complained that these books contained poems of Cowper and speeches of Webster which Southern children should not read, and he was certain that if parents knew their whole contents "they would demand expurgated editions for the use of their children." All schoolboys know that the kind of books complained of contain, for the most part, the choice selections of English literature—works that have survived owing to their elevation of thought and beauty of expression. Such attacks were a condemnation of literature itself, for from Homer down the master-spirits of many ages have reprobated slavery.

History, as well as literature, needed expurgation before it was adapted to the instruction of Southern youth. Peter Parley's "Pictorial History of the United States" was complained of, because the author, although a conservative Whig and far from being an abolitionist, deemed it necessary, in the course of his narrative, to mention slavery, the attempts at colonization, and the zeal with which some people labored "in behalf of immediate and universal emancipation." [1]

It was likewise necessary to prepare the historical reading of adults with care. In an editorial notice in *De Bow's Review* of the current number of *Harper's Magazine*, which had a large circulation at the South, it was suggested that the notice of the Life of Toussaint "had been better left out, so far as the South is concerned." [2] To what absurdities did this people come on account of their peculiar institution! Toussaint, as a brilliant historian of our day has told us, exercised on our history "an influence as decisive as that of any European ruler." [3] He was one of the important links in that chain of historical events of which Napoleon and Jefferson were the others, that gave us Louisiana and New Orleans.

These comments which have been cited are not taken

---

[1] See *De Bow's Review*, vol. xx. p. 74.   [2] See ibid., vol. x. p. 492.
[3] Henry Adams's History of the United States, vol. i. p. 378.

from a periodical without influence and published in a corner. *De Bow's Review* was devoted to economical and social matters; it was one of the ablest exponents of the thinking people and best society of the South. Moreover, it had received the endorsement of fifty-five Southern senators and representatives in Congress for the "ability and accuracy of its exposition of the working of the system of polity of the Southern States." De Bow was professor of political economy in the University of Louisiana, and his *Review* was published in the commercial metropolis of the South. Indeed, the provision for education in harmony with their institutions was a subject of grave consideration by thinking men, and a thoroughly representative body— the Southern commercial convention which was held at Memphis in 1853—paid it marked attention. The convention earnestly recommended to the citizens of the Southern States: "The education of their youth at home, as far as practicable; the employment of native teachers in their schools and colleges; the encouragement of a home press; and the publication of books adapted to the educational wants and the social condition of these States."[1]

It is no wonder such recommendations were thought necessary, for many delegates must have remembered the difficulty which attended the publication of the works of Calhoun, although South Carolina appropriated ten thousand dollars for the purpose. A Charleston newspaper complained: "The writings of Mr. Calhoun were edited in Virginia; the stereotyped plates were cast in New York; they were then sent to Columbia, where the impressions were struck off; the sheets were thence transferred to Charleston in order that the books might be bound; and now that they are bound, there is really no publisher in the State to see to their circulation."[2]

---

[1] *De Bow's Review*, vol. xv. p. 268.

[2] Charleston *News*, cited in the New York *Independent*, Oct. 30th, 1851; see also estimate of the book-publishing business of 1856 in Recollections of a Lifetime, S. G. Goodrich, vol. ii. p. 387, in which the business of the

I.—23

If we contrast the North and the South in material prosperity, the South will appear to no better advantage than it does in respect of intellectual development. Yet the superiority of the North in this regard was by no means admitted. The thinking men of the South felt, if this were proved, a serious drawback to their system would be manifest. We find, therefore, in the Southern literature many arguments to show that the contrary was true; most of them take the form of statistical demonstrations, in which the census figures are made to do strange and wondrous duty. Parson Brownlow, of Tennessee, in a joint debate at Philadelphia, where he maintained that American slavery ought to be perpetuated, brought forward an array of figures which demonstrated to his own satisfaction that the material prosperity of the South was greater than that of the North; at the time he was speaking it seemed to him that his section was smiling with good fortune, while the Northern industries were crippled by the loss of Southern trade and by the financial panic of 1857.[1] A favorite method of argument was to make a comparison between two representative States. Georgia and New York were contrasted in the light of the census of 1850, with the result of convincing the Southern mind that in social, political, and financial conditions Georgia was far superior to New York.[2] A paper was read before the Mercantile Society of Cincinnati to demonstrate that, as between Maryland and Massachusetts, Virginia and New York, Kentucky and Ohio, the slave States were the more prosperous. "Virginia," says the author, "instead of being poor and in need of the pity of the much poorer population of the North, is perhaps the richest community in

---

Southern and Southwestern States is given at $750,000, in a total of $16,000,000; in the first-named figures are included Baltimore and Louisville, which were by far the most important publishing cities in the South.

[1] Debate between Brownlow and Pryne at Philadelphia, 1858, pp. 258 and 265.

[2] De Bow's Industrial Resources, vol. iii. p. 122.

the world." After a comparison of the census figures, the conclusion is that the free people of the slave-holding States are much richer than those of the non-slave-holding States. De Bow, in introducing this paper to his public, said that, although it had been angrily assailed by the abolition press, it had never been refuted or invalidated in any material respect.[1] Arguments, of which these are examples, are made by men who go with preconceived ideas to the statistics, and select therefrom what they deem will sustain their thesis. Such reasoning does not proceed from earnest seekers after truth. The speciousness of such deductions was shown over and over again. Indeed, it needed no extensive marshalling of statistics to prove that the welfare of the North was greater than that of the South. Two simple facts, everywhere admitted, were of so far-reaching moment that they amounted to irrefragable demonstration. The emigration from the slave States to the free States was much larger than the movement in the other direction; and the South repelled the industrious emigrants who came from Europe, while the North attracted them. "Leave us in the peaceable possession of our slaves," cried Parson Brownlow, "and our Northern neighbors may have all the paupers and convicts that pour in upon us from European prisons."[2] This remark found general sympathy, because the South ignored, or wished to ignore, the fact that able-bodied men with intelligence enough to wish to better their condition are the most costly and valuable products on earth, and that nothing can more redound to the advantage of a new country than to get men without having been at the cost of rearing them.[3] This was occasionally appreciated at the

---

[1] *De Bow's Review*, vol. xxii. p. 623. The paper was read in 1848 and based on the census of 1840. See also *De Bow*, vol. vii. p. 140.

[2] Debate between Brownlow and Pryne, p. 263.

[3] One of the imports of the United States, "that of adult and trained immigrants, . . . would be in an economical analysis underestimated at £100,000,000 a year."—Thorold Rogers, Lectures in 1888, Economic Interpretation of History, p. 407.

South,[1] and sometimes the greater growth in wealth and population of the North would break in upon the mind of Southern thinkers with such force that they could not hold their peace.[2] Sometimes the truth would be owned, but its dissemination was prevented, for fear that the admission of it would furnish arguments to the abolitionists.[3]

Two of the most careful observers who ever considered the differences between the South and the North are unimpeachable witnesses to the greater prosperity of the latter. Washington noted, in 1796, that the prices of land were higher in Pennsylvania than in Virginia and Maryland, "although they are not of superior quality." One of the important reasons for the difference was that Pennsylvania had passed laws for the gradual abolition of slavery, which had not been done in the other two States ; but it was Washington's opinion that "nothing is more certain than that they must, at a period not far remote," take steps in the same direction.[4]

De Tocqueville was struck with the external contrast between the free and the slave States. "The traveller who floats down the current of the Ohio," he wrote, "to the point where that river joins the Mississippi may be said to sail between liberty and slavery ; and he only needs to look around him in order to decide in an instant which is the more favorable to humanity. On the Southern bank of the river the population is thinly scattered ; from time to time one descries a gang of slaves at work, going with indolent air over the half-desert fields ; the primeval forest unceasingly reappears ; one would think that the people were asleep ; man seems to be idle, nature alone offers a picture of activ-

---

[1] See a thoughtful article in the Augusta *Chronicle*, cited in Niles's Register, April, 1849, vol. lxxv. p. 271.

[2] See citation from Richmond *Enquirer*, Cotton Kingdom, vol. ii. p. 365 ; also Richmond *Whig*, cited in Life of Garrison, vol. i. p. 252.

[3] See proceedings in regard to an address to the farmers at a Virginia agricultural convention, Cotton Kingdom, vol. ii. p. 366.

[4] Sparks, vol. xii. p. 326.

ity and life. From the Northern bank, on the contrary, there arises the busy hum of industry which is heard afar off; the fields abound with rich harvests; comfortable homes indicate the taste and care of the laborer; prosperity is seen on all sides; man appears rich and content; he labors."[1] The difference was greater when De Tocqueville visited this country than in Washington's day; and it was greater in 1850 than when the philosophic Frenchman recorded his observations in the book which is a classic in the science of politics. The difference was of a nature that must become intensified with the years.

What was the reason of the marked diversity between the two sections of the country? The only solution of the question is that which presented itself to the mind of De Tocqueville. "Almost all the differences which may be remarked between the Southerners and Northerners had their origin in slavery;"[2] for the settlers of both sections of the country belonged "to the same European race, had the same customs, the same civilization, the same laws, and their shades of difference were very slight."[3] It is true that the Cavalier colonized Virginia, and the Puritan Massachusetts. Yet after the Revolution of 1688 the Cavalier and Puritan in England began coming nearer together, until, by the middle of the nineteenth century, there was no longer a line of demarcation. After the American Revolution, however, the difference between the Virginian and the man of Massachusetts increased so that it became the remark of travellers, the theme of statesmen, and finally a subject for the arbitrament of the sword. In that contest the Scotch-Irishman of South Carolina fought on one side, and the Scotch-Irishman of Pennsylvania fought on the other; but in the seventeenth century, on their native soil, they would have stood shoulder to shoulder in a common cause.

---

[1] De la Démocratie en Amérique, vol. ii. p. 311. See also H. Martineau, Society in America, vol. i. p. 304.   [2] De Tocqueville, vol. ii. p. 316.

[3] Ibid., p. 310; see also article of Prof. A. B. Hart, *New England Magazine*, November, 1891, p. 376.

Nor will the diversity of climate account in any considerable degree for the difference between the South and the North in material prosperity and intellectual development. The climate of Virginia and Kentucky was like that of Pennsylvania and Ohio ; yet the contrast was seen in a marked degree between those communities. The climate of the slave States as a whole was not warmer than that of Italy or Spain, and those countries have been the seat of an energetic and intellectual people.[1] An illustration showing that the physical conditions of the South did not require slavery was seen in the German colony settled in Texas. By 1857 the Germans made up nearly one-half of the white population of Western Texas, and constituted a community apart. They believed in the dignity of labor; those who had not land were willing to work for the proprietors, and those who had capital would not purchase slaves. They were industrious, thrifty, fairly prosperous, and contented. They brought from their homes some of the flowers of civilization, and were an oasis in the arid desert of slavery. Olmsted had a happier experience among these people than in his journey from the Mississippi to the James, where he failed to see the common indications of comfort and culture.[2] Among the Germans of Texas, he wrote, " you are welcomed by a figure in blue flannel shirt and pendent beard," quoting Tacitus; you see " Madonnas upon log walls ;" coffee is served you " in tin cups upon Dresden saucers ;" and you hear a symphony of Beethoven on a grand piano.[3] These Germans loved music and hated slavery. In 1854, after their annual musical festival at San Antonio, they resolved themselves into a po-

---

[1] " Contemplated in the mass, facts do not countenance the current idea that great heat hinders progress."—Sociology, Herbert Spencer, vol. i. p. 19. " High degrees of moral sentiment control the unfavorable influences of climate ; and some of our grandest examples of men and of races come from the equatorial regions—as the genius of Egypt, of India, and of Arabia."—Emerson's Lecture on Civilization.

[2] See p. 349.

[3] Olmsted's Texas Journey, p. 430.

litical convention, and declared that slavery was an evil which ought eventually to be removed.[1]

In giving the South credit for producing able politicians, we have not exhausted the subject of the virtues of her social system. The little aristocracy, whose nucleus was less than eight thousand large slave-holders,[2] had another excellence that deserves high esteem. While in the North their manners were often aggressive, in their own homes they displayed good breeding, refined manners, and dignified deportment. And these were more than outside show; the Southern gentleman was to the manner born. In society and conversation he appeared to the best advantage. He had self-assurance, an easy bearing, and to women a chivalrous courtesy; he was "stately but condescending, haughty but jovial."[3] Underneath all were physical courage, a habit of command, a keen sense of honor, and a generous disposition. The Southerners were fast friends, and they dispensed hospitality with an open hand. They fitted themselves for society, and looked upon conversation as an art. They knew how to draw out the best from their guests; and, with all their high self-appreciation, at home they did not often indulge in distasteful egotism. They amused themselves with literature, art, and science; for such knowledge they deemed indispensable for prolonging an interesting conversation. They were cultured, educated men of the world, who would meet their visitors on their own favorite ground.[4]

If we reckon by numbers, there were certainly more well-bred people at the North than at the South; but when we compare the cream of society in both sections, the palm must be awarded to the slave-holding community. The testi-

---

[1] Olmsted's Texas Journey, p. 435 *et ante*.   [2] See p. 346.

[3] Cotton Kingdom, vol. ii. p. 335.   "We justly admire the easy, graceful politeness of our Southern brethren." — Todd's Student's Manual, p. 235.

[4] "The people [of the South] seem to be fine, open-hearted."—Lieber to Sumner, 1835, Life and Letters of Lieber, p. 109.

mony of English gentlemen and ladies, few of whom have
any sympathy with slavery, is almost unanimous in this respect. They bear witness to the aristocratic bearing of
their generous hosts. Between the titled English visitors
and the Southern gentlemen there was, indeed, a fellow-feel-
ing, which grew up between the two aristocracies separated
by the sea. There was the concord of sentiments. The
Southern lord, like his English prototype, believed that the
cultivation of the soil was the finest and noblest pursuit.[1]
But nearly all educated Englishmen, whether belonging to
the aristocracy or not, enjoyed their intercourse with Southerners more than they did the contact with the best society
at the North, on account of the high value which they
placed on good manners. The men and women who composed the Brook Farm community, and the choice spirits
whom they attracted, were certainly more interesting and
admirable than any set of people one could meet in Richmond, Charleston, or New Orleans;[2] but society, properly
so called, is not made up of women with missions and men
who aim to reform the world. The little knot of literary
people who lived in Boston, Cambridge, and vicinity were a
fellowship by whom it was an honor to be received; but
these were men of learning and wisdom; they were " inac-
cessible, solitary, impatient of interruptions, fenced by eti-
quette;" and few of them had the desire, leisure, or money
to take part in the festive entertainments which are a necessary accompaniment of society.

When the foreign visitors who came here during the generation before the war compared Northern and Southern

---

[1] " You know I am engaged entirely on my estates at present, and
solely occupied, thank God ! in the finest and noblest pursuit—the cultivation of the soil."—Letter of F. W. Pickens, of South Carolina, to James
Buchanan, Life of Buchanan, Curtis, vol. i. p. 608; see also Memorials of
a Southern Planter, Smedes, p. 115.

[2] " Je ne trouve pas à la Nouvelle Orleans la même vie intellectuelle,
le même mouvement scientifique qu'à Boston, à New York, à Philadel-
phie."—J. J. Ampère, Promenade en Amérique, tome ii. p. 155.

society, they had in their minds the people whom they met at dinners, receptions, and balls; the Northern men seemed frequently overweighted with business cares, and, except on the subjects of trade, politics, and the material growth of the country, were not good talkers. The merchant or manufacturer of Boston, New York, or Philadelphia was a busy man; he had not the leisure of his Southern brother to cultivate the amenities of life, and he lacked that abandon of manners which Englishmen found so charming in the slaveholding lords.

This superiority of the best Southern society undoubtedly grew out of the social system of which slavery was the basis; but there went with it two drawbacks. In these circles where conversation was a delight, one subject must be treated with the utmost delicacy. The Englishman could argue with his Southern host that a monarchy was better than a republic, but he might not exult over the emancipation of the slaves in the West Indies. The German could deny the inspiration of the Bible, but he might not question that their institution of slavery was divine. One was made to feel in the most emphatic manner that his host desired no expression on the subject other than an opinion that the relation which existed between the whites and the blacks at the South was the necessary one.

The high sense of personal worth, the habit of command, the tyranny engendered by the submission of the prostrate race, made the Southern gentleman jealous in honor, sudden and quick in quarrel. While the duello was not an outgrowth of slavery, its practice in the South was more savage and bloody than anywhere else in the civilized world. The custom of going about fully armed to be prepared for an enemy, the readiness with which pistols were used on slight provocation, the frequent occurrence of deadly street fights, were an anomaly among a people so urbane and generous; but they were the result of slavery.

From youth the slave-holder was accustomed to have his word regarded as law; when he insisted, others yielded.

Accustomed to irresponsible power over his dependants, he could not endure contradiction, he would not brook opposition. When one lord ran against another in controversy, if the feelings were deeply engaged the final argument was the pistol. The smaller slave-holders, influenced partly by the same reason and partly actuated by imitation of the aristocracy, settled their disputes in like manner, but more brutally, for they also used the bowie-knife in their encounters. The poor whites aped their betters. The consequence was a condition of society hardly conceivable in a civilized, Christian, Anglo-Saxon community. In the new States of the Southwest, it was perhaps explainable as incident to the life of the frontier; but when met with in the old communities of Virginia and the Carolinas, it could admit but of one inference—that it was primarily due to slavery.[1] But slavery itself and these attendant phenomena were survivals in the South, more than in any other contemporary enlightened community, of a passing militant civilization.[2]

I have endeavored to describe slavery and its effects as it might have appeared to an honest inquirer in the decade before the war. There was no difficulty in seeing the facts as they have been stated, or in arriving at the conclusions drawn. There was a correct picture of the essential features

---

[1] My authorities for this description of the manners of the South are Olmsted's Cotton Kingdom and Seaboard Slave States; Kemble's Journal; Martineau's Society in America; Buckingham's Slave States of America; Mackay's Life and Liberty in America; De Bow's Resources; Basil Hall's North America; America and the Americans, by Achille Murat; Pro-slavery Argument; *De Bow's Review;* Promenade en Amérique, J. J. Ampère.

"L'influence de l'esclavage, combinée avec le caractère anglais, explique les moeurs et l'état social du Sud."—De la Démocratie en Amérique, vol. i. p. 46. See also Hurrygraphs, N. P. Willis, p. 302.

[2] For distinction between militant and industrial organizations, see Herbert Spencer's Sociology, *passim;* also Data of Ethics, p. 135, where Spencer writes: While militancy "is dominant, ownership of a slave is honorable, and, in the slave, submission is praiseworthy;" but as industrialism "grows dominant, slave-owning becomes a crime, and servile obedience excites contempt."

of slavery in " Uncle Tom's Cabin," the book which everybody read. The author of it had " but one purpose, to show
the institution of slavery truly just as it existed." [1] While
she had not the facts which a critical historian would have
collected—for the " Key to Uncle Tom's Cabin" was not
compiled until after the novel was written—she used with
the intuition of genius the materials gained through personal observation, and the result was what she desired. If
we bear in mind that the novelist, from the very nature of
the art, deals with characteristic and not with average persons, the conclusion is resistless that Mrs. Stowe realized her
ideal. Fanny Kemble wrote to the London *Times* that she
could bear witness to the truth and moderation of " Uncle
Tom's Cabin" as a representation of the slave system in the
United States, and added that her testimony was " the experience of an eye-witness, having been a resident in the
Southern States, and having opportunities of observation such
as no one who has not lived on a slave estate can have." [2] It
was certain, she proceeded, that the incident of Uncle Tom's
death was not only possible, but it was unfortunately a very
probable occurrence.[3] Olmsted came to the conclusion that
cases like the Red River episode were not extremely rare.[4]

The fidelity to truth of that portion of the novel was sometimes questioned in a curious way. Bishop Polk assured an
English clergyman that he " had been all over the country
on Red River, the scene of the fictitious sufferings of Uncle
Tom, and that he had found the temporal and spiritual welfare
of the negroes well cared for. He had confirmed thirty black
persons near the situation assigned to Legree's estate." [5]

A Northern doctor of divinity who wrote a book in defence of slavery based on a three months' sojourn at the
South, admitted that " some of the warmest advocates of
slavery [at the South] said that they could parallel most of

---

[1] Introduction to new edition of Uncle Tom's Cabin, p. 12.
[2] Kemble's Journal, p. 300.   [3] Ibid., p. 301.
[4] Cotton Kingdom, vol. i. p. 356.   [5] Ibid., vol. ii. p. 213.

the abuses in slavery mentioned in the book out of their own knowledge; and on speaking of some bad master and wishing to express his tyrannical character and barbarous conduct, they would say, 'He is a real Legree;' or, 'He is worse than Legree.'"[1] A Southern Presbyterian preacher who published a book of speeches and letters to maintain that "slavery is of God," and ought "to continue for the good of the slave, the good of the master, and the good of the whole American people," said: "I have admitted, and do again admit, without qualification, that every fact in 'Uncle Tom's Cabin' has occurred in the South;" and again he speaks of it as "that book of genius, true in all its facts, false in all its impressions."[2] The great desire of the author to be impartial was evident from the portrayal of slave-holders; the humane and generous men were even more prominent in the story than the inhuman ones. She did justice to the prevailing and correct sentiment at the South that Northerners were harder masters than Southern men, by making Legree, whose name became a synonym for a brutal slave-holder, a son of New England.

Mrs. Stowe was felicitous in her description of the negro character. There was a fitness in the secondary title of the book, "Life among the Lowly." It was the life she had studied with rare human sympathy, and in its portrayal the author's genius is seen to the best advantage. Some critics objected that Uncle Tom was an impossible character, and that the world, in weeping at the tale of his ill-treatment and sufferings, exhibited a mawkish sentimentality. But the author knew his prototype.[3] Frederick Douglass also describes a colored man whose resemblance to Uncle Tom was "so perfect that he might have been the original of Mrs. Stowe's Christian hero."[4] Rev. Noah Davis, who wrote

---

[1] South-side View of Slavery, Nehemiah Adams, p. 158.
[2] Slavery Ordained by God, Ross, pp. 5, 38, 53.
[3] Preface to new edition of Uncle Tom's Cabin, p. vii.
[4] Life of Douglass, p. 94.

in a little book the narrative of his own life, certainly equalled Uncle Tom in piety, self-denial, and industry.[1]

The author's most conspicuous failure as a portrayer of manners is in the descriptions of the best society at the South. Nor is this surprising. Her life was an earnest working one, and she had no conception of a society where dinner-parties, receptions, and balls made up the lives of its votaries. Her associates were ministers, devoted to their calling, and hard-working college professors, who esteemed learning above all ; their thoughts were so engrossed in their serious occupations that the lighter graces of life seemed like folly and idleness. It is, then, no wonder that the subtle charm which exquisite manners spread over plantation life and New Orleans society completely eluded the observation of the author.

The Southern people desired to stand well at the great tribunal of modern civilization.[2] As their peculiar institution was under the ban of the most enlightened portion of the world, they made repeated efforts to set themselves in the right. As long as the argument followed the line of admitting the evil, while averring that for the present, at least, slavery seemed the most advantageous relation between the two races at the South, the slave-holders had much sympathy from the North and from England. It was conceded that if the slaves were freed, civil rights must eventually be accorded them. That condition staggered many who hated slavery. In those Northern States where the negro had the right to vote, that right was exercised only with great difficulty and some danger ; but the blacks were few in number, and patiently submitted to a practical annulling of their privilege. But the fact was ap-

---

[1] A Narrative of the Life of Noah Davis, a colored man, written by himself, published at Baltimore, 1859. I am informed by a colored man who knew him well that Davis was truly a religious man, and had the confidence and respect of all classes of citizens.

[2] Webster's expression when speaking on slavery, Works, vol. v. p. 304.

preciated that at the South, owing to the great number of negroes, the problem would be a far different one. There was, therefore, considerable sympathy with the opinion of McDuffie, that if the slaves were freed and made voters, no rational man could live in such a state of society.[1] Basil Hall, who travelled in this country in 1827 and 1828, believed that the slave-holders were "a class of men who are really entitled to a large share of our indulgence;" that no men were more ready than were most of the American planters to grant " that slavery is an evil in itself and eminently an evil in its consequences;" but to do away with it seemed " so completely beyond the reach of any human exertions that I consider the abolition of slavery as one of the most profit-less of all possible subjects of discussion."[2] The difficulty did not escape the philosophic mind of De Tocqueville. " I am obliged to confess," he wrote, "that I do not regard the abolition of slavery as a means of putting off the struggle between the two races in the Southern States. . . . God forbid that I should justify the principle of negro slavery, as some American writers have done; but I only observe that all the countries which formerly adopted that execrable principle are not equally able to abandon it at the present time."[3]

Owing, however, to the efforts which Southern statesmen made for the extension of slavery, it became necessary to maintain the proposition that slavery is a positive good. The logic of the abolitionists likewise had influence in goading the Southern reasoners to this position. " Twenty years ago," wrote W. Gilmore Simms, " few persons in the South undertook to justify negro slavery, except on the score of necessity. Now, very few persons in the same region question their perfect right to the labor of their slaves; and, more, their moral obligation to keep them still subject as

---

[1] Life of Garrison, vol. ii. p. 62.
[2] Basil Hall's North America, vol. ii. p. 62.
[3] De la Démocratie en Amérique, vol. ii. p. 338.

slaves, and to compel their labor, so long as they remain the inferior beings which we find them now, and which they seem to have been from the beginning. This is a great good, the fruit wholly of the hostile pressure." [1]

The book from which this passage is taken contains all that can be said in favor of slavery. The jurist, the statesman, the *littérateur*, and the educator — the most distinguished writers of the Southern States united in a publication of collected essays which they had written for Southern magazines, and gave them to the world under the title of " The Pro-slavery Argument." As I have already had occasion to refer many times to this work, an extended abstract of it would be profitless. In the light of our day it is melancholy reading. It is the waste of varied ability in a doomed cause.

Chancellor Harper devotes the larger part of his essay to arguing the good of slavery as an abstract question. Governor (afterwards Senator) Hammond applies himself to proving two texts: First, that the domestic slavery of these States is " not only an inexorable necessity for the present, but a moral and humane institution, productive of the greatest political and social advantages;" [2] and, " I endorse without reserve the much-abused sentiment of Governor McDuffie, that 'slavery is the corner-stone of our republican edifice;' while I repudiate, as ridiculously absurd, that much-lauded but nowhere accredited dogma of Mr. Jefferson, that 'all men are born equal.' " [3] Simms's contribution to this volume, entitled " Morals of Slavery," was a criticism of Harriet Martineau's description of the peculiar institution. He felt that, as a candid man, he must make some damaging admissions, and that ultimately he would be obliged to resort to recrimination; he therefore fortified his reasoning in advance by demanding, " Why should we account to these

[1] Pro-slavery Argument, p. 179.   Published at Charleston by Walker, Richards & Co., 1852.
[2] Pro-slavery Argument, p. 100.   [3] Ibid., p. 110.

people? What are they, that they should subject us to the question? . . . The Southern people form a nation, and, as such, it derogates from their dignity that they should be called to answer at the tribunal of any other nation. When that call shall be definitely or imperatively made, they will answer with their weapons, and in no other language than that of war to the knife." [1]

Dew, the professor of history, metaphysics, and political law at William and Mary College, Virginia, propounded two questions : " Can these two distinct races of people, now living together as master and servant, be ever separated ?" and " will the day ever arrive when the black can be liberated from his thraldom and mount upward in the scale of civilization and rights, to an equality with the white ?" [2] He answered both of these questions with a decided negative; his article, full of deductions from history and law, and abounding in wealth of illustration, essayed to prove that any such consummation was either undesirable or impossible. He narrowed the question to Virginia; but the inference was plain that what applied to Virginia could with greater force be urged in reference to most of the other slave States. The author arrived at this conclusion : " There is slave property of the value of $100,000,000 in the State of Virginia, and it matters but little how you destroy it, whether by the slow process of the cautious practitioner, or with the frightful despatch of the self-confident quack; when it is gone, no matter how, the deed will be done, and Virginia will be a desert." [3]

We can only regard with pity these arguments that were retailed in the select circles of the South, and used to per-

---

[1] Pro-slavery Argument, p. 184.   [2] Ibid., p. 287.

[3] Ibid., p. 384.   This essay of Prof. Dew was a review of the debate in the Virginia legislature, 1831–32 (see p. 57), attracted much attention, and had great influence on public sentiment in Virginia at the time. The argument was regarded as convincing, and worthy of publication in connection with essays of a later date.

suade willing Northern and English visitors. When we
meet them in their balder form, we can only turn away
with disgust. A representative from Louisiana, during the
debate on the compromise of 1850, said in the House:
"A union is not worth a curse as long as distinction exists between negroes and horses."[1] "Niggers are property, sir," an illiterate slave-holder told Olmsted, "the
same as horses and cattle; and nobody has any more right
to help a negro that has run away than he has to steal a
horse."[2]

A writer in *De Bow's Review* maintained that slavery
of the negro was no worse than slavery of the ass.
"God made the world," he tells us. "God gave thee
there thy place, my hirsute brother; and, according to
all earthly probabilities and possibilities, it is thy destiny therein to remain, bray as thou wilt. From the
same great power have our sable friends, Messrs. Sambo,
Cuffee & Co., received their position also. . . . Alas,
'my poor black brother!' thou, like the hirsute, must do
thy braying in vain. Where God has placed thee, there
must thou stay."[3] A unique book of several hundred
closely printed pages was published at Natchez in 1852,
entitled "Studies on Slavery, in Easy Lessons." A considerable portion of it was devoted to combating the views
of Wayland as found in his "Moral Science," and of Channing as elaborated in his treatise on "Slavery." The author
takes issue with Channing on the statement, " Now, I say,
a being having rights cannot justly be made property ; for
this claim over him virtually annuls all his rights." The
Southern apostle rejoins: " We see no force of argument
in this position. It is also true that all domestic animals
held as property have rights. ' The ox knoweth his owner,
and the ass his master's crib.' They all have 'the right of

---

[1] Rise and Fall of the Slave Power, Wilson, vol. ii. p. 286.
[2] Cotton Kingdom, vol. ii. p. 92.
[3] De Bow's Resources, vol. ii. p. 198.

I.—24

petition,' and ask in their way for food; are they the less property?" [1]

So long as Southern reasoners maintained that the negro race was inferior to the Caucasian, their basis was scientific truth, although their inference that this fact justified slavery was cruel as well as illogical. But the assertion that the negro does not partake of the nature of mankind is as repugnant to science as it is to common-sense. The chimpanzee is not so near in intellect to the blackest Congo as is this negro to Daniel Webster. The common possession of language creates a wide gulf between man and the highest of the other animals.[2]

The chief argument in favor of slavery was drawn from the Bible. The Mosaic law authorized the buying and holding of bondmen and bondmaids; it was therefore argued that if God's chosen people were not only permitted but enjoined to possess slaves, slavery must certainly be an institution of the Deity. Texts of approval from the New Testament were more difficult to find. Although slavery in the Roman empire was an obtrusive fact, Christ was silent on the subject. The apologists of slavery made the utmost of Paul's exhortation to servants to obey their masters; yet of all the writings of the apostle of the Gentiles, the one of chief value to these special pleaders was his shortest epistle. It was used as a triumphant justification of the Fugitive Slave law. Paul sent back the runaway slave Onesimus to his master Philemon, the inclination to retain him being outweighed by the justice of his owner's claim.[3]

The most weighty scriptural argument, however, was that

---

[1] Studies on Slavery, by John Fletcher, p. 183. This book had reached the fifth thousand when the *Independent* noticed it, Aug. 26th, 1852.

[2] "What is it that separates mind from nature—that gives human intelligence an existence of its own, distinguished from general existence? . . . Is it not language?"—Religion of Philosophy, Perrin, p. 246.

[3] See an article in *De Bow's Review*, entitled Slavery and the Bible, vol. ix. p. 281.

based on the curse of Canaan. This reasoning had been used by the fathers of the Christian church,[1] but its force was vastly greater as employed to justify negro slavery. It seems amazing that a few verses of a chapter of Genesis should be sincerely deemed sufficient warrant for the degradation of more than three million human beings. The unscientific use of the Bible in the nineteenth century to defend slavery finds a striking parallel in its use in the seventeenth and eighteenth centuries[2] to defend the belief in witchcraft against the attacks of science. Jefferson Davis, in the debate upon the compromise measures, asserted that slavery "was established by decree of Almighty God" and that "through the portal of slavery alone has the descendant of the graceless son of Noah ever entered the temple of civilization."[3] The persistence with which such statements were urged, and the fact that they were believed in good faith, gave the institution a rooted strength which it could not have gained from reasoning based only on human considerations. When doubts of the right of slavery would rise in the minds of religious men at the South, they were checked by the thought that this was to question the mysterious ways of an inscrutable Providence. Noah had said, presumably with authority from on high:

---

[1] See Lecky's Morals, vol. ii. p. 70, note.

[2] This peculiar use of the biblical narrative was a characteristic of the decade between 1850-60. Horace Mann, whose religious ideas were liberal, said, in 1853, in his inaugural address at Antioch College, that it was "morally impossible for God to have created in the beginning such men and women as we find the human race now to be." He appealed to the records of the book of Genesis, "which contains the earliest annals of the human family." For the first 2369 years "not a single instance is recorded of a child born blind, or deaf, or dumb, or idiotic, or malformed in any way! . . . Not one man or woman died of disease. . . . No cholera infantum, scarlatina, measles, small-pox — not even toothache! So extraordinary a thing was it for a son to die before his father that an instance of it is deemed worthy of special notice."—New York *Nation*, Aug. 6th, 1891.

[3] *Congressional Globe*, vol. xxii. p. 153.

"Cursed be Canaan [the son of Ham]; a servant of servants shall he be unto his brethren." Blessed be Shem, and blessed be Japheth, and Canaan shall be their servant.

Nor was the influence of this argument confined to the South. It seemed to many Christians at the North that it was flying in the face of Providence to wish a change in the divinely ordered relation of master and slave between the descendant of Japheth and the descendant of Ham. Stranger yet does it seem to us, who are willing to accept the conclusions about the origin of race which have been arrived at by the patient and brilliant investigators of our day, that Emerson, who was one to go beyond the letter and grasp the spirit, should have been so profoundly swayed by the Mosaic explanation of the blackness of the negro. "The degradation of that black race," he said, "though now lost in the starless spaces of the past, did not come without sin."[1]

But the biblical argument in favor of slavery did not remain unchallenged. Between 1850 and 1860, the anti-slavery people received large accessions from Christian ministers and teachers, and with as firm faith in the inspiration of the Bible as the Southern religionists, they took up the gauntlet and joined issue on the chosen ground. Whether the Bible and the Christian religion sanctioned slavery, was a prominent topic in the joint debates that were held in Northern cities. The anti-slavery literature is full of such discussions. From a logical point, there is no question that the Northern reasoners had altogether the better of the argument.[2] The spirit of Christianity was certainly opposed to slavery; under the Roman empire it had ameliorated the condition of the slaves, and during the middle ages

---

[1] Memoir of Emerson, Cabot, p. 428.

[2] See especially Debate between Brownlow and Pryne, and Blanchard and Rice; The Church and Slavery, by Albert Barnes. For the refutation of the Ham argument, from the Unitarian point of view, see Life of Parker, Weiss, vol. ii. p. 81.

it had been the chief influence in the abolition of slavery in Europe.[1]

The fact that the slaves had their material wants supplied and were without anxiety for the morrow was urged without ceasing as one of the benefits of the system. When Seward visited Virginia he was told that they were the "happiest people in the world."[2] Frederika Bremer was convinced that under a good master the slaves were "much better provided for than the poor working people in many parts of Europe."[3] Lyell quotes the observations of a Scotch weaver who had spent several weeks on cotton plantations in Alabama and Georgia, and who asserted that he had not there witnessed one fifth of the real suffering he had seen in manufacturing establishments in Great Britain. This agreed with Lyell's own experience.[4] Lady Wortley was impressed by the fact that the slaves "seemed thoroughly happy and contented."[5] Mackay was convinced that the slaves were "better clad, fed, and cared for than the agricultural laborers of Europe or the slop tailors and sempstresses of London and Liverpool."[6] Achille Murat, who became a Florida

---

[1] See Lecky's History of Morals, vol. i. pp. 70 and 76; Macaulay's History of England, chap. i.   [2] Life of Seward, vol. i. p. 779.

[3] Homes of the New World, vol. i. p. 296.

[4] Second Visit, vol. ii. p. 78. "To one who arrives in Georgia direct from Europe, with a vivid impression on his mind of the state of the peasantry there in many populous regions, their ignorance, intemperance, and improvidence, the difficulty of obtaining subsistence, and the small chance they have of bettering their lot, the condition of the black laborers on such a property as Hopeton will afford but small ground for lamentation or despondency."—Ibid., vol. i. p. 262.

The women "are always allowed a month's rest after their confinement, an advantage rarely enjoyed by hard-working English peasants." —Ibid., p. 264; see also Diary of a Southern Planter, Smedes, p. 78.

[5] Travels in the United States, vol. i. p. 218.

[6] Life and Liberty in America, vol. i. p. 311. "The general condition of the Southern slave is one of comparative happiness and comfort, such as many a free man in the United Kingdom might regard with envy." —London Times, Sept. 1st, 1852, quoted in Notes on Uncle Tom's Cabin,

planter, maintained that the slaves were happier than the
laborers in the large English manufacturing towns and
than European peasants in general; but he likewise wrote
that slavery, when viewed from afar, has quite a different
physiognomy from that which presents itself when viewed
on the spot; "that which appears rigorous by law becomes
lenient by custom."[1]

The opinions of these foreign travellers, with the exception of the Scotch weaver who supported himself by manual
labor and only saw the lower society, were greatly influenced by the generous hospitality of Southern gentlemen.
Harriet Martineau had found that hospitality so remarkable
and grateful that she appreciated the lurking danger in it of
blinding many to the real evils of slavery. In those spacious
country-houses everything was so "gay and friendly," there
was "such a prevailing hilarity and kindness," that one forgot the misery on which this open-handed way of living was
based.[2] The liberality and heartiness of Southern entertainments made a powerful impression on Lyell, who has
left a graceful testimony of "the perfect ease and politeness
with which a stranger is made to feel himself at home."[3]

The character in which the slave-holding lord wished to
appear to the world is well illustrated by a fanciful account
in *The Southern Literary Journal* of a visit by a nineteenth-
century Addison to Sir Roger de Coverley's plantation.
The Carolina de Coverley is described as having all the
virtues of the famous English knight, whose faithful old do-
mestics, grown gray-headed in the service, are paralleled by

---

p. 74. Ampère arrived at the conclusion that the lot of the slaves was
not very hard (see tome ii. p. 142), but he is severe on those who attempt
to justify slavery, see p. 148. Thackeray wrote from Richmond in 1853:
"The negroes don't shock me, or excite my compassionate feelings at all;
they are so grotesque and happy that I can't cry over them. The little
black imps are trotting and grinning about the streets; women, work-
men, waiters, all well fed and happy."—Letters, p. 168.

[1] America and the Americans, pp. 67 and 77.

[2] Society in America, vol. i. p. 229.   [3] Second Visit, vol. i. p. 245.

"healthy, laughing, contented" negroes, who are "comfortably provided for," whose "sleep is sweet," and who "care not for the morrow." The devotion of the ancient servants to the English Sir Roger, their joyful welcome when he returned from a journey, the mixture of the father and the master of the family in his conduct to his dependants, is likened to the "endearing relation" which exists between the slaves and the Carolina lord.[1] Yet in this imitation of one of the most graceful sketches of English literature, one trait is added which sets in a clear light the foul blot of slavery on an otherwise charming picture of rural life. "Cleanliness is indispensable to health," says Sir Roger de Coverley of Carolina, "and makes the slave prolific. I have at this time a hundred and fifty of these people; and their annual increase may be estimated as adding as much to my income as arises from all other sources."[2] The love of art as well as the love of liberty would have prevented Joseph Addison from putting such words into the mouth of Sir Roger; for had he spoken thus, he would have been no longer the old-fashioned country gentleman of high honor and rare benevolence that remains as one of the characteristic creations of English literature.

A well-known result of slavery was the denial of free speech at the South. While Southern advocates of the rightfulness of slavery were heard willingly at the North in joint debate, or from the lyceum platform, the life of Garrison and of Parker would have been forfeited had they gone South and attempted to get a hearing. The circulation of anti-slavery newspapers and books was suppressed as far as possible. One book, however, and the most dangerous of

---

[1] "In 'the days that are no more,' so confiding and affectionate was the relation of the master and the slave, and we, who personally loved many of them, cannot now easily become reconciled to the attitude of alienation in which the negroes stand towards us."—Mrs. Davis in 1890, Memoir of Jefferson Davis, vol. i. p. 311.

[2] Slave States of America, Buckingham, vol. i. p. 60

all, found many readers.   The desire to read "Uncle Tom's Cabin" was too great to be crushed by the usual efforts at repression.[1]

It must, however, be confessed that reason enough existed for the denial of free speech and a free press.   The first duty of a society is self-preservation.   Whether or not the danger of slave insurrections was great, it is certain that the fear of them was real and ever present.   "I speak from facts," said John Randolph, "when I say that the night bell never tolls for fire in Richmond, that the frightened mother does not hug her infant the more closely to her bosom, not knowing what may have happened.   I have myself witnessed some of the alarms in the capital of Virginia."[2]   De Tocqueville was struck by the inevitable danger of a struggle between the blacks and whites in the slave States.   While he found the subject discussed freely at the North, it was ignored at the South; yet the tacit foreboding of servile insurrection in that community seemed more dreadful than the expressed fears of his Northern friends.[3]   Men in the slave States were wont to deny the danger,[4] but Fanny Kemble testified that all Southern women to whom she had spoken about the matter admitted that they lived in terror of their slaves.[5] Never elsewhere had she known "anything like the pervading timidity of tone," and it was her belief that the slave-

---

[1] See letter of Francis Lieber, Feb. 3d, 1853: "Apropos of slavery: Uncle Tom's Cabin sells here [in Columbia, S. C.] rapidly.   One bookseller tells me that he cannot supply the demand with sufficient rapidity."—Life and Letters, p. 257; see also Olmsted's Cotton Kingdom.

[2] House of Representatives, Dec., 1811.

[3] "Dans les États du Sud, on se tait; on ne parle point de l'avenir aux étrangers; on évite de s'en expliquer avec ses amis; chacun se le cache, pour ainsi dire, à soi-même.   Le silence du Sud a quelque chose de plus effrayant que les craintes bruyantes du Nord."— De la Démocratie en Amérique, vol. ii. p. 334.

[4] See Kemble, p. 295; Pro-slavery Argument, p. 74; Society in America, vol. ii. p. 120.

[5] See Kemble, p. 295.

holders lived in a "perpetual state of suspicion and apprehension."[1] Olmsted saw "more direct expression of tyranny in a single day and night at Charleston than at Naples,
under Bomba, in a week."[2] Mackay, who was favorably
disposed towards the South, was impressed with the surveil-
lance, strict as martial law, to which the negroes were subjected at Charleston.[3] Further evidence of this sort need
not be adduced. The legislation, the daily conduct of the
whites, the great alarms excited by slight provocation, go to
show that the Roman proverb, "As many enemies as slaves,"
acquired the same force in the South after Nat Turner as it
had in Rome after the revolt of Spartacus.[4]

Even had the material condition of the slaves been as
good as the apologists of slavery were in the habit of assert-
ing, the fact that nearly every negro was eager for liberty
was a grave indictment of the system. The evidence of
this is so overwhelming that the statement will not be disputed. One of the finest touches in "Uncle Tom's Cabin"
is the joyful expression of Uncle Tom when told by his
good and indulgent master that he should be set free and
sent back to his old home in Kentucky. In attributing the
common desire of humanity to the negro, the author was as
true as she was effective.

---

[1] Kemble, p. 268. "Ten years ago an eminent Southern statesman told
us that he never retired to rest on his plantation without carefully ex-
amining his pistols and rifle, which hung by his bedside, to make sure
that they were ready for instant use; and a mother of Virginia told us
years ago that if accidentally awakened at night by any noise in the
neighborhood, her first impulse was one of terror lest it should proceed
from a revolt of negroes."—New York *Tribune*, 1859.

[2] Cotton Kingdom, vol. ii. p. 350.

[3] Life and Liberty in America, vol. i. p. 310; see also Seaboard Slave
States, p. 404. Thackeray wrote from Richmond in 1853: "Crowe has
just come out from what might have been and may be yet a dreadful
scrape. He went into a slave-market and began sketching; and the people rushed on him savagely and obliged him to quit."—Letters, p. 168.

[4] See account of Henry S. Foote of excitement in Central Mississippi
in 1835, Casket of Reminiscences, p. 250 *et seq.*

A good deal of currency was given to stories of slaves who escaped and afterwards came to their old masters and voluntarily surrendered themselves.[1] Clay grew eloquent when he told of a slave in his own family, who, having been enticed away, "addressed her mistress, and begged and implored of her the means of getting back from the state of freedom, to which she had been seduced, to the state of slavery, in which she was so much more happy."[2] There is no doubt that similar instances occurred, but the very prominence given to isolated cases shows that they were the exceptions and not the rule. The small number of fugitive slaves was sometimes urged to show that the dissatisfaction with the servile condition was not general. Only about one thousand negroes escaped yearly into the free States, and only about two thousand were annually manumitted.[3] Yet this argument was fallacious. The count of fugitives who reached the North cannot be taken to measure the number of negroes who escaped from their masters. In the cotton States the chance of getting to the land of freedom was small, yet slaves frequently ran away; they were often caught alive by the dogs, occasionally shot, and sometimes they remained for months in the swamps, or in mountainous regions kept secreted among the hills.[4]

The number of all sorts of fugitives, however, was small compared with the negroes who yearned for freedom, but, owing to insurmountable obstacles, were deterred from making the attempt. Frederick Douglass, one of the brightest and most intelligent of slaves, held notions of geography so vague and indistinct that the eastern shore of Maryland,

---

[1] See Retrospect of Western Travel, vol. i. p. 242.

[2] Speech on the compromise resolutions, Last Years of Henry Clay, p. 330.

[3] The number of fugitives escaping into the free States in 1850 was 1011, or one in each 3165 held in bondage; in 1860, 803, or one to about 5000. Twenty thousand slaves were supposed to have been manumitted between 1850 and 1860. United States Census Report.

[4] See Cotton Kingdom, under "Runaway Slaves."

where he wrought as a bondman, seemed a vast distance from Pennsylvania; and his description of the difficulties that lay in the way of eager fugitives is a sufficient explanation of why their number was so small.[1] The vilest and most ignorant of slaves in the cotton States knew that freedom was in the direction of the north star; the wisest of them knew little more, except that the distance was great and that the route lay through a country where everybody kept on the watch, and where their color itself was a grave object of suspicion.

What will the judgment of history be on the Southern men? Must not coming ages ratify the opinion of the moralist and the philosopher who lived in slave times, who loved liberty and yet were able to take a charitable view? "Slavery is the calamity of our Southern brethren, and not their crime," wrote Channing.[2] "The misfortune of the planter," said Emerson, "is at least as great as his sin."[3] Least of all may the North or England cast a stone at the South, for each had a hand in the establishing of negro slavery. Yet it does not follow that the Southern men of the generation before the war can plead innocence at the judgment bar of history. They may be arraigned for taking steps backward from the position held by the leaders of Southern opinion when the Constitution was framed. Jefferson made an effort to abolish slavery in his own State. It is true he might have done more; and he was subject to the influence of his environment to the extent that, in his later years, he found a palliation of slavery which his pen would have refused to record in the days when he wrote the Declaration of Independence.

Jefferson, and the great Virginians who were associated with him, freed a country and established a nation. Is it not asking too much that they should have solved the social question and freed a race? Yet that was the duty of the generation which succeeded. Calhoun was the intellectual

---

[1] Life of Douglass, p. 159.
[2] Webster's Works, vol. v. p. 367.   [3] Life of Emerson, Cabot, p. 426.

heir of Jefferson,[1] and if he had continued to hold the national views with which he started in public life, he might have done much to shatter the system that he consecrated his later years to uphold.[2]   The mantle of Calhoun fell on Jefferson Davis, who translated into action the logic of his master.   The judgment of posterity is made up: it was an unrighteous cause which the South defended by arms; and at the tribunal of modern civilization, Calhoun and Davis must be held accountable for the misery which resulted from this appeal to the sword.

It is true that had Calhoun espoused the cause of freedom, his influence would have been less; he would not have been idolized as the Southern hero and have received the affectionate devotion of his aristocratic order.[3]   Calhoun and Davis were leaders because in them the feelings of the Southern oligarchy found the ablest expression.   It is therefore fitting that the judgment which is meted out to the Southern leaders should be shared by their followers who failed to grapple with the problem sincerely and boldly, and foremost of these were the slave-holding lords.   The smaller proprietors, who imitated their betters, were not guiltless; but the most lenient judgment should fall upon the poor whites, who were hoodwinked into fighting for a cause which, though deemed holy, was in reality an instrument in their own degradation.   Yet, while making these reflections, the historian cannot forget that in the heat of the conflict the great leader could say: " Both [the North and

---

[1] This is pointed out by Henry Adams.   " A radical democrat, less liberal, less cultivated, and much less genial than Jefferson, Calhoun was the true heir to his intellectual succession." — History of the United States, vol. i. p. 154.

[2] Harriet Martineau has an interesting passage on Calhoun, Retrospect, vol. i. p. 241; see also conversation between Calhoun and John Quincy Adams, March, 1820, Memoirs of J. Q. Adams, vol. v. p. 10.

[3] " Calhoun sways South Carolina by pampering her vanity."—Francis Lieber, Life and Letters, p. 171.

the South] read the same Bible and pray to the same God. It may seem strange that any men should dare to ask a just God's assistance in wringing their bread from the sweat of other men's faces; but let us judge not, that we be not judged."[1] Nor is it an impossible supposition that if the Puritan had settled Virginia and the Cavalier had settled Massachusetts, while the question would have remained the same, the Puritan might have fought for slavery and the Cavalier for liberty.

Then, too, it may be that the peculiar institution was so interwoven with the political and social life of the South, that to inaugurate a movement there which should result in the abolition of slavery might have required a genius by the side of whom Calhoun and Davis would seem intellectual pygmies. The mighty Cæsar, the sovereign ruler, although convinced of the evil of large slave estates, did not venture to assail the practice of slavery in Rome. Our civilization is certainly superior in the virtue of humanity to that of the ancient world in the time of Cæsar, and a man as able and energetic as the Roman imperator might, under republican forms, have worked out the salvation of the South.

But one is struck by the absence of any well-directed effort towards the abolition of slavery. Nor were the slave States willing to entertain any plan involving emancipation with compensation.[2] No doubt whatever exists that the moral sentiment of the North would have favored employing the treasure and credit of the general government to pay for the slaves, had the Southern owners been willing to emancipate them;[3] and while such a course was not without practical and political difficulties, these were by no means insuperable. Yet no such project was entertained; for even had the North made such an offer, it would have been spurned by the South. The Colonization Society, whose object was to remove the negroes to Africa and colonize

---

[1] From President Lincoln's second inaugural.
[2] See Seward's Works, vol. i. p. 87.
[3] See Emerson's speech, 1855, Cabot, p. 593.

them at Liberia, undoubtedly proved a salve to the tender consciences of many; but as a means of putting an end to the evil, its operations were a fit subject of ridicule. Garrison charged that seven times as many slaves were annually smuggled into the South as had been transported to Africa in fifteen years by the Colonization Society.[1]

The Southern lord would not make the sacrifice of his ease to examine the question honestly. Lyell, who was inclined to be partial to the South, was of the opinion that steps ought long ago to have been taken towards the gradual emancipation of the slaves.[2] Jefferson Davis and his fellow-planters, who were fond of books and delighted in the study of ancient history, might have read in the year 1857 an impressive lesson; and had their minds been open to the reception of the truth, the words of Mommsen would have appeared to them the highest philosophy; for he furnished an example of a social system strikingly similar to that the Southern lords extolled; he drew the parallel and let the consequence be seen. "Riches and misery," wrote the historian of Rome, "in close league drove the Italians out of Italy, and filled the Peninsula partly with swarms of slaves, partly with awful silence. It is a terrible picture, but not one peculiar to Italy; whenever the government of capitalists in a slave State has fully developed itself, it has desolated God's fair world in the same way. . . . All the arrant sins that capital has been guilty of against nation and civil-

---

[1] Life of Garrison, vol. i. p. 295. "Mr. Madison, the president of the colonization society, gave me his favorable views of it. Mr. Clay, the vice-president, gave me his. So did almost every clergyman and other member of society whom I met for some months. . . . But I am firmly persuaded that any clear-headed man, shutting himself up in his closet for a day's study of the question, . . . can come to no other conclusion than that the scheme of transporting the colored population of the United States to the coast of Africa is absolutely absurd; and if it were not so, would be absolutely pernicious." — H. Martineau, Society in America, vol. i. p. 346. "It is a tub thrown to the whale."—Ibid., p. 349.

[2] Lyell's Second Visit, vol. i. p. 208.

ization in the modern world remain as far inferior to the abomination of the ancient capitalist States as the free man, be he ever so poor, remains superior to the slave; and not until the dragon-seed of North America ripens will the world have again similar fruits to reap." [1]

When the war ended with the abolition of slavery, the general opinion at the North was that the negro question was settled. This was an illusion; yet no one fully conversant with the literature of slavery in the decade of 1850–60, and with the literature of the race question at the present time, can doubt that the negro problem was a graver one in 1850 than it is in 1892. This the historian may affirm with confidence and yet feel the seriousness of the present situation, which demands the wisdom of action on the part of the South, and the wisdom of forbearance on the part of the North. The North better than ever before appreciates the feeling that induced Madison, in the closing years of his useful life, to give vent to the ardent wish that he might be able to work a miracle; were that power given him, he would make all the negroes white, for then he could in one day abolish slavery. [2]

---

[1] Vol. iv. p. 621.

[2] See Society in America, Martineau, vol. i. p. 382. On the subject of this chapter generally, see article in the *Andover Review*, Aug., 1891, entitled "Slavery as Seen by a Northern Man in 1844," by A. P. Peabody.

I desire here to acknowledge my obligations to my friend Raymond S. Perrin, who read with me a large portion of the manuscript of this work, and to whom I am indebted for valuable suggestions. And I wish to mention the assistance received from my friend Professor Bourne, of Adelbert College, who read carefully the whole manuscript, and gave me the benefit of his historical knowledge and literary criticism.

CHAPTER V

FRANKLIN PIERCE, the youngest man who up to this time had taken the presidential oath, was inaugurated March 4th, 1853. The ceremony was more imposing than usual, and was witnessed by the largest number of strangers who had ever gathered in Washington to assist at the installation of a new chief magistrate. When he took the oath he did not, as is ordinary, use the word "swear," but accepted the constitutional alternative which permitted him to affirm that he would faithfully execute the office of President of the United States. Nor did he kiss the book, as was the Southern fashion, but laid his left hand upon the Bible and held his right hand aloft, having previously bared his head to the falling snow. He did not read the address, but spoke without manuscript or notes in a clear and distinct voice, with a graceful manner. The inaugural was a well-turned literary composition, delivered by an effective speaker, and made a striking impression upon the many auditors.[1] He began : "My countrymen ! It is a relief to feel that no heart but my own can know the personal regret and bitter sorrow over which I have been borne to a position so suitable for others rather than desirable for myself." This was an allusion to the sudden taking-away of his only living child, a bright boy of thirteen, by a railroad accident which happened in the early part of January. The boy, to whom Pierce was devotedly attached, was travelling with his father and mother, when his brains were dashed out before their eyes. Some Whig journals criticised this allusion as being a trick of the orator

---

[1] New York *Herald*, March 5th, 1853; *National Intelligencer*.

to awaken personal interest before proceeding to unfold his public policy; but the people who heard the words felt only sympathy for the handsome young President who thus frankly disclosed his private grief, knowing that he would gladly resign the most glittering of earthly prizes if only his son might have been restored to him.

The President hinted strongly that during his term of office it might be his part to add Cuba to the common country. "The policy of my administration," he said, "will not be controlled by any timid forebodings of evil from expansion. Indeed, it is not to be disguised that our attitude as a nation, and our position on the globe, render the acquisition of certain possessions, not within our jurisdiction, eminently important for our protection."

He affirmed the principle of the Monroe doctrine. He intimated that the Whigs should be turned out of the offices to make room for Democrats. Yet he was not hampered by promises made before nomination or election; he had no "implied engagements to ratify," so that in the disposal of patronage he should not be subject to the dictation of the politicians. "I acknowledge," he declared, "my obligations to the masses of my countrymen, and to them alone."

He made a vigorous appeal for the Union, holding that the compromise measures of 1850 were strictly constitutional, and should be "unhesitatingly carried into effect." While the Fugitive Slave act was not mentioned by name, everybody knew that this expression meant that the President would vigorously enforce that law, as it was the only part of the compromise on which executive action was now needed.

The enthusiastic cheers and noise of the cannon which greeted the President when he closed his address was typical of the joy of Democrats all over the country on their restoration to power. In truth, they had felt, ever since the first election of Jackson, that the duty of administering the government belonged rightfully to them, and that in their hands only were the interests of the whole people properly

I.—25

protected. Aristocratic cabals and money combinations certainly fared better at the hands of the Whigs, but a party
whose support was largely derived from those elements did
not, the Democrats thought, deserve popular success. The
Whigs had twice elected a President, but it was by means
of the trick of playing upon the universal fancy for military prestige. It was now the general Democratic feeling
that the installation of Pierce into office was a restoration
simply of the power and patronage justly due the Democrats.

The inaugural was well received; it was generally satisfactory to the business interests. The disposition always
exists on the part of the successful party to hail their new
chief as a paragon of wisdom or virtue; nor, in the first days
of the administration, do the defeated party bear rancor,
but are willing to look on with charity, feeling that the new
President deserves a fair chance. Especially was this the
case when Franklin Pierce took the reins of government.
He was very popular on election day, and so overpowering
had been his success that he was still more popular on the
day of his inauguration. If the general acclaim augured
well for the prosperity of the new administration, few Presidents have started with auspices so favorable. Yet the
anti-slavery Whigs, and a few anti-slavery Democrats whose
principles were stronger than their desire to see the old
party cemented, could not but tremble for their country
when they saw in this cautious exposition of principle and
announcement of programme that the President, whose hold
on the people was apparently so powerful, did not regard
human slavery as an evil, but was anxious to acquire more
slave territory. It did not allay their apprehensions when
he said that the new territory should be obtained " with a
view to obvious national interest and security, and in a manner entirely consistent with the strictest observance of national faith ;" for the intrigue by which Texas was annexed
was too fresh in their minds. It was patent that the Southern men who composed the slavery propaganda, while strict-

ly honorable in private life, were ready to use any means to extend the influence of their dear institution. It was a prime article of Southern faith that Texas had been honorably acquired; and if one were a true Democrat, he must believe the war with Mexico to have been just and holy.

A mere reading of the inaugural was sufficient to give rise to a suspicion that in President Pierce the Southern leaders had found a man who would do their bidding; but had one known what was going on in the inner councils of the party, the feeling would have been more than a suspicion. In the month following the election, Pierce had written a letter to Buchanan asking suggestions and advice, to which the Pennsylvania statesman was glad to respond fully and freely. He pointed out where lay the path of glory. " The foreign affairs of the government," he wrote, " and especially the question of Cuba, will occupy the most conspicuous place in your administration. I believe that Cuba can be acquired by cession upon honorable terms, and I should not desire to acquire it in any other manner. The President who shall accomplish this object will render his name illustrious, and place it on the same level with that of his great predecessor, who gave Louisiana to the Union." [1]

Pierce, shortly after his election, sent a message to John A. Dix, of New York, requesting a personal interview. When Dix repaired to Concord he was offered, in the most cordial manner, the position of Secretary of State under the new administration, the President-elect assuring him that he was the man of all others whose presence in the cabinet would be especially desirable and gratifying. But when this became known to the party leaders, the extreme Southern politicians and the pro-slavery New York Democrats protested earnestly against the appointment, on account of Dix's connection with the Free-soil party in 1848, when he had been their candidate for governor. Thereupon a second

---

[1] Life of Buchanan, G. T. Curtis, vol. ii. p. 72.

interview between Pierce and Dix took place, and as it was
quite evident that the President-elect desired to be relieved
from his obligation, Dix at once released him.[1]

Far different was the treatment of Jefferson Davis, who
early received an offer of the position of Secretary of War.
He at first declined the appointment,[2] but Pierce was so
earnest in his solicitations that Davis came to Washington
the day after the inauguration, and was finally prevailed
upon to accept the position.[3] This appointment, highly satisfactory to the Southern states-rights men, and in the
main agreeable to the South, was decidedly objectionable to
the Union party in Mississippi.[4] One frequently heard the
remark at the North that Davis was the only member of
the cabinet who had opposed the compromise measures of
1850. The difference in the treatment of Dix and of Davis,
both of whom had similar personal claims on Pierce, was
evidence that the extreme Southern faction of the party
would receive more consideration than the Northern Democrats who were tinctured with Free-soilism.

The cabinet nominations were not sent to the Senate until
three days after the inauguration. The President appointed
William L. Marcy, of New York, Secretary of State; James
Guthrie, of Kentucky, Secretary of the Treasury; Jefferson
Davis, of Mississippi, Secretary of War; James C. Dobbin,
of North Carolina, Secretary of the Navy; Robert McClelland, of Michigan, Secretary of the Interior; James Campbell, of Pennsylvania, Postmaster-General; and Caleb Cushing, of Massachusetts, Attorney-General.

The courteous action of Dix in permitting Pierce to retract the offer of the State portfolio did not relieve him
from all embarrassment in regard to the leading position in

---

[1] Life of J. A. Dix, by Morgan Dix, vol. i. p. 271.
[2] Davis's wife urged him to decline the offer. Memoir of Jefferson Davis,
by his wife, vol. i. p. 476.
[3] Life of Jefferson Davis, Alfriend, p. 89.
[4] Casket of Reminiscences, Foote, p. 90.

the cabinet. Desirous of giving this place to a New York man, he was perplexed by the bitter factional contest among the Democrats of that State. Although all differences had been sunk during the Presidential canvass, the split which began in 1848 broke out afresh as soon as the party gained the signal victory, and, while no principle seemed to be at stake, the fight was earnest for proper recognition in the distribution of the offices. It is undeniable that a few among those who were called Free-soilers remained true to their former declarations; but most of them were becoming merged in the faction called " Softs," whose endeavor was to unite the jarring elements of the party in order to control elections, and who after 1848 became the link of connection between the Free-soilers and the " Hunkers " or " Hards," as the regular Democrats were called.[1] Dix was a " Soft," with Free-soil antecedents ; while Marcy, though the chief of the "Softs," had been decidedly opposed to the Free-soil movement. To satisfy the greatest number was the aim of the President, to whom it became the subject of serious thought and many councils; and although the whole cabinet, as finally announced, was published in the newspapers one week before the inauguration,[2] Pierce did not really decide who should be his Secretary of State until he had actually been one day in office, for up to the morning of March 5th that portfolio had not been offered to Marcy.[3]

Marcy was the best-known man in the cabinet; he was an adroit politician; his intellectual qualities were solid rather than brilliant, but he had a strong mind and honest purposes. Jefferson Davis and Caleb Cushing also brought to the council board talents of a high order.

The first appearance of Davis in national public life was

---

[1] The distinction is well described in Rise and Fall of the Slave Power, vol. ii. p. 141 ; see also Dickinson's Letters and Speeches, vol. i. p. 394.

[2] New York *Herald*, Feb. 25th.

[3] See Letter of Marcy to Buchanan, Washington, March 5th, 1853, Life of Buchanan, Curtis, vol. ii. p. 75.

in the House of Representatives at the age of thirty-seven. He was fortunate in having a liberal training that made him well fitted for the political arena. A graduate of West Point, he had served as lieutenant in the Blackhawk and other Indian wars. He then resigned his commission and for eight years, from the age of twenty-seven to thirty-five, he lived in retirement on his cotton plantation, superintending the work in the manner common to the Southern planter, but for the most part devoting himself to a systematic course of reading and study, for which his taste amounted to a passion. When he quitted the life of a recluse to engage in the affairs of State he was a man of culture, well read in the classical writers of England, and deeply versed in political history and economy.

His maiden speech in the House of Representatives attracted the attention of John Quincy Adams, who said: "That young man is no ordinary man. He will make his mark yet, mind me."

Davis served as colonel in the Mexican war. His admirers asserted that his brilliant movement at Buena Vista carried the day, and that his tactical conception was worthy of a Cæsar or a Napoleon. He was afterwards United States senator for four years, resigning the position in 1851 to make the contest for governor of Mississippi as state-rights candidate against Foote, who led the Union party.[1] After his defeat he remained in private life until called forth by Pierce, with whom he held friendly personal relations. He was now in his forty-fifth year, and one could see that he was gradually reaching the position to which he aspired—a position which by 1860 he attained—that of leader of the Southern people, and successor of John C. Calhoun.[2]

Cushing owed his appointment primarily to the fact that

---

[1] See p. 226.

[2] In this characterization of Davis I have used Life of Davis, by Alfriend; Life of Davis, by Pollard; Our Living Representative Men, by John Savage.

he was one of the New England politicians who had striven
to bring about the nomination of Pierce; moreover, the
President-elect, himself an educated man, was not unwilling
to make known to the country that all the scholars did not
belong to the Whig party. That steadfast Whig State, Massachusetts, furnished the scholar of the cabinet for Pierce, as
she had likewise done for Polk.

Cushing was one of those men who seem to have taken
all knowledge for their province. Scholar, author, lawyer,
statesman, diplomatist, general, and judge, in at least four
of these callings he achieved distinction. " I started from
the same point," he once wrote, " so far as regards education, atmosphere, and mental culture, with Everett and Bancroft. Their lives have been of a more learned and medita-
tive cast than mine, and mine of a more adventurous and active complexion than theirs." [1] Born in 1800, he graduated
from Harvard when he was seventeen, became a tutor of
natural philosophy and mathematics at that college, then
studied law, and at twenty-five entered the legislature of his
State. In 1829 he went to Europe, remained there two
years, and, like many other Americans of culture, finding
Spain the most interesting of countries, stayed there long
enough to get the spirit and material for an interesting book
which he wrote upon his return. During a three years'
term in Congress he acquired the reputation of being a fas-
cinating public speaker; his utterances smacked of the study,
for he quoted from the Iliad with the same facility as did
other members from the Bible. President Tyler sent him
as minister to China, where he was successful in negotiating
a treaty which for the first time opened up diplomatic relations with the celestial empire. He served as general in the
Mexican war, and, when appointed a member of the cabinet,
was Justice of the Supreme Court of Massachusetts.

Cushing was one of the most indefatigable of workers.

---

[1] Private letter of Cushing to C. E. Lester, Feb. 19th, 1853, published in
the New York *Times*, Oct. 17th, 1853.

While well versed in the ancient languages, he could also speak fluently several modern tongues, and it was noted that at diplomatic dinners, while the Secretary of State could converse only in his own vernacular, the Attorney-general carried on conversation with all the ambassadors in their proper languages. Thoroughly acquainted with the best English literature, he yet read every new book, and remembered what he read.[1] A writer of books and an honored contributor to the stately *North American Review*, he wrote, while Attorney-general, an editorial nearly every day for the Washington *Union*, the organ of the administration. His habits were temperate, his health robust, he had wealth both inherited and earned, and he was altogether an agreeable member of society.

It is, indeed, a pity to mar the portrait of such a man, but it cannot be denied that he lacked moral sense. Admired by everybody for his learning and ability, he was trusted by few. Nor was it due alone to his political inconsistency that he forfeited the confidence of his fellow-men. Starting in public life a Whig, he apostatized with Tyler, and remained a Democrat. Other men have changed their politics, yet have retained their reputation for sincerity. But it was the general opinion that personal interest and not principle accounted for Cushing's political unsteadiness. When he was a candidate for governor of Massachusetts, James Russell Lowell struck the popular note in the following verses:

> " Gineral C. is a dreffle smart man :
>   He's been on all sides that give places and pelf;
>   But consistency still wuz a part of his plan,
>   He's been true to one party—and that is himself."[2]

---

[1] When living at Newburyport, it was his custom to look over all books that came to the bookseller before they were exposed for sale. He was also known as the man who had read Webster's Dictionary through twice.—Story told by the Boston *Herald*, cited by the New York *Tribune*, Jan. 7th, 1879.

[2] Biglow Papers. This was written in 1847.

Pierce, it was said, believed Cushing's fickleness to be intellectual, not moral, and that he only needed the influence of a man of stable judgment to keep him straight. His advice was well esteemed by the President-elect, and it is more than probable that he confirmed Pierce in the design, if he did not originally make the suggestion, of offering a cabinet position to Jefferson Davis.[1]

Next in importance to the cabinet appointments was the selection of men for the principal diplomatic posts. "Should you desire to acquire Cuba," Buchanan had written the President-elect, "the choice of suitable ministers to Spain, Naples, England, and France will be very important."[2] Buchanan was appointed minister to England; which gave notice to the country and to the European powers concerned that a leading object of the administration would be the acquisition of Cuba. While Secretary of State under Polk, Buchanan had offered one hundred million dollars for it. His political position, however, was so high, and his diplomatic experience so useful, that no criticism could be fairly made of his selection by Pierce.

---

[1] In this characterization of Cushing, I have consulted Forney's Anecdotes of Public Men, vol. i.; Our Living Representative Men, Savage; the New York Herald, 1853; Letters and Times of the Tylers, vol. ii.; North American Review, vol. xxxvii.; Public Men and Events, Sargent, vol. ii.; New York Nation, vol. xviii.; Twenty Years in Congress, Blaine; Casket of Reminiscences, Foote; Men and Measures of Half a Century, McCulloch; Memoirs of John Quincy Adams, vol. ix.; Reminiscences by Ben: Perley Poore; History of Journalism, Hudson. Thos. Benton's opinion, expressed in a speech delivered in 1856, will be of interest: "Of all these [the members of the cabinet] the Attorney-General is the master spirit. He is a man of talent, of learning, of industry — unscrupulous, double-sexed, double-gendered, and hermaphroditic in politics, with a hinge in his knee, which he often crooks, that thrift may follow fawning. He governs by subserviency; and to him is deferred the master's place in Mr. Pierce's cabinet. When I heard that he was to come into the cabinet I set down Mr. Pierce for a doomed man, and foresaw the swift and full destruction which was to fall upon him."—Quoted by Von Holst, vol. iv. p. 263, note.

[2] Dec. 11th, 1852, Life of James Buchanan, Curtis, vol. ii. p. 73.

The case was far otherwise in regard to the appointment of Soulé, of Louisiana, as minister to Spain. This could be construed in no other way than that President Pierce meant to carry out as well as he was able the desires of the Southern propaganda who were bent on getting Cuba by hook or by crook. The opinion of Soulé was no secret; he had declared it in open Senate in the January preceding his appointment. He took occasion then to speak enthusiastically of the followers of Lopez and Crittenden, who joined in the expedition to Cuba. Their heroic devotion and "the morality of their aspirations," he said, "deserve the praise that is freely accorded to Lafayette and Kosciusko." Soulé was opposed to purchasing Cuba. It could be acquired in a better way, he thought. It was useless for Spain to ignore the fact that Cuba could not much longer remain a Spanish dependency; that she was certain to secure her independence; and if the Cuban people revolted against Spain, we should sympathize with them, because the independence of the island would be as desirable as its annexation to this country. Cannot Southern senators see, he asked, that they ought to long for the annexation of Cuba on account of weighty domestic reasons, and cannot they understand that the intrigues of England are directed towards the abolition of slavery in that island? As Lord Palmerston avows, "if the negro population of Cuba were rendered free, that fact would create a most powerful element of resistance to any scheme for annexing Cuba to the United States, where slavery exists." [1]

If the object had been to bully Spain into giving up the possession she held so dear, something might be said in favor of this appointment; but if the object were to gain the island by patient, careful, and wise negotiation, a more objectionable appointment could not have been made. It gave much annoyance to the Spanish court, and the government

---

[1] This speech of Soulé was made Jan. 25th, 1853. See *Congressional Globe*, vol. xxvii. p. 118.

organ contended in a carefully prepared article that Soulé ought not to be received. The London *Times* called it an extraordinary choice, and it would have been no surprise had the Spanish government absolutely refused to hold relations with one who extolled rebellion against Spain, diplomatic precedents being ample to warrant such a course.[1]

On his way to Europe, Soulé received a deputation of Cuban exiles, to whom he made a speech, assuring them that when a man became a minister abroad he did not cease to be an American citizen; "and as such he has a right to carry wherever he goes the throbbings of that people that speak out such tremendous truths to the tyrants of the old continent."[2]

The French mission was offered to Dix, but, though accepted, the appointment in form was never made. Southern politicians objected strenuously on the ground that Dix was an abolitionist. He was certainly no friend to the extension of slavery; and although sufficiently affected by the manifest destiny doctrine of his party not to oppose the honorable annexation of Cuba, he could not be depended upon to play the part which was assigned to the minister at Paris in the scheme already brewing.[3]

John Y. Mason, a Virginian of the old school, received the appointment. Hawthorne described him as "a fat-brained, good-hearted, sensible old man."[4] He hated an abolitionist, as is shown by the fact that when Sumner was in Paris, seeking advice for the injury sustained by the assault of Brooks in the Senate chamber, Mason declared emphatically that he would not treat the Massachusetts senator with any politeness or consideration.[5] There was no reason to

---

[1] See New York *Herald*, May 30th and 31st, 1853.
[2] *Harper's Magazine*, Oct., 1853, p. 693.
[3] Life of John A. Dix, vol. i. p. 273, also vol. ii. p. 328.
[4] Hawthorne and his Wife, vol. ii. p. 174.
[5] Memories of Many Men, Field, p. 63.

doubt that Mason would favor zealously the plan of the Southern propaganda, or at least be as clay in the hands of the astute Buchanan and the impetuous Soulé.

Of the consular appointments, one deserves mention on account of being at once a graceful bestowal by the President and an honor to the country. Nathaniel Hawthorne was named for the lucrative position of consul at Liverpool. He at first shrank from accepting office from his friend, as it seemed too much like receiving pay for his campaign biography out of the public purse, and argument was needed to vanquish his scruples.

It is agreeable to record an instance where the bonds among the members of the republic of letters proved stronger than the alienation which might have arisen from political differences. "'Good! good!' I exclaimed aloud on the floor of the Senate as your nomination was announced," wrote Sumner to Hawthorne from the Senate chamber. "'Good! good!' I now write you on its confirmation." [1] Hawthorne was a man of such fine honor that he called forth the truest attachments and noblest friendships. So much has been published about him; his daily life has been presented to our view with detail so minute; every scrap which would show his mental processes being so fully divulged, that it is given us to know Hawthorne as he was known to his intimate friends and devoted family. That with this knowledge our respect for him remains undiminished is perhaps the highest tribute to his character.

In after-years, in the midst of the war, when Pierce, on account of his undisguised Southern sympathies, had lost the favor of the Northern people, and Hawthorne had reached that point of a successful writer's career where the most trivial productions of his pen were awaited with eagerness, the popular author dedicated to the unpopular ex-President, in the most complimentary of inscriptions, his work, " Our

---

[1] Study of Hawthorne, Lathrop, p. 248.

Old Home." For the most part, the men who read books were earnest for the prosecution of the war and the destruction of slavery, and Hawthorne's publishers remonstrated with him for the dedication of the book. His reply, absolutely refusing to withdraw either the dedication or dedicatory epistle, displays a manliness of temper which it is a pleasure to record. "If," wrote Hawthorne, "Pierce is so exceedingly unpopular that his name is enough to sink the volume, there is so much the more need that an old friend should stand by him. I cannot, merely on account of pecuniary profit or literary reputation, go back from what I have deliberately felt and thought it right to do; and if I were to tear out the dedication, I should never look at the volume again without remorse or shame."[1]

It is a curious fact that an unobtrusive politician like Hawthorne should have owed to his connection with politics the necessary prompting and opportunity for his two greatest works.[2] The loss of his place in the custom-house impelled him to write "The Scarlet Letter;" the consulship gave him the opportunity of visiting Europe, which enabled him to write "The Marble Faun." It is the contrast between these two romances, together with their similarities, which make the deepest impression on the minds of those who admire this literary artist. The one portrays the manners of the narrow-minded Puritan community, making us enter into the inmost thoughts and feelings of those men who founded a State; the other takes us among the gay, light-hearted Italians. We enjoy for the moment their sensuous existence, and share with them the feeling that life is one long holiday. Both are tales of sin and remorse, yet so marked is the power of the artist in the setting of his pictures that to us it seems the New England sky must be al-

---

[1] Study of Hawthorne, p. 321   The Old Home was published in 1863.
[2] But Hawthorne wrote, March 15, 1851: "*The House of the Seven Gables*, in my opinion, is better than *The Scarlet Letter*."—Letter to Horatio Bridge, *Harper's Magazine*, February, 1892, p. 371.

ways gray, nature ever taking on a sombre hue to be in keeping with the gloomy story.[1]

In the tale of Italy everything is bright. A flood of sunshine pours upon the remorseful souls in their most bitter moments. One can scarce believe, such is the powerful physical impression made by these stories, that the sun shines as brightly, and that the clear blue sky is as common, in New England as in Italy. The criticism has sometimes been made that as Hawthorne did not know Italian he could not penetrate into the inner life of the people, and seize upon their essential characteristics. Yet, in truth, he seemed to know Rome better than his birthplace, and to have known it longer. " Rome certainly does draw into itself my heart," he wrote, " as I think even London, or even little Concord itself, or old sleepy Salem, never did and never will." [2] Rome does not belong to Italy, but to the western world. One must indeed be an Aryan to appreciate its worth, but every one who speaks a language of the European branch of that race has a part in the historic and artistic possessions of the imperial city. This view powerfully influenced Hawthorne, and the elaboration of it in the descriptive portions of " The Marble Faun" has made it the best of Roman guide-books.

As long as these romances are read, people fond of metaphysical subtleties will interpret variously the meaning of the author, argue about the motive, and seek the underlying meaning of these tales of sin, suffering, and remorse. But if there were nothing but the plot and the moral to give merit to his books, they would have been forgotten by the generation who first read them. It is because Hawthorne wrote the best English prose of the century that he may be reckoned among the immortals. " Where," asked Mot-

---

[1] Hawthorne wrote, Feb. 4, 1850: " *The Scarlet Letter* lacks sunshine. . . . It is . . . a story, into which I found it almost impossible to throw any cheering light."—Ibid., p. 369.

[2] See articles in New York *Nation*, vol. xlix. pp. 32, 48, and references to Italian Note Books, vol. ii. pp. 189, 216.

ley of him, after reading "The Marble Faun," "oh, where is the godmother who gave you to talk pearls and diamonds?"[1]

While the diplomatic appointments were under consideration, the parcelling-out of offices which brought profit rather than honor was also going on. It has been noted above that the crowd of people at the inauguration was unusually great. A large number remained at Washington after the ceremonies to seek reward for their exertions in bringing back again to power the Democratic party. During the canvass it had been openly proclaimed that if the Democrats were successful, a clean sweep of offices would be made. The President stated in his inaugural, in courtly terms, that the general expectation would be realized. Everybody was agreed about the policy; but when it came to the division of the spoils there were ten applicants for nearly every important office, and the disappointment of the many was more noticeable than the complacency of the few.

The importunate begging for official positions in a republic where it was so easy to earn a living was nothing less than disgraceful. Office-seekers crowded the public receptions of the President, and while greeting him in the usual way, attempted at the same time to urge their claims, actually thrusting their petitions into his hands. "There never was a fiercer time than this among the office-seekers," wrote Hawthorne to a friend.[2]

The usual trouble about the New York City offices existed, and the factional fight in the party made it extremely difficult to decide between the conflicting interests. The President and his cabinet applied themselves diligently to the work, and in less than two months after the inauguration it could be said that practically all the fat places in the

---

[1] A Study of Hawthorne, p. 262.

[2] To R. H. Stoddard, who had applied for his influence. The letter is worth reading, as a commentary on the spoils system in 1853. Hawthorne and his Wife, vol. i. p. 461.

gift of the administration at home and abroad had been filled.[1]

In this proscription, Fillmore Whigs received no more consideration than the followers of Seward. The fact that they had fought side by side with the Northern Democrats for the compromise and had counselled submission to the Fugitive Slave law counted for nothing. The popular verdict was interpreted as a demand that all the Whigs should be turned out of office, and it is the most noteworthy feature of the situation that the Whigs tamely acquiesced in this wholesale proscription, surrendering their positions without a murmur. Nor did the opposition press teem with articles censuring the administration for its course. None of those journals were violent in denunciation, some even approved the policy, and all appeared to regard it as a matter of course. From the time when Jackson began the practice of making party fealty the test for appointment to the civil service, the opposition press had denounced vigorously the removal of political opponents at every partisan change of administration. The acquiescence in the practice now may have arisen in some degree from the crushing defeat which the Whigs had sustained; but a more powerful reason for this silent submission lay in the fact that the constant practice and advocacy of the policy by party leaders had so debauched public opinion that a change of officers in the civil service had come to be regarded as a necessary accompaniment of a change of party control. From the year 1853 we must date the cordial recognition by politicians and people of the principle "To the victors belong the spoils."

The summer of 1853 was one of political quiet and business prosperity, but many Southern cities were afflicted by a scourge more terrible than political turmoil or financial disaster. The dreaded yellow fever made its appearance. In New Orleans its ravages were the greatest. Never had

---

[1] See New York *Herald*, April 22d, 1853. I have, in this account of office-seeking, consulted that newspaper carefully from March 4th.

New Orleans been so prosperous and gay as during the winter season of 1853; never had the city been so full of people.[1] The largest cotton crop ever produced in the United States up to that time was being marketed at favorable prices. Never had the sugar plantations yielded such rich returns. One hundred and thirty million dollars' worth of produce of all kinds had been landed upon the levees of New Orleans. The Jackson railroad was building, and a great system of iron roads was projected. Real estate was active. Louisiana had not indulged in threats of secession or in dreams of a Southern confederacy, such as were common in the sister States of South Carolina and Mississippi; for her citizens appreciated that her prosperity was bound up in the Union, and the triumphant election of Pierce was interpreted as being favorable to the allaying of sectional controversies.

If the smiling material conditions of New Orleans were a tribute to the energy of the American population, the many places of amusement, nightly open, denoted that the desire of distraction, so characteristic of the French, prevailed in this cosmopolitan city. At one theatre the elder Booth astonished the audience by his intensely natural impersonation of Richard III.; at another, Anna Cora Mowatt delighted the old-fashioned play-goers; at another, Lola Montez, who had not yet outlived the notoriety of causing a revolution in Munich and the abdication of a king, fascinated crowds of gay and frivolous people by representing on the mimic stage a story of her disorderly adventures in Bavaria,[2] and by dancing in voluptuous measure the swift, whirling tarantella. One place of amusement was devoted to French opera, which had become a necessity of the winter to the lovers of music; Dan Rice had a hippodrome; Ole Bull with the violin, and Gottschalk with the piano, enchanted their hearers by their brilliant execution; Adelina Patti was

---

[1] New Orleans *Picayune*, Jan. 9th, 1853.
[2] The play was called Lola Montez in Bavaria: a Drama in Five Eras.

I.—26

just beginning in the concert hall that career which has entitled her to the name of the queen of song. Those who
loved science were gratified by a course of lectures from
Louis Agassiz on his favorite subjects. The Southern people heard him gladly, for his theory of the origin of man
denied emphatically that the Caucasian and negro had a
common ancestor, and this hypothesis was construed to
justify the enslaving of the inferior race.

Every Sunday those who were fond of the sport could
choose between the attractions offered at three rival race-
courses. Private hospitality was lavishly dispensed, and to
those whose social position was high, and who were able to
take part in all the gayeties of the season, life seemed a car-
nival.[1] The public balls were numerous. When Mardi-
gras came, although many bewailed that the usual street
parade was given up, and regretted the glories of bygone
days, it was acknowledged by every one that the brilliant
fancy-dress parties and balls were a compensation.

Isolated cases of yellow fever began to occur in the early
part of May, and although during the month there were
deaths from the disease, no alarm whatever was felt, for
this was but a repetition of the experience of every year
since the epidemic of 1847. Those who intimated that
the vile condition of the streets was such as to augment a
pestilence, if not to invite it, were frowned upon as defam-
ers of the city. It was pleasanter to discuss magnificent
future schemes of improved drainage than to take immediate and practical steps towards setting the city in order.
The travel to the North and Europe during the spring and
early summer was larger than usual; not, however, because
the rich and the fashionable had any forebodings of the
dismal fate in store for their beloved city, but because the
spring, being warmer than common, prompted an earlier

---

[1] "At the time of my first visit, in the winter of 1856–57, New Orleans
was socially the most delightful city in the Union."—Episodes in a Life
of Adventure, Laurence Oliphant, p. 91.

departure from the Southern climate ; and, as money was abundant, the desire for travel could be gratified as soon as born.

By the latter part of June the situation looked ominous. For the week ending June 25th there were nine deaths from yellow fever, and for that ending July 2d twenty-five. Yet if one had depended upon the newspapers for knowledge of passing events, he would never have dreamed that the dreaded epidemic had begun, since the journals made no mention whatever of the startling fact. The commercial interest of the city insisted strenuously that the state of affairs should not be made public, and the real-estate speculators were wild with alarm lest the truth should be told. The next week, when the deaths had more than doubled, there were editorial expressions of fear that the present season would be a sickly one ; but when July 16th arrived and two hundred and four deaths by yellow fever for the week were reported, it was felt that concealment was no longer possible, and the newspapers · became again the chronicles of the time. The jaunty air with which a serious condition had been treated now gave place to panic-stricken fear. All who were able, and who were not detained by duty, fled. The city government failed completely to grasp the situation ; the board of aldermen resolved, the last week in July, that the yellow fever in the city had not become epidemic, and adjourned till October; the cowardly went North, the brave remained, and as citizens did duty which their associates would not let them do officially.

As frequently happens, however, in American cities, when the constituted authorities have broken down, the best men of the community came to the front and went to work with discretion and heroism. Chief among the agencies of good was the Howard Association, composed of active, energetic men, whose mission during an epidemic was to take care of the poor and destitute sick, and provide them with proper medical attendance and nursing. A record of the work of this noble body during the fatal summer was written by one of their number, and, while it vies in interest with any romance, it is simply the truthful tale of an unassuming "Samaritan;" [1] but the fascination of the book lies in the accounts of the conversation and action of the men and women whom the approach of death made sincere.

The premonitory symptoms of yellow fever were not unmistakable, nor such as to cause intense anxiety; they were the same that precede the most ordinary diseases. It began with a cold, a hardly perceptible chill, an aching in the head, an apparently insignificant fever, and, a little later, pains in the back ensue. These warnings were made light of by the laboring poor. Those who lived from hand to mouth could not afford to lie by on account of ill feelings, which strong men living in a malarious climate learn to slight. In such cases, the poison of the insidious disease had coursed through the veins of the body before the man took to his bed or called a physician. Only about one-half of those attacked with yellow fever recovered; an apparent cessation of the ravages of the disease was with many but a premonition of a fatal issue.

The weather was unfavorable, being characterized by sudden changes; there was much rain, and for ten days July seemed like January. Woollens were worn, people slept under blankets, windows were kept shut, and the thin-blooded lighted their fires. The death-rate increased. On the last day of July there were one hundred and thirty-seven deaths from yellow fever, and in August the number of victims became constantly greater until the 21st, which, by common consent, was called the black day of the plague. Two hundred and thirty deaths from yellow fever were reported that day, but the actual number was nearer three hundred—a daily mortality more than double the ordinary weekly death-rate of New Orleans.

---

[1] Diary of a Samaritan, by a Member of the Howard Association of New Orleans. The writer was W. L. Robison, a gentleman of good social and business position and high character. (Harper & Brothers, 1860.)

The weather now became intensely hot, but the atmosphere was full of humidity, and the analytical chemists said there was a lack of ozone in the air. To purify the atmosphere, the Board of Health ordered that four hundred discharges should be fired from several six-pound cannons; but the thunder of the artillery had a fatal effect on many of the sick, throwing them into convulsions. Then another mode of clearing the air was tried. Barrels filled with tar were burned all over the city. "At sunset," wrote the "Samaritan" in his diary, "when all were simultaneously fired, a pandemonium glare lighted up our city. Not a breath of air disturbed the dense smoke, which slowly ascended in curling columns until it reached the height of about five hundred feet. Here it seemed equipoised, festooning over our doomed city like a funeral pall, and there remaining until the shades of night disputed with it the reign of darkness." [1]

In the latter part of August there were new developments in the disease, and greater difficulty in treating it. After a few days of convalescence, the patient failed to gain appetite or strength, distressing boils appeared on the body, and a fatal relapse was not uncommon. Another characteristic appeared in some patients on the second day of their attack. "Round purple spots, the size of a dime, with the edges darker than the centre," were discovered on their bodies. "If they survived the third day, the side on which they lay for a few hours became of the same color, as if mortification had set in from interruption to a free circulation through the laggard veins." [2] These symptoms suggested to physicians who had not forgotten their classical reading the descriptions of Thucydides and Lucretius, and gave rise to the conjecture that the spots indicated a modified type of the most famous of plagues.

When the historian writes that the physicians were faith-

---

[1] Diary of a Samaritan, p. 153.
[2] Ibid., p. 208.

ful, brave, and untiring, he simply adds another to the many tributes to the character of the American medical profession. The yellow fever of 1853 was the most aggravated type ever known. The doctors early recognized this fact, and appreciated that different treatment was required from that which had hitherto been in vogue. Cupping, which in former epidemics had been deemed indispensable, was now only employed in rare cases, and even then with the greatest caution. The differences in treatment among the native physicians were not very material except on one point; and that was as to whether quinine should be administered, and if so, whether in large or small quantities. The physicians not only worked nobly, but with rare good sense. In the presence of the appalling scourge, they felt that petty wrangles were unworthy of their profession, and adjourned their disputes until the epidemic was over, when they carried them on in the columns of newspapers and magazines instead of in the sick-chamber or hospital.

The "Samaritan," who seems to have been a man of discernment and good judgment, made some curious observations. The only quarrel he reported was the case of two German doctors who, by a mistake, were asked to visit the same patient. Both prescribed; each condemned the treatment of the other; and each, at every visit, threw the medicine of his rival into the street. The poor patient could not venture to decide between the two, and therefore took the physic of neither, but drank copiously of iced water. He was soon beyond danger and convalesced rapidly.

Two patients in a hospital had their cots changed by some accident, and as the doctor prescribed by number, the convalescent got the medicine of the one who had been sick but thirty-six hours, while he in turn took physic which, according to the directions of the faculty, was neither proper nor useful until the disease had been eight days in progress. Both patients finally recovered.

A physician who had a diploma from the college of medicine at Paris came to the hospital stricken with the disease,

and claimed the right of prescribing for himself. He was
a friend to the heroic treatment, had himself cupped and
bled frequently and freely, and swallowed the strongest of
drugs; his strength failed him, he had no power to resist
the disease, and fell its victim.

A circumstance worthy of note is the difference of treatment among physicians of different nationalities. It was
the aim of the Howard Association to send respectively to
sick Frenchmen, Spaniards, and Germans doctors of their
own country. The Spanish physician would give to his
patients on the first day of convalescence the juice of fresh
oysters; the German, at the height of the disease, advised
strong fluid nourishment, and in convalescence hard-boiled
eggs; the French physicians would give hot drinks or cold
drinks, and enjoin close covering or no covering at all.
Each treatment seemed to be equally successful.

The doctors, recognizing that careful nursing was as important as skilful medical attendance, made many visits
simply of counsel and suggestion to their assistants. Nurses
were plentiful, and good ones easily obtained. The fever
did not attack negroes or quadroons, and white persons once
having the disease rarely suffered from it again. Thus there
was a large class of people available for ministering to the
sick. The Sisters of Charity received a special tribute
from the "Samaritan," though he was not of their religion.
"Chief above all," he writes, "do I record the praise of the
Sisters of Charity. . . . They do good by stealth. . . . I have
seen them in the silent rounds of duty, in the infirmaries,
hospitals, and rickety tenements of the poor, comforting
their own sex of all religions, castes, and conditions, fearless
of contamination, dressing loathsome wounds and inhaling
the most nauseating odors. . . . The world may be bad in
the main, but a redeeming feature is this institution, which
is as a golden connecting link between heaven and earth."[1]

Many strange experiences does this observer record.

---

[1] Diary of a Samaritan, p. 196.

His walk led him among the poor, but he found people of
education and refinement; he gave succor to a woman from
France whom he thought more beautiful than the Venus of
Praxiteles; he witnessed among destitute families the strongest attachments, the most bitter grief at separations, and the
most heroic self-sacrifice; he saw Christians die with heroism, and infidels without fear. The " Samaritan " was especially struck with the carelessness of an Italian soldier who,
though sick unto death and perfectly conscious, remained in
gay spirits, and attempted to cheer his companions in the
hospital by his philosophy. He spoke of quitting life as losing "a thing which none but fools would keep," and when
enjoined to sleep, replied, " Sleep! have we not all eternity
to sleep in ?"

The most incongruous circumstance which came under the
"Samaritan's" observation was the case of an old man who
was employed as a hospital nurse. The sick who were past
recovery had for him a serpent-like fascination : when there
was agony in the face or when the body writhed in contor-
tions, he would chuckle; when the fatal symptom of the
black vomit manifested itself, he grinned with a strange delight; and the death-rattle was music to his ear. It turned
out that the man had suffered from misfortune, deceit, and
ingratitude, and had become a hater of his kind, to whom
remained no joy but that of seeing his fellow-man in trouble
and in pain.

When all attempt to conceal the truth became useless, and
the full horror of the situation broke upon the people of
New Orleans, dismay and despair succeeded for a while
levity and hope. The newspapers, as if to atone for their
first silence, now spoke of nothing but the epidemic; the
editors studied the history of former plagues, and in their
articles imitated the many graphic accounts found in literature, which are remembered, not so much for their historical
and scientific value, as for the thrilling interest which the
writers have transfused into their narratives. The one item
of news anxiously awaited was the daily bulletin of the

Board of Health giving the interments of the day previous, which was posted up in many frequented places. As the number of deaths by the epidemic mounted up to an alarming degree, this intelligence caused blanched cheeks and sinking hearts. Business was suspended; the levee was a desert; pleasure was hardly thought of; the bar-room and club-houses were scarcely visited. Vice was cowed; the haunts of the libertine were deserted. One passion alone proved too strong for the prevailing fear to overcome: gambling held its votaries, the excitement of high play making them forget that the pestilence stalked through their city.

But the lawlessness, the bold and illicit indulgence in the pleasure of the moment, of which Thucydides speaks; the disregard of human laws and religious vows, the voluptuous riot which Boccaccio has related of the plague of Florence; the work of thieves and the excesses of blasphemers which augmented the horrors of the great plague of London, if De Foe's account be true—from all these New Orleans was spared. Mention is made, however, of hilarious parties who drove along the shell road to the lake to escape for a while the deadly atmosphere that hung over the doomed city. There, in a fine hotel, might gentlemen and ladies partake of dainty food and generous wines. Yet revelry which in ordinary times would be counted innocent jarred harshly on the ears in this season of distress. The streets of the city were given up to doctor's gigs, to cabs conveying the sick to the hospital and hearses carrying the dead to the grave. "The morning train of funerals," wrote the "Samaritan," "as was the evening's, crowded the road to the cemeteries. It was an unbroken line of carriages and omnibuses for two miles and a half." [1]

When the number of deaths grew rapidly, it was for a while impossible to bury the dead. The situation of the city below the level of the river, and the nature of the soil,

---

[1] Diary of a Samaritan, p. 152.

which is almost semi-fluid at the depth of two or three feet, added to the difficulty. The living brought the remains of their relatives and friends to the cemeteries, but men could not be had to dig the graves. The white laborers seemed to have disappeared; they were either dead, sick, or tending the sick. In some cases the mourners dug the graves for their own dead, and when the task was completed threw aside the spades, dropped on their knees, and solemnly repeated a funeral prayer. At times a dozen or more processions would meet at the cemetery; abuse of the authorities and strife for precedence marred sadly the impressiveness of the place and occasion. Quarrels became so frequent that it was necessary to detail a strong police force to preserve order at the graveyards.

But most horrible of all were the cases of the poor who had no friends, or of families who were all victims of the pestilence and were buried by the city authorities. The dead coming faster than they could be interred, seventy coffins were at one time left on the ground exposed to the powerful action of the August sun. The bodies swelled, the roughly constructed board coffins of the corporation burst open, and the poisonous effluvia were wafted by breezes from the lake over the stricken city. The attention of the public was drawn to this hideous scene; it called forth notices from the journals; the turgid style of the editors in describing this cumulation of horrors shows the excitement under which they labored. Order, however, was soon restored and a system adopted which prevented the recurrence of such dreadful incidents. The chain-gang was ordered to the work by the mayor; negroes were hired at five dollars per hour and an unstinted supply of strong liquor to bury the dead. Trenches, seven feet wide and one hundred feet long, were dug, into which the coffins were closely packed three to four feet deep, without intermediate earth.[1] The pits made by the corporation were not more than two feet

---

[1] Diary of a Samaritan, p. 151.

in depth. Custom soon reconciled the laborers to their work,
and moved them to ribald jokes more unseemly than the
jesting of the grave-diggers at Ophelia's grave. It was
strange that in this time of dire distress the poor should
have thought to object to the name of Potter's Field as
the place of interment for their relatives and friends, but
in the very height of the epidemic the designation of that
cemetery was officially changed to "Cypress Grove, Number 2."

"As we passed the cemeteries," wrote the "Samaritan,"
"we saw coffins piled up beside the gate and in the walks,
and laborers at work digging trenches in preparation for
the morrow's dead. . . . A fog, which hung over the moss-
enveloped oaks, prevented the egress of the dense and putrid
exhalations. The atmosphere was nauseating to a degree
that I have never noticed in a sick-room."[1] The experiences
of this month of August were the most awful in the event-
ful history of New Orleans. The city "was one vast charnel-
house."[2] Men now went around with carts, knocking at
every door and crying out, "Who have dead to bury?"
The atmosphere in the streets was stifling and fetid. Emigrants just landed were nearly all attacked by the plague.
Whole families died, leaving not a trace behind them; parents left young children who grew up, not only in ignorance
of a father or mother, but who never knew their own proper
names, or from what country they came. When the sub-
urbs and country were blasted with the fell disease, "the
poultry, horses, and mules fell dead in the fields."[3]

New Orleans was a field for heroism, nor was heroism
lacking. The rich gave money freely for the relief of the
destitute, the energetic devoted their time and ability for
the general good, and brave, hopeful souls cheered those
who were on the brink of despair. All accounts agree that,
with rare exceptions, the clergy of all denominations remained at their posts, ministering to the sick, smoothing

[1] Diary of a Samaritan, p. 187.   [2] Ibid., p. 209.   [3] Ibid., p. 186.

the pillow of the dying, and speaking words of comfort to the mourners. An excess of zeal led many to overwork, and these became an easy prey to the epidemic. Those who received aid from the Howard Association were nearly all Catholics, so that the "Samaritan" saw much of the labor and devotion of the priest, who was on duty from early morn until late at night; caring nothing for comforts, and seemingly above fatigue; working for the glory of his church and the relief of those in her communion; holding the crucifix before the eyes of the dying, and always on hand in the hospital to administer the rite of extreme unction. "The sympathy of the priest and the dying penitent was complete."

Thus wrote the "Samaritan," who felt deep gratitude for the assistance he received from ministers of a religion not his own. On one occasion, in response to an urgent request, he visited one of those unhappy women whom the more favored of their sex call the scourge, and whom philosophers have called the safeguard, of society. She had fallen a victim to the plague, but worse than the rage of the fever was her bitter remorse as she thought of the life she had quitted to become an inmate of a house of sin. She felt that her peace could not be made with Heaven until she had confessed and received absolution from a priest of the church, and she begged that such a one might be brought to her. The "Samaritan" went in search of a priest, and stated to him clearly who the woman was and in what manner of house she lived, expecting that objection would be made; but the good father quickly responded: "Such as you speak of have my readiest service, for truly do they stand in need of the consolations of religion." The priest shrived the patient, feeling rewarded that he had given peace to the soul of another Magdalene, and he could not murmur that, while the Angelus was ringing, she passed away.

When September came the weather changed and the fever was more successfully treated. But this epidemic lasted longer than its predecessors; sixty days was the usual term, but this did not cease its ravages until after three months. The 2d of September was observed as a day of fasting in response to a proclamation of the mayor calling upon all citizens to keep it "as a day of special prayer for the repose of the souls of the dead, for the stay of the epidemic, for the well-being of the survivors, and for gratitude that the hearts of so many have been led to share of their abundance with this afflicted city." The North had contributed money liberally for the work of the Howard Association. The board of health officially declared the city free of the epidemic on the 13th of October. The number of deaths from this visitation is variously stated, but no doubt remains that they exceeded eight thousand. Never before or since has New Orleans suffered so severely from the yellow fever. In making a comparison with other plagues, confusion arises from the fact that the actual population of the city and the number of unacclimated persons who remained during the epidemic are matters only of estimate; but it is not a rash assertion to make, that, reckoning the proportion of deaths to the probable number of people subject to the disease, the mortality of the yellow fever at New Orleans in 1853 was equal to that of the great plague of London or the yellow-fever epidemic at Philadelphia in 1798.[1]

---

[1] My authorities for this account of the yellow fever are, first and foremost, The Diary of a Samaritan (see p. 404, note); article by Dr. A. W. Ely, of New Orleans, *De Bow's Review*, Dec., 1853; an article in *Harper's Magazine*, Nov., 1853, by one who was present during the epidemic; the New Orleans *Picayune;* the New York *Times*, Sept., 1853, and March 3d, 1854; Dr. McFarlane in *De Bow's Review*, May, 1854; Dr. E. D. Fenner in *De Bow's Review*, July, 1854. I have derived valuable information on the yellow fever in general from vol. ii. of Principal Diseases of North America, by Dr. Daniel Drake. The New Orleans epidemic bears no comparison in severity with the great plague of the fourteenth century. "The plague [of 1348] raged in Florence from April to September. . . . The deaths in Florence averaged 600 a day; and three-fifths of the population are recorded to have perished." —History of Florence, T. A. Trollope, vol. ii. p. 90. "The memorable plague, described with so much eloquence by Giovanni Boccaccio, and

The prevalence of the yellow fever in the Southern cities excited much sympathy at the North, but it was not mixed with apprehension, for every one felt confident that the epidemic would be confined to the South. Political repose and signal activity in trade characterized the year. One of the victories of peace was the Industrial exhibition in the Crystal Palace at New York. It was a private enterprise, suggested by the London exhibition of 1851, and called by the high-sounding name of a World's Fair. The edifice was admirable. George William Curtis called it Aladdin's palace because of the light elegance in its architectural lines, which were "worthily surmounted and crowned by the dome." "It is," he adds, "a dome of Oriental characteristics. But there is nothing in architecture more pleasing. It seems to have been borne in upon a zephyr, and the slightest breath would lift it away. Blown like a bubble in some happy moment of a Jinn's inspiration, it floats over the whole, imparting an aerial grace, not to be comprehended without being seen." [1]

Rarely has there been a more creditable result to a specu-

---

by which Florence lost 96,000 souls." — History of Florence, Machiavelli. "In Florence there died of the black plague 60,000; in Venice, 100,000; in Paris, 50,000; in London, at least 100,000. . . . In all Germany, according to a probable calculation, there seem to have died only 1,244,-434 inhabitants; this country was, however, more spared than others. Italy, on the contrary, was most severely visited. It is said to have lost half of its inhabitants. . . . The whole period during which the black death raged with destructive violence in Europe was, with the exception of Russia, from the year 1347 to 1350. . . . Of all the estimates of the number of lives lost in Europe, the most probable is that altogether a fourth part of the inhabitants were carried off. It may be assumed without exaggeration that Europe lost during the black death 25,000,000 of inhabitants." — Hecker on the Black Death, Buckle's Commonplace Book, p. 557. The plague of 1349 "probably killed a third of the population" of England. The Economic Interpretation of History, Thorold Rogers, p. 22. See also article of Andrew D. White, *Popular Science Monthly*, Sept., 1891.

[1] *Harper's Magazine*, Nov., 1853, p. 844.

lative enterprise. No sooner was the building begun than a
furious speculation took place in the stock of the company.
The shares steadily advanced until they reached eighty per
cent. above par. The President opened the exhibition ; distinguished people from the country and Europe were present. It was not asserted that the fair would equal its London predecessor ; the head of the enterprise said that the
attempt was made to do on a smaller scale what had been
done so magnificently in London.[1] The exhibition commenced in midsummer, but at first the number of visitors
was small. The summer was hot, and in August there occurred a heated spell which put a stop to business and pleasure. Nearly everywhere at the North the mercury for several days rose to 100° in the shade ; in New York City two
hundred and thirty deaths were in one day caused by the
heat, and the mortality for a week was great.[2] When the
cooler days of September came, people began to attend the
exhibition and appreciate its value. Those who had sneered
at the enterprise now admired the display. The most
graceful commenter on passing events wrote that beneath
the dome of the Crystal Palace, " in cheerful rivalry meet
all the nations, as of old kings met upon a field of cloth of
gold. But this is a tournament of friendship ; this is a joust
of justice. Denmark sends the solemn group of Thorwald-
sen, and France her rarest and most delicate tapestries and
porcelains, and England her solid silver and earthen ware,
and hydra-headed Germany a hundred varieties in every
kind, and Italy, Belgium, and Holland each their best.
While America, like a host of infinitely various hospitality,
receives each with a kindred welcome, meeting the useful
and beautiful of every art and of every country upon its

---

[1] See article " Our Crystal Palace," by Parke Godwin, *Putnam's Magazine*, Aug., 1853.

[2] New York *Tribune, Harper's Magazine,* and *American Almanac.*
Official reports from the Smithsonian Institution show 1853 to be the
hottest summer since 1798. New Orleans *Picayune*, Aug. 23d, 1853.

own ground. . . . The true success of the exhibition lies in
its justification of the American pride. We have grown
tired of hearing that we were such a great nation; but the
Crystal Palace inclines us to tolerate the boast. It will
teach us the high-minded humility we want, by showing us
what actual and undeniable successes we have achieved.
Lyons and Manchester and Paris and Vienna must look to
their laurels."[1]

The material progress of the country was, indeed, great.
Railroads were building everywhere. The extension of the
system was bringing the rich grain-fields of the prairies into
easy communication with the seaboard; and as the iron rails
were laid westward, the comforts and luxuries of civilization
were brought within the reach of the pioneers. But the operation of the railroads left much to be desired. Travelling
was attended with danger. In the first eight months of the
year sixty-five fatal railroad accidents occurred, one hundred
and seventy-seven persons were killed, and three hundred
and thirty-three injured.[2] These accidents were for the
most part charged against the carelessness of the officials, the
greed of the directors, and the desire of the public for high
speed. "Our fast age is growing rapidly faster," wrote the
moralist of the time;[3] and while the journals and magazines inveighed against the railroad management, and each
casualty caused a fresh outburst of indignation, this was
succeeded by indifference, and nothing was done to remedy
the evil. It could hardly be denied, therefore, that a disregard of human life characterized the nation.

Contemporaneous with the glorification of our industries
by the Crystal Palace exhibition came a vigorous assertion
from the Secretary of State of the power and protection
afforded by American nationality, which caused deep exulta-
tation. Martin Koszta, a Hungarian, took part in the un-

---

[1] Editor's Easy Chair, *Harper's Magazine*, Nov., 1853, p. 844.
[2] New York *Herald*, quoted by *De Bow's Review*, Oct., 1853, p. 429.
[3] *Harper's Magazine*, July, 1853, p. 272.

successful revolution of 1848, escaped to Turkey, was confined there for a while, and then came to the United States,
where he declared, under oath and before a proper officer,
his intention to become a citizen of this country. After residing here nearly two years he returned to Smyrna, Turkey, upon business of a temporary nature, and placed himself under the protection of the American consul. The
Austrian consul-general tried to get authority from the
Turkish governor for his arrest, but, failing in this, insti-
gated some desperadoes to kidnap him. He was taken on
board the Austrian brig-of-war the *Huszar*, and put in irons.
The American representatives made the proper protests, but
the demand for his release was unsuccessful. Meanwhile
there arrived in the harbor of Smyrna the United States
sloop-of-war *Saint Louis*, under the command of Captain
Ingraham, who, becoming convinced that a design was set
on foot by the Austrian officials to remove Koszta clandes-
tinely to Trieste, an Austrian port, demanded his release,
and to enforce it brought the guns of the *Saint Louis* to
bear upon the *Huszar*. A compromise, however, was effected, by virtue of which the prisoner was delivered to the custody of the French consul-general until the two governments
should agree in regard to his disposal. The Austrian government addressed to various courts a protest against the
action of Captain Ingraham, and instructed Hülsemann, the
imperial *chargé d'affaires* at Washington, to ask the government of the United States "not to interpose any obstacle to
the extradition of Koszta to Austria," "to disavow the conduct of its agents," and "to call them to a severe account
and tender to Austria a satisfaction proportionate to the magnitude of the outrage." Such an opportunity could make
Marcy well believe that the stars were in his favor. Ardently desiring the next Democratic nomination for President, he set himself to write a diplomatic paper that should
gain the good-will of the people. He acquitted himself,
however, with credit and dignity, equal to that of Webster
and Everett on similar occasions. His reply to Hülsemann

I.—27

is a state-paper carefully considered and clearly expressed; and while it may be criticised as raising too many questions, the main reason for refusing Austria's request is cogently argued, and, to an American, his position seems irrefutable. This manifesto had a remarkable reception, not confined to section or party, and for the moment Marcy was certainly the most popular man in the United States.

From a careful and precise statement of the facts, the Secretary of State shows that "Koszta was seized without any rightful authority." And although he had not yet become a naturalized citizen, he had established his domicile in the United States and become thereby clothed with the national character; "he retained that character when he was seized at Smyrna; . . . he acquired the right to claim protection from the United States, and they had the right to extend it to him." The course of Captain Ingraham was fully justified, the disavowal of the acts of American agents refused, the satisfaction asked for by Austria respectfully declined, and the request to put no obstacles in the way of the delivery of Koszta to the Austrian consul-general at Smyrna was denied. Marcy made one declaration which has the flavor of the stump-speech, but it was of a nature to thrill the American heart with delight, for never had the national aggressiveness been so strong as at this time. "Whenever," he wrote, "by the operation of the law of nations, an individual becomes clothed with our national character, be he a native-born or naturalized citizen, an exile driven from his early home by political oppression, or an emigrant enticed from it by the hopes of a better fortune for himself and his posterity, he can claim the protection of this government, and it may respond to that claim without being obliged to explain its conduct to any foreign power; for it is its duty to make its nationality respected by other nations and respectable in every quarter of the globe." Yet there was little of buncombe about Marcy's paper. His important point was well taken and has been sustained by eminent American authorities on international law; and his

successors in the State department have followed the principle he laid down. In the end Koszta was allowed to return to the United States. Congress showed its satisfaction
by a joint resolution thanking Captain Ingraham and conferring on him a medal.[1]

The President needed all the glory he could get from the
State department to prevent his administration from sinking
into contempt. Undoubtedly the most popular man in the
country when he delivered his inaugural address, he was,
by the time that he sent his first message to Congress, regarded by most of the leaders of his own party as incom-
petent for his position. To distribute the offices in a manner that should subserve the best interests of the party

---

[1] See Executive Documents, 1st Sess. 33d Cong., vol. i. part 1, House
Document 1. Marcy's doctrine is approved by Woolsey, International
Law, § 81, and in a qualified way by G. B. Davis, Outlines of International
Law, p. 105. Calvo, the eminent South American authority, sustains
Marcy. See Wharton, § 198. Halleck's International Law, edited by
Sir Sherston Baker, Bart., an English barrister, thoroughly supports
Marcy's position, and says the allegations of the Austrian government
" were most clearly and satisfactorily disproved in the masterly despatch
of Mr. Marcy," vol. i. p. 202. See also Boyd's edition of Wheaton; also
Woolsey's International Law, sixth edition (1891), Appendix III. Hall,
however, an English authority, says, "Marcy's contention was wholly
destitute of legal foundation," International Law, § 72. Marcy's position
is questioned by Von Holst, vol. iv. p. 280, who adds: "The question is
permissible, too, whether both Ingraham and the President would not
have proceeded more gently if they had had to do with England instead
of Austria." This statement leads me to emphasize what I have already
alluded to in the text. The fact is, that the American of 1853 feared no
nation, and thought his country fully able to cope with any European
power. Marcy was too good a lawyer and too just a man to take an un-
tenable attitude towards a weak nation, and too brave not to maintain the
rights of his country against a strong nation. Moreover, nothing pleased
one section of the Democratic party better than to defy England; and as
the Crimean war was already looming in the distance, no Democratic
Secretary of State would have bated a jot of a just demand on England.
For public opinion in the matter, see Harper's Magazine, Nov., 1853,
p. 834, and Dec., 1853, p. 130; also the debate in Congress.

would have been an herculean task for a wise man, but the inherent difficulty of the situation was increased by the President's lack of executive ability. He would make up his mind in the morning and change it in the afternoon. He would receive an applicant for office effusively, put on his most urbane manner, listen to the claim with attention, giving the aspirant for public place every reason to feel that the position was surely his. For Franklin Pierce could not say no; and when he was not able to give a direct promise, he would give an implied one. This failing caused him trouble without end. In more than one case the same important office was promised to two different men, and indirect assurances of executive favor were almost as numerous as visitors at the White House.

It was a common saying that Pierce treated everybody with the same marked kindness and seeming confidence.[1] People soon perceived that the President lacked firmness, and by the time that Congress assembled there had arisen general distrust of his capacity. No one could deny that he had grown less by his elevation, like a little statue on a great pedestal.

In New York State, Pierce was accused of being tinctured with Free-soilism, because in the distribution of the patronage his personal affiliations had led him to lean to the faction of Softs. Marcy's influence, moreover, was very apparent and was exercised in a manner to take care of the faction of which he was the admitted chief. But in Massachusetts the liberty-loving Democrats were alienated; for Cushing, who unquestionably had the ear of the President, had written a letter which gave no uncertain sound on the slavery question. " If," wrote the Attorney-General, " there be any purpose more fixed than another in the mind of the President and those with whom he is accustomed to consult, it is that that dangerous element of abolitionism, under whatever

---

[1] "The President has a *very* winning way in his manners."—Seward to his wife, March 30th, 1853, Life of Seward, vol. ii. p. 202.

guise or form it may present itself, shall be crushed out so far as this administration is concerned." [1]

In one part of the South, however, Pierce was regarded as an abolitionist, for it was believed that John Van Buren, the soul of the Democratic Free-soil movement, was closeted daily with him and had undisguised influence with the administration; while in Mississippi, where the contest between the Union and the secession faction had been bitter, it was thought that Pierce had thrown himself into the arms of the states-rights men, from his avowed political and personal friendship with Jefferson Davis. [2]   But in spite of factional disaffection, the position of the President and the Democratic party was apparently an enviable one when Congress came together on the first Monday of December. In the Senate there were thirty-seven Democrats, twenty-one Whigs, and two Free-soilers; in the House there were one hundred and fifty-nine Democrats, seventy-one Whigs, and four Free-soilers. Moreover, the unpopularity of the administration with the leaders and politicians of the party had not spread to the mass of voters.   Indeed, it would not have been surprising had the Democrats lost ground in the elections of 1853 as compared with their remarkable success one year earlier.   After such an astounding victory, under ordinary circumstances even, a reaction might have been expected.   It is now a maxim in American politics that the first year of a new administration is the trying one; and it was undeniable that the difficulties of the unfavorable year had been increased by many unwise acts on the part of the President.   Yet with one notable exception, there was no evidence of this in the State elections of the year, for where they occurred every State that had voted for Pierce but New York went Democratic.   Here the Hards and Softs each nominated a State ticket, which resulted in a plurality

---

[1] This letter was published in the New York *Tribune* of Nov. 3d.

[2] See Foote's speech at a public dinner at Washington, Richmond *Whig*, Jan. 24th, 1854.

for the Whigs, but the combined Democratic vote was thirty thousand in excess of that received by the Whig candidates. As a partial set-off, Tennessee, which Scott had carried, now elected a Democratic governor, and some States gave increased Democratic majorities as compared with the presidential year. Thus, the Democrats had not only the executive and a large majority in Congress, but they had the governors and the legislatures of nearly every State.

The President in his message to Congress mentioned that negotiations were on foot with Great Britain to settle a dispute about the fisheries and certain embarrassing questions which had arisen between the two governments regarding Central America. The relations with Spain were touched upon lightly, and no inkling was given of the scheme of which the minds of the President and his Southern advisers were full. There being a surplus of revenue over expenditures, it was Pierce's opinion that the reduction of the tariff was a matter of great importance, and he asked a careful and candid consideration of the plan of the Secretary of the Treasury, which was "to reduce the duties on certain articles, and to add to the free list many articles now taxed, and especially such as enter into manufactures, and are not largely, or at all, produced in this country." He also recommended to Congress that it should aid by all constitutional means the construction of a railroad to the Pacific coast.

This Congress would have been notable for a reduction of the tariff, and still more notable for giving a start to a railroad across the continent, had there not been in the Senate a man powerful enough to change the course of history.

The Democratic party now occupied high vantage-ground. It certainly never entered the heads of that party's magnates that anything could endanger its supremacy in the government for many years; and he would have been indeed a rash Whig who cast a doubt on the prediction that the Democrats had secured for themselves a long lease of power. The nearly unanimous opinion of the country was that he who should receive the Democratic nomination for President in 1856 would be elected, and that without a formidable opposition. Never in the history of the party, when the nomination had been open to active competition, had it seemed so glittering and sure a prize. Pierce had tasted the sweets of office and wanted to succeed himself.[1] Puffed up with the vanity of power, looking on everything with an optimistic eye, full of good humor with himself and the world, he little dreamed of the attacks on him which were whispered in corners or talked openly on the streets.[2] If he saw, or heard of, the criticisms in the newspapers of his own party, he could ascribe them in the main to ungratified desires; and before Democratic members, on the floor of the House, called in question his motives and policy, a public measure engrossed his attention and made this factional contest seem like a petty quarrel.

The four prominent candidates of 1852 still cast longing eyes on the next Democratic nomination for President. Marcy[3] felt that he had gained an advantage in the Koszta affair; but if Cuba could be honorably acquired, he was certain that the people would call him, instead of the President, the second Jefferson.

Buchanan had accepted the English mission with reluctance, because the negotiations in regard to all the disputed questions between this country and Great Britain had not been put in his hands. The Central American affair was

---

[1] As early as May, 1853, this was noted by Buchanan: "I had not been in Washington many days before I clearly discovered that the President and his cabinet were intent upon his renomination and re-election."— Life of Buchanan, Curtis, vol. ii. p. 80.

[2] An occasional correspondent of the New York *Evening Post*, who knew Pierce well, gives a noteworthy account of the impression he got on seeing the President at about this time. See the *Post*, Feb. 13th, 1854.

[3] Buchanan thought in May, 1853, that Governor Marcy would "probably cherish until the day of his death the anxious desire to become President."—Curtis, vol. ii. p. 80.

confided to him, but out of that little glory was to be had.[1]
He had written a public letter stating his intention to retire
from active politics on the completion of his mission,[2] but
his rivals regarded those expressions as conventional rather
than sincere. A private letter written by Buchanan soon
after his arrival in England is evidence that he mentally reserved a loop-hole through which he might evade this positive declaration. " I have neither the desire nor the intention," he wrote, " again to become a candidate for the presidency. On the contrary, this mission is tolerable to me alone
because it will enable me gracefully and gradually to retire
from an active participation in party politics. . . . But
while these are the genuine sentiments of my heart, I do
not think I ought to say that in no imaginable state of circumstances would I consent to be nominated as a candidate." [3]

General Cass had not yet given up all hope of the presidency, and there was considerable rivalry between him and
Douglas, as they were both representatives of the Northwest. Douglas was the boldest of all the aspirants, and on
the 1st day of January, 1854, of the five candidates for the
Democratic succession he was the least popular with the
South. He had not grown in favor since 1852, when he had
the smallest following from that section in the convention
which nominated Pierce. Although Douglas had married a
Southern lady and had agreeable personal relations at the
South, the politicians did not trust him. It may be that
they thought he was too practical a champion of free labor,
for he liked to boast of his early poverty and the fact that
when a boy he had worked at a trade. The result of the
previous convention, however, had taught Douglas that he
could not be nominated without the aid of Southern votes.
He might get nearly the whole support of the West and he
might hope for assistance from New York, but he could ex-

---

[1] Life of Buchanan, Curtis, vol. ii. p. 92 *et ante.*   [2] Ibid., p. 93.

[3] Letter to Ben: Perley Poore, Reminiscences, vol. i. p. 437.

pect nothing from New England and Pennsylvania. While the term "the solid South" had not come into use, politicians were beginning to think what a force there might be in the fact. The South would have one hundred and seventeen votes in the next convention, and, it being pretty well understood that there was no chance of the nomination of a Southern man, it was evident that if this strength could be concentrated on a favorite son of the North, it would, added to his home support, assure him the nomination. Thoughts and calculations like these must have passed through Douglas's mind during his trip of recreation to Europe the preceding summer; and when he came to Washington to survey the ground, one way was manifest in which he might commend himself to Southern favor. The acquisition of Cuba was out of his province. While free trade was popular at the South, the senator had no taste for economical questions, and the Pacific railroad was a Western measure. But the organization of the new territories might be handled in a satisfactory manner; this, moreover, was the favorite field of Douglas, and he was chairman of the committee on territories. A bill for the organization of the territory of Nebraska had passed the House at the previous session and was reported to the Senate. This bill was in the usual form, but made no reference whatever to slavery. It encountered opposition in the Senate, as involving bad faith with the Indians; and as it came up late in the session, there was not sufficient time for its consideration, so it failed to become a law. The same bill was introduced into the Senate in December, 1853, and referred to the committee on territories.[1] On the 4th of January, 1854, Douglas made a report which was the introduction to a project whose importance cannot

---

[1] It is well to bear in mind that so far as any affirmative legislation was concerned, the committee on territories was Douglas. It was composed of Douglas, Johnson of Arkansas, Jones of Iowa, Houston, Democrats, and Bell and Everett, Whigs. The last three named are well-known men, but were all opposed to the Nebraska bill.

be overestimated. The territory of Nebraska comprised what is now [1] the States of Kansas, Nebraska, the Dakotas, Montana, part of Colorado, and Wyoming. It was part of the Louisiana purchase, and contained four hundred and eighty-five thousand square miles, a territory more than ten times as large as New York, and larger by thirty-three thousand square miles than all the free States then in the Union east of the Rocky Mountains. In this magnificent domain were less than one thousand white inhabitants; but as soon as it should be opened to settlement by proper legislation, there was certain to be a large immediate increase of population.[2]

This report of Douglas began with the announcement of the discovery of a great principle which had been established by the compromise measures of 1850. They " were intended to have a far more comprehensive and enduring effect than the mere adjustment of difficulties arising out of the recent acquisition of Mexican territory. They were designed to establish certain great principles, which would not only furnish adequate remedies for existing evils, but, in all time to come, avoid the perils of similar agitation by withdrawing the question of slavery from the halls of Congress and the political arena, committing it to the arbitration of those who were immediately interested in, and alone responsible for, its consequences. . . . A question has arisen in regard to the right to hold slaves in the territory of Nebraska, when the Indian laws shall be withdrawn and the country thrown open to emigration and settlement. . . . It is a disputed point whether slavery is prohibited in the Nebraska country by *valid* enactment. . . . In the opinion of those

---

[1] In 1890.

[2] One of the objections made to the organization of the territory was on account of insufficient population, but it was not well taken. Douglas was well informed on this point, and showed clearly that if the restrictions in favor of the Indians were removed, there would be a large influx of settlers. Benton, who opposed the Nebraska bill of Douglas, was positive that a territorial government ought to be at once established for Nebraska. See *Harper's Magazine*, Dec., 1853, p. 121.

eminent statesmen who hold that Congress is invested with no rightful authority to legislate upon the subject of slavery in the territories, the eighth section of the act preparatory to the admission of Missouri is null and void." The reader may be reminded that the gist of the Missouri Compromise lay in this eighth section, which provided that slavery should be prohibited in all the Louisiana territory lying north of 36° 30' north latitude, not included within the limits of the State of Missouri. The report of Douglas continued: "The prevailing sentiment in large portions of the Union sustains the doctrine that the Constitution of the United States secures to every citizen an inalienable right to move into any of the territories with his property, of whatever kind and description, and to hold and enjoy the same under the sanction of law." Yet the committee did not propose to recommend the affirmation or the repeal of the eighth section of the Missouri act. The report concluded with the statement, "The compromise measures of 1850 affirm and rest upon the following propositions:

"First—That all questions pertaining to slavery in the territories, and the new States to be formed therefrom, are to be left to the decision of the people residing therein, by their appropriate representatives, to be chosen by them for that purpose.

"Second—That 'all cases involving title to slaves' and 'questions of personal freedom' are to be referred to the jurisdiction of the local tribunals, with the right of appeal to the Supreme Court of the United States.

"Third—That the provision of the Constitution of the United States in respect to fugitives from service is to be carried into faithful execution in all 'the organized territories,' the same as in the States."

The bill reported by the committee as first printed contained the provision that the territory of Nebraska, or any portion of the same, when admitted as a State or States, "shall be received into the Union with or without slavery, as their Constitution may prescribe at the time of their admission." This language was borrowed from the Utah and New Mexico bills, which were a part of the compromise of 1850. Three days after the bill was first printed another section was added, which incorporated into the bill these closing propositions of the committee's report.

Douglas professed to have discovered a way by which the slavery question might be put to rest. But everybody North and South, as well as Douglas himself, knew that this report would certainly open up again the agitation. The country was at peace. Business was good; evidences of smiling prosperity were everywhere to be seen. The spirit of enterprise was rampant; great works were in progress, others were projected. Political repose was a marked feature of the situation. The slavery question seemed settled, and the dream of the great compromisers of 1850 seemed to be realized. Every foot of land in the States or in the territories seemed to have, so far as slavery was concerned, a fixed and settled character. The obnoxious part of the compromise to the North, the Fugitive Slave law, was no longer resisted. Another era of good feeling appeared to have set in. The earnest hope of Clay, that the work in which he had so large a share would give the country rest from slavery agitation for a generation, did not seem vain. There has been restored, said the President in his message, "a sense of repose and security to the public mind throughout the confederacy." This quiet was ruthlessly disturbed by the report of Douglas, which, although it professed in one part not to repeal the Missouri Compromise, closed with a proposition which certainly set it aside. The Missouri Compromise forever prohibited slavery in what was now the territory of Nebraska. Douglas proposed to leave to the inhabitants of Nebraska the decision as to whether or not they would have slavery. From the circumstances under which the Missouri Compromise was enacted, from the fact that it received the seal of constitutionality from an impartial President and a thoroughly representative cabinet, it had been looked upon as having the moral force of an article of the Constitution itself. For what purpose was the repose of the country disturbed by throwing a doubt on the constitutionality and application of an act which had been acquiesced in and observed by both parties to the compact for thirty-four years?

The motives which actuate men who alter the current of their time are ever an interesting study; and in this case no confidential letters or conversations need be unearthed to arrive at a satisfactory explanation. We may use the expression of the Independent Democrats in Congress and say that the dearest interests of the people were made "the mere hazards of a presidential game;" or we may employ the words of John Van Buren, an astute politician who was in the secrets of the party, and ask, " Could anything but a desire to buy the South at the presidential shambles dictate such an outrage?"[1]   And this true statement and the inference from this trenchant question explain the motives prompting Douglas to this action. Even those who were very friendly to the measure did not scruple openly to express this opinion. One wrote that Douglas had betrayed " an indiscreet and hasty ambition;"[2] another granted that the object of Douglas " was to get the inside track in the South."[3]   The defences made by Douglas and his friends at the time and in the succeeding years, when his political prospects depended upon the justification of his course, are shuffling and delusive. None are satisfactory, and it may

---

[1] Private letter of John Van Buren to ex-Senator Clemens, Feb. 3d, 1854, published in the New York *Evening Post*, Feb. 11th, 1854.

[2] Washington correspondence Richmond *Enquirer*, quoted by Richmond *Whig*, Jan. 31st, 1854. I am indebted to the New York Historical Society for permission to examine their file of the Richmond *Whig*.

[3] New York *Herald*, Feb. 21st. I am indebted to the Society Library of New York for permission to examine their file of the New York *Herald* and the New York *Courier and Enquirer*. These expressions were used after the formal repeal of the Missouri Compromise had been incorporated into the Kansas-Nebraska bill.

with confidence be affirmed that the action of the Illinois senator was a bid for Southern support in the next Democratic convention. In truth, Douglas might have used the words of Frederick the Great when he began the unjust war against Austria for the conquest of Silesia : " Ambition, interest, the desire of making people talk about me, carried the day, and I decided " to renew the agitation of slavery.

Douglas subsequently, veiling his own ambition under the wish to promote the interests of the Democratic party, confessed in part the truth of this impeachment. He said " that his party, in the election of Pierce, had consumed all its powder, and therefore, without a deep-reaching agitation, it would have no more ammunition for its artillery." [1] Yet it was patent to every one—and none knew it better than Douglas, for he was the ablest politician of the party—that the Democrats needed to make no fresh issue ; that to let things drift along and not turn them into new channels was the safest course, and that appeals to past history were the best of arguments. An economical administration, a reduction of the tariff, a vigorous and just foreign policy, were certain to keep the Democrats in power as long as man could foresee. There was, it is true, one element of uncertainty. The factious quarrel in New York had led to defeat at the last State election ; but the party was so strong that even without the Empire State it could retain its ascendency in the nation, and there was, moreover, good reason to hope that this trouble would be patched up before another presidential election.

To become the acknowledged and dominating leader of so strong a party seemed to an ardent partisan an object worthy of any exertion and any sacrifice. It was the ambition of Douglas to hold the same position among the Democrats that Clay had held among the Whigs. Clay attained that position by being the originator of important legislative

---

[1] Kapp, Geschichte der Sklaverei, quoted by Von Holst, vol. iv. p. 313. This was in the fall of 1855.

measures and by carrying them to a successful issue. The
ability of Douglas lay in this direction, and he, like Clay,
was a natural leader of men. Indeed, they were men of
similar parts, strong natures whose private vices were
hardly hidden. But Clay had profound moral convictions
which, although sometimes set at naught in the heat of
partisan conflict, were of powerful influence in his political
career; in the view of Douglas, moral ideas had no place in
politics.

Douglas prepared the bill without consultation with any
Southern men. First submitted to two Western senators,
after their approval was given, it was shown to their Southern friends.[1] It became the object of some of those opposed
to the Nebraska bill to show that the project was dictated
by the South. Much credence was given to a boast of senator Atchison, made under the inspiration of the invisible
spirit of wine, that he had forced Douglas to bring in such
a bill.[2] It was also charged that Toombs and Stephens had
been the potent influence which had brought about the ac-

---

[1] This was the statement of Douglas in the Senate in 1856, *Congressional Globe*, vol. xxxiii. p. 393. I have never seen any well-attested evidence which contradicts this statement. Butler, of South Carolina, said
in the Senate during the debate: "I have had very little to do with this
bill, and I believe the South has had very little to do with the provisions
of the bill." At the time of the greatest unpopularity of this legislation,
Douglas said in the Senate (Feb. 23d, 1855): "The Nebraska bill was
not concocted in any conclave, night or day. It was written by myself,
at my own house, with no man present. Whatever odium there is attached to it, I assume it. Whatever of credit there may be, let the public award it where they think it belongs." The earliest premonition of
the report which I have found is in the New York *Herald* of Jan. 2d,
1854: "It is understood that the territory of Nebraska is to be admitted
into the confederacy upon such terms as will leave it at the option of her
people to make it either a slave or free territory."

[2] This speech was made at Atchison, Kan., Sept. 26th, 1854, reported
in the Parkville *Luminary* Sept. 26th, copied in the New York *Tribune*
Oct. 10th; see also the New York *Tribune*, June 4th, 1855, and see Wilson's remarks in the Senate, April 14th, 1856.

tion. The Illinois senator, in April, 1856, denied both of these imputations,[1] and all the circumstances support the truth of this denial.[2]   Douglas was a man of too much independence to suffer the dictation of Atchison, Toombs, or Stephens.   He always wanted to lead, and was never content to follow.

Immediately on the publication of the report the anti-slavery people of the North took alarm.   The newspapers which were devoted to freedom saw the point at once and made clear the scheme which was in progress.   One journal said it was a " proposition to turn the Missouri Compromise into a juggle and a cheat ;" it was "presented in so bold and barefaced shape that it is quite as much an insult as it is a fraud."[3]   Another called it an overt attempt to override the Missouri Compromise.[4]   Another termed the project low trickery, which deluded the South with the idea that it would legalize slavery in Nebraska, and at the same time cheated the North "with a thin pretence of not repealing the existing prohibition."[5]   The anti-slavery press responded more quickly than the people whose sentiment they both represented and led.   The people of the South were as much surprised at the report as those of the North.   Not counting upon Douglas as one of their adherents through thick and thin, they at first viewed the proposition with distrust,

[1] *Congressional Globe*, vol. xxxiii. p. 393.

[2] In 1886, Jefferson Davis, in a letter to a friend, said : " So far as I know and believe, Douglas and Atchison never were in such relation to each other as would have caused Douglas to ask Atchison's help in preparing the bill, and I think the whole discussion shows that Douglas originated the bill, and for a year or two vaunted himself on its paternity."—Memoir of Jefferson Davis, by his wife, vol. i. p. 671.

[3] New York *Evening Post*, Jan. 7th, 1854.

[4] New York *Tribune*, Jan. 11th, 1854.

[5] New York *Independent*, Jan. 7th. The *Herald*, which approved of the report of Douglas, said : " Senator Douglas's report has created a great sensation among the abolitionists and their aiders and abettors in this city. Already the *Post* and *Tribune*—and the *Times* will soon follow with the other abolitionist organs—are out in full swoop against the report."

and some even regarded it as "a snare set for the South."[1] But the senators and representatives from the slave-holding States understood the matter better than the people and the press, and knew that Douglas had taken a long stride in their direction. As he could not retrace his steps, he could therefore be easily influenced to alter his bill in a manner that should make it conform pretty nearly to their cherished wish.

On Monday, the 16th of January, Dixon, a Whig senator from Kentucky, who was filling the unexpired term of Henry Clay, offered an amendment to the Nebraska act, which provided in set terms for the repeal of the slavery-restriction feature of the Missouri Compromise. The Senate was astonished and Douglas was startled. He went at once to Dixon's seat and remonstrated courteously against the amendment. He said that in his bill he had used almost the same words which were employed in the Utah and New Mexico acts; and as they were a part of the compromise measures of 1850, he hoped that Dixon, who had been a zealous friend of that adjustment, would do nothing to interfere with it or weaken it before the country. Dixon replied that it was precisely because he was a zealous friend of the compromise of 1850 that he had introduced the amendment; in his view, the Missouri Compromise, unless expressly repealed, would continue to operate in the Territory of Nebraska; and while the bill of Douglas affirmed the principle of non-intervention, this amendment was necessary to carry it legitimately into effect. That being the well-considered opinion of Dixon, he was determined to insist upon his amendment.[2]

On the 17th of January, Sumner offered an amendment to

---

[1] Richmond *Whig*, Jan. 20th; also see Cullom's speech, *Congressional Globe*, vol. xxix. p. 54.

[2] Letter of Dixon to Henry S. Foote, Sept. 30th, 1858, Spring's Kansas, p. 3; Life of Douglas, by a Member of the Western Bar, New York, 1860. Dixon's letter is referred to by Nicolay and Hay, in History of Lincoln, as having been published in the Louisville *Democrat*, Oct. 3d, 1858.

I.—28

the Nebraska act which expressly affirmed the slavery restriction of the Missouri Compromise.

A few days after Dixon had surprised the Senate, Douglas called to see him and invited him to take a drive. The conversation turned upon the subject which was uppermost in their minds, and, to the great delight of Dixon, the Illinois senator proposed to take charge of his amendment and incorporate it in the Nebraska bill. As Dixon reports the familiar talk, Douglas in substance said: "I have become perfectly satisfied that it is my duty, as a fair-minded national statesman, to co-operate with you as proposed in securing the repeal of the Missouri Compromise restriction. It is due to the South; it is due to the Constitution, heretofore palpably infracted; it is due to that character for *consistency* which I have heretofore labored to maintain. The repeal, if we can effect it, will produce much stir and commotion in the free States of the Union for a season. I shall be assailed by demagogues and fanatics there, without stint or moderation. Every opprobrious epithet will be applied to me. I shall probably be hung in effigy in many places. It is more than probable that I may become permanently odious among those whose friendship and esteem I have heretofore possessed. This proceeding may end my political career. But, acting under the sense of duty which animates me, I am prepared to make the sacrifice; I will do it." Dixon relates that Douglas spoke in an earnest and touching manner; the Kentucky senator was deeply affected and showed emotion in the reply that he made. "Sir," he said, "I once recognized you as a demagogue, a mere party manager, selfish, and intriguing. I now find you a warm-hearted and sterling patriot. Go forward in the pathway of duty as you propose, and though all the world desert you, *I never will.*"[1]

It was a pretty comedy. The words of Douglas are those of a self-denying patriot, and not those of a man who was

---

[1] Letter of Dixon, Life of Douglas, p. 172.

sacrificing the peace of his country, and, as it turned out, the success of his party, to his own personal ambition. Between the Monday on which the amendment repealing the Missouri Compromise was introduced, and the day of the drive with Dixon, Douglas resolved to take a further step in the path on which he had entered. Of course, all sorts of influences were brought to bear upon him by Southern men, and there was one powerful argument from the Democratic point of view. While the difference between Democrats and Whigs at the South was no longer essential, the party organizations remained intact, and each endeavored to win an advantage over the other by taking more pronounced ground in the interest of slavery. It would not do, therefore, to have a measure of so obvious advantage to the South fathered by a Whig, even by one who truly felt, as he afterwards stated in the Senate: " Upon the question of slavery, I know no Whiggery and I know no Democracy." This and other arguments undoubtedly had their influence on Douglas; but, in truth, he had laid out his course when he made the report of the 4th of January. He had then crossed the Rubicon; he was now preparing to burn his bridges behind him.

Unquestionably Douglas would have preferred to stand on the proposition as at first introduced. It is the testimony of two personal and political friends that he was reluctant to incorporate in his bill a clause virtually repealing the Missouri Compromise.[1] The ambiguous character of the first project was not without design, and suited his purpose exactly. At the South it could be paraded as a measure in her interest, while at the North there might be honest differences of opinion whether or not the slavery restriction was set aside; and in the inception of this movement it is probable that Douglas thought that, no matter what legislation was had, none but free States would be formed out of

---

[1] Cox, Three Decades of Federal Legislation, p. 49; Foote, Casket of Reminiscences, p. 93.

this territory. This was certainly his opinion in 1850, when he maintained that "the Missouri Compromise had no practical bearing upon the question of slavery—it neither curtailed nor extended it an inch. Like the ordinance of 1787, it did the South no harm, the North no good."[1] And in the same speech he expressed the opinion that the Nebraska territory would be forever free, and out of it would be formed at least six free States. It was rumored at the time, and was always believed by many of the friends of Douglas, that what finally decided him to shape the bill in accordance with Dixon's views was because he had reason to believe that if he did not take that step Cass would forestall him, support the repeal of the Missouri Compromise, and thereby gain an important advantage in the race for the Democratic nomination.[2]

Douglas had written his report and prepared his first bill without any consultation with the President, but the rising tide of Northern sentiment against the measure, and the certainty that the murmur would become a roar, admonished him that nothing could be safely omitted which would aid the passage of the act through both houses of Congress. He felt confident that success in the Senate was certain, but the power and influence of the administration might be necessary to insure a majority in the House. He sought, therefore, the assistance of the President. Pierce, through his own organ, the Washington *Union*, which faithfully represented his opinions,[3] had approved the report of the com-

---

[1] Speech on the compromise measures, March 13th, 1850.

[2] This was a view presented to me by ex-Senator Bradbury, of Maine. Cass regarded the rumor of enough importance to deny it in open Senate. "I am aware," he said, "it was reported that I intended to propose the repeal of the Missouri Compromise; but it was an error. My intentions were wholly misunderstood."—*Congressional Globe*, vol. xxix. p. 270. See also the St. Louis *Democrat*, quoted in the New York *Tribune* of Jan. 30th; also Washington *Union*, Jan. 19th, referred to in Nicolay and Hay's History of Lincoln, *Century Magazine*, vol. xi. p. 699.

[3] "While I was one of the editors of the National Democratic organ

mittee on territories;[1] but he did not regard with favor the amendment of Dixon, and on January 20th the *Union* argued against it.[2]

On Sunday morning, January 22d, Douglas, in company with other gentlemen, members of Congress, called on Jefferson Davis, and stated to him the proposed change in the Nebraska bill. They further desired that he would procure them on that day an interview with the President, who, as they knew, was strictly opposed to receiving visits or discussing political affairs on Sunday; but it was highly important to introduce the substitute on the following day, and Douglas would not do so without consulting the President. Davis went with them to the White House. He stood on such friendly footing with Pierce that the door was always open to him, and, leaving his companions in the reception-room, he proceeded at once to the private apartments of the President and unfolded the object of their visit. Afterwards the President met the gentlemen, listened

---

during Pierce's administration, Attorney-General Cushing, although deeply immersed in the business of his department, hardly let a day pass without sending me an editorial on some subject."—Forney, Anecdotes of Public Men, vol. i. p. 229.

[1] Douglas "has arrived at conclusions which seem to us unassailable. . . . We commend Mr. Douglas's report not only for the ability with which it is prepared, but for the sound, national, Union-loving sentiments with which it abounds."—Washington *Union*, Jan. 5th.

"The Nebraska bill is drawn upon the same principles [*i. e.*, those of 1850] and presents an opportunity for a practical vindication of the policy of the administration."—Ibid., Jan. 6th.

[2] "To repeal the Missouri Compromise might, and according to our view would, clear the principle of congressional non-intervention of all embarrassment; but we doubt whether the good thus promised is so important that it would be wise to seek it through the agitation which necessarily stands in our path. Upon a calm review of the whole ground, we yet see no such reasons for disturbing the compromise of 1850 as could induce us to advocate either of the amendments proposed to Mr. Douglas's bill." — Washington *Union*, Jan. 20th. The amendments referred to are Dixon's and Sumner's.

to the reading of the bill, gave attention to the arguments of Douglas explanatory of the proposed alteration, and in the end promised the support of the administration.[1] We may feel certain, however, that it was the persuasion of Davis at the private interview which induced the President to give his approval. He could not have forgotten that, less than two months previously, when in his message he mentioned that in regard to the slavery and sectional question there had been "restored a sense of repose and security to the public mind throughout the confederacy," he had added, "That this repose is to suffer no shock during my official term, if I have power to avert it, those who placed me here may be assured." On this Sunday he had the power to fulfil the solemn pledge he had given the nation and its representatives; but his hankering after a renomination made him easily susceptible to the influences which were brought to bear upon him.

Douglas had reckoned wisely when he applied to Davis for help in gaining the President. There were two opposing influences in the administration, one represented by the Secretary of State and the other by the Secretary of War, and Douglas knew that in this affair it was Davis that he should call upon. Pierce loved and trusted Davis,[2] who had, moreover, the backing of the Southern Democracy, which the President was now anxious to conciliate in order to effectually contradict reports current in the South that the administration was tinctured with Free-soilism. Yet Pierce was also solicitous for the support of Marcy in this

---

[1] The Rise and Fall of the Confederate Government, Jefferson Davis, vol. i. p. 28; Life of Davis, Alfriend, p. 94; Life of Davis, Pollard, p. 49; Memoir of Jefferson Davis, by his wife, vol. i. p. 669. See also Washington correspondence of the New York *Courier and Enquirer*, March 25th; New York *Herald*, Jan. 24th.

[2] At the end of his term of office, Pierce said to Davis: "I can scarcely bear the parting from you, who have been strength and solace to me for four anxious years, and never failed me."—Memoir of Jefferson Davis, by his wife, vol. i. p. 530.

affair, and requested Douglas and his companions to call upon
him for consultation. This wish was, of course, complied
with, but the Secretary of State was not found at home.[1]

On Monday, January 23d, Douglas offered a substitute
for his preceding bill. It differed from the other in two
particulars. It affirmed that the slavery restriction of the
Missouri Compromise " was superseded by the principles of
the legislation of 1850, commonly called the compromise
measures, and is hereby declared inoperative;" and it divided the great territory into two parts, calling the northern
portion Nebraska, and the southern Kansas. The northern
and southern boundaries of Kansas were the same as those
of the present State, but the western limit was the Rocky
Mountains, and the total area one hundred and twenty-six
thousand square miles.[2]

We cannot clearly trace the ways leading up to this division of Nebraska, which apparently formed no part of the
original plan. Nor is the explanation of Senator Douglas
sufficient.[3] It is almost certain that if there had been no
question of slavery, this change would not have been made.
A steadfast Northern follower of Douglas has acknowledged
that the purpose which he had in view by this division was
to make one slave and one free State;[4] and there is much
in the contemporaneous evidence to lead one to this conclusion. In the summer and fall of 1853, a movement began

[1] Rise and Fall of the Slave Power, Wilson, vol. ii. p. 383.

[2] Spring's Kansas, p. 17.   The present State of Kansas has 81,700 square
miles.

[3] See *Congressional Globe*, vol. xxviii. p. 221.

[4] Three Decades of Federal Legislation, S. S. Cox, p. 49.   Of the close
relation of Cox to Douglas, see his eulogy on the death of Douglas, House
of Representatives, July, 1861, when he said : " It may not be improper
to refer to the fact that I was among the many young men of the West
who were bound to him by a tie of friendship and a spell of enthusiasm
which death has no power to break;" and he also speaks of the "unbroken association of friendship with him from the first year of my political life."

in western Missouri with the avowed object of making Nebraska slave territory.[1] In that portion of the State there
were fifty thousand slaves, worth perhaps twenty-five millions of dollars, and the interests of their owners seemed to
demand that the contiguous country should be devoted to
slavery. Senator Atchison urged this view warmly, showing
that the only obstacle to their wishes lay in the Missouri
Compromise. Coming to Washington on the opening of
Congress, he felt that he had an aggressive sentiment behind him which demanded the repeal of the slavery restriction.[2] His eyes, and those of his constituents, were cast
longingly on the country which is now Kansas, and in which
they hoped slavery might gain the foothold it had in Missouri. The Missouri border abounded in adventurous spirits
who were ready for any enterprise; Atchison and his fellow
slave-holders were confident that if the restriction were removed, these men could be used to advantage in establishing
a slave State. Kansas was all they wanted, and the territory,
if divided, would be easier to manage. That all this was
known to the Southern Democrats and Whigs in Congress
and to Senator Douglas is indisputable. The supporters of
the Nebraska bill came together so frequently in caucus
and conference[3] that, if all the features of the situation
were not discussed, they must certainly have been well understood. Indeed, the expectation that Kansas would become a slave State was openly expressed on the floor of the
House.[4] It follows plainly enough, therefore, that the division of the territory was in the interest of slavery; and
if Douglas had not been brought to the point of actually

---

[1] Spring's Kansas, p. 24. See a very noteworthy article in the New
York *Tribune* of Nov. 12th, 1853.

[2] Spring's Kansas, p. 24.

[3] See speech of Senator Benjamin, May 8th, 1860.

[4] " I will not now detail my reasons, but I have a strong faith that *Kansas will become a slave State*."—Zollicoffer, Whig representative from Tennessee, May 9th, quoted by Von Holst.

conceding that Kansas should be a slave State, he at least knew that there was a well-devised scheme in progress to make it one.

Tuesday, the 24th of January, was a notable day in the history of the Kansas-Nebraska bill. Dixon stated in the Senate that he was entirely satisfied with the amendment Douglas had incorporated in his bill; and the Washington *Union* had a carefully written editorial which was the fruit of the conference of the preceding Sunday. After endorsing the substitute of the committee on territories, the organ of the President went on to say: " We cannot but regard the policy of the administration as directly involved in the question. That policy looks to fidelity to the compromise of 1850 as an essential requisite in Democratic orthodoxy. The proposition of Mr. Douglas is a practical execution of the principles of that compromise, and, therefore, cannot but be regarded by the administration as a test of Democratic orthodoxy. The union of the Democracy on this proposition will dissipate forever the charge of Free-soil sympathies so recklessly and pertinaciously urged against the administration by our Whig opponents; while it will take from disaffection in our ranks the last vestige of a pretext for its opposition."

On this same day (January 24th) was published the " Appeal of the Independent Democrats in Congress to the People of the United States." [1] Chase wrote the paper from a draft made by Giddings, and it received some verbal correc-

---

[1] There was considerable confusion about the date of this address. As published in the New York *Times* and *National Era* of the 24th, it was dated the 22d, which was Sunday. Douglas made a great point of the date, charging that the abolition confederates had assembled in secret conclave on the holy Sabbath. The date was an error. The New York *Tribune*, when it copied the address from the *Times*, changed the date to the 23d. It appears in the *Congressional Globe* as of Jan. 19th, but a postscript is added which could not possibly have been written until the 23d.

tions from Sumner and Gerrit Smith.[1]   These men signed it,
as did also Edward Wade and Alexander De Witt, representatives from Ohio and Massachusetts. All of the signers
were Free-soilers. Like so many political manifestoes, composed in the midst of agitating events and under the influence of powerful emotion, the Appeal of the Independent
Democrats is strong in expression; but few partisan documents will stand so well the test of time. It expresses
earnest feeling, but it relates truthful history. The historical argument is incontrovertible. The reasoning is earnest,
but the writers felt that, having history and justice on their
side, they needed only to make fair statements, and that the
straining of any point was unnecessary. Viewing it in the
calm light of the present, criticism is silent. Had the language been less strong, the writers would not have shown
themselves equal to the occasion. It is a brave, truthful,
earnest exposition.

It should be remarked that all of the address except the
postscript was written before Douglas introduced his substitute of January 23d, and has reference to the report and
first bill of the committee on territories. The Appeal
states at the outset that, should the project receive the sanction of Congress, it "will open all the unorganized territory
of the Union to the ingress of slavery." Therefore, "We
arraign this bill as a gross violation of a sacred pledge; as a
criminal betrayal of precious rights; as part and parcel of
an atrocious plot to exclude from a vast unoccupied region
immigrants from the Old World and free laborers from our
own States, and convert it into a dreary region of despotism
inhabited by masters and slaves." The history of the Missouri Compromise is then related,[2] and the truthful statement is made: "For more than thirty years—during more
than half the period of our national Constitution—this com-

[1] Life of Chase, Schuckers, p. 140; History of the Rebellion, Giddings,
p. 300; Life of Wade, Riddle, p. 225.
[2] See Chap. I.

pact [*i. e.*, the Missouri Compromise] has been universally regarded and acted upon as inviolable American law." And now it is proposed to cancel this compact. " Language fails to express the sentiments of indignation and abhorrence" which the Nebraska act inspires. " It is a bold scheme against American liberty worthy of an accomplished architect of ruin. . . . Shall a plot against humanity and democracy so monstrous, and so dangerous to the interest of liberty throughout the world, be permitted to succeed? We appeal to the people. We warn you that the dearest interests of freedom and the Union are in imminent peril. . . . Let all protest, earnestly and emphatically, by correspondence, through the press, by memorials, by resolutions of public meetings and legislative bodies, and in whatever other mode may seem expedient, against this enormous crime."

The postscript, which was written just before the Appeal was given to the press, relates to the substitute of January 23d. The truth of the emphatic statements with which it closes has never been successfully impugned, and they may justly receive the seal of impartial history. " This amendment," the Appeal says, " is a manifest falsification of the truth of history. . . . Not a man in Congress, or out of Congress, in 1850 pretended that the compromise measures would repeal the Missouri prohibition.[1] Mr. Douglas himself never advanced such a pretense until this session. His own Nebraska bill, of last session, rejected it. It is a sheer afterthought. To declare the prohibition inoperative may, indeed, have effect in law as a repeal, but it is a most discreditable way of reaching the object. Will the people permit their dearest interests to be thus made the mere hazards of a presidential game, and destroyed by false facts and false inferences?"[2]

This appeal was published in nearly all the newspapers of

---

[1] There may possibly be one exception to this statement. It will be considered later.

[2] *Congressional Globe*, vol. xxviii. p. 281.

the free States.   The field had been well prepared for the
sowing of this seed.   Connected with the journals of this
time were many able and earnest men full of enthusiasm for
a righteous cause.   Almost without exception, the conspicuous editors at the North took ground from the first against
the Nebraska act, and their papers abounded in sharp criticisms of the author of the measure and in entreaties to the
friends of freedom not to permit the consummation of the
infamy.   Some regarded the measure with anger, others with
grief, and all with apprehension.   The public mind was in a
state that could not fail to be profoundly affected by an authoritative and impressive protest from Washington.   It is
true that the Free-soil congressmen had not a large political
following; but their arguments were so cogent that they
convinced and roused many men who had been accustomed
to regard the authors of the Appeal with mistrust.   If the
politicians at Washington, wrote one earnest journalist, have
any doubt about the public opinion, let them put their ears
to the ground and they " will hear the roar of the tide coming in." [1]

When Douglas came into the Senate on the morning of
January 30th, he was a prey to angry excitement, and
shortly after his entrance he took the floor to open the debate on the Kansas-Nebraska bill.   The reason of his rage
was soon apparent.   It was caused by the Appeal of the Independent Democrats and by the indications of public sentiment which had already reached Washington, and which
Douglas was inclined to attribute wholly to the prompting
of this address.   In deference to the wishes of Chase and
Sumner, he had postponed the consideration of the bill for
six days, and now he charged Chase with having come to
him " with a smiling face and the appearance of friendship,"
begging for delay, merely in order to get a wide circulation
for the Appeal and forestall public opinion before an exposition of the measure was made by its author.   The address,

---

[1] New York *Evening Post*, Feb. 3d, 1854.

he said, grossly misrepresented the bill, arraigned the motives and calumniated the characters of the members of the
committee, and the postscript applied coarse epithets to
himself by name. Chase endeavored to interrupt the
speaker, and an excited colloquy followed; Douglas lost his
temper completely, and emphatic language was used by both
senators, so that they were at different times called to order
by the president. This, one may gather from the official
report in the *Congressional Globe;* but it was stated that
Douglas carefully corrected his remarks before publication,
and struck out many opprobrious words he had used.[1]
Several Washington correspondents agree in their description of the manner and language of Douglas. One speaks
of his "senatorial billingsgate," and of the "vulgarity and
vehemence of the abuse which he poured out upon Senator
Chase;"[2] another described the scene as one of "intemperate violence," and maintained that the course of Douglas
was "indecorous and a most reprehensible violation of the
dignity of the body," and that his style of attack was "more
becoming a pot-house than the Senate;"[3] and another spoke
of his speech as "violent and abusive."[4] In spite of the
fact that the display of temper at the outset lost Douglas in
a certain degree the respect of his audience, the speech was
conceded by his opponents to be able and ingenious, indeed
the very best that could be made in a very bad cause.[5] An
earnest abolitionist paid a tribute to the remarkable force
and adroitness of the argument.[6]

---

[1] See New York *Times*, Feb. 2d; also letter in the New York *Independent* of March 16th.

[2] See New York *Times*, Feb. 1st.

[3] Washington correspondence New York *Courier and Enquirer*, Jan.
30th.

[4] New York *Tribune*. It may be remarked that all these journals were
hostile to Douglas. The anger of Douglas was raised when he referred
to the affair five years later. See Constitutional and Party Questions, J.
M. Cutts, p. 94.   [5] New York *Times*.

[6] T. W. Higginson, letter in the *Liberator*, Feb. 24th.

Douglas stated that by the Missouri Compromise of 1820 a geographical line had been established, north of which slavery was prohibited, and south of which it was permitted. When New Mexico and California were acquired, a logical adherence to that principle required the extension of this line to the Pacific Ocean. On his motion in 1848, the Senate had adopted such a provision; but it failed in the House, being defeated "by Northern votes with Free-soil proclivities." [1] This refusal to extend the Missouri Compromise line to the Pacific Ocean gave rise to a furious slavery agitation, which continued until it was quieted by the compromise measures of 1850. In that series of acts, the principle established was: " Congressional non-intervention as to slavery in the territories; that the people of the territories . . . were to be allowed to do as they pleased upon the subject of slavery, subject only to the provisions of the Constitution." Although the only territorial bills which were a part of the plan of 1850 were those organizing Utah and New Mexico, yet the Missouri Compromise line, in all the unorganized territory not covered by those bills, was superseded by the principles of that compromise. " We all know," said the senator, "that the object of the compromise measures of 1850 was to establish certain great principles, which would avoid the slavery agitation in all time to come. Was it our object simply to provide for a temporary evil? Was it our object just to heal over an old sore and leave it to break out again? Was it our object to adopt a mere miserable expedient to apply to that territory, and that alone, and leave ourselves entirely at sea, without compass, when new territory was acquired or new territorial organizations were to be made? Was that the object for which the eminent and venerable senator from Kentucky [Clay] came here and sacrificed even his last energies upon the altar of his country? Was that the object for which Webster, Clay, and Cass, and all the patriots of that day, struggled so long

* See p. 96.

and so strenuously? Was it merely the application of a temporary expedient in agreeing to stand by past and dead legislation that the Baltimore platform pledged us to sustain the compromise of 1850? Was it the understanding of the Whig party when they adopted the compromise measures of 1850 as an article of political faith, that they were only agreeing to that which was past and had no reference to the future?" By no means. In the legislation of 1850 a principle was adopted—the principle of congressional non-interference with slavery, and when the two party conventions resolved to acquiesce in the compromise measures, they were giving pledges that in their future action they would carry out that principle. Now it is necessary to organize the territory of Nebraska. The Missouri Compromise restriction is inconsistent with this later principle and should give place to it. "The legal effect of this bill," continued Douglas, "is neither to legislate slavery into these territories nor out of them, but to leave the people do as they please. . . . If they wish slavery, they have a right to it. If they do not want it, they will not have it, and you should not force it upon them."

Did Douglas describe the workings of his own mind between January 4th and 23d, when he said, in graphic words: "I know there are some men, Whigs and Democrats, who . . . would be willing to vote for this principle, provided they could do so in such equivocal terms that they could deny that it means what it was intended to mean, in certain localities." But he went on to say: "I do not wish to deal in any equivocal language. If the principle is right, let it be avowed and maintained. If it is wrong, let it be repudiated. Let all this quibbling about the Missouri Compromise . . . be cast behind you; for the simple question is, will you allow the people to legislate for themselves upon the question of slavery? Why should you not?" For the benefit, probably, of what he called "tender-footed Democrats," he maintained that it was worse than folly to think of Nebraska being a slave-holding country. Nor did the manifestations of public sentiment averse to the measure frighten Douglas. "This tornado," he said, "has been raised by abolitionists, and abolitionists alone."

The senator made an argument based on the fact that the boundary lines of New Mexico and Utah, as constituted, annulled the Missouri Compromise in a part of the territory to which it applied. While this at the time was considered ingenious reasoning, it was effectually refuted by Chase and Everett, and Douglas did not allude to it in his speech which closed the debate; nor was this the argument he relied on in the many defences he made of his present course in after-years.

When Douglas sat down, Chase obtained the floor and made a defence of the Appeal of the Independent Democrats. They meant exactly what they said; it was not an occasion for soft words; they considered the Missouri Compromise a sacred pledge, and its proposed abrogation "a criminal betrayal of precious rights." "What rights are precious," demanded the senator, "if those secured to free labor and free laborers in that vast territory are not?" The attempt of Douglas to shield himself under the ægis of Clay and Webster was not overlooked; the Illinois senator knew it to be a strong point, and in after-years elaborated it into a statement that he had given the "immortal Clay," lying on his death-bed, a pledge that his energies should be devoted to the vindication of the principle of leaving each State and territory free to decide its institutions for itself, and he had also given the same pledge to the "godlike Webster."[2] On the day when this justification was first broached, Chase must have felt that if he held his peace, the stones would cry out against it, and he emphatically asserted: "When the senator vouches the authority of Clay and Webster to sustain him, he vouches authorities which would rebuke him could those statesmen speak from their graves."

On the 3d of February, Chase made his mark in an elab-

---

[2] Speech at Bloomington, Ill., 1858, Life of Douglas, Flint, p. 125.

orate speech against the Kansas-Nebraska bill, and on that day he took a place in the foremost ranks of the statesmen who devoted themselves to anti-slavery principles.

He was, with perhaps the exception of Sumner, the handsomest man in the Senate, and as he rose to make his plea for the maintenance of plighted faith, all felt the force of his commanding presence. More than six feet high, he had a frame and figure proportioned to his height; with his large head, massive brow, and smoothly shaven face, he looked like a Roman senator; and the similitude was heightened by his coming to plead against the introduction of Punic faith into the Congress of the United States. He appreciated the gravity of the situation, and attributed the crowded galleries, the thronged lobbies and the full attendance of the Senate to the transcendent interest of the theme. Chase was not a fluent and easy speaker; he had less of the spirit of the orator than Douglas; he could not sway an audience of the Senate as could the Little Giant.[1] Nevertheless, the dignity of his manner and the weight of his words obtained him a careful hearing, and he was listened to with attention by senators and visitors.[2]

When Congress met, he said, "no agitation seemed to disturb the political elements." The two great political parties "had announced that slavery agitation was at an end;" the President "had declared his fixed purpose to maintain the quiet of the country. . . . But suddenly all is changed. . . . And now we find ourselves in an agitation the end and issue of which no man can foresee. Who is responsible for this renewal of strife and controversy? . . . It is slavery. . . . And what does slavery ask for now? It demands that a time-honored and sacred compact shall be rescinded — a compact which has endured through a whole

---

[1] Warden's Life of Chase, p. 340.

[2] Washington correspondence New York *Times*, published Feb. 6th. I am indebted to Mr. R. C. Parsons, of Cleveland, who knew Chase intimately, for a vivid description of him as he was in his senatorial career.

I.—29

generation; a compact which has been universally regarded
as inviolable, North and South; a compact the constitutionality of which few have doubted, and by which all have
consented to abide." The ground on which it is proposed
to violate this compact is supposed to be found in the doctrine that the restriction of the Missouri Compromise is
superseded by the principles of the compromise measures of
1850. This is a "statement untrue in fact and without
foundation in history." It is, continued the senator, "a
novel idea. At the time when these measures were before
Congress in 1850, when the questions involved in them were
discussed from day to day, from week to week, and from
month to month, in this Senate Chamber, who ever heard
that the Missouri prohibition was to be superseded? What
man, at what time, in what speech, ever suggested the idea
that the acts of that year were to affect the Missouri Compromise? . . . Did Henry Clay, in the report made by him
as chairman of the committee of thirteen, or in any speech
in support of the compromise acts, or in any conversation, in
the committee or out of the committee, ever even hint at
this doctrine of supersedure? Did any supporter or any
opponent of the compromise acts ever vindicate or condemn
them upon the ground that the Missouri prohibition would
be affected by them? Well, sir, the compromise acts were
passed. They were denounced North and they were denounced South. Did any defender of them at the South
ever justify his support of them upon the ground that the
South had obtained through them the repeal of the Missouri
prohibition? Did any objector to them at the North ever
even suggest, as a ground of condemnation, that that prohibition was swept away by them? No, sir! No man, North
or South, during the whole of the discussion of those acts
here, or in that other discussion which followed their enactment throughout the country, ever intimated any such opinion." After effectually refuting the argument of Douglas
drawn from the constitution of the boundaries of New
Mexico and Utah, and giving an account of the anti-slavery

opinions of the fathers of the government, Chase related briefly and correctly the history of the Missouri Compromise, and in a few words he stated the obligations which that act imposed on the South. He said: " A large majority of Southern senators voted for it; a majority of Southern representatives voted for it. It was approved by all the Southern members of the cabinet, and received the sanction of a Southern President. The compact was embodied in a single bill containing reciprocal provisions. The admission of Missouri with slavery, and the understanding that slavery should not be prohibited by Congress south of 36° 30′, were the considerations of the perpetual prohibition north of that line. And that prohibition was the consideration of the admission and the understanding. The slave States received a large share of the consideration coming to them, paid in hand. Missouri was admitted without restriction by the act itself. Every other part of the compact, on the part of the free States, has been fulfilled to the letter. No part of the compact on the part of the slave States has been fulfilled at all, except in the admission of Iowa and the organization of Minnesota; and now the slave States propose to break up the compact without the consent and against the will of the free States." Chase gave a brief but able review of the slavery question in this country. He rose to the height of noble prophecy as he spoke of his faith in progress and his hope of the future of the republic, and he closed with an earnest appeal to the senators to reject this bill, as it was " a violation of the plighted faith and solemn compact which our fathers made, and which we, their sons, are bound by every sacred tie of obligation sacredly to maintain."

This speech of Chase was great. As an earnest protest against a measure which violated the sentiment of justice, and whose iniquity the speaker felt in every fibre of his being, it must ever take high rank. In it were united the understanding of the lawyer, the elevation of the statesman, and the gravity of the moralist; the warmth of the advocate is tempered by the fairness of the judge. His state-

ments are lucid, his arguments unanswerable. He seems to
feel a profound regret that the question of slavery should
be agitated again; but his strong moral nature had burning
convictions, and he was bound to express them. The matter is made plain, history is truthfully related, his reasoning
is careful, and the conclusions irresistible.

Wade, Seward, and Sumner made powerful speeches
against the bill. Their point of view was the same as that
of Chase. All thought slavery an evil whose power must
be circumscribed, and all looked to a time when it should be
eradicated. The line of argument which they pursued was
substantially the same as that of Chase, but each had a peculiar following in the country, to whom their arguments
were addressed as well as to the Senate. The rasping language of Wade offended some Eastern critics,[1] but the farmers of Northern Ohio, whom he represented, loved plain
speaking, and were glad that their senator did not mince
his words when he protested against a rank injustice. He
had a ready wit, and, while his set speech was soon forgotten,
a retort that he made during the debate is still remembered.
In it there lurked a strong argument, and it states incisively
the difference between the apologists and the assailants of
slavery.

Badger, of North Carolina, had rehearsed the ancient argument for the dilution of slavery, and in a feeling manner had
asked: "Why, if some Southern gentleman wishes to take
the nurse who takes charge of his little baby, or the old
woman who nursed him in childhood, and whom he called
'Mammy' until he returned from college, and perhaps afterwards too, and whom he wishes to take with him in his old
age when he is moving into one of these new territories for
the betterment of the fortunes of the whole family—why, in
the name of God, should anybody prevent it?" Wade was
glad to answer this question. "The senator," he said, "entirely mistakes our position. We have not the least objec-

---

[1] See Washington correspondence New York *Times*, Feb. 6th.

tion, and would oppose no obstacle to the senator's migrat-
ing to Kansas and taking his old 'Mammy' along with
him. We only insist that he shall not be empowered to *sell*
her after taking her there." [1]

Seward was not an effective speaker, but his high political
position gave him an attentive hearing at Washington, and
his words were listened to not only by his followers in New
York, but they had a marked influence on all the anti-slavery
Whigs in the country. His speech was translated into German and extensively circulated among the Germans of Western Texas under the frank of Senator Houston. [2] It probably
affected the minds of more men than any speech delivered
on that side of this question in Congress; and, though lacking the force, feeling, and decision of that of Chase, it was a
clever legal argument. The speech of Chase was the argument of an indignant moralist, the pathetic appeal of a patriotic statesman; that of Seward was the reasoning of a
politician who could not conceal his exultation that the
Democrats had forsaken their high vantage-ground and
played into the hands of their opponents. [3] But he could
not feel entirely certain whether a new anti-slavery party
would be formed, or whether there was still a reason for the
existence of the Whig party, and thought it not well to use
words so harsh that a deadly breach would be made between the Northern and Southern Whigs. He had declined,

---

[1] Rise and Fall of the Slave Power, Wilson, vol. ii. p. 388. Compare
Life of Wade, Riddle, p. 232.

[2] See letter of Yeoman from San Antonio, Texas, of April 18th, 1854,
New York *Times*, May 13th. Yeoman was the name under which Frederick Law Olmsted wrote.

[3] Montgomery Blair wrote to Gideon Welles, May 17th, 1873: "I shall
never forget how shocked I was at his [Seward] telling me that he was
the man who put Archy Dixon, the Whig senator from Kentucky in 1854,
up to moving the repeal of the Missouri Compromise as an amendment to
Douglas's first Kansas bill, and had himself forced the repeal by that
movement, and had thus brought to life the Republican party."—Lincoln
and Seward, Welles, p. 68.

therefore, to sign the Appeal of the Independent Democrats.[1]

Yet Seward made some pregnant assertions that may not be omitted in an account of this debate. If, said he, it had been known that the Missouri Compromise was to be abrogated, directly or indirectly, by the compromise of 1850, not a representative from a non-slaveholding State would have at that day voted for it, while every senator from the slaveholding States would have given it his support. Nor, he asserted, does it weaken my opposition to this measure " to be told that only a few slaves will enter into this vast region. One slave-holder in a new territory, with access to the executive ear at Washington, exercises more political influence than five hundred freemen." [2]

Sumner spoke to the cultured people of Massachusetts, to the professors and students of colleges, and to clergymen of advanced political views. The moral side of the question appealed to him forcibly, and he approached it inspired by the same sentiment that had moved Chase. His illustrations delighted scholars, and his quotations pleased lovers of literature; but the speech lacked the cogency that distinguished the effort of the Ohio senator. No doubt can remain in the minds of impartial men that the speech of Chase was the greatest which was made in either House in opposition to the Kansas-Nebraska bill. It was so regarded by Douglas. Five years afterwards, in speaking of the senatorial debates on this subject, he said: " Seward's and Sumner's speeches were mere essays against slavery. Chase was the leader." [3]

In eloquent periods Sumner depicted the nature of the question which now agitated the country. He showed that

---

[1] Life of Chase, Schuckers, p. 160. Many Western papers published the Appeal with Seward's name signed to it. The *Tribune* said, when the Appeal was made, " Seward was at home in Auburn in consequence of serious illness in his family, and accordingly neither signed it, nor had any knowledge of it whatever."—New York *Weekly Tribune*, Feb. 11th.

[2] Seward's Works, vol. iv. p. 442.

[3] Constitutional and Party Questions, J. M. Cutts, p. 123.

the issue was made up. Slavery, he said, "is the only subject within the field of national politics which excites any
real interest. The old matters which have divided the
minds of men . . . have disappeared, leaving the ground to
be occupied by a question grander far. The bank, sub-
treasury, the distribution of the public lands, are each and
all obsolete issues. And now, instead of these superseded
questions, which were filled for the most part with the odor
of the dollar, the country is directly summoned to consider
face to face a cause which is connected with all that is divine in religion, with all that is pure and noble in morals,
with all that is truly practical and constitutional in politics.
Unlike the other questions, it is not temporary or local in its
character. It belongs to all times and to all countries.
Though long kept in check, it now, by your introduction,
confronts the people, demanding to be heard. To every
man in the land, it says with clear, penetrating voice, ' Are
you for freedom or are you for slavery ?' And every man
in the land must answer this question when he votes." [1]

Edward Everett also made a speech against the bill in the
Senate. His utterances were important, not only for the
weight of his argument, but because he spoke for the conservative Whigs of the North, those who had supported the
compromise of 1850 and had been the followers of Webster
or Fillmore. Chase and Seward in the Senate, and Sumner
and Wade out of it, had opposed that adjustment. The
character of the opposition had led Douglas to assert that
every one in either House of Congress who had supported
the compromise of 1850 was now in favor of the Kansas-
Nebraska bill; and this speech of Everett gave that statement the first effective denial. [2] As had been the case when
the other senators who have been mentioned spoke, so now
crowds filled the Senate Chamber ; the House was deserted.
The senator was listened to with profound attention, in

---

[1] Wade spoke Feb. 6th, Seward Feb. 17th, and Sumner Feb. 21st.
[2] Everett's speech was made Feb. 8th.

which curiosity in regard to his position was mingled with interest, for it had been reported that he would favor the bill.[1]   But all doubts regarding Everett's position were soon dispelled as he gradually unfolded his argument, which, though expressed in too courtly phrase to suit the radical spirits, was very forcible.   Being of a deprecatory nature, it would hardly have fitted the leader of the opposition.[2]   Yet it appealed to men whom the more radical utterances of Chase, Wade, and Sumner could not reach, and it was of great importance as reflecting, and at the same time mould-ing, a certain public sentiment.[3]

Everett showed conclusively, by an argument drawn from the letter of the acts and from the very nature of the legis-lation itself, that the principle of non-intervention on the part of Congress in the question of slavery was not enacted in the territorial bills of 1850.   Furthermore he asked : "How can you find in a simple measure applying in terms to these individual territories, and to them alone, a rule which is to govern all other territories with a retrospective and with a prospective action ?   Is it not a mere begging of

---

[1] Everett was a true conservative. "You are quite right," he wrote Greeley in 1862, "in calling me a ' conservative,' but I am so, not from any bigoted attachment to the past or to the established, as such. We should all strive to preserve what is good as well as contest what is evil. . . . Few men succeed in living up to their ideal of character, but I have tried to obey the apostolic rule in both parts—' to prove all things : hold fast that which is good.' " This letter was called out by a complimentary biographical notice that Greeley had written for the New York *Ledger*, and a copy of it was kindly furnished me by Mr. Gordon L. Ford, of Brooklyn, who owns the original. I take this occasion to say that I have been under many obligations to Mr. Ford, and to his son, Mr. Paul L. Ford.

[2] See Washington correspondence New York *Times*, Feb. 8th ; see also New York *Evening Post*, especially letter from Boston criticising this speech, published March 11th.

[3] The New York *Courier and Enquirer* called this speech of Everett the most brilliant and effective effort of the session.   Editorial of Feb. 9th. The Washington correspondent of the New York *Tribune* spoke of his "eloquent, impressive, and truthful words."

the question to say that those compromise measures adopted in this specific case amount to such a general rule?"

He then went on to consider the spirit of the compromise measures of 1850, and what was the understanding of their scope by their chief supporters. While, said he, " I was not a member of Congress and had not heard the debates . . . I inquired of those who had heard them, I read the reports, and I had an opportunity of personal intercourse with some who had taken a prominent part in all of those measures. I never formed the idea—I never received the intimation until I got it from this report of the committee—that those measures were intended to have any effect beyond the territories of Utah and New Mexico, for which they were enacted. I cannot but think that if it was intended that they should have any larger application, if it was intended that they should furnish the rule which is now supposed, it would have been a fact as notorious as the light of day." The well-known personal and political friendship existing between Webster and Everett[1] gave a peculiar force to these expressions; and it was heightened when the orator proceeded to relate his familiar intercourse with the expounder of the Constitution in 1851, brought about by the fact that he had by request undertaken to edit Webster's works and write the biographical memoir prefaced to them. He had occasion to discuss the 7th-of-March speech with its author; and, while the question of 1854 was not mooted, for little had they dreamed that any such construction would ever be put upon the legislation of 1850, Everett spoke with authority when he expounded the meaning of Webster. He had not the slightest doubt that the great Massachusetts senator considered the Missouri restriction a compact which the government could not in good faith repeal.

Everett touched upon the absurdity of the principle of Congressional non-intervention on the subject of slavery in the territories; and in conclusion he gave vent to words

---

[1] See p. 293.

eminently proper for a philosophic historian, but which
sounded strange enough in the midst of a heated debate.
He said : " I share the opinions and the sentiments of the
part of the country where I was born and educated. . . .
But in relation to my fellow-citizens in other parts of the
country, I will treat . . . their characters and feelings with
tenderness. I believe them to be as good Christians, as good
patriots, as good men as we are."

The speeches in the Senate in favor of the Kansas-
Nebraska bill were not, with the exception of those of
Douglas, remarkable. There was considerable curiosity in
regard to the position of Cass. Although in the early part
of January it was reported that he would take advanced
ground in favor of the repeal of the Missouri Compromise,
an opinion became current, after Douglas had in substance
incorporated the Dixon amendment in his bill, that Cass was
wavering and would vote against the Kansas-Nebraska act.[1]
" He," wrote a prominent Democratic representative from
New York City, "evidently looks upon the whole movement, and the manner in which it has been made, as a des-
picable piece of demagogism on the part of Douglas, though
he does not like to say so."[2] John Van Buren had hopes
that Cass might be induced even to head the opposition.
"There are but two men," he wrote to Clemens, " who can
do any good in this crisis—one is General Cass, the other
yourself. If you will agree to the Nebraska bill of last year,[3]
it will be promptly and triumphantly passed."[4] Cass voted
for one of the amendments with which Chase badgered
Douglas, and he explained that he did so because he did not
like the phraseology of the bill. In order to meet this objection, Douglas still further amended his bill so that the

---

[1] See correspondence New York *Courier and Enquirer*, Jan. 31st.
[2] Letter of Mike Walsh, New York *Herald*, Feb. 13th.
[3] See p. 425.
[4] John Van Buren to ex-Senator Clemens, Feb. 3d, 1854, New York
Evening Post, Feb. 11th.

crucial section should read: "which [the Missouri Compromise act] being inconsistent with the principles of non-
intervention by Congress with slavery in the States and
territories, as recognized by the legislation of 1850, commonly called the compromise measures, is hereby declared
inoperative and void, it being the true intent and meaning
of this act not to legislate slavery into any territory or
State, nor to exclude it therefrom; but to leave the people
thereof perfectly free to form and regulate their domestic
institutions in their own way, subject only to the Constitution of the United States." The alteration lay in the use of
the words "being inconsistent with" instead of "was superseded by," and in the more elaborate explanation of the intention of the act; in this shape it finally became a law.
This satisfied Cass, who declared that he would support the
measure,[1] and two weeks later he delivered a long and formal
speech advocating it.

Among the supporters of the bill, two distinct conceptions
were developed of what would be the practical working of
the act. One was the notion of Douglas and Cass, agreed
to by most of the Northern Democrats, and in the main by
the Southern Whigs. It was their idea that the inhabitants
of the territories themselves should protect or prohibit slavery. As that part of the country to which the act applied
was practically unsettled, they eluded the decision as to
when this sovereignty should begin, or as to how great a
number of settlers there should be in the territory before
they might legislate on this subject. Cass, goaded to define
the doctrine of which he was the author[2] by the questions
of Southern Democrats, said that he did not seek "in the
science of arithmetic the principles of the science of political
institutions;" and he maintained that the world had never

---

[1] This amendment was not formally introduced until Feb. 7th; but the
vote on the Chase amendment was on the 6th. This amendment was then
outlined by Douglas, and declared satisfactory by Cass.

[2] See the Nicholson letter.

seen a truer basis of government than that established by
the one hundred and one Pilgrims when they landed at
Plymouth.

The Southern Democrats, however, believed in the doctrine of Calhoun; that as slaves were property, those owning them had the same right under the Constitution to carry
their negroes into the new territories as they had to take
their horses and mules, and no law could rightfully be made
to prevent their exercise of this right. It was true that the
Missouri restriction in set words prohibited slavery in the
Nebraska territory; but the Southern Democratic senators
were all sure that it was unconstitutional, and would be so
decided when the question should be brought before the
highest tribunal. Yet to have the Missouri restriction declared inoperative and void by Congress was more speedy
and direct than to have it decided unconstitutional by the
Supreme Court, and the Kansas-Nebraska act, therefore, met
their approval. But if it became a law, they held that they
would have a right to take their slaves into these territories,
and that such property would be entitled to the same protection as any other property. When the people of a territory came to the point of applying for admission as a State,
then it would be decided by the voice of those inhabitants
whether the new State should be free or slave.

Chase laid great stress upon this difference of views between the supporters of the bill, and he endeavored, by an
amendment and pertinent suggestions, to have the Senate
declare precisely what was meant by the act. He averred
that in its present shape it settled nothing, and that misun-
derstandings were sure to arise in its construction. But his
amendment only received ten votes, and his suggestions were
contemptuously rejected. The reason of this is plainly apparent. If the act stated that the first settlers of the territory might prohibit slavery, it would not receive the full
Southern Democratic vote; if, on the other hand, it declared
the doctrine of Calhoun, hardly a Northern senator would
dare to give it his support. This difference of opinion was

frequently discussed in caucus; and as the bill looked either way, it was decided to put it through and leave it to the Supreme Court to determine which of the two constructions was correct.[1]

Toombs made a noteworthy contribution to the discussion when he denied the declaration so frequently made, that in 1850 no one pretended that the compromise measures were inconsistent with the Missouri restriction. He said that in Georgia he had been severely criticised for having supported the compromise, and that in an address made to the people of his State to vindicate his action, he had maintained that a great principle, compromised away in 1820, had " been rescued, re-established, and again firmly planted in our political system" by the legislation of 1850. Yet Toombs did not say that the Missouri restriction was abrogated; and if that were his meaning, he would have been practically alone in his opinion. His statement did not, therefore, invalidate in the slightest degree the argument drawn from the spirit of the compromise measures or the intent of their originator and supporters.

Douglas managed the bill in an adroit and energetic manner, but it was objected that he was at times dictatorial to the friends of the measure. Anxious to have the debate proceed rapidly, he objected to a postponement, no matter how reasonable might be the cause. He chafed at the delay that Everett asked for in order to examine and consider carefully the last amendment of Douglas before speaking to the subject, and he was urgent that Clayton should continue speaking when physically unable to do so. It was foreign to the nature of Douglas to be discourteous, but he felt the necessity of haste. While he could at no time have had any doubt about carrying the measure through the Senate, he had anxiety about the bill in the House; for that

---

[1] Speech of Benjamin in the Senate, May 8th, 1860; see also speech of Bell, May 24th and 25th, 1854; and speech of Douglas in the Senate, Feb. 23d, 1859.

body was more amenable to public opinion, and by the 1st of February Douglas knew that the current of Northern sentiment was setting strongly against his measure. The longer the delay, the greater was the chance of representatives being influenced by the manifest feeling of their constituents. Douglas was always present in the Senate, and eagerly watched the progress of the debate. His political prospects were bound up in this measure, and he could not afford to miss a single trick. He did not, however, speak as often as Clay did on the compromise measures, but these were before the Senate more than six months, while the debate on the Kansas-Nebraska act lasted but thirty-three days.

Chase tacitly took the position of the leader of the opposition. He was ready in debate, and quick to see and lay bare the weak points of the adversary. Yet he was frank in his replies, even when forced to answer questions he would rather have left unanswered; for while he knew he could not be too radical for his Free-soil supporters, he felt that the time had come when he must appeal to a larger constituency. His manner was described by Badger " as cool and unimpassioned earnestness."

Some of the Southern Whig senators justified their support of the bill, because the offer of the repeal of the Missouri Compromise came from the North; if it were a compact between the North and the South, the two parties to the contract had the right to annul it; and as the restriction was manifestly in the interest of the Northern people, they had, in a spirit of magnanimity, offered through their senators to yield their advantage. Could it be expected that the South would refuse this generous proffer?[1]

It was, indeed, strange that honorable men could shield

---

[1] This was the argument of Dixon, Jones of Tennessee, and Clayton of Delaware. The latter, indeed, did not vote for the bill. " Clayton speaks for the bill, but will vote against it. Cass speaks against the bill, but will vote for it."—New York *Evening Post*, March 2d.

themselves under such a miserable subterfuge ; for no fact was ever more certain or easier to be seen than that the Northern people utterly repudiated the action of the Illinois senator and his supporters.   Never but thrice in our history has a feeling so spontaneous, fierce, and sincere spread over the North.   For a parallel to the sentiment of February, 1854, we must look backward to that inspired by the shedding of American blood at Lexington, or forward to the grand uprising of 1861.   " The storm that is rising," wrote Seward, " is such a one as this country has never yet seen." [1]   In every way that was possible a free and earnest people expressed their opinion.   The power of the newspapers was exercised in a manner to justify all the praise that has ever been bestowed upon an unrestrained press.   Ability and zeal combined marked every step.   Greeley and Dana, of the New York *Tribune;* Bryant and Bigelow, of the *Evening Post;* Raymond, of the *Times;* Webb, of the *Courier and Enquirer;* Bowles, of the Springfield *Republican;* Thurlow Weed, of the Albany *Journal;* Schouler, of the Cincinnati *Gazette*—all bore an honorable part in exciting and guiding public opinion.   And they had coadjutors, young men full of enthusiasm for a righteous cause, who were glad to begin a journalistic career under the inspiration of the noble principle of opposition to the spread of slavery.   Some of them have written their reminiscences, which are a record of pure and unselfish labors in a holy war.   In reading carefully the leading articles in the journals of this period, one is struck with the vigor of the reasoning, and the sincere motives which prompted it.   Apparently the editors determined their course without ulterior thoughts as to what the effect might be on their pecuniary interest, or whether it would suit their party or faction.

What was true of the prominent newspapers which have been named may be affirmed, in general, of the opposition press all over the North.   The Whig journals were unani-

---

[1] Seward to his wife, Feb. 19th, Life of Seward, vol. ii. p. 222.

mously opposed to the bill; the Democratic press was divided. In the main it could be said that the newspapers which favored it had their policy dictated from Washington.[1] The journals which opposed the repeal of the Missouri Compromise were aggressive in tone; their articles had the ring of sincerity and earnestness; they were fervent protests against the violation of plighted faith and against opening the door to an extension of slavery.[2] On the other hand, the arguments of the newspapers favoring the bill were shuffling, and sounded as if the heart of the writers was not in the cause they were paid to advocate.[3]

---

[1] See New York *Evening Post*, Feb. 7th. In New York State the Albany *Argus* stated that thirty-seven "Hard" papers and two "Soft" supported the bill, while thirty-eight "Soft" papers opposed it; cited by Von Holst, vol. iv. p. 418, note. In Ohio, thirteen Democratic journals were for it, forty-one against it. *National Intelligencer*, March 25th. In Wisconsin, four Democratic papers supported and eleven opposed the bill. Boston *Atlas*, Feb. 21st. In Illinois, but one daily journal supported it. Ibid. The five daily newspapers of Chicago, one of which Senator Douglas had a prominent share in establishing, were against it. New York *Evening Post*, Feb. 20th. Only two daily papers in Indiana were in favor of the bill; and it was about the same way in Michigan and Iowa as in Indiana and Illinois. Boston *Atlas*. "In some hundred newspapers which we have just looked over, the expression of an indignant disapproval of the Nebraska bill is almost unanimous. It is a perfect chorus of condemnation and remonstrance."—New York *Evening Post*, Feb. 15th.

[2] One of the notable contributions to the discussion may be found in the New York *Tribune* of Feb. 22d. Greeley, who obviously wrote the article, says: "We know Henry Clay did not deceive us with regard to his views and purpose in urging that compromise [the compromise of 1850]; we are morally sure that no idea of repealing or 'superseding' the Missouri Compromise entered into his mind. Others may have been deeper in his confidence; but he deceived no man, and he discussed the whole subject freely with us, and ever regarded it as one wherein the territories [*i. e.*, Utah and New Mexico] were to inure to free labor, and that the practical business was to save the South from all needless and wanton humiliation."

[3] A good example of this may be seen in the able paper, the New York *Journal of Commerce*. The remarks in the text will not apply to the New York *Herald*, which advocated the bill in a positive and flippant manner.

Public opinion generally acts more quickly through the press than through public meetings. People will not assemble to pass resolutions on any subject until they have had time to get at the facts, to discuss them with their neighbors, and to make up their minds. But the Kansas-Nebraska bill was a measure whose provisions, clearly stated, were its own condemnation; and the newspapers and the Appeal of the Independent Democrats had made the intent of the bill easily intelligible. Public meetings of protest began to be held early. New York City was one of the first to lead off.[1] On January 30th, two or three thousand conservative people met at the Broadway Tabernacle. They were, for the most part, the solid merchants and leading lawyers of the city, who had been active in 1850 in working up public sentiment in favor of the compromise measures. This meeting, with but one negative vote, declared against the repeal of the Missouri Compromise, and asserted that such action "would impair the confidence of the country in the integrity of the South."[2] A gathering in Chicago on the 8th of February attracted great attention, for the proceedings were directed by men who, though they had been warm personal and political friends of Senator Douglas, could not follow where he led. These spoke in earnest tones against the passage of the Kansas-Nebraska act.[3] On the 18th of February a people's meeting was held at the Broadway Tabernacle, New York City. The building was crowded; people were glad to stand in the aisles and lobbies for the sake of hearing the speeches, and many were turned away because they could not get inside the doors. The meeting was addressed by John P. Hale and Henry Ward Beecher, who created great enthusiasm. Resolutions denouncing the Kansas-Nebraska bill and calling upon the

---

[1] The first meeting of which I have found any notice was at Cleveland on Jan. 28th.

[2] New York *Tribune*, Jan. 31st; see also the *Liberator*, Feb. 10th, and the New York *Evening Post* of Jan. 31st.

[3] Boston *Atlas;* New York *Tribune.*

I.—30

President to veto it, if passed, were adopted with demonstrations of intense feeling.[1]

Boston likewise had two meetings in Faneuil Hall to protest against the repeal of the Missouri Compromise. The radical gathering was addressed by Theodore Parker; the conservative meeting was composed largely of the same element that had assembled together to endorse Webster's 7th-of-March speech, and was presided over by Samuel Eliot, the Boston representative who had voted for the Fugitive Slave law.[2]

These meetings which have been mentioned were simply a representation of what was taking place all over the North. In every city and every town, people of the same mind came together and expressed their sentiments. The newspapers had columns in each issue which were entitled " The Voice of the Free States on the Nebraska Question,"[3] or " The Voice of the North, No Slavery Extension,"[4] and these were devoted to brief accounts of public meetings the tenor and action of which were always the same. At last one journal which had devoted a great deal of space to these expressions of opinion felt impelled to say : " If the *Evening Post* were three times as large as it is, and were issued three times a day, we should still despair of finding room for anything like full reports of the spontaneous gatherings which are every day held throughout the North and West " to protest against the passage of the Kansas-Nebraska act.[5] Up to the 15th of March two to three hundred large popular meetings had been held to denounce the bill, while there had not been at the North half a dozen gatherings to sustain it.[6] " We have never known," said the Richmond *Whig*, " such unanimity of sentiment at the North upon any ques-

---

[1] New York *Times ;* New York *Tribune.*

[2] The *Liberator ;* New York *Tribune,* Feb. 24th.

[3] New York *Evening Post.*   [4] New York *Tribune.*

[5] Cited by the *Liberator,* April 7th.

[6] New York *Courier,* March 15th, cited and verified by the Washington *National Intelligencer* of March 18th.

tion affecting the rights of the South as now prevails in opposition to the Missouri Compromise repeal." [1]

The expression of the authoritative representatives of the people, with one notable exception, was all in the same direction. Between January 1st and March 15th, ten of the legislatures of the free States were in session, and these bodies, in Maine, Massachusetts, Rhode Island, New York, and Wisconsin, protested against the passage of the Kansas-Nebraska bill. [2] The legislatures of Pennsylvania, New Jersey, and Ohio, although strongly Democratic, refused to vote on resolutions concerning the subject. California took no action. A large amount of influence and work was brought to bear upon Illinois, with the result of obtaining a reluctant approval of the measure from her legislature. [3]

---

[1] March 21st. The description of the opinion of New England by a Southerner visiting there may be interesting: "They are 'boiling over' here upon the Nebraska bill; all parties, Whigs and Democrats, Silver Grays and Woolly Heads, Softs and Hards, anti-slavery and even the little handful of pro-slavery folks."—Private letter to a Washington lady, dated Boston, Feb. 18th, published in *National Intelligencer*, Feb. 28th. The Boston correspondent of the New York *Journal of Commerce* wrote Feb. 16th: "It must be acknowledged that persons who have hitherto been quite conservative on the questions before the country are now giving unmistakable symptoms in the opposite direction. . . . They begin to feel that they must oppose with all their might the further extension of slave-holding on this continent, and that the North has hitherto been too lukewarm on this subject." "The protest against the Nebraska bill of Senator Douglas from the Northwest will be long and loud. It comes not from anti-slavery men, but from men of all parties."—Letter from Iowa, dated Jan. 26th, published in New York *Independent*.

[2] In Maine, the resolutions passed the Senate by a vote of 24 to 1, the House by 96 to 6; in Massachusetts, the Senate was unanimous, the House 246 to 13. The Rhode Island Legislature passed the resolutions unanimously. In New York, the Senate stood 23 to 6, the Assembly 80 to 27; in Wisconsin, the majorities for the resolutions were large. New York *Courier*, March 15th, cited and corrected by the Washington *National Intelligencer* of March 18th. Maine, Rhode Island, and Wisconsin were Democratic States.

[3] Ibid. The vote in Illinois stood: Senate, 14 to 8; House, 30 to 22; but

Petitions and memorials against the Kansas-Nebraska act poured in to Congress. "We know not," said the *Liberator*, " how many remonstrances have been sent to Congress from all parts of the free States against the passage of the Nebraska bill : we only know that we cannot keep pace with them ; while the first memorial, approving the bill, has yet to be presented to that body." [1]   " Sir," said a great man at Washington to a friend, "every ten signatures to a remonstrance against this bill make a pale face at Washington." [2]

Those who have read the preceding chapter will not expect any such display of sentiment in favor of the measure at the South as there was against it at the North. There had, indeed, been exciting political contests at the South, but they were generally connected with the strife of candidates for office, at which time interest in the struggle had been aroused by impassioned appeals from the stump. But a healthy public opinion which was not worked up by politicians, and which manifested itself in engrossing private discussion, in countless letters to the newspapers, in large popular meetings, and in petitions to Congress without number, was almost absolutely unknown at the South. [3]   A portion of the Southern press and a large part of the Southern aristocracy, who were the only people that did any political thinking in their section, were at first disposed to regard this measure of Douglas as a gift of the Greeks. It is true that, in 1848, Calhoun had originated the doctrine that the Missouri Compromise was unconstitutional, and Southern thinkers had embraced that theory ; but Calhoun himself had never proposed its abrogation ; and, indeed, at the previous session of Congress, Atchison, who was one of the chief

---

the affirmative vote in both branches made up less than one-half of the legislature.

[1] April 14th.   [2] New York *Evening Post*, Feb. 20th.

[3] The South does not speak by petitions to Congress, said Toombs; " she speaks through her representatives and senators."—Senate, May 25th, 1854.

apostles of slavery, had admitted that while the Missouri Compromise was a great error, the error was irremediable and must be submitted to, for it was evident that the restriction could never be repealed. And now "no public meeting of the people, no private assembly, no convention, no legislative body, had asked that the Missouri restriction should be set aside; and no Southerner in Congress had ever proposed its repeal." [1]

But when the scope of the Kansas - Nebraska act came to be thoroughly understood, when it was noted that the friends of Southern institutions in Congress were earnest in its favor and that the abolitionists were vehemently opposed to it, the newspapers began to praise Douglas warmly and to advocate his measure with zeal. [2] The exceptions were few, and were practically confined to New Orleans and the commercial cities of the border States. [3] While some observers reported a feeling of indifference in regard to the measure, this arose from the fact that it was not perfectly understood, or because its passage would be regarded as a barren victory. [4] There was no doubt, however, that the Charleston *Courier* faithfully represented Southern opinion when it remarked, "We cherish slavery as the apple of our eye, and

---

[1] See speech of Cullom, Whig representative of Tennessee, April 11th.

[2] Compare the Richmond *Whig* of Jan. 25th and Feb. 14th. Jan. 25th it is "that tricky demagogue, Douglas;" Feb. 14th, Douglas has "exhibited a disinterested fearlessness." See New York *Times*, Feb. 4th; also article in the Columbia (S. C.) *Times* of March 4th. "Senator Douglas deserves well of his country for having originally proposed it."—Charleston *Courier*, Feb. 16th; also letters in the Washington *National Intelligencer*, Jan. 31st and Feb. 14th.

[3] The New Orleans *Commercial Bulletin* was strongly opposed to it; see articles of Jan. 23d, 27th, Feb. 18th, 24th, and March 8th. The New Orleans *Crescent* thought the measure one of bad policy for the South; see article of Feb. 24th, cited in the New York *Times*, March 8th. The Louisville *Journal* and Baltimore *American* gave it a qualified condemnation, and the St. Louis *Democrat* was outspoken against it. See New York *Evening Post*, Feb. 4th.

[4] New York *Evening Post*, March 17th; New York *Times*, Feb. 16th.

are resolved to maintain it, peaceably if we can, forcibly if
we must;" and it may confidently be stated that when the
Kansas-Nebraska bill was understood to be of benefit to
slavery, Southern sentiment at that moment became concentrated in its favor.[1]   "The South flies to the bill," wrote
Francis Lieber from South Carolina, "as moths to the
candle."[2]

The legislatures of the slave States were slower to act
than those of the North.   Before the bill passed the Senate,
only Georgia had spoken.   Her House unanimously, and the
Senate with only three dissenting votes, adopted resolutions
strongly in favor of the bill, and instructed her delegation to
vote in Congress accordingly.   In Tennessee the Senate endorsed the principles of the Kansas-Nebraska act, but the
House laid a similar resolution on the table.[3]   Not until
after the bill had passed the United States Senate did the
legislatures of Mississippi and Louisiana adopt resolutions
approving it.[4]

And now the day had come when a vote on the bill was
to be taken.   The Senate met on the 3d of March at the
usual hour, and an animated discussion of the measure consumed the afternoon and evening.   The floor was full and
the galleries were crowded when Douglas rose, a half an
hour before midnight, to close the debate.   He offered to
waive his privilege in order that they might proceed to vote;
but many senators protested, and begged him to go on.   The
importance of the occasion and the influence which this
speech might have on his future career might well make
even as ready a speaker as Douglas tremble when he thought
what he must confront.   The bill had passed to a third read-

[1] Charleston *Courier*, Feb. 16th.   The Richmond *Whig* said, March 14th:
"The South are united for the removal of the Missouri restriction."
[2] Life and Letters of Francis Lieber, p. 269.
[3] New York *Courier*, March 15th, cited and corrected by the *National Intelligencer* of March 18th.
[4] *National Intelligencer*, April 1st and 4th.

ing the day previous by a vote of twenty-nine to twelve, so
that argument in the Senate was needless; but the people
of the North were almost unanimously against the measure
and its author, and it was to them that Douglas spoke with
extraordinary energy and ability, persuading and imploring
them to reverse their verdict. A feeling of regret that he
had provoked this controversy must have mingled with the
excitement of the combatant in the contest; but there was
no trace of it in his manner as he applied himself vigorously
to the work of justifying himself, of defending his bill, and
of hurling defiance at his opponents.

The appearance of Douglas was striking. Though very
short in stature, he had an enormous head, and when he rose
to take arms against the sea of troubles which opposed him,
he was the very picture of intellectual force. Always a
splendid fighter, he seemed this night like a gladiator who
contended against great odds; for while he was backed by
thirty-seven senators, among his fourteen opponents were
the ablest men of the Senate, and their arguments must be
answered if he expected to ride out the storm which had
been raised against him. Never in the United States, in
the arena of debate, had a bad cause been more splendidly
advocated; never more effectively was the worse made to
appear the better reason.

The opponents of the bill, he said, had misrepresented the
issue to the country; they wished the people to believe that
the paramount object of the bill was to repeal the Missouri
Compromise. "That which is a mere incident they choose
to consider the principle. They make war on the means by
which we propose to accomplish an object instead of openly
resisting the object itself. The principle which we propose
to carry into effect is this: *That Congress shall neither legislate slavery into any territories or State, nor out of the same;
but the people shall be left free to regulate their domestic concerns in their own way, subject only to the Constitution of the
United States.* In order to carry this principle into practical operation, it becomes necessary to remove whatever legal

obstacles might be found in the way of its free exercise.
It is only for the purpose of carrying out this great fundamental principle of self-government that the bill renders"
the Missouri restriction inoperative and void.

Douglas then went on to show, by extracts from his
speeches, that as he thought now, so had he thought in
1850; and at that time the legislature of his State believed
that the principle should be so applied.[1] We are contend-
ing, he maintained, for "the great fundamental principle of
popular sovereignty;" and as the Missouri restriction is inconsistent with that principle, it ought to be abrogated. Instead of the opponents of this bill talking about "the sanctity of the Missouri Compromise and the dishonor attached
to the violation of plighted faith, . . . why do they not
meet the issue boldly and fairly and controvert the sound-
ness of this great principle of popular sovereignty in obedience to the Constitution?" It is because "the doctrine of
the abolitionists—the doctrine of the opponents of the Nebraska and Kansas bill and of the advocates of the Missouri
restriction—demands congressional interference with slavery, not only in the territories, but in all the new States to
be formed therefrom. It is the same doctrine, when applied
to the territories and new States of this Union, which the
British government attempted to enforce by the sword upon
the American colonies. It is this fundamental principle of
self-government which constitutes the distinguishing feature
of the Nebraska bill. . . . The onward march of this great
and growing country," he continued, made it necessary for
the committee on territories to give a government to Nebraska; and then we met this question of slavery. It could
be settled on the principle of 1820, which was congressional
interference, or on the principle of 1850, which was non-
interference. "We chose the latter for two reasons: first,
because we believed that the principle was right; and, second, because it was the principle adopted in 1850, to which

---

[1] See Appendix, *Congressional Globe*, vol. xxix. p. 327.

the two great political parties of the country were solemnly pledged." If we will adopt this principle, the senator further argued, "it will have the effect to destroy all sectional parties and sectional agitations." If the slavery question is withdrawn from the political arena and removed to the States and territories, each to decide for itself, there can be no more agitation of slavery. If this vexed question is removed from politics, the agitators will be deprived of their vocation. There will be no further necessity for bargains between the North and the South.

"I have not," said Douglas at the close of his argument, "brought this question forward as a Northern man or as a Southern man. I am unwilling to recognize such divisions and distinctions. I have brought it forward as an American senator, representing a State which is true to this principle, and which has approved of my action with respect to the Nebraska bill. I have brought it forward not as an act of justice to the South more than to the North. I have presented it especially as an act of justice to the people of those territories, and of the States to be formed therefrom, now and in all time to come. I have nothing to say about Northern rights or Southern rights. I know of no such divisions or distinctions under the Constitution. The bill does equal and exact justice to the whole Union, and every part of it; it violates the rights of no State or territory, but places each on a perfect equality, and leaves the people thereof to the free enjoyment of all their rights under the Constitution."

The foregoing extracts will give an idea of the line of argument which Douglas pursued; but nearly the whole speech must be read to comprehend the skill with which specious arguments were urged, and duly to estimate the dexterity with which an historical account of the Missouri Compromise and succeeding events was used. The kindly feeling of the audience towards him from the first was increased by his audacity, and with artful management he gained their sympathy. He told how he had been maligned all over the country. He had been burned in effigy in all the abolition towns of Ohio because they believed the misrepresentations of Chase; he had been hanged in effigy in Boston, owing to the influence of Sumner; but that he considered an honor, for this same Boston had closed Faneuil Hall to the immortal Webster. A remonstrance had been presented to the Senate in which he was called "a traitor to his country, to freedom, and to God, worthy only of everlasting infamy;" and he had even received insulting letters from Ohio, rejoicing at his domestic bereavements,[1] and praying that still greater calamities might befall him. The state of public sentiment of which these were the manifestations was, the senator averred, due to the misrepresentations of his opponents, and particularly to those which were contained in the Appeal of the Independent Democrats.

In spite of his warmth of argument and vehemence of attack, Douglas showed the most perfect courtesy to his antagonists. When Seward, Chase, or Sumner, to whom he especially addressed himself, desired to interrupt him to correct a statement or briefly reply to an argument, Douglas cheerfully yielded the floor; but every rejoinder showed that in debate he was more than a match for any one of these senators. The politeness with which he complied with their requests for a hearing, and the force of his answers, caused Seward to burst out, in admiration, "I have never had so much respect for the senator as I have to-night."

In the course of his speech, Douglas took up Everett's argument, and showed by the construction he put upon Webster's 7th-of-March speech that he could twist the language of the clearest of speakers to his purpose as well as he could distort the facts of history.

While the suavity of Douglas during the whole night was remarkable, he did not propose to let Chase and Sumner off as easily as he had Seward and Everett. Their charge that his measure was offered as a bid for Presidential votes was

---

[1] The wife of Douglas died Jan. 19th, 1853.

a rankling wound, and he demanded with a show of sincere indignation if they were "incapable of conceiving that an honest man can do a right thing from worthy motives?" Nor did he think that these senators were proper judges of his character or principles, for he intimated that they had obtained their seats in the Senate "by a corrupt bargain or dishonorable coalition." This angered Chase, who met it with an indignant denial, and Sumner made a calm refutation. In the excited colloquy which followed between Chase and a Democrat from California, who insisted on charging directly what Douglas had only implied, the "Little Giant" was cool, and, restraining the impetuosity of his supporter, continued the defence of his own motives; and, with the address of a master of parliamentary art, he made it appear, by the most delicate implication, that he was a self-sacrificing patriot, while Chase was actuated by an "unworthy ambition."

Douglas spoke until daybreak, and the crowd remained to hear the last words of the giant, who seemed to exult in his strength and who was flushed with victory. Senator Houston explained why he could not consent to a violation of the Missouri Compromise; and then the vote was taken. The Senate was composed of sixty-one members,[1] of whom fifty-one were present, and the vote stood 37 in favor to 14 against the bill. There were recorded in the affirmative fourteen Northern Democrats, fourteen Southern Democrats, and nine Southern Whigs; while four Northern Democrats, six Northern Whigs, two Free-soilers, one Southern Whig, and one Southern Democrat voted in the negative. The negative vote is a roll of legislative honor, and deserves detailed mention. It was composed of Dodge of Wisconsin, Hamlin of Maine, James of Rhode Island, Walker of Wisconsin, Houston of Texas, Democrats; Fessenden of Maine, Fish and Seward of New York, Foot of Vermont, Smith of Connecticut, Wade of Ohio, and

---

[1] There were thirty-one States, but there was one vacancy.

Bell of Tennessee, Whigs; and Chase and Sumner, Free-soilers.[1]

As the senators went home on this sombre March morning, they heard the boom of the cannon from the navy-yard proclaiming the triumph of what Douglas called popular sovereignty. Chase and Sumner, who were devoted friends, walked down the steps of the Capitol together, and as they heard the thunders of victory, Chase exclaimed: "They celebrate a present victory, but the echoes they awake will never rest until slavery itself shall die."[2]

Before the bill passed, an amendment of Badger of North Carolina was incorporated in it to the effect that nothing in the act should be construed to revive the old Louisiana law which protected slavery in the whole of that territory. An amendment of Clayton was likewise adopted; this provided that only citizens of the United States should have the right of suffrage and of holding office in the territories, it being intended to work against emigrants from Europe who might settle there. This amendment was only carried by a vote of 22 to 20; and it is noticeable, as indicating the feeling towards the foreign population, that all the senators but one who favored this amendment were from the slave States, and all who opposed it were from the free States, Douglas voting with Chase, Seward, Sumner, and Wade.

[1] It will be noted that Everett's name does not appear in the negative. He remained in the Senate until half-past three o'clock in the morning, but was ill and could not remain longer. *National Intelligencer*, March 4th, and Everett's explanation, March 7th. He showed excessive sensitiveness to attacks that were made upon him for his failure to vote against the bill. A certificate soon appeared, signed by Seward, Wade, Fish, Smith, and Foot, vouching his inability to be present. This did not help the matter. See New York *Evening Post*, April 10th, 11th, and 15th; also Reminiscences of a Journalist, C. T. Congdon, p. 278, which undoubtedly refers to Everett. See also private letters of Seward, Life of Seward, vol. ii. p. 225. Clayton was also ill, but would have voted against the bill; he stated his reasons in the Senate, March 7th.

[2] Life of Chase, Schuckers, p. 156.

This speech of Douglas, which closed the debate, has been considered at length, for it was an epoch-making event in the decade of 1850–60. Cass was the author of the doctrine which Douglas so warmly embraced, but until now it had been known as congressional non-intervention, or squatter sovereignty.[1] Douglas this night gave it the name of popular sovereignty, and the name was a far greater invention than the doctrine. The ardent advocacy of the sovereignty of the people was certain to have a powerful influence;[2] and while at this moment the fate of Douglas seemed trembling in the balance, he was destined to rise above the wave of popular indignation which now threatened to overwhelm him. Using his principle of popular sovereignty to oppose the encroachments of slavery, he would in the future enlist under that banner many who now regarded his work with execration.

The doctrine of popular sovereignty died with slavery. At the best it was a makeshift. As expounded by Douglas, it meant that Congress, which represented the political wisdom of an educated people, should abdicate its constitutional right of deciding a question, which demanded the most sagacious statesmanship, in favor of a thousand, or perhaps ten thousand, pioneers, adventurers, and fortune-seekers who should happen to locate in a territory. As an expedient to settle an angry controversy, and as one of a series of compromises, congressional non-intervention in Utah and New Mexico was justified in 1850; but, used as a principle to unsettle a time-honored settlement, it can receive at the bar of history only an unqualified condemnation.

A spirit had been roused by the introduction of this bill which the politicians must reckon with. On the 13th of March, Hamilton Fish, senator from New York, presented a petition, signed by clergymen of different denominations in New York City and its vicinity, remonstrating against the passage of the Kansas-Nebraska act. The bish-

---

[1] Douglas made a distinction between squatter and popular sovereignty. See Cutts, p. 123.   [2] See Life and Times of Samuel Bowles, vol. i. p. 115.

op of the Episcopal Church headed the memorial, and it was subscribed by a majority of the clergymen of New York City.[1] This petition attracted no attention, and it was ordered to lie upon the table in the usual manner. But the next day Everett presented a remonstrance against the passage of the Nebraska bill, signed by three thousand and fifty clergymen of all denominations and sects in the different States of New England. There were in that section of country three thousand eight hundred ministers,[2] and this memorial was therefore the expression of the sentiments of a very large proportion of the whole number.[3]

The petition was couched in strong language. It said: "The undersigned, clergymen of different religious denominations in New England, hereby, in the name of Almighty God, and in his presence, do solemnly protest against the passage of what is known as the Nebraska bill. . . . We protest against it as a great moral wrong, as a breach of faith eminently unjust to the moral principles of the community, and subversive of all confidence in national engagements; as a measure full of danger to the peace and even the existence of our beloved Union, and exposing us to the righteous judgments of the Almighty."[4]

---

[1] Among the names subscribed to it were: J. M. Wainwright, Stephen H. Tyng, G. T. Bedell, Isaac Ferris, George B. Cheever, R. S. Storrs, Jr., Theo. L. Cuyler, Samuel Osgood, Henry W. Bellows, Thomas K. Beecher. The *Independent* said that if there had been time to circulate the petition more widely, many more names would have been obtained. The *Independent*, March 23d.

[2] See Everett's statement, *Congressional Globe*, vol. xxviii. p. 617.

[3] Among the names subscribed to this memorial were: Lyman Beecher; Manton Eastburn, Episcopal bishop of Massachusetts; C. A. Bartol; Theodore Parker; T. D. Woolsey, Pres. of Yale College; F. Wayland, Pres. of Brown University; Mark Hopkins, Pres. Williams College; Edward Hitchcock, Pres. Amherst College; G. Burgess, Episcopal bishop of Maine; Horace Bushnell, Hartford; E. Ballou, Montpelier. See the *Liberator*, April 14th.

[4] The petition was dated March 1st, and the purpose was to present it to the Senate before the bill passed.

The reading of this memorial created a sensation in the Senate. Douglas made some fierce and sarcastic remarks, and rebuked the clergymen for quitting their proper vocation and meddling in an affair which they did not understand. They had, he said, "desecrated the pulpit and prostituted the sacred desk to the miserable and corrupting influence of party politics."

Somewhat more than a month later, Douglas himself presented a petition against the bill of five hundred and four clergymen of the Northwestern States, which emanated from Chicago, and which was similar in language to the New England petition. He made this the text of a speech which criticised severely the interference of preachers in affairs of State.

Douglas and the Southern senators might cry down these manifestations, but in truth they were the inception of a movement which was destined to have a powerful influence towards the abolition of slavery. On the compromise measures clergymen had been divided; indeed, many of high station had counselled submission to the Fugitive Slave law. Now, however, they were practically united, and they considered it their duty to preach sermons against what they believed to be a violation of plighted faith.[1]

It will be generally conceded that on political questions which are those of mere expediency the minister should be silent. It would to-day[2] shock the church-going community to hear from the pulpit arguments directed to show that a high tariff or free trade was demanded by the law of God; but when the paramount political issue becomes intertwined with a sacred moral principle, it is the duty of the preacher to declare that principle, and to urge his hearers to make

---

[1] Douglas said that on one day in New England fifteen hundred to two thousand sermons were preached against the bill. Appendix, *Congressional Globe*, vol. xxix. p. 656. The religious and secular newspapers of this time are full of reports of sermons on the subject.

[2] 1892.

their political action conform to the behests of the moral law. The slavery question had a moral as well as a political side. The ministers would have been recreant to their calling had they not proclaimed from their pulpits what the spirit of their religion prompted them to speak. This widespread agitation from the pulpit is a striking evidence of the deeply stirred-up feeling at the North. It was patent that the preachers spoke to willing listeners, and that their congregations would stand by them in the position they had taken.

The bill now went to the House of Representatives, and the first action of this body showed that it paid attention to the uprising of popular sentiment which the Senate had depreciated and disregarded. On the 21st of March, the Senate Kansas-Nebraska bill came up in order, and Richardson,[1] who was thoroughly devoted to Douglas and his interests, moved that it be referred to the committee on territories, of which he was the chairman. Cutting, a member from New York City, and who belonged to the faction of "Hards," at once moved that it be referred to the committee of the whole on the state of the Union, and demanded the previous question. He stated that he was in favor of the principle of the bill; but the representatives owed it to the country to consider this "grave and serious question" carefully, to correct whatever imperfections there were in the measure as it had come from the Senate, and to make plain to the people of the North what was intended by this legislation; for it was undeniable that, "since its introduction into Congress, the North would seem to have taken up arms, and to have become excited into a sort of civil insurrection." In spite of the protest of Richardson that such a reference of the bill "would be killing it by indirection," Cutting's motion prevailed by a vote of 110 to 95. This action was a defeat for the friends of the measure, and especially incensed Breckinridge, of Kentucky, who said that,

---

[1] Richardson was from Illinois.

having been done "under the guise of friendship to the bill, it was the act of a man who throws his arm in apparently friendly embrace around another saying, 'How is it with thee, brother?' and at the same time covertly stabs him to the heart." Some of the opponents of the bill were disposed to think that it could not possibly pass the House at this session; but those who had the best knowledge and clearest judgment thought, with the New York *Tribune*, that the snake was scotched, not killed.[1] As a matter of fact, this reference placed the bill at the foot of the calendar; there were fifty bills ahead of it, and it could not be reached in the regular course of legislation.[2]

The shrewd anticipation of Douglas, that the help of the administration would be needed to carry the measure through the House, was realized. Marcy, however, who had more influence with the representatives than any other member of the cabinet, was indifferent to the fate of the measure. Indeed, after Douglas introduced the substitute, Marcy's apprehensions of the effect of it on the Democratic party were so grave that he entertained the idea of resigning his position, and took advice from his personal and political friends regarding his line of duty. The drift of their opinion was that he ought to remain. The "Softs" had now an equal amount of the patronage and influence of New York State; but should Marcy retire, it was feared that the "Hards" would gain the supremacy.[3] It may be presumed that in Marcy's mind a higher motive was mixed with the lower, and that he felt that, if he resigned, a secretary of state might be chosen who would truckle to the Southern propaganda, and give them effective aid in carrying out schemes prejudicial to the country.

---

[1] March 23d.   [2] See *Congressional Globe*, vol. xxviii. p. 762.

[3] Wilson's Rise and Fall of the Slave Power, vol. ii. p. 382. This was stated on the authority of Reuben E. Fenton, a "Soft" representative from New York. See also Washington correspondence New York *Courier and Enquirer*, Jan. 31st and Feb. 25th.

I.—31

The vacillation of the President undoubtedly gave uneasiness to the supporters of the measure. When under the influence of Davis and Cushing, he was an enthusiastic friend of it, and expressed himself warmly in favor of the principle of the bill;[1] when chilled by the doubts of Marcy, he wavered. "You ask me," wrote Dix, "what General Pierce's opinion is. I do not know. Some say he is for the repeal of the Missouri Compromise—others as confidently that he is against it."[2] The result of the New Hampshire election might well make him halt between the two opinions. His native State, which had given him a handsome majority for President, was now only carried with great difficulty by the Democratic governor; and, what was of more importance, the lower House of the legislature was so strongly anti-Nebraska that it would insure the choice of two opposition senators in the place of Norris and Williams, who had voted for the Kansas-Nebraska act. But, in spite of internal dissensions and the unsteadiness of the President, the authoritative public expressions of the administration were all one way. It was announced that the patronage would be used in the interest of those representatives who voted for the bill;[3] and the morning after the House had consigned it to the committee of the whole, the organ declared that the Kansas-Nebraska project had become a prominent measure of President Pierce's administration. "If it be defeated in the House, it will, it must be admitted, be a defeat of the administration."[4] Important appointments were withheld in order that they might be used to reward the constant friends of the bill; alluring bait was held out to those who were lukewarm, and threats were

---

[1] See letter of Jeremiah Clemens to Franklin Pierce, March 24th, *Washington Union*, March 26th.

[2] Letter of Dix to J. C. Curtis, Feb. 25th, Memoirs of J. A. Dix, vol. i. p. 285.

[3] *Washington Union*, March 7th, quoted by Von Holst.

[4] *Washington Union*, March 22d.

employed to coerce the representatives who were disposed to rebel against the dictates of the party leaders. All the members of the cabinet, except Marcy and McClelland, were working for the measure, and Davis and Cushing were earnest and indefatigable advocates.

As the bill slept in the committee of the whole, some of its friends and some of its enemies began to think that the project would not be revived this session.[1] But they little knew Douglas who thought one check would daunt him. He thoroughly understood the situation. He was aware that many Northern Democratic representatives would secretly delight if the bill were never brought to a vote in the House, yet these same men would feel constrained to give it their voice when the question was actually put. They would not dare to resist the power of the administration and that party discipline which, having been instituted by Jefferson, had gained force by use, and was never so powerful as now.

On the 8th of May the result of the pressure became manifest. On that day Richardson, the trusted lieutenant of Douglas, obtained the floor after the reading of the journal, and moved that the House resolve itself into the committee of the whole on the state of the Union. He frankly avowed that his object was to have the committee lay aside all bills which had the precedence of the Kansas-Nebraska bill, so that they might at once proceed to its consideration. While the Senate act had been placed at the foot of the calendar, there were but eighteen bills ahead of the House bill, which had been reported by the House committee of territories, and which was the same as the Senate bill before it had been amended. Richardson now moved to lay aside one by one

---

[1] "The Nebraska bill lies quietly in the committee of the whole. . . . The Nebraska bill is considered dead. . . . Killed by Cutting."—New York *Herald*, April 6th. "We now believe it most improbable that any bill repudiating the Missouri restriction can be forced through the present House."—New York *Tribune*, April 27th. The latter is quoted by Von Holst.

these bills. The question was put eighteen times, and each
time the majority voted with their leader. The House Kansas-Nebraska bill was then reached, when Richardson proposed as a substitute a bill which was the same as the Senate
act, with the exception of the Clayton amendment. This
was, the next two days, debated in committee. On Thursday, May 11th, Richardson obtained the floor almost immediately after the reading of the journal, moved that the debate close the next day at twelve o'clock, and on that motion
called for the previous question. At this, the pent-up feeling of the opponents of the measure broke forth. They implored Richardson for more time ; they protested against
this summary closing of debate as rank injustice. An in-
formal discussion was permitted by the speaker, in order to
see whether an understanding could not be arrived at ; but
the feeling was so intense that heated expressions were not
avoided, and the breach became wider. One member roused
the wrath of others by calling the bill a "swindle." Alexander H. Stephens expressed the willingness of the majority
to give the minority a reasonable time for debate, provided
they would then allow a vote to be taken ; but he emphatically declared that if factious opposition were made, it would
be met "as factious opposition in this House has always been
met." Lewis D. Campbell[1] cried, amidst shouts of approval:
" I will resist the further progress of this bill by all the means
which the rules of the House place in my power, even though
gentlemen may call it faction." Then filibustering under
the leadership of Campbell began. Motions to adjourn,
motions to adjourn to a fixed time, motions for a call of the
House, followed one another. Then a member would ask
to be excused from voting, and a friend would move that
he be excused ; and on all these motions the yeas and nays
were called for. In short, all kinds of dilatory motions were
used with skill by men who thoroughly understood the rules
of the House, and they were supported by a determined

---

[1] Of Ohio.

minority. The session continued all day Thursday, all of Thursday night, and all day Friday, without reaching any result. At times the monotonous call of the yeas and nays would cease, and attempts would be made by the more moderate of both sides to come to some arrangement, when a remark would be interjected by some member which would provoke an angry reply, and the uproar and confusion would begin again. Douglas was on the floor of the House a large share of the time for the purpose of directing his followers, but he and Richardson did little but watch and wait for a subsidence of the excited feeling. It was after eleven o'clock on Friday night when, as a result of a talk between Campbell and Richardson, the latter stated that, as a number of the opponents of the bill had signified their desire that they might have until the next day for deliberation, he would move an adjournment. The House was now in a very excited state. The nervous tension caused by loss of sleep, irregular hours, and powerful emotion was manifest. Those who were accustomed to stimulate themselves in times of excitement were inflamed by strong drink. It had been freely talked that a disturbance was liable to occur, and many members came to the House armed for the fray. A spark only was needed to produce an explosion.

Hunt, a Whig from Louisiana opposed to the measure, who many times had tried to pour oil upon the troubled waters, now made a patriotic and amicable appeal to Richardson to give his friends until Monday for consideration. Richardson made a courteous reply, saying it was beyond his power to grant the request, but hoped that on the morrow a desirable result might be reached. Had the speaker[1] then put the question, trouble would have been avoided; but, with praiseworthy intentions, he permitted a desultory discussion, during which Alexander Stephens made some fiery remarks. This brought Campbell to his feet, who was pro-

---

[1] Linn Boyd, of Kentucky, was speaker, but at this moment Orr, of South Carolina, was in the chair.

ceeding to reply when he was called to order by Seward, of Georgia. It must be understood that this discussion was by unanimous consent, no debatable question being before the House, and no member could speak if called to order by another. The interposition of Seward was unfair, and cries of order went up from all parts of the hall. Above the confusion could be heard the voice of Campbell: "I shall resist this measure to the bitter end. I say so, never minding the gentleman who calls me to order." Amidst repeated shouts of "Order!" Seward retorted: "There are other places instead of this where personal difficulties may be settled." Confusion was now confounded. Members crowded around Campbell. Many got on the tops of the desks. Above the din Campbell vehemently exclaimed: "I tell you, gentlemen, that I shall resist this measure with all the power that I can to the bitter end." Members still continued to crowd around Campbell, and it was reported that weapons were drawn, and that an attempt was made to use one by Edmundson, of Virginia. The speaker did his best to preserve order; he prayed all lovers of order to assist him, and he commanded the sergeant-at-arms to use the emblem of authority. The sergeant-at-arms, advancing with the mace of the House, arrested Edmundson, compelled members to resume their seats, and was successful in partially restoring order. The speaker then cut off all further attempts at discussion, and, as soon as possible, put the motion of Richardson, and declared the House adjourned. By his prompt action he undoubtedly prevented a bloody affray. It deserves to be noted that among the gentlemen who effectually assisted the speaker in preventing a disgraceful brawl were Aiken and Keitt, of South Carolina. The sitting came to a close at twenty-seven minutes before midnight, the House having been in continuous session nearly thirty-six hours.[1]

_____

[1] See *Congressional Globe*, Washington correspondence New York *Courier and Enquirer*, New York *Times*, and New York *Herald*.

The next day's session of the House was short, and nothing was done. On this Saturday, May 13th, an enthusiastic anti-Nebraska meeting of five thousand people was held in the City Hall Park, New York City, the assemblage being composed chiefly of mechanics. The speeches were heard attentively, and the resolutions responded to with earnestness. One of these declared that they would vote for no representative who gave his voice in Congress for the repeal of the Missouri Compromise.[1]

On Monday, May 15th, Richardson proposed to give until Saturday for debate. This offer would undoubtedly have been made before, had not a special order on the Pacific Railroad bill stood in the way. To postpone this now, a suspension of the rules was necessary, and eighteen Northern Democrats, who had hitherto voted in the opposition, gave their voices on the side of the majority, which made the requisite two-thirds vote; and it was then decided that the debate should close on the Saturday following. The action of these Democrats was severely criticised by the Whigs, and they were charged with being recreant to principle and dominated by party considerations; but, in truth, such questioning of motives was liable to be unjust. It must always occur to some congressmen of the minority, as it does to the philosophic observer, that filibustering is an inane mode of accomplishing an object. It rarely defeats the aim of the majority, although indeed it may postpone action. It is true that there was abundant reason to suppose that if action were not reached on the Kansas-Nebraska bill this session, it would not be revived at the next; but it was also true that the majority was large enough and determined enough to keep the House in session until the measure was passed. The assertion of the minority that the majority wanted to stifle debate was, of course, a subterfuge. Already, Richardson stated, eighty speeches had been made in the House on the question, which was more

---

[1] New York *Times*, May 15th.

than had ever been made on any previous measure;[1] and before the bill came to a vote this number was increased to one hundred.[2]

The discussion proceeded quietly the remaining days of the week, the House holding long sessions. On Saturday, the 20th, the members came together at nine o'clock. The debate closed soon after twelve; the opposition badgered the majority the rest of the day by offering amendments and speaking to them under the five-minute rule. On Monday, May 22d, the House met and went immediately into committee. Stephens then moved to strike out the enacting clause of the bill, avowing that his object was to cut off all amendments, and have the bill reported to the House so that a vote might be taken on it. This unusual proceeding caused a great sensation. Indeed, Stephens had great difficulty in getting the leaders to agree to this mode of action.[3] One member declared that it was apparent the majority purposed to ride rough-shod over the minority. Another, in the midst of the excitement, called upon his friends not to vote upon the question, and cried: "Oppose tyranny by revolution!" The motion to strike out the enacting clause was, however, agreed to. The committee rose and reported to the House. Then ensued a stubborn contest. The minority used every means in their power to prevent a vote; but the management of Richardson[4] was skilful, and he had Douglas at hand to prompt him. The House refused to concur in the report of the committee, which struck out the enacting clause of the bill. Well might Stephens write, "I took the reins in hand, applied whip and spur, and brought the

---

[1] *Congressional Globe*, vol. xxviii. p. 1161.

[2] Washington *Sentinel*, quoted by New York *Herald*, May 23d. In the House, 45 speeches were made for the bill, 55 against; in the Senate, 17 for, 11 against. Total number of set speeches to May 21st, 128.

[3] Life of Alexander H. Stephens, Johnston and Browne, p. 277.

[4] Campbell afterwards (June 27th) said that the course of Richardson on the Nebraska bill was "open, frank, and manly."

'wagon' out."[1] It was nearly midnight when a vote was reached. The Kansas-Nebraska bill was then passed by 113 yeas to 100 nays. Forty-four Northern and fifty-seven Southern Democrats voted for the bill, and these were reinforced by twelve Whigs from the slave States; against the bill were forty-five Whigs and forty-two Democrats from the North, two Democrats and seven Whigs from the slave States. The names of these nine, with whom respect for plighted faith was more powerful than the supposed interest of their section, deserve a record. They were : Puryear and Rogers of North Carolina, Bugg, Cullom, Etheridge, and Taylor of Tennessee, Hunt of Louisiana, Whigs; and Millson of Virginia and Thomas H. Benton, Democrats.[2]

No man in either House of Congress brought so much intelligence and experience to bear upon his vote as did Benton. He had come into political life on the Missouri Compromise. His State had kept him in the Senate for thirty years; and when the legislature would no longer elect him, he had appealed to the people of his district and they had sent him to the House. He was not only a statesman of experience, but he was writing a history of the events in which he had been an actor and on which he had looked as a spectator. Certainly his protest should have been regarded. He spoke as a statesman whose memory and judgment were enlightened by the investigation of an historian. He declared that the movement for the abrogation of the Missouri Compromise began " without a memorial, without a petition, without a request from a human being;" that this scheme was directed against a compromise which was not a "mere statute to last for a day," but one which " was intended for perpetuity, and so declared itself."   When he came to analyze the Kansas-Nebraska bill, he referred to the explanation which Douglas had incorporated in his substitute in

---

[1] Johnston and Browne, p. 277.
[2] This analysis is taken from the New York *Tribune*.

words which were remembered as long as Douglas was a candidate for the presidency.[1]

As the House bill had left out the Clayton amendment, it was necessary that it should go to the Senate before becoming a law. An interesting debate of two days occurred, in which important revelations were made of the efforts used to dragoon a few objecting Southern Whigs into support of the measure. The difference, moreover, in the construction of the act by its friends became again apparent. Judged by the succeeding events, the most remarkable expressions came from Sumner, for he had an insight into the future. This bill, he said, " is at once the worst and the best bill on which Congress ever acted. It is the worst bill, inasmuch as it is a present victory of slavery. . . . It is the best bill, . . . for it prepares the way for that ' All hail hereafter,' when slavery must disappear. It annuls all past compromises with slavery, and makes all future compromises impossible. Thus it puts freedom and slavery face to face, and bids them grapple. Who can doubt the result ?"

The bill, as it had come from the House, was ordered to a third reading by a vote of 35 to 13, and passed the Senate May 25th. It was approved by the President May 30th.

It is safe to say that, in the scope and consequences of the Kansas-Nebraska act, it was the most momentous measure that passed Congress from the day that the senators and representatives first met to the outbreak of the civil war. It sealed the doom of the Whig party; it caused the formation of the Republican party on the principle of no extension of slavery; it roused Lincoln and gave a bent to his great political ambition.[2] It made the Fugitive Slave law a

---

[1] Benton said that the clause " It being the true intent and meaning of this act, etc.," was " a little stump speech injected in the belly of the bill."

[2] Life of Lincoln, Herndon, p. 361; Life of Lincoln, Arnold, p. 115. He wrote to a friend : " I was losing interest in politics when the repeal of the Missouri Compromise aroused me again."—E. B. Washburne on Lincoln, Reminiscences of A. Lincoln, North American Publishing Company.

dead letter at the North; it caused the Germans to become Republicans; it lost the Democrats their hold on New England; it made the Northwest Republican; it led to the downfall of the Democratic party.

It may be asserted with confidence that no man in the country except Douglas could have carried this measure through the necessary stages of becoming a law. Five years later, in familiar talk with his Boswell, he said: "I passed the Kansas-Nebraska act myself. I had the authority and power of a dictator throughout the whole controversy in both houses. The speeches were nothing. It was the marshalling and directing of men, and guarding from attacks, and a ceaseless vigilance preventing surprise,"[1] that led to the success of the measure. It is certain that in after-years Douglas came to believe that his doctrine of popular sovereignty was a great political principle; and it is probable that even now he half believed that there was some occult virtue in it as a rule of action. Persistent advocacy often convinces the advocate. Yet, laying aside entirely the moral view, the action of Douglas as a statesman, as a politician and leader of a party, was characterized by a lamentable lack of foresight and the utter absence of the careful reflection which far-reaching measures of legislation demand. Douglas had asserted in 1849 that all the evidences of public opinion seemed to indicate that the Missouri Compromise "had become canonized in the hearts of the American people, as a sacred thing which no ruthless hand would ever be reckless enough to disturb."[2] Having once had that conviction, therefore, he owed it to his country, and to his party as well, not to broach this measure until he had given it deep study and prolonged consideration. For Douglas loved his country; his party was his religion, the Constitution was his creed; and in following the leading of an inordinate ambition he did not imagine that he was sacrific-

---

[1] Constitutional and Party Questions, Cutts, p. 122.
[2] Quoted by Cullom, Appendix, *Congressional Globe*, vol. xxix. p. 539.

ing his party and injuring his country. He made up his
mind quickly; confiding, like all spoiled children of fortune
who have been endowed with rich natural gifts, in his in-
tuitive judgment, he thought that he had no need of close
application and methodical reasoning. "His library was
never clear from dust," said a friend and follower;[1] and
Greeley, who in these days denounced him without stint,[2]
wrote truly after his death that, if Douglas had been a hard
student, "it would have been difficult to set limits to his
power."[3] He, like his greater Illinois rival, was a fine math-
ematician,[4] but he did not, like Lincoln, wrestle in manhood
with the problems of Euclid for mental discipline.[5] He
hardly knew any history but that of his own country; he
cared not to learn of the development of the world, except
when Alexander, Cæsar, and Napoleon were on the stage
of action, and of them he could not read too much.[6]

Of all the descriptions of Douglas at this time, none seem
to seize the essential characteristics of the man so well as
that of a journalist whose soul was wrapped up in the anti-
slavery cause. The writer was impressed with his "pluck,
persistency, and muscular self-assurance and self-assertion."
To see and hear him was to "comprehend the aptness of
that title of 'Little Giant.'" Never was a characteristic
name better applied. The historian must sympathize with
the regret expressed by this journalist that one who cham-
pioned bad measures with such indomitable ability was not
upon the right side; and the thought cannot fail to come,
"of what infinite value this remarkable man might have

---

[1] S. S. Cox, Eulogy, July, 1861.

[2] "We presume that three more tricky and managing politicians don't
live than Pierce, Cushing, and Soulé. If we were to add a fourth, we
should of course name S. A. Douglas."—New York *Tribune*, May 13th,
1854; evidently written by Greeley.

[3] Recollections of a Busy Life, p. 358.

[4] See *Atlantic Monthly*, vol. viii. p. 203.

[5] Herndon's Life of Lincoln, p. 308.

[6] *Atlantic Monthly*, vol. viii. p. 206; Forney's Anecdotes of Public Men.

been to the cause of liberty if the fortune of politics had made him a leader of it." [1]

Douglas had the quality of attaching men to him; he was especially fond of young men, and they repaid his complaisance by devotion. No American statesman but Clay ever had such a personal following. He now became the leader of the Democratic party; he retained the leadership of the Northern Democrats to the last; and since Andrew Jackson, no man has possessed the influence, received the confidence, or had the support that it was the lot of Douglas to enjoy from the Democrats in the northern half of the Union.   From 1854 to 1858, he was the centre of the political history of the country; from 1858 to 1860, he was the best-known man in the United States; but after the contest with Lincoln in 1858, it became apparent that the "Little Giant" had met his match in that other son of Illinois.

Douglas was generous and faithful to his friends. He had large ideas in business; he made money easily and spent it lavishly. It was stated during this controversy that he was furthering the interests of slavery because he was himself a slave-holder, but the allegation was untrue. Douglas had, indeed, been offered the gift of a plantation with a large number of slaves by his father-in-law, but he had refused it, being unwilling to accept such a responsibility. He answered this charge in the Senate with dignity.[2] Indeed, those who sought a mercenary motive as a key to the course of Douglas strangely misapprehended his character.[3]

---

[1] Reminiscences of a Journalist, C. T. Congdon, p. 286.

[2] Life of Douglas, Sheahan, p. 437.

[3] My authorities for the view of Douglas are, besides those I have named, the two biographies of him by Sheahan and Flint; Constitutional and Party Questions, J. M. Cutts; Representative Men, Savage; Forney's Anecdotes of Public Men; Blaine's Eulogy on Garfield. I have received valuable hints concerning him from Senator John Sherman, General Logan, and my friend Mr. George H. Stone; but for his personal characteristics more than to any other source I am indebted to my father and mother, who were intimately acquainted with him and very often saw

In comprehensive views he was a true representative of the West. No public man has ever had more of the spirit of the boundless prairie or has been such a faithful type of the resistless energy that characterizes the city of Chicago. He understood the West, but it is plain that he had not thought out the results of the repeal of the Missouri Compromise, for he seemed to have little apprehension of the political revolution that was destined to take place in his beloved section of country.[1] On January 1st, 1854, Indiana, Illinois, Michigan, Wisconsin, and Iowa were Democratic States;[2] all their senators were Democrats; of twenty-nine representatives only five were Whigs. None but Indiana remained reliably Democratic. Michigan, Wisconsin, and Iowa at once became Republican, and Illinois would have immediately ranged herself at their side had it not been for the strong personal influence of Douglas.

Some writers and many men who were contemporary with the event have maintained that the civil war would not have taken place had it not been for the abrogation of the Missouri Compromise. This will probably not be the mature verdict of history. The more the subject is studied, the more profound will appear the prophetic saying of John Quincy Adams: "I am satisfied slavery will not go down until it goes down in blood."[3] Yet it must be adjudged that Douglas hastened the struggle; he precipitated the civil war.

The North was now in a ferment. At the Connecticut State election in April the Democrats had failed to elect

---

him familiarly. Having seen him frequently when a child, my own recollection of his personal appearance and manner of speaking from the stump is vivid.

[1] See his speech, May 25th, 1854.

[2] Minnesota was not a State. "What gain had freedom in the admission of Iowa into the Union? Are Alabama and Mississippi more devoted to the despotic ideas of American panslavism than are Indiana and Illinois?"—New York *Tribune*, March 29th, 1854.

[3] Life of Seward, vol. i. p. 672. This remark was made in 1843.

the legislature or governor.   While both Whig and Democratic conventions had protested against the repeal of the
Missouri Compromise,[1] the result of the election was obviously a rebuke to the dominant party for their support of
the Kansas-Nebraska bill.   The newly elected legislature
passed resolutions averse to the proposed measure; these
were presented to the House the day on which the con-
cluding vote was taken, and to the Senate before its final
action on the bill.   The Whig convention of Pennsylvania
resolved against the disturbance of the legislation of 1820,
while the Democratic convention of that State was silent.[2]

One phase of the public sentiment has been barely alluded
to.   The foreign immigration had become a factor in politics of which heed must be taken.   The Germans and Irish,
for the most part, had joined the Democratic party; but the
Germans, from the first, were opposed to the repeal of the
Missouri Compromise, for they were against the extension of
slavery.[3]   Of eighty-eight German newspapers, eight were
in favor of the Kansas-Nebraska bill, while eighty were decidedly opposed to it.[4]   This change was of enough consequence to determine the political character of Wisconsin
and Iowa, and was a great element of anti-slavery strength
in Ohio.

The cannon roared in Washington when the Senate enacted the measure, but gloom overspread the minds of Northern men.   Pierce and Douglas, said Greeley, have made
more abolitionists in three months than Garrison and Phillips could have made in half a century.[5]   Crowds of people

---

[1] *National Intelligencer*, March 2d.   [2] Ibid, March 18th.

[3] See New York *Evening Post*, Feb. 4th and 7th; the *Liberator*, April
21st; *National Intelligencer*, April 15th.

[4] List made by Cincinnati *Gazette*, cited by Von Holst, vol. iv. p. 429.
See Von Holst's remarks on this subject in his history; also his criticism
of Bryce's American Commonwealth.   See *The Nation*, April 24th, 1890,
which refers to an article in the *Historische Zeitschrift*, neue Folge, vol.
xxviii. pp. 1–50.

[5] New York *Tribune*, May 17th.

who had heretofore severely criticised Garrison, Phillips, Parker, and their methods, now flocked to hear them, and were glad to listen to the arguments of these earnest men.[1] It was at once urged by the press and from the platform that an effort should be made to have Kansas enter the Union as a free State, and a systematic movement was begun with this end in view.

The author of the bill was regarded with execration; his middle name was Arnold, and this suggested a comparison to Benedict Arnold. The term which is used in every Christian land as a synonym of traitor was likewise applied to him, and one hundred and three ladies of an Ohio village sent him thirty pieces of silver.[2] He could travel, as he afterwards said, "from Boston to Chicago by the light of his own effigies." Horace Bushnell, a noted preacher in Hartford, applied to Douglas the bitter prophecy of the Hebrew prophet: "Tidings out of the east and out of the north shall trouble him; therefore he shall go forth with great fury to destroy and utterly to make away many, yet he shall come to his end, and none shall help him." A journal which had opposed the Kansas-Nebraska measure with pertinacity asked, in derision, "Who names Douglas for the next President now?"[3] Not a response came from the North.

"Never was an act of Congress so generally and so unanimously hailed with delight at the South" as was the Kansas-Nebraska act, wrote Alexander Stephens six years after its passage.[4] This may be accepted as a fact, although there were some exceptions to the almost universal acclaim. Many people in New Orleans did not like it; such, also, ap-

---

[1] Life of Garrison, vol. iii. pp. 407, 408; New York *Tribune.* See Bell's speech in the Senate, *Congressional Globe*, Appendix, vol. xxix. p. 943.

[2] The *Liberator*, vol. xxiv. p. 43.

[3] New York *Times*, May 23d.

[4] Life of Alex. H. Stephens, Johnston and Browne, p. 360, letter of May 9th, 1860.

peared to be the feeling in Texas.[1] Indifference as to the
fate of the bill while it was pending was reported from
Charleston, from other parts of South Carolina, and from a
city of Mississippi.[2] The leading state-rights organ of
Charleston did not scruple to condemn the tactics of Stephens as a violation of the rights of the minority and as of
a dangerous tendency.[3] But as the measure gradually came
to be understood as a victory for slavery and a defeat of the
abolitionists, the general feeling fully justified the assertion
of Stephens. It was thought in the border States that if a
new slave State could be created it would add five per cent.
to the value of slaves, which was already very high.[4] The
planters in the cotton States, being buyers of negroes, did not
regard the rise of values as an unmixed good; but they did
not grumble: they cast about for a remedy, and did not look
for it long. The reopening of the African slave-trade began to be discussed seriously in South Carolina and Mississippi.[5]

There were Southern members of Congress whom Atchison could not convince that Kansas would enter the Union
as a slave State.[6] But they felt that if Atchison were too

---

[1] See the New Orleans *Crescent*. Gen. Houston says: " The people of
the South care nothing for it; it is the worst thing for the South that has
ever transpired since the Union was first formed."—Washington correspondence New York *Tribune*, June 5th.

[2] See Charleston *News*, cited in *National Intelligencer*, May 25th and
27th; Charleston *Mercury*, June 21st, cited in *National Intelligencer*, June
27th; see private letter from Beaufort, S. C., to New York *Courier and
Enquirer*, dated May 15th; letter from Natchez, Miss., to the *National
Intelligencer*, cited by *Courier and Enquirer*, May 31st. There was a
strong feeling against the measure in Eastern Tennessee, see letter from
Knoxville, ibid.

[3] Charleston *Mercury*, cited in New York *Tribune*, May 31st.

[4] See letter of Yeoman, New York *Times*, May 13th. For the high price
of slaves see Mobile *Advertiser*, cited in New York *Evening Post*, Jan. 30th.

[5] New York *Tribune*, May 31st; see Pike, First Blows of the Civil War,
cited by Von Holst, vol. iv. p. 437.

[6] See *Congressional Globe*, Appendix, vol. xxix. p. 939.

I.—32

sanguine, and even if the Kansas-Nebraska act did not recognize the Calhoun dogma, it did at any rate make a quie-
tus of the Wilmot proviso doctrine. As the establishment
of a principle it was of great benefit to the South; for when
the bill was introduced negotiations were in progress which
were expected to result in the accession of an important
piece of territory from Mexico. That Cuba would be ours
by the close of the year was not deemed an unwarranted
expectation. Nor was it a wild dream to expect that before many years the United States would extend to the
isthmus. The acquisition of Mexico, Central America, and
Cuba, to be cut up into slave States, was an object worth
striving for, and the Kansas-Nebraska act seemed to assert
a principle that could properly be applied if this territory
were gained to achieve such a consummation. The better
the measure was understood, the more complete seemed the
humiliation of the North, and the greater reason there appeared for the exultation of the South.

"The Fugitive law did much to unglue the eyes of men,
and now the Nebraska bill leaves us staring," said Emerson.[1]
The repeal of the Missouri Compromise emphasized every
argument against the Fugitive Slave act, and gave to the
story of "Uncle Tom's Cabin" the force of solid reasoning.
The uprising against this law of 1850 is a well-known fact
of the decade between 1850–60, but the distinction between
the excitement which followed its passage and that which
grew out of the Kansas-Nebraska act is not always carefully borne in mind. Yet the difference is of transcendent
importance. The excitement of 1850 and 1851 was transi-
tory. It was vehement while it lasted, for the abolitionists
and extreme anti-slavery men prompted it, but all their agitation did not prevent the public mind from settling into
the conviction that the Fugitive Slave law was only one un-
palatable article of a good contract. Public opinion at the
North in 1852 was well expressed by the Democratic and

---

[1] New York *Evening Post*, March 8th.

Whig platforms.[1] Even the brilliant speech of Sumner on the subject[2] did not produce a ripple of excitement, and in 1853 the acquiescence was complete. When the Fugitive Slave law was enforced it was done quietly, with sometimes a lack of zeal[3] on the part of the officers, and with little or no resistance from the people. It seemed to be one of those laws which a law-abiding community believe wrong to resist, though inexpedient to put in force.

But in 1854 there began to be a smarting sense of the injustice of the Fugitive Slave law, which was never allayed until there was no longer reason for its existence. We shall see, in the course of this work, that one political party made, in its political platforms, obedience to this act a test of fidelity, and that the other remained silent on the subject; we shall see that Lincoln, on first taking the oath of his high office, virtually announced his purpose of enforcing it. Yet, after the passage of the Kansas-Nebraska act, the majority of men at the North, and by far the greater number of intelligent and moral people, felt that they had been cheated, and that the Fugitive Slave law was a part of the cheat. They reasoned that the South set aside the Missouri Compromise because it no longer operated in their favor; and as the Fugitive act was to them the obnoxious part of the compromise of 1850, they would consider the breach of it more honorable than the observance.

In March a colored man had been claimed as a fugitive slave and committed to jail at Milwaukee, Wis. He was rescued by a party of sympathizers. Booth, a journalist, who was one of these, was arrested on a warrant of the United States commissioner; he applied to an associate justice of the State Supreme Court for a writ of habeas corpus and his discharge. The justice ordered his discharge on two grounds, one of which was that the Fugitive Slave law was unconstitutional. This decision was afterwards

---

[1] See pp. 249, 253.   [2] See p. 266.
[3] See the Richmond *Whig*, Jan. 19th, 1854.

affirmed by a full bench of the Wisconsin Supreme Court, only one justice dissenting.[1]

"If the Nebraska bill should be passed, the Fugitive Slave law is a dead letter throughout New England," wrote a Southerner from Boston to a friend.[2] "As easily," he continued, "could a law prohibiting the eating of codfish and pumpkin-pies be enforced as that law be executed." The events which followed hard upon the action of the House of Representatives showed that the stranger had accurately judged the drift of opinion.

On the evening of the 24th of May, Anthony Burns, a negro who had escaped from servitude about three months previously, was arrested in the heart of Boston. The next morning he was taken manacled to the United States Court-room for examination by Commissioner Loring. The news of his arrest had not got into the papers, and the proceedings would have been summary had not Richard H. Dana, Jr., a prominent lawyer of anti-slavery opinions, chanced to pass the court-house at about nine o'clock and received an intimation of what was going on. He entered the court-room and offered Burns his professional services. The negro declined them. "It is of no use," he said; "they will swear to me and get me back; and if they do, I shall fare worse if I resist."[3] Meanwhile, Theodore Parker and other gentlemen who had accidentally heard of the arrest had entered the court-room, and Parker had a conference with Burns. He told the frightened fugitive that he was a minister, that by a meeting of citizens he had been appointed the special pastor of fugitive slaves, and he asked whether Burns did not want counsel. The negro replied: "I shall

---

[1] 3 Wisconsin Reports, edited by Abram D. Smith, pp. 1–144. The case was carried to the Supreme Court of the United States and the decision of the Wisconsin Supreme Court reversed. Chief-Justice Taney gave the decision. See 21 Howard, p. 506.

[2] Letter dated Feb. 18th, *National Intelligencer*, Feb. 28th.

[3] R. H. Dana's Diary, Life by C. F. Adams, vol. i. p. 265.

have to go back. My master knows me. His agent knows
me. If I must go back, I want to go back as easily as I
can." "But surely," rejoined Parker, "it can do you no
harm to make a defence." "Well," said Burns, "you may
do as you have a mind to about it." "He seemed," Parker
afterwards related, "to be stupefied with fear."

The news of the arrest, and the circumstances connected
with it, spread quickly through the city and found a great
change in public opinion from that which had prevailed
three years before, when Sims was arrested.[1] The fugitive
had now the active or passive sympathy of nearly every
one. Inflammatory handbills were circulated; they were
drawn up with skill, appealing at the same time to the fiery
abolitionist and to the compromiser of 1850. Invectives
against kidnappers and man-stealing were joined to a statement which expressed the overpowering thought in the
minds of New England men. "The compromises," one of
the placards said, "trampled upon by the slave power when
in the path of slavery, are to be crammed down the throat
of the North."[2] On Friday morning, the 26th, a call for a
meeting at Faneuil Hall that evening was issued, the object
of which was stated to be: "To secure justice for a man
claimed as a slave by a Virginia kidnapper;" and the notice
ended: "Shall he be plunged into the hell of Virginia slavery by a Massachusetts judge of probate?"[3] By Friday
evening the city was in a ferment. Not since the massacre
in revolutionary days had there been such wild excitement.
Agitators were running to and fro, setting all the city in
an uproar. The pent-up feeling produced by the repeal
of the Missouri Compromise broke forth with fury. The
crowd that gathered in Faneuil Hall were agitated by pas-

---

[1] See p. 211; also Life of R. H. Dana, C. F. Adams, vol. i. pp. 269, 285,
286. For a similar change in Iowa, see Life of Grimes, Salter, p. 73.

[2] A copy of these placards may be found in Life and Correspondence
of Theo. Parker, Weiss, vol. ii. p. 132.

[3] Loring was judge of probate as well as United States commissioner.

sion; and when Wendell Phillips rose to speak, they were in that state which orators delight to see when they would urge their fellow-men to violent deeds. Phillips had the manner of Brutus, but his words were like those of Mark Antony, fitted to stir up mutiny. "See to it," he said, "that to-morrow, in the streets of Boston, you ratify the verdict of Faneuil Hall, that Anthony Burns has no master but his God. . . . Will you adhere to the case of Sims and see this man carried down State Street between two hundred men? . . . Nebraska, I call knocking a man down, and this is spitting in his face after he is down." Thus Phillips went on, the audience hanging breathless on his every word.

When he had finished, Theodore Parker delivered a wild, incoherent, and vindictive harangue. "Men and brothers," Parker said, "I am an old man; I have heard hurrahs and cheers for liberty many times; I have not seen a great many *deeds* done for liberty. I ask you are we to have *deeds* as well as words? . . . Gentlemen, there was a Boston once, and you and I had fathers—brave fathers; and mothers who stirred up fathers to manly deeds. . . . They did not obey the stamp-act. . . . You know what they did with the tea." He ended with the proposition that when they adjourned it should be to meet the next morning at nine o'clock in Court-house Square. "To-night," shouted a hundred voices in reply. The excitement was now intense. The people were in a tumult. Above the roar of voices might be heard cries, "To the court-house!"[1] "To the Revere House for the slave-catchers!" Parker tried in vain to still the storm he had raised, but he could not get a hearing. Phillips then ascended the platform and a few well-chosen words sufficed to allay the tumult. He had almost persuaded the audience to disperse quietly, when a man at the entrance of the hall shouted: "Mr. Chairman, I am just

---

[1] The United States leased a portion of the court-house. Burns was imprisoned in the jury-room of the United States Court.

informed that a mob of negroes is in Court Square attempting to rescue Burns. I move that we adjourn to Court
Square." The hall became quickly empty. The crowd
rushed to the scene of action. There they found a small
party under the lead of Thomas W. Higginson attempting
to break down one of the doors of the court-house with a
large stick of timber used as a battering-ram. The Faneuil
Hall men lent a hand. Those who could not work rent the
air with shouts; others hurled stones or fired pistol-shots at
the court-house windows. It was an angry, excited crowd
of two thousand, bent on the rescue of Burns.[1] At last a
breach was made in the door, but the place was defended.
In the mêlée one of the marshal's posse was killed, and
Higginson was wounded by a sabre-cut. Several of Higginson's companions were arrested, after which no further
attempt was made to break into the court-house. Two
companies of artillery were immediately ordered out by the
mayor to preserve the peace.

It was a foolish attempt for the rescue of Burns. Under
a government like ours there can be no justification for an
attack upon the constituted authorities. It pleased the multitude to call the Boston Court-house the Bastille; but the
recollection of the event which was thus conjured up strikes
one with the contrast between the Paris of 1789 and the
Boston of 1854, and not with their likeness. Yet it is an
evidence of the deep feeling that, although this attempt
was widely condemned, it did not weaken the public sympathy for the fugitive or the indignation against the United
States functionaries. This attack enabled the marshal to
appear as a vindicator of the law; he immediately called out
two companies of United States troops, reported his action
to the President, and received the reply: "Your conduct is
approved. The law must be executed."

On the following Monday the examination began. An
eye-witness relates that "the court-house had the air of a

---

[1] A Bronson Alcott was in the mob.—*The Nation*, March 8, 1888.

beleaguered fortress." [1] Every window was guarded by
Massachusetts or United States soldiery. Only one door of
the court-house was open, and at that was stationed a strong
force of city police. None but functionaries could enter
without a permit from the marshal. The counsel for the
fugitive made a strong defence. Burns was undeniably the
slave of the claimant, although the proofs were clumsy, and
on technical grounds he might have been set free. The
United States officers, however, were determined to win.
On the 2d of June, Commissioner Loring adjudged the negro to his owner.

The most instructive act in the whole drama was now to
be played. The fugitive slave must be sent out of Boston.
The city was full of people; during the whole week men
from the suburban towns and from all parts of Massachusetts had been flocking into Boston. The President had
just signed the Kansas-Nebraska act. There was earnest
indignation against Congress, the President, and the United
States authorities of Boston; but these Massachusetts men
were, for the most part, on a peaceful errand bent. The
United States district attorney, the marshal, and the mayor
of the city were determined, however, to be prepared for a
mob and an attempt at rescue. A large body of city police
and twenty-two companies of Massachusetts soldiers guarded in detachments the streets through which Burns and his
guard must pass. The streets were cleared by a company
of cavalry. The procession was made up of one United
States artillery battalion, one platoon of United States
marines, the marshal's civil posse of one hundred and
twenty-five men guarding the fugitive, two platoons of marines, a field-piece, and one platoon of marines as a guard
to the field-piece. Windows along the line of march were
draped in mourning; from a window opposite the old State-
house was suspended a black coffin on which were the
words, "The funeral of liberty;" further on was an Amer-

---

[1] Anthony Burns, Stevens, p. 80.

ican flag, the union down, draped in mourning. The solemn procession was witnessed by fifty thousand people, who hissed, groaned, and cried " Shame ! shame !" as it went by. A weight of suspense hung over the crowd, and it seemed as if a slight occasion might precipitate an outbreak with terrible consequences. The fugitive was marched to the wharf, and was soon on a United States revenue-cutter, sailing towards Virginia.[1]

To this complexion had it come at last. In a community

---

[1] About fourteen thousand dollars were paid out of the United States Treasury for services rendered by the Massachusetts militia. Anthony Burns, Stevens, p. 133. The cost of returning Burns to the federal government was not far from forty thousand dollars. New York *Times*, June 9th. Henry A. Wise said it cost the government a hundred thousand dollars. Speech at Alexandria, Feb., 1855.

My chief authority in this account is Anthony Burns, a History, by C. E. Stevens, published in 1856. The writer states in his preface : " My materials have been derived chiefly from original sources. . . . I was present at the Faneuil Hall meeting from its commencement to its close, and I witnessed the attack on the court-house." I have also used the Life of R. H. Dana, by C. F. Adams ; the Life of Theodore Parker, by Weiss ; and I have carefully read the contemporary accounts in the Boston *Journal*, the *Liberator*, and the Boston *Courier*. The latter was a very conservative Whig newspaper. The sequel of this affair is interesting. Burns, after undergoing persecution and hardship in Virginia, was sold to go to North Carolina, was ransomed in 1855 by money collected by a Boston colored preacher ; was sent to Oberlin College ; afterwards became the pastor of a colored society at St. Catherines, Canada, and died in 1862. " Burns was the last fugitive slave ever seized on the soil of Massachusetts."—Life of R. H. Dana, C. F. Adams, vol. i. p. 265. Indictments were found against Parker, Phillips, Higginson, and others. A test case was made of one, and Judge Curtis quashed the indictment. Rise and Fall of the Slave Power, Wilson, vol. ii. p. 443.

Loring had previously been appointed lecturer to the law-school of Harvard University, but the board of overseers refused to confirm the appointment. The legislature sent an address to the governor requesting him to remove Loring from the position of probate judge ; this the governor declined to do. The agitation against Loring was, however, kept up, and when Banks became governor in 1858 he made the removal of the probate judge on an address from the legislature.

celebrated all over the world for the respect it yielded to law, and for obedience to those clothed with authority; in a community where the readiness of all citizens to assist the authorities had struck intelligent Europeans with amazement—it now required to execute a law a large body of deputy marshals, the whole force of the city police, eleven hundred and forty soldiers with muskets loaded, supplied with eleven rounds of powder and ball and furnished with a cannon loaded with grape-shot. If anything were needed to heighten the strangeness of the situation, it may be found in the fact that the marshal's deputies were taken from the dregs of society, for no reputable citizen would serve as a slave-catcher.

As the men of Boston and the men of New England reflected on what had taken place, they were persuaded, as they had never been before, that something was rotten in the United States, and that these events boded some strange eruption to our State.[1] Nor was the significance of the transaction entirely lost upon the South. "We rejoice at the recapture of Burns," said a fiery organ of the slavery propaganda, "but a few more such victories and the South is undone."[2]

---

[1] "The tables under the Fugitive Slave law are beginning at last to turn against the law and in favor of humanity. There is deep and painful suspense here."—Seward to his wife from Washington, May 28th. Life of Seward, vol. ii. p. 230.

[2] Richmond *Enquirer*, cited in the *Independent*, June 8th.

END OF VOL. I.